SICKNESS AND HEALING

SICKNESS
AND HEALING
An Anthropological Perspective

ROBERT A. HAHN

Yale University Press   New Haven and London

This book was written by Robert A. Hahn in his private
capacity. No official support or endorsement by Centers
for Disease Control and Prevention is intended or should
be inferred.

Designed by Jill Breitbarth and set in Garamond No. 3 type
by Keystone Typesetting, Inc., Orwigsburg, Pennsylvania.
Printed in the United States of America by BookCrafters, Inc.,
Chelsea, Michigan.

Library of Congress Cataloging-in-Publication Data
    Sickness and healing : an anthropological perspective / Robert A. Hahn.
        p.   cm.
    Includes bibliographical references and index.
    ISBN 0-300-06088-2 (cloth: alk. paper)
        0-300-06871-9 (pbk.: alk. paper)
    1. Medical anthropology.   2. Social medicine.   I. Title.
    [DNLM: 1. History of Medicine.   2. Disease.   3. Anthropology,
Cultural.   WZ   40   H371s   1995]
GN296.H35   1995
306.4'61—dc20
DNLM/DLC
for Library of Congress   94-3382
                                                                    CIP

A catalogue record for this book is available from the British Library.

The paper in this book meets the guidelines for permanence and durability of
the Committee on Production Guidelines for Book Longevity of the Council on
Library Resources.

10   9   8   7   6   5   4   3   2

CONTENTS

v

ACKNOWLEDGMENTS

In preparing this book, I am fortunate to have lived and worked with excellent colleagues and friends and to have experienced many diverse research opportunities. I thank my parents, Lili and Peter Hahn, and my friends and colleagues Melanie Anderson, Sevgi Aral, Howard Brody, Esther Brown, Peter Brown, Noel Chrisman, Elliott Churchill, Atwood Gaines, Deborah Gordon, Alan Harwood, Brigitte Jordan, Sharon Kaufmann, Sarala Krishnamurthy, Cathy Lutz, Jim Mendlein, Marjorie Muecke, Tracy Paget, Michael Phillips, Andrea Sankar, Michele Shedlin, Ron Simons, Ginny Soules, Howard Stein, and others for thoughtful and supportive attendance in the long gestation of this work. I am grateful also for the inspiration and support of pioneers at the frontiers of anthropology and health—Arthur Kleinman, Arthur Rubel, and Renée Fox. Early versions of chapters 4 and 6 were written with Arthur Kleinman, and chapter 7 was guided by Arthur Rubel and Renée Fox. I am thankful, too, for the encouragement and clarification of editors Ellen Graham and Gladys Topkis at Yale University Press.

For the past eight years the U.S. Centers for Disease Control and Prevention has provided me an outstanding environment in which to work. This book, however, was written in my private capacity, and no official support or endorsement by the CDC is intended or should be inferred.

Chapters 3, 5, and 10 appear here for the first time. Chapter 1 is a reincarnation of Hahn 1984; chapter 4 an expansion of Hahn 1985. Chapter 2 is revised from an article published in *Social Science and Medicine* (21 [1985]:165–71); chapters 8 and 9 are revised from articles first published in *Medical Anthropology Quarterly* and its predecessor; and chapter 7 is a revision of a chapter in Hahn and Gaines 1985. I thank the publishers of these sources for permission to reuse previously published material. I also thank Appleton-Century-Crofts for permission to reproduce the frontispiece of early editions of *Williams Obstetrics* and the American College of Obstetricians and Gynecologists for the photograph and for access to its excellent library. Thanks are due also to many nimble librarians in Seattle and Atlanta for numerous searches into obscure places.

For this project and other new things, Stephanie Sherman has shared with me a haven for which gratitude has no measure.

INTRODUCTION

At its best anthropology has always been subversive. By describing different social, cultural, and psychological arrangements, it challenges commonly accepted ways of perceiving, articulating, and understanding the world.

—*Crapanzano 1990:145*

In all epochs and everywhere, sickness and healing are primal human concerns. Yet the understanding of sickness and the response to sickness through healing vary greatly from time to time and place to place, fundamentally shaped by historical and cultural circumstance. Contemporary Westerners are accustomed to taking their own views of sickness and healing for granted—the way things are, reality. Such-and-such diseases exist, and there may be specific techniques for their treatment. Although Westerners recognize that their medicine, Biomedicine,* is imperfect in detail, still, its underlying principles of pathology and therapeutics are presumed to be correct. Alternative, non-Western views are generally regarded as primitive, mystical, and essentially misguided and their occasional benefits—for example, medicinal plants—as empirical serendipity.

THE ANTHROPOLOGICAL PERSPECTIVE

In this book, I attempt to step aside from the Western perspective. I examine the world of sickness and healing from an anthropological perspec-

---

* I capitalize "Biomedicine" to indicate the name of the biologically oriented medicine that predominates in Western societies.

1

tive that differs from the prevailing Western view in regarding systems of sickness and healing everywhere as cultural systems—that is, organized patterns of thinking, judging, and behaving shared by the members of a society. In the first half of the book, I explore ways of conceiving sickness and healing in which the reality of Western medicine is not taken for granted. In the second half, having willfully suspended the perspective of Western medicine, I return to reflect upon it. I seek familiarity in the exotic, the exotic in the familiar.

The anthropological perspective has an egalitarian theme: although beliefs about sickness and practices of healing clearly differ from society to society, all are equally cultural systems. By translating across cultural boundaries, anthropologists seek a wider audience for the voices of others. They treat their "informants" in different cultural settings as teachers. They are particularly tolerant abroad and unusually skeptical at home—both sometimes to excess.

Anthropologists take as real the "new" forms of sickness discovered in foreign settings, sicknesses that may appear strange and implausible on first encounter. They also take seriously "new" ways of healing witnessed beyond their own cultural boundaries. What is "new" depends on where one has been and what one has seen. Anthropologists attempt to understand the concepts and theories and values that underlie forms of sickness and healing that are not part of their own tradition. By representing a broader range of human variation, they may expand Western ideas about humanity. The goal of this cross-cultural encounter is not to synthesize all variations into one gigantic, panhuman hodgepodge but to promote mutual respect, communication across boundaries, and exchange where it may be beneficial.

I deliberately say that I "attempt" to step aside from the Western perspective. I do not pretend to understand sickness and healing entirely from the perspective of another culture or all cultures, totally free of my own cultural assumptions. To do so would be to deny the fundamental anthropological tenet that the concepts and premises that guide the way people understand the world—their "worldview"—are profoundly shaped by the cultural setting they inhabit. Like patients, physicians, and other healers, anthropologists are creatures of their culture. I do not deny my cultural roots.

Nor do I deny the unprecedented knowledge of twentieth-century Biomedicine. I am astonished daily by its remarkable discoveries and inventions. When sick, I, too, resort to Biomedicine for medical care—not simply because it is relatively convenient but because I believe that for many conditions it offers the best treatment available anywhere. In my epidemiological research as well, I build on findings of Biomedicine. I am a Westerner and have grown up in a society where Biomedicine prevails.

Medical anthropologists commonly confront an essential dilemma and a profound ambivalence toward Biomedicine, resulting in uncertainty about the validity of their own framework. Although they seek to compare medical systems across cultural boundaries without bias for or against any one perspective, they themselves are often rooted in the perspective of Biomedicine. Much of what they believe about sickness and healing has been learned from the teachings of Biomedicine and the broader culture.

The socialization of many anthropologists in societies where Biomedicine prevails has led to two visions within the field of medical anthropology as a whole, sometimes to double vision within single practitioners. One vision professes a fundamentally hierarchical view of the universe of sickness. At the superior level are the basic truths of Biomedicine; below are the distorted or simplified views of patients and the practitioners of non-Western medicines. Corresponding to the hierarchy of sickness is another hierarchy of participants—physicians as masters of Biomedical truths, nurses and other paramedical personnel, as well as patients and practitioners of other medicines, as adherents of simpler, less valid perspectives.

In the second vision, common in analyses of non-Western medical systems, researchers have professed to reveal the local medical "reality" in its own terms; in their concern not to impose their own vision on those they study, these researchers have assumed that the local, indigenous explanations of the world of sickness and healing are valid (Kenny 1983). In this relativism, researchers may minimize, ignore, or even explicitly deny universal biological and pathological realities (as formulated in their own culture).

The first vision, which assumes that the analyst's culture possesses exclusive truths, is "ethnocentric," and the second vision might be described as "xenocentric," now assuming that the cultures of *others* have exclusive access to the truth—at least in their home setting. I believe that both visions are false. That beliefs are part of a cultural system—our own or someone else's—argues neither for nor against their validity. There is no reason to assume that exclusive truth is to be found in any given system of beliefs before examining it. Moreover, the ability to understand foreign beliefs depends in the first place upon various assumptions on the part of the observer, assumptions that are most likely to come from his or her own culture (Quine 1960; Hahn 1973). Conclusions about another's logic and beliefs may be as much the product of one's own preconceptions or prejudices as of the processes of thought imputed to others. The xenocentric assumption that one can apprehend the cultural beliefs of others "as they are," independent of one's own beliefs, belies the basis of one's observations in just such cultural beliefs.

The observer needs a place to stand. Observation and understanding are built from categories, hypotheses, and principles of knowledge. Even among positivist philosophers in the early part of the twentieth century, it was recognized that one could not begin the reconstruction of knowledge without a conceptual platform and that the platform available was the builder's own tradition. Otto Neurath wrote: "We are like sailors who must reconstruct our ship on the open sea, without ever dismantling at a dock and rebuilding with the best of parts" (quoted in Quine 1960:vii; my translation).

The challenge of anthropology—and of other disciplines that seek an understanding of human phenomena rather than of the phenomena found only in the observer's home setting—is to develop an observational framework that is as explicit, rational, and consistent as possible and that is at the same time receptive to the alternative truths of other cultural frameworks. If we begin from the culture in which Biomedicine prevails, we must first make our Biomedical framework as clear and systematic as possible. But, at the same time, we should not assume that the premises of this system are final or exclusive truths. Ours is not the only place to stand.

As they use the term *ethnobotany* (from the Greek *ethnos,* a "nation or people") to refer to a society's botanical thought and *ethnoicthyology* to its ideas about fish, so anthropologists have coined the awkward but useful term *ethnomedicine* to refer to the part of a society's cultural system concerned with sickness and healing. The total culture of a society consists of several *cultural systems*—for example, science, religion, economics, and medicine—each of which may be thought of as having three basic features: a distinctive *domain* of knowledge and practice; a means of *socialization*—the teaching of this domain to specialists and others; and an *arena* in which the activities of this domain are conducted.

The *domain* defines what a cultural system is about. The domain of medicine distinguishes things that are "medical" from those that are not. Included within the domain are the goals, values, knowledge, and techniques of both practitioners and laypersons. The domain also includes ideas about proper behavior (for both patients and healers) and about sanctions for misbehavior, such as the feigning of sickness by patients or the neglect of standards of practice by healers. In many "traditional," non-Western societies, the domain of medicine is not clearly differentiated from that of religion, politics, and the rest of social life; sickness may involve the world of ancestral spirits, and healing may require the resolution of social conflict.

Socialization is the way in which a cultural domain is inculcated in novices—for example, in the vision quests of shamanism and the premedical education, medical school, internship, and residency of Biomedicine. Through socialization, a society produces and maintains the personnel, such as its healers and specialists, who occupy its roles. In Biomedicine as well as in many traditional medical systems, the socialization of healers involves a prolonged and arduous apprenticeship in which expert practitioners play a leading role. Socialization is also the way in which a society educates its population about sickness and healing; it informs patients how to behave when sick, both in and outside of medical settings.

Finally, a cultural system has a defined *arena* in which its activities are carried out. The arena may include institutions and settings, such as hospitals and doctors' offices, as well as designated roles—for example, "doctor," "pediatrician," "surgeon," "psychiatrist," "nurse," "lab technician," "patient." In traditional societies, healing activities may not have a fixed place but may be marked by time and ritual.

SICKNESS

If the meaning of "sickness" varies widely from one cultural setting to another, what, then, do cultures have in common that might be called "sickness"? How can "sickness" be defined so that we know what to look for in a comparative study?

Broadly speaking, the essence of "sickness" is an unwanted condition in one's person or self—one's mind, body, soul, or connection to the world. What counts as "sickness" is thus determined by the perception and experience of its bearer, the patient (from the Latin *pati-*, as in "passion," to suffer, to bear affliction). Sicknesses represent and express the particularities of individual patients within a society. What counts as sickness and health may differ for a four-minute miler, a lower-limb amputee, an opera singer, and most of the rest of us. What *causes* the sickness may be environmental conditions or pathogens, the patient's physiology, or harmful behaviors. What *defines* the event for which we seek a cause, however, may be not the patient's body, behaviors, or potentially harmful environmental occurrences— its possible causes—but rather his or her subjective experience and values.

It is not commonly recognized in the West that ideas about what a "person" and a "self" are and should be differ greatly from one cultural setting to another. Indeed, the individuated person, separate from the rest of society and the universe, is a distinctly Western notion (Dumont 1965; Lutz 1985b); in many non-Western societies, persons are regarded as essentially and inextricably linked with other beings, human and nonhuman. Autonomy and independence are also largely Western values about desirable connections with others. Consequently, in other societies, ideas about "something wrong and undesirable in one's person or being" may differ greatly from Western ideas. For example, whereas disturbances in the capacity for *independence* may be thought of as pathological in the West, disturbances in the capacity for *interdependence* may be regarded as pathological elsewhere.

Sickness often obstructs or threatens to obstruct the everyday activities or life plans of persons. Often, though not always, sick persons themselves know best when they are sick. Often, but not always, afflicted persons suffer in their sicknesses either directly, from the pains of sickness itself, or indirectly, from actual or threatened impairment.

However much a society's worldview shapes its members' perceptions of their sicknesses, it is primarily how a person works well in the world according to his or her own vision that defines the person's sickness—as loss or as threat to this desired capacity and function. The labeling of persons as "sick" who deviate from the standards of others, as has been reported, for example, in Soviet psychiatry in the mid- and later twentieth century, is a political abuse of diagnosis in which the purported well-being of society is imposed upon its members with a pretense of interest in the so-called patient. But, rather than label existing sickness, such societal acts are more likely to cause suffering, if not sickness. The societal labeling of conditions is akin to what has been called the "tertiary gain of illness" (Dansak 1973), in which a person's consociates support his or her pathological condition for some benefit of their own; in this case, the "illness" is a fiction.

Included as sicknesses are broken limbs, cancers, and "neurotic" habits that get in one's way. Where hunting is thought to indicate one's connection with the animal world (as in some Amazonian tribes) or with ancestral spirits (as in some traditional African societies), difficulties in hunting may be regarded as sicknesses and treated by healers. Also included are traumatic events such as automobile fatalities; although the victim may not have had time to experience these mortal events as wrong and undesirable, we expect that, unless suicidal, he or she would have made such judgments of the outcome. Childbirth is commonly a healthy event, which, however, produces levels of pain (and pleasure as well) exceeding most other events; it is not sickness unless taken to be an unwanted condition of the mother's self or body. Grief, too, may bring much suffering, yet may be a healthy reaction to loss; it may also be pathological when it plays into psychodynamic processes not directly related to the loss itself.

Unemployment and poverty are likely to be unwanted conditions, but they are not necessarily conditions *in* one's self or one's connection with the world. Yet they may become a part of the self, incorporated, and in this case would reasonably be regarded as sicknesses. What of personality characteristics such as greed or arrogance or shyness, and what of emotions such as rage—are these sicknesses? Again, I believe they are reasonably regarded as sicknesses when they are a part of the self and are unwanted. The same holds for bodily states—being fat, skinny, weak, clumsy, unable to carry a tune. Some of these states are *causes* of sickness. They may themselves *be* sicknesses when they play a conscious role in one's life and when they become subjects of regret.

On the other hand, we may exclude as "sickness" the result of immunization in which pathogenic matter is deliberately injected or ingested to enhance the body's defenses. We may also exclude otherwise "sick" conditions such as pneumonia, "the old man's friend," among the elderly or others who, following rational reflection, wish to die. Though with side effects, immunization and the old man's friend produce desired outcomes.

The conception of sickness outlined here differs substantially from the conception found widely in Biomedicine. The anthropological notion I formulate defines sickness essentially from the perspective of the patient, who determines the work of the healer. In Biomedicine sickness is defined as disturbance in bodily or behavioral function in ways determined by the physician, who defines the problem of the patient, independent of and sometimes contrary to the patient's judgment.

HEALING

Given this conceptualization of sickness, a definition of "healing" is relatively straightforward. Broadly speaking, healing is the redress of sickness. The words *heal* and *health* may derive from the Germanic terms for "whole, uninjured, of good omen." If one adopts this concept, ideas of healing will vary with notions of "whole," which, like notions of "self" and "person," vary greatly from setting to setting and epoch to epoch. I include as healing not only the remedy or cure of sickness—that is, the restoration of a prior healthy state—but also rehabilitation—the compensation for loss of health—and palliation—the mitigation of suffering in the sick.

Healing is a sequence of events, some of which may be deliberately caused, others unintended (Dunn 1976). Although we generally designate as healers persons who specialize in intentional healing, this designation can be misleading. Healers may facilitate healing, but they may also hinder it; and healing may occur without or in spite of their interventions. Patients themselves, their bodies and minds—often considered the passive recipients of healing—may and commonly do play a prominent role in their own healing. Other persons not regarded as healers may heal as well, intentionally or not. And nonpersonal forces, too—for example, the physical environment—may play a healing role.

PLAN OF THE BOOK

In the first half of this book, I develop an anthropological framework for examining sickness and healing in all cultural settings, without assuming that the perspective of any one culture is true or better than others. Chapter 1, "The Universe of Sickness," explores issues in the classification of sickness and elaborates a definition of sickness in which the underlying reality is not, as assumed in Biomedicine, the patient's biology as assessed by a physician but rather the patient's perception of suffering and disturbance in him- or herself. Patients' anatomy and physiology may play a prominent role in the etiology and remedy of sicknesses. It is the patient, however, with his or her concepts, theories, and goals, who determines in the first place that he or she is sick.

Chapter 1 also proposes three basic kinds of accounts of sickness that may be held in different cultural settings: *disease accounts,* such as the theory of

Biomedicine, in which the patient's body is regarded as the seat of the causation and remedy of sickness; *illness accounts,* such as ideas about stress in recent popular thought in the West, in which the person, including his or her mind, body, and social environment, is seen as the focus of sickness causation and treatment; and *disorder accounts,* such as that of traditional Chinese medicine, in which imbalances in cosmic forces are seen as the source of sickness and the means of its redress.

Chapter 2, "Culture-bound Syndromes Unbound," argues that the notion of culture-bound syndromes, used by psychiatrists as well as by anthropologists, is itself also culturally biased. Supposedly, culture-bound syndromes are manifestations of sickness thought to be found only in delimited cultural settings. Running "amok," a behavior originally described in Malaysia, is the most infamous of culture-bound syndromes. Culture-bound syndromes are commonly described as congruent and largely explainable in terms of their settings. I claim that the idea of culture-bound syndromes assumes that some conditions are bound by their cultural settings and that others are not. I suggest, rather, that *all* conditions of sickness are affected by their cultural setting as well as by human biology, psychology, and the physical and social environment. I conclude that the category "culture-bound syndrome" is misleading and should be abandoned.

Chapter 3, "Three Theories of Sickness and Healing," reviews the wide range of theories that anthropologists have proposed to account for variations in the medical systems found in different settings. Some have argued that medical systems, and indeed cultures as wholes, are largely determined by adaptation to their physical environment. At the other extreme, some anthropologists appear to believe that medical systems, like the rest of human cultures, are arbitrary albeit systematic mental fabrications, minimally constrained, if at all, by the physical environment; the world becomes the way it is believed to be. I argue that both extremes are incorrect and propose a view between the two.

Chapter 4, "The Role of Society and Culture in Sickness and Healing," presents a wide range of evidence that the mind, social relationships, and societal organization profoundly affect processes of sickness and healing in a causal manner. The placebo effect is a good example of the role of beliefs— largely shaped by the patient's cultural setting—in events of healing (and of sickness as well). This view of sickness and healing as causally associated with the social and cultural environment in the same way that they are associated with pathogens and medicines runs counter to a fundamental premise of Biomedicine. The sociocultural model is proposed to complement rather than replace the Biomedical model.

Chapter 5, "Anthropology and Epidemiology: One Logic or Two?" reconsiders the relationships between two basic approaches to the understanding of sickness and healing. Some anthropologists and many epidemiologists believe that the basic methods of these disciplines are entirely distinct, if not contradictory. I describe what practitioners of these disciplines believe them-selves to do in their work. I then show how fundamental assumptions made by practitioners of each discipline are based on principles of the other disci-pline and how practitioners of each thus practice the other discipline without knowing it. I recommend exploration of basic commonalities to enhance the practice of both disciplines. I illustrate the potential of collaboration in plausible solutions to the problem of understanding the persistent gap be-tween white and black infant mortality rates in the United States.

The second half of the book examines several facets of Biomedicine from an anthropological perspective. Chapter 6 portrays "Biomedicine as a Cultural System," concentrating on its preeminent practitioners, physicians. The chapter describes the way in which physicians define the domain of medi-cine—focusing on the body—and the way the body is divided by medical specialties. The chapter then describes the process of medical education, one of the most grueling rituals of socialization known. Finally, it describes the rules that guide relationships between physicians and their patients.

Chapter 7 illustrates the culture of Biomedicine in "A World of Internal Medicine: Portrait of an Internist." Internal medicine is the rational heart of Biomedicine. I observed an internist I call "Barry Siegler" for several months to understand how he thought of his work and how he treated colleagues and patients.

By reviewing the development of the principal textbook of obstetrics, *Williams Obstetrics,* from the first edition, published in 1903, to the eigh-teenth, published in 1985, chapter 8, "Divisions of Labor: Obstetrician, Woman, and Society in *Williams Obstetrics,*" analyzes the twentieth-century evolution of Biomedical ideas about women patients and their suffering and about the distribution of authority in the medical setting. This text has likely guided the training of most obstetricians and the conduct of most deliveries in the United States since the turn of the century. Particularly in earlier editions, women are depicted as childbearing machines; they are treated mechanically, without attention to their experience. Editions of *Williams* in the 1950s introduced an effort to attend to the women themselves. Recent editions have given limited choice to women patients but have also given prominence and authority to a "new" obstetrical patient, the fetus.

Chapter 9, "Between Two Worlds: Physicians as Patients," explores the gulf between physicians and their patients by examining the experiences of approximately twenty physicians who became sick and wrote about their ex-perience, thus revealing the encounter of two worlds—patient and healer—in one person. For the most part, there are commonalities among the experi-ences of these physician/patients—their initial clinical treatment of their own sickness, the subsequent recognition that they are suffering, their adop-tion of the patient role, their awareness of distance and coldness in their physicians and in the medical system, their acknowledgment of the need for external social support, and their ambivalent return from patienthood to normal life. Many of these physicians are awakened by their journeys between two worlds; they alter their vision and their practice of medicine upon return.

Chapter 10, "From Medical Anthropology to Anthropological Medicine," suggests that an anthropological approach may address several dilemmas of contemporary Biomedicine. On the part of patients, there are often false expectations of what medicine can and should do, excessive optimism and excessive skepticism, dissatisfaction with a biological and fragmentary approach to their sickness, and resentment at not being listened to or heard. Physicians, too, are concerned with false expectations on the part of patients, with their difficulties in persuading patients to comply with what they, the physicians, think best, with the adversarial climate this promotes, with the excessive demands of medical work, and with the encroachment of corporations and government into medical decision making. An anthropological approach to medicine is proposed not as a panacea to these problems but as a critical element in their solution.

part one | AN ANTHROPOLOGICAL PERSPECTIVE

1

THE UNIVERSE OF SICKNESS

A good cook changes his knife once a year—because he cuts. A mediocre cook changes his knife once a month—because he hacks. I've had this knife of mine for nineteen years and I've cut up thousands of oxen with it, and yet the blade is as good as though it had just come from the grindstone. There are spaces between the joints, and the blade of the knife has really no thickness. If you insert what has no thickness into such spaces, then there's plenty of room—more than enough for the blade to play about in. That's why after nineteen years the blade of my knife is still as good as when it first came from the grindstone.

—*Ting, cook to Lord Wen-hui, in* Chuang Tzu, *translation by Watson 1964:47*

Although most of us are sick at least from time to time, none of us is ever sick in quite the same way twice. And each of us is sick in a way different from others. We are sick not only from different "things," or "causes," but we are sick in a manner corresponding to our singular bodies, our unfolding biographies, our cultural and historical positions, and our current circumstances. Each event of sickness is unique.

THE NAMES OF SICKNESS

Given the vast universe of all sicknesses that have ever occurred, how can we classify the diversity into this, that, and the other kind of sickness? Are there such "things" as "depression," "cholera," or "broken legs"? Which ones are there, and how do we know? What makes all occurrences of "cholera" significantly alike—so that we can reasonably call all of them cholera—and each significantly different from occurrences of "rabies," "influenza," "heart attack," and "schizophrenia"? When and why do we then distinguish different forms of "one" sickness—for example, cholera of the el Tor and classic biotypes and the Inaba, Ogawa, and Hikojima serotypes, and more than one hundred recognized strains? Short of the listing of single

13

occurrences of sickness in individuals, what is the limit of such sub-sub- . . . specification?

And further, what about forms of sickness that have labels in other societies, but may not in our own? Are there sicknesses that are not captured in our thought or that are conceived of in very different ways? *Susto,* for example, is a condition referred to by many Indian and mestizo peoples in Latin America (Rubel, O'Nell, and Collado-Ardon 1984). Persons afflicted with susto are thought to suffer a loss of their soul because of fright; they commonly lose their appetite and strength; they are listless and restless, depressed, withdrawn, and lacking in motivation. They must be cured by restoration of their soul. Another example, *amok* is a syndrome diagnosed in Southeast Asia in which violent and homicidal outbursts follow a period of brooding (Carr 1978). A third example, *pora-keri dohari,* is a condition believed by the Desana of the Amazon Basin in Colombia to be caused by a malevolent shaman who puts a fence around the uterus of a pregnant woman and turns her fetus to the breech position, blocking its birth (Reichel-Dolmatoff 1971). Pora-keri dohari is relieved when a benevolent shaman ascertains the position of the fetus, turns it for proper birth, and gives it food for strength. Are conditions such as susto, amok, and pora-keri dohari any less a part of the reality of sickness than cholera, hypertension, and depression? Is susto another label for depression, pora-keri dohari simply the breech position misconceived? Is amok in Malay the same as amok borrowed in English? Is there one reality of sickness differently named or are there multiple realities?

In this chapter I explore the range and dimensions of the universe of human sickness and the classification of its forms. I consider whether the varieties of sickness found are so diverse that no commonality can be discerned or whether, in contrast, sickness has an essence. I formulate a definition of sickness as *a condition of the self unwanted by its bearer.* With certain caveats, the range of human sickness is all those conditions of selves that have been or might be unwanted by their bearers. I consider preconditions that must exist in order for persons to know their own sicknesses. I then describe four interrelated aspects of sickness found in all settings: (1) accounts of sickness, (2) sickness experiences, (3) sickness roles and institutions, and (4) causes of sickness. I consider how one compares sicknesses in different cultural traditions; and I examine the question of the relative truth of different medical systems. I conclude that the Biomedical conception of sickness as physiological malfunction confuses conditions and their causes. To comprehend human sickness in diverse settings, the Biomedical view must be revised and greatly expanded. The universe of sickness is refracted in multiple realities.

A classification of the forms of sickness is referred to as a *nosology* (from the ancient Greek, *-logy,* "discourse on," and *nos-,* "disease"). A nosology is to forms of sickness what the classificatory schemes of Linnaeus are to the kingdoms of plants and animals, and what the nomenclature of contemporary nuclear physics is to the elementary particles of the universe—electrons, muons, quarks, Z°s, and so on. Nosologies group events of sickness on the basis of criteria that are detectable and deemed significant. A nosology is useful if it helps us understand sicknesses, if it allows prediction of their course, if it facilitates communication of our experiences of sickness, if it enables a more effective response, preventing, curing, or palliating sickness.

Nosologies are critical in research on the causes, possible cures, or other measures against sickness. Before we demonstrate causes or cures, we must appropriately specify which particular conditions constitute the sickness of interest and which do not. If our definitions are too broad, we may not be able to evaluate hypotheses, since possible causal connections may be obscured by unrelated conditions. The generic category of cancer hinders etiological research because it includes heterogeneous phenomena. On the other hand, the specific diagnosis of adenocarcinoma of the vagina allowed determination that DES (diethylstilbesterol), a medicine taken by pregnant women in the 1940s and 1950s to prevent fetal loss, was a highly potent cause of this cancer in their daughters (Herbst, Ulfelder, and Poskanzer 1971). The category of squamous cell lung cancer allows investigation of cigarette smoke as a cause. On the other hand, if our definitions are too narrow, we may also be unable to find associations because a common cause may contribute to phenomena not included.

A nosology is an element of a broader medical system and a still broader total culture—a society's system of ideas, values, and ways of doing things. Anthropologists have referred to the systems of medicine found in different cultures as folk or ethnomedicines. Contemporary Biomedicine is an ethnomedicine as are the shamanistic medicine of the Amazonian Desana Indians and the traditional medicine of China. All ethnomedicines have their own nosologies and medical theories. Nosologies and the medical theories of which they are a part vary widely among societies.

NOSOLOGIES IN THREE SOCIETIES
The Subanun

The Subanun, described as a pagan population, inhabit a mountainous region on the Philippine island of Mindanao; they are slash-and-burn farmers (Frake 1961). Subanun have no designated diagnosticians or healers; patients call upon their own knowledge and that of kin and neighbors for diagnosis and for herbal and other treatment. Charles Frake, an anthropologist who studied Subanun life in the 1960s, reports that, after legal matters and the plant life of their environment, sickness is the third most common topic of conversation among the Subanun. All Subanun are active and informed participants in the classification of and response to sickness. They

most often agree in their theoretical discussions of sickness, even though they
may differ in specific applications.

Frake systematically elicited Subanun diagnostic categories and found a
total of 186 basic diagnoses. Categories were distinguished by four criteria:
(1) Most conditions were distinguished on the basis of symptoms. (2) Other
conditions were distinguished by their causal agents and mechanisms. Causal
agents included not only the parts of particular plants and microscopic
animals—for example, mites—but also stress, objects thought to enter the
body, symbolic acts, and the loss of one's soul. (3) Some conditions were
distinguished on the basis of "prodromes"—that is, the set of symptoms that
preceded the sickness. (4) The remaining conditions were distinguished by
their personal etiology—the circumstances that caused the particular occurrence of sickness. Etiologic determination required divination or seance with
supernatural beings, costly procedures reserved for instances in which ordinary medicinal treatment had failed.

Early in the course of his field research, Frake had an infected swelling on
his leg. He took the occasion to learn about Subanun diagnostics. He found
29 distinctive diagnoses for dermatologic conditions, collectively called
nuka; diagnoses included *pugu,* rash, *nuka* (again), eruption, *beldut,* sore, and
buni, ringworm. Subanun made various diagnoses of his infection, at least in
part because his informants were responding to different levels of specificity—for example, skin diseases, or sore, or distal ulcer. (Frake does not say
how or by what means his infection was resolved—presumably satisfac-
torily.) Subanun commonly use diagnoses to select among 724 botanical
medicines for treatment and among 61 named offerings made to propitiate
supernatural beings. It is the gods who effect cure.

The Ndembu

Spirits also pervade the world of sickness of the Ndembu, a tribal
people of Zambia. Victor Turner studied Ndembu social organization, ritual,
and symbolism in the 1950s and early 1960s. Ndembu regard sickness as one
of several kinds of misfortune, which also include "bad luck at hunting,
reproductive disorders, physical accidents, and the loss of property." Turner
claims that the Ndembu "are obsessively logical, though on the basis of
mystical premises. . . . [They] consider that calamities and adversities of all
kinds are caused by mystical forces generated or evoked and directed by
conscious agents. These agents may be alive or dead, human or extrahuman"
(1967:300). The Ndembu are said not to distinguish "natural" from "supernatural" conditions.

Turner describes twenty-two examples of Ndembu diagnostic categories
and their therapies. The categories are distinguished on the basis of symptoms—for example, *mbumba yaluzong'a,* a disease that causes people to lose
toes and fingers (most likely leprosy in the Biomedical classification), *kaseli*

kamashi, a disease with bloody urine (most likely schistosomiasis), and *mu-song'u wachingongu,* a disease that leaves pockmarks (most likely smallpox). Also included are conditions whose symptoms are paralysis, insanity, and fits.

Ndembu diagnosis makes visible the forces hidden behind particular conditions. Much of Ndembu therapy is thought to work by a form of sympathy: manipulation of a substance representing the disease produces a parallel effect on the disease itself. For example, kaseli kamashi, blood in the urine, is treated by consumption of a medicine made of the red gum of a certain tree. Turner suggests that the curative principle here is homeopathic. If this treatment fails, a white gum medicine is used. Sickness in general is associated with blackness, health with whiteness.

Treatment for insanity involves medicines concocted from the old bones of a mad dog, a fruit associated with revelation and clarity, parts of the leopard (which kills without reason), the wild pig (which moves at random), and the *muvundu* fish (which may swim upside down). The leaves of a plant from the top of termite hills are used because the insane seem to be above things. "He wanders about in the air . . . talks in the air. . . . This disease of insanity comes in the air" (Turner 1967:319). Its remedy works through mimicry.

Biomedicine in Western Society

Western medicine is most often assumed (by Westerners) to be rational and systematic, based on empirical evidence and inductive and/or deductive logic. Its nosology is formally codified in the *International Classification of Diseases* (World Health Organization 1978), now in its ninth revision, known as ICD-9. Included in ICD-9 are places for 999 conditions, from "001, Cholera" to "999, Complications of Medical Care, Not Elsewhere Classified," and for more specific forms of many conditions—for example, along with "001, Cholera" is "001.1 Due to *Vibrio cholerae* el tor." Psychiatric conditions are included between ICD-9 codes 290 and 319, followed by "Diseases of the Nervous System and Sense Organs" (from which psychiatric conditions are thus, presumably, distinct); they are more fully defined in the American Psychiatric Association's *Diagnostic and Statistical Manual of Mental Disorders—III,* or "DSM-III" (American Psychiatric Association 1980). There is no apparent reason, other than coincidence or numerologic fancy, why the number of sicknesses allotted in the universe should accord so closely with the decimal system, $10^3 - 1$.

Diseases come and change and go in succeeding editions of the *International Classification of Diseases.* There are also vacant ICD-9 code numbers waiting for a disease—for example, ICD-9 codes 89 and 119. Conditions that are AIDS-related were assigned ICD-9 codes 42–44 in 1987. Smallpox, although eradicated in 1977, remains coded ICD-050; perhaps if and when known laboratory reservoirs of the infectious agent variola virus are destroyed, this ICD code will be vacated. The DSM-III code 302.0, "homosexuality," was replaced in 1973 with "sexual orientation disturbance," and then in DSM-III with "ego dystonic homosexuality"; thus homosexuality came to be regarded as a disease only when unwanted and accompanied by heterosexual desires. (There are no parallel conditions specified for unwanted heterosexuality or bisexuality.) Definitional decisions are political and judgmental as well as scientific.

The overall rationale for the ICD-9 classification is not spelled out. I am not aware of principles by which certain human problems are included (and excluded) in ICD-9 in the first place and then, once included, distinguished from one another. A wide variety of criteria underlies the ICD-9 classification: diseases are classified by causal agent, vector of the agent (for example, the mosquito that carries the parasite that causes malaria), affected body part, organ or system, symptoms, pathologic process, stage of disease, and behavior of patient, and by various combinations of these factors. Variable principles of classification may correspond to differences in the conditions themselves, to what is known about them, and to the historical circumstances of their discovery.

The multinational authors of ICD-9 seek both to be exhaustive—to include all conditions—and to ensure that no particular event of sickness will be classified under more than one code number. The ICD-9 seeks coverage of all known conditions by use of categories such as "001.9, Cholera, *unspecified*," "727.3, *other* bursitis," or "——, not elsewhere classified"; this allows for comprehensive classification despite incomplete knowledge of the range or characteristics of each condition. The ICD-9 avoids overlapping classifications by a variety of explicit statements excluding categories defined by other codes—for example, "297.1, Paranoia, *Excludes:* paranoid personality disorder (301.0)." Thus, the ICD-9 is logical by fiat.

Fundamental questions underlie the elaboration of a nosologic system, though nosologic systems such as the ICD-9 are most often developed without providing clear or explicit answers. The comparison of nosologies across cultural boundaries raises fundamental questions:

- What kind of thing, force, event, or process is a sickness? What distinguishes sickness from health and from other kinds of problems? Does sickness have an essence?
- How do we measure sickness? What are its dimensions—location, shape, acuteness, pain, severity, duration, cause, cost? By what criteria do we say that a sickness has begun, is ongoing, or has ended?
- How is knowledge of sickness and healing distributed—for example, among healers and patients, between Western societies and others? Who knows best when someone is sick?
- How do we know whether two sicknesses labeled in two languages are similar or different? How do we know which terms are valid?

Answers to these questions are vital for the way sickness and healing are understood and confronted in societies. A society in which sickness is thought to be defined and caused by anatomical and physiological alterations will focus on these physical characteristics of persons in seeking prevention or cure; since afflicted persons may be unable to assess their own anatomy and physiology, such a system of medicine may not listen to their complaints or accounts. In contrast, a society in which sickness is thought to be defined by human experience and caused by human interactions—physiological as well as social—may attend more to its social organization and the under-standings of its patients in addressing prevention and cure. How we think of sickness and the different kinds of sickness shapes our response, diagnosis, and treatment.

THE UNITY OF SICKNESS

In the course of an analysis of the roles of storytelling in medical practice and in the process of healing itself, physician and philosopher How-ard Brody argues that it is both futile and misleading to search for an essence of sickness (Brody 1987). What concept or principle could possibly unify such diverse conditions as warts, AIDS, schizophrenia, and paraplegia? Brody recommends that, beyond the abstract analysis of philosophy, we should study the range of stories (fictional and factual) of individual patients who have (or might have) suffered particular sicknesses. Brody quotes Oliver Sacks who equates persons with their biographies, their stories:

> If we wish to know a man, we ask "what is his story, his real, inmost story?," for each of us *is* a biography, a story. Each of us *is* a sin-gular narrative, which is constructed continually and unconsciously by, through, and in us—through our perceptions, our feelings, our thoughts, our actions; and, not least, through our discourse, our spoken narrations. Biologically, physiologically, we are not so differ-ent from each other; historically, as narratives, we are each of us unique.   (Sacks 1985:12)

Brody claims that "suffering is produced, and alleviated, primarily by the meaning one attaches to one's experience" (1987:5); thus, healing requires listening and responding to the patient's story.

Brody notes that most if not all attempts to formulate a definition of sickness have been either too restrictive—excluding conditions that most of us would include—or too broad—including conditions that usually would not be counted. He proposes that, instead of seeking a single definition, we look for a loosely connected "family resemblance" among the variety of phenomena referred to as "sickness." He sketches five themes that might connect the members of this "family":

1. To be sick is to have something wrong with oneself in a way regarded as abnormal when compared to a suitably chosen reference class.
2. To be sick is to experience both an unpleasant sense of disruption of body and self and a threat to one's integrated personhood.
3. To be sick is to have the sort of thing that medicine, as an evolving craft, has customarily treated.
4. To be sick is to undergo an alteration of one's social roles and relationships in ways that will be influenced by cultural belief systems.
5. To be sick is to participate in a disruption of an integrated hierarchy of natural systems, including one's biological subsystems, oneself as a discrete psychological entity, and the social and cultural systems of which one is a member.   (Brody 1987:22)

The third of these themes is peculiar. There may be sicknesses not treated by medicine (perhaps because medicine is currently incapable, perhaps because it is unaware) and other conditions treated that may not be sicknesses. The reverse definition seems more plausible—medicine as a craft intended to treat sicknesses.

Brody suggests that the last theme in his list—the systems view of humans and their internal and external environments—is the most comprehensive. But, more important, he is wary of all such generalizations; he warns that "each [generalization] should be seen as an approach to a further investigation of particular sickness episodes spanning the entire range of illness experiences, and not as a shortcut making such an investigation unnecessary" (1987:22). It is as if the term *sickness* were a homonym—as if, on hearing of *sickness*, we had to ask, "Are you speaking of sickness in the wart-sense, the schizophrenia-sense, or some other sense?"

Brody's argument against the search for a unifying notion follows the philosophical approach formulated by Wittgenstein (1958) and more recently advanced by Rorty (1979). This perspective transforms philosophy from an analytic discipline that criticizes the logic of other disciplines to reveal the true nature of concepts and the world into an observational discipline that, like anthropology and lexicography, more modestly describes how people use concepts and language. Wittgenstein professed, "Don't look for the meaning of a word, look for its use" (1958). The new philosophy would not attempt to discover by abstract reasoning what sickness "really is," but would examine the diverse ways in which the term *sickness* is used in different settings. Thus, individual stories of sickness become critical. (It should be noted, however, that traditional, non-Wittgensteinian philosophers also rely on stories—examples and counterexamples—to define the limits of their own or other analyses.)

I agree that the description of language usage has an important place in understanding the meaning of concepts such as sickness. But I also believe that the critical analysis of concepts and ideas should play a fundamental role in the practice of disciplines. Moreover, resort to stories does not avoid the problem of definition. In response to the recommendation that the understanding of sickness requires listening to stories of sickness, we may ask what makes a given story a story of sickness rather than a story of another of life's problems? Particularly in a foreign setting, how do we know we are listening to a story of sickness? We are forced to return to the question said to be unanswerable and misleading—what is sickness? While philosophy could profitably employ the descriptive and comparative practices of anthropology, anthropology should also adopt the critical habits of analytic philosophy.

The discussion of whether or not sickness has an essence continues a debate about the fundamental relationship between words and things that has persisted at least since the days of Plato. Plato and his "realist" heirs argue that the phenomena labeled by words share essential properties—precisely those that allow us to properly call these things by the given word and to distinguish these things from others. In contrast, "nominalists," such as Brody and other followers of Wittgenstein, believe that words are arbitrary and conventional labels for collections of objects (or events or other sorts of things) that have no common essence. In an extreme form of nominalism, because concepts and words are defined by and are appropriate in the cultural context in which they are used, the use of concepts and words from one tradition to describe phenomena in another becomes logically impossible. Nominalists may be trapped and isolated in their own thought and language.

I take a position between realism and nominalism, perhaps closer to the realist stance. As a realist, I believe that the phenomena labeled by sickness terms, such as *schizophrenia, cholera, paraplegia,* or *warts,* share essential characteristics—namely, those that allow the determination of whether or not they fall into one of these categories. It is a group of signs and symptoms caused by cholera organisms (though not by these organisms alone) that leads us to refer to specific events of sickness as *cholera* and to exclude other events as *not cholera.* Assessment of the applicability of sickness terms to given conditions is the work of diagnosis. The diagnosis of other conditions—for example, schizophrenia—may not be as clear-cut as that of cholera, because the characteristics of the condition are not clearly defined and/or because defined characteristics may be difficult to assess. Nevertheless, the same semantic principle applies—phenomena are grouped under a common label because of shared characteristics.

As a nominalist, I believe that the characteristics chosen to distinguish among specific sicknesses (such as symptoms or causal agents) are somewhat arbitrary and vary among societies and historical periods. Choosing different characteristics might lead to different groupings of sickness events. And the labels used are conventional and also arbitrary—certainly they, too, vary among societies and historical periods. But given the criteria chosen and the system of labels available, the conditions grouped under each label are no longer arbitrary but subject to rational determination.

THE ESSENCE OF SICKNESS

I propose that *sicknesses are unwanted conditions of self, or substantial threats of unwanted conditions of self*. Unwanted conditions may include states of any part of a person—body, mind, experience, or relationships. Unwantedness comes in degrees, and individuals may have different thresholds regarding just how seriously unwanted a condition must be in order to qualify as sickness.

If sickness is a matter of unwanted conditions of self, then the patient's story retains a central defining role, because the story is an account of which conditions are wanted and unwanted. He or she may not be able to determine when a substantial threat of unwanted conditions exists; but it is his or her desires and conceptions of well-being that define in the first place what threats there are.

This formulation bears similarities to a proposal of Clouser, Culver, and Gert (1981). "We believe," they write, "that there are objective definitional criteria, and that they apply equally to mental and physical conditions" (1981:29). They examine the term *malady,* because it includes many other concepts—disease, illness, injury, and disability. They develop a compact definition as follows: "A person has a malady if and only if he or she has a condition, other than a rational belief or desire, such that he or she is suffering, or at increased risk of suffering, an evil (death, pain, disability, loss of freedom or opportunity, or loss of pleasure) in the absence of a distinct sustaining cause" (1981:36). In other words, a malady is a condition that produces or threatens to produce suffering. Rational beliefs or desires are exempted because such conditions—for example, rationally mournful thoughts about the death of a companion—though they may cause suffering, need not be pathological. "Absence of a distinct sustaining cause" indicates that whatever external force may have initiated the condition is no longer present; a malady is incorporated in the patient. Brody criticizes this definition because some of its criteria ("increased risk," for example) are themselves in need of definition and also because, by including "loss of freedom and opportunity," the proposed definition is too broad—it would include pregnancy, menstruation, and sleep.

Like Clouser, Culver, and Gert (1981), I also note that sickness conditions lie *within* the self—they are *of* the self, physically and/or mentally. Unemployment and poor television reception may be unwanted conditions, but unless one has absorbed them into one's person (being obsessed about the television, say, or seriously lacking self-esteem because of unemployment), these conditions would not count as sicknesses.

A principal difference between the definition of *malady* proposed by Clouser, Culver, and Gert and what I have proposed for *sickness* is that, whereas maladies are the same for all persons in all cultures and at all times, sicknesses may vary by person, culture, and time. Sicknesses are unwanted by their *individual* bearers, but maladies are said to be diverse "evils" that have in common that "*no one* wants them" (Clouser, Culver, and Gert 1981:31; emphasis added). Malady restricts suffering to conditions unwanted by everyone; sickness allows suffering according to unique personal, cultural, and historical circumstances. Do not wanted and unwanted conditions depend on one's circumstances and individual character? Can sprinters, marathoners, scholars, surgeons, and pianists not suffer different conditions that are evil for one but not for all? What is a major sickness for one may be a minor irritation for another. Broken legs, rabies, and heart attacks may be universally unwanted, but there are other conditions that will be unwanted because of individual circumstances. Thus, it is more appropriate to define the universe of sicknesses by the biographical conditions of each patient rather than by the common denominator of all. Sicknesses are not only *of* the self; they are in essence determined *by* the self.

Although the matter has not been systematically studied, there is evidence that notions akin to sickness as I have described it exist in widely differing societies. The Subanun, for example, refer to *miglaru*, translated as "being sick"; they have numerous *njalan mesait en*, "disease names," each corresponding to a group of symptoms and treatments (Frake 1961).

Similarly, Turner reports of the Ndembu,

> Ndembu conceive disease or illness (*musong'u*) as a species of misfortune (*malwa, khualwa, kuyindama*, or *kubula kutooka*—this last term signifying "to lack whiteness or luck or purity"). . . . The Ndembu, like the Azande, consider that calamities and adversities of all kinds are caused by mystical forces generated or evoked and directed by conscious agents. . . . For Ndembu talk of different kinds of *nyisong'u*, "illnesses" or "diseases," and recognize that specific symptoms are connected with each of them.   (1967:300–301)

Among the Desana of the Colombian rain forest, Reichel-Dolmatoff writes, "The concept of disease is called *dore*, a term that denotes a complex symbolism that, at first sight, obscures the sequence of interconnected ideas. The word *dore* is derived from *doreri*/to order, to send. Illness is thus commonly interpreted as a mandate, or the product of a mandate, sent by or through a supernatural agency" (1971:175).

Among Mayan Indians of the Chiapas highlands, Manning and Fabrega report that despite "a lack of a conception of the *self* which is internally located, autonomous, and separate from that of other 'objects' (that is, persons, things, dieties, animals)," there is a concept of sicknesslike phenomena. "The theory of disease that prevails . . . can best be described as a *sociological* theory, although illness is nonetheless an event of significance to the individual" (1973:263).

Anthropological observers in a variety of non-Western settings have noted that, in addition to roughly equivalent generic terms, sickness is connected to two broader phenomena: cosmological or religious forces, and social relationships and interpersonal conflict. Yet, though commonly embedded in distinctive worldviews, there is nevertheless a shared concept akin to unwanted states of self.

Since an essential feature of sickness is its recognition and unwantedness by the patient, a prerequisite to the existence of sickness is the effective functioning of the person's capacities of perception and desire. Potential patients must be able to perceive conditions and to evaluate them as desirable or not. Ordinarily this is not a problem—most of us are capable of recognizing conditions in ourselves, or of understanding what others report to us about ourselves (for example, about an asymptomatic condition). And we are then capable of judging what we recognize as desirable or not.

In some cases, however, we identify an unwanted condition, but incorrectly describe its characteristics or its causes. For example, we can often correctly and precisely locate a noxious stimulus, say, a pin prick or a burn, but our sensations can be misleading. One normal effect of neurological connections is "referred pain," in which physical damage in one part of the body is experienced as pain in another part. Appendicitis is commonly sensed in the upper middle of the abdomen instead of deep in the lower right where it actually occurs. Angina pectoris is experienced across the upper chest and down the left arm rather than near the heart. And inflammation of the diaphragm is commonly sensed as pain in the shoulder (Melzack and Wall 1982). Such conditions are symptomatic, but deceptively so. They are recognized by their patients, but they are misplaced.

Inability to assess conditions of self may also arise in persons whose perceptual or emotional capacities are abnormal or impaired. I refer to pathologies that obstruct the assessment of sickness as "metapathologies"; they are sicknesses that, in turn, constrain the capacity of patients to recognize their own sickness. A functioning self is a prerequisite for self-knowledge of sickness; as Sacks notes, "If a man has lost a leg or an eye, he knows he has lost a leg or an eye, but if he has lost a self—himself—he cannot know it, because he is no longer there to know it" (1985:36–37). In the extreme, we would not accept at face value the statements of an insane man about when or how he is sick.

In some instances, metapathology results from trauma and neurological damage. In the "phantom limb" phenomenon, for example, pain and other sensations are experienced in limbs that have been (and that are known by the patient to be) amputated. Oliver Sacks (1985) has described other metapathologies in which neurological defects in patients have altered their experiential capacities—for example, a woman without proprioception (the ability to sense events in one's own body) and a man who incorrectly conceptualizes objects and literally "mistakes his wife for a hat." These disturbances impair the capacity of patients to know and judge their own conditions.

Another form of metapathology, similar to referred pain, might be called "altered reference." In somatization, for example, psychological conditions and stressful mental or interpersonal conditions are experienced as bodily conditions. The patient identifies an unwanted condition, but incorrectly identifies its source. Somatization is reported common in Taiwan and China, where the expression of mental conditions is stigmatized and physical symptoms are more readily acceptable (Kleinman 1980). Less well recognized is psychologization—conceptually the opposite of somatization—in which conditions judged by others to be physical are experienced by patients as states of mind. The doctrines of Christian Science explain all physical pathology as an illusion arising from the patient's lack of spiritual harmony; it is believed that only through proper religious faith can purportedly physical conditions be eliminated.

Personal knowledge of sickness may also be affected by "altered scaling" in which the patient's response appears either to exaggerate a condition (hyperaesthesia) or to minimize it (hypoaesthesia), to the extreme of denial. Hypochondriasis may be regarded as a form of hyperaesthesia, in which ordinary sensations are interpreted as symptoms. In "medical student's disease," a common occurrence in the course of Biomedical education, students (erroneously) believe themselves to have the pathological conditions they are studying (Mechanic 1972). In the contrary event of denial, patients assert that a condition does not exist when it is apparent to others that it does exist. Denial is common in alcoholism and other addictions.

Most infamous among metapathologies is the Munchausen syndrome (named for the notorious German fabulist Baron Karl von Münchausen) in which patients (often themselves medical personnel) feign or even fabricate sickness in themselves and then seek medical treatment for their "symptoms." They may claim pains or simulate scars or other physical damage; or they may cause physical harm to themselves—for example, by injecting feces or other pathogenic substances into their bloodstream. Whereas in denial patients deny the existence of pathologies observable to others, in the Munchausen syndrome, patients claim or create pathology not observable to others. Instances of "Munchausen syndrome by proxy" have been described in which one person (say, a parent) causes factitious disease in someone else (a child) and then seeks care in medical settings. One paradoxical case has been reported in which the patient sought treatment claiming, perhaps undeniably, to have Munchausen syndrome (Gurwith and Langston 1980). When patients with Munchausen syndrome are recognized by hospital personnel for their dissemblance, they commonly move on to another hospital, beginning the cycle again. Though they have been described as false patients, persons afflicted with Munchausen syndrome are truly sick; but their sickness lies not in the sickness they present but in their experience and presentation of sickness.

More generally, acts in which people deliberately inflict harm on themselves or others should be regarded as sicknesses, even if the perpetrators derive pleasure from these acts and feel nothing wrong or undesirable in themselves. We would not want to count as healthy such forms of behavior as sadism, torture, homicide, genocide, and other forms of abuse. Reference to such conditions as "sickness" may violate the patient's sense of self—the condition may not be unwanted. It is likely, however, that metapathology could be demonstrated—that is, impairment of the patient's capacity to experience sickness.

There is one critical exception to the characterization of the deliberate harm of self as sickness. Suicide might be regarded as the ultimate act of self-destruction, and impulsive suicide or suicide in which there is little rational reflection may reasonably be considered a form of sickness. But rational suicide, in which the so-called victim has decided on self-destruction following a clear weighing of his or her life and its possibilities, should not be included as sickness. Under these circumstances, suicide may be the best means of fulfilling an integral life. Similarly, living wills define the physical limits beyond which a person no longer considers his or her life worthy of sustaining; violation of the living will might then be considered a form of battery. It is inappropriate to refer to acts that complete the self as self-harm.

Since sicknesses compromise desired capacities or states, they are most often disvalued and rejected, but patients may be ambivalent toward and attached to their sicknesses. Chapter 9 describes patients who, despite their rational wishes to return to healthy life, are fearful of the end of their sickness; they have become engaged in the society and the machinery of the hospital; they are uncertain if they can succeed without these supports.

Sicknesses are recognized to bring "gains" to patients and to others as well. A sickness may give its patient a "primary gain" by diverting the patient's attention from a more disturbing problem. Patients may also be exempt from difficult or tiresome duties, and they may receive the sympathy and care of others—benefits referred to as "secondary gain." Secondary gains are thought to be motivating factors in conditions such as Munchausen syndrome. When secondary gains play a role in the intentional initiation of a sickness, the sickness is referred to as malingering. Others, too, may benefit from a patient's sickness—for example, by being able to exercise a desired caring role. Such "tertiary gains" may impede recovery and contribute to the persistence of sickness (Dansak 1973).

DIMENSIONS OF SICKNESS

I now propose a framework for thinking about sickness that allows for the validity of phenomena envisioned by Biomedicine without assuming these to be ultimate or exclusive truths. Elements in the framework are persons and their environments, including their society, culture, and physical environment. Each person has a body and a self that includes a mind, subjective experience, and relationships with the social and physical environment. Persons affect and are affected by their environments; and each part of a person (body, mind, experience, relationships) may affect other parts.

Accounts of Sickness

Sicknesses may be thought of as self-inflicted or inflicted by another—perhaps a spirit, an ancestor, or some other force. They may be held to be lodged in the body, the mind, or the soul, or to be more widely dispersed in the web of relations among beings of the world. They may be accepted passively as natural or fated, or they may be actively resisted as obstacles to personal fulfillment or social duty. I refer to alternative conceptions and understandings of sickness as "accounts." Accounts of sickness explain the "who?" "what?" "where?" "when?" and "why?" of sickness.

Accounts are akin to what Nichter has referred to as "idioms of distress" (1982), to what I have previously called "ideologies of suffering" (Hahn 1984), to Brody's "stories of sickness" (1987), and to what Kleinman has called "explanatory models" (1980) and "illness narratives" (1988). For each event of sickness, the explanatory model is said to be specific and to address five issues: etiology, occurrence, pathophysiology, course, and treatment (Kleinman 1980).

Accounts of sickness and of the different forms of sickness are elements of larger cultural systems that assume that the world consists of certain kinds of "things" and "forces" of which events of sickness are instances. As elements in cultural systems, accounts of sickness also make assumptions about the sources and means of medical knowledge; these assumptions provide standards that allow the members of a society (for example, patients and healers) to assess conditions and remedies and to evaluate proposed accounts. Accounts of sickness also assume a system of values by which to judge states of sickness, their causes, and responses to them—as moral or immoral, worthy or unimportant, and so on.

Accounts may themselves play a role in the causation of events of sickness. The placebo phenomenon, described in greater detail in chapter 4, is a well-known form of causation in which beliefs affect the occurrence of the events believed in—persons are healed because they believe in the causal efficacy of certain things, even though these things are known not to have the independent effect credited them.

The diverse accounts of sickness may be usefully classified by expanding the terminology developed by Kleinman, Eisenberg, and Good (1978). The classification of disease, illness, and disorder accounts of sickness divides the conceptual space centered on and surrounding the patient as follows:

Disease accounts focus on the body of the patient as the source of sickness; disease is located within the body, at or beneath the skin, and most often "below" the mind. Diseases, write Kleinman, Eisenberg, and Good (1978), are "abnormalities in the structure and function of body organs and systems." Accordingly, bodily interventions are regarded as the principal means by which to relieve sickness. The Biomedical explanation of sickness is epitomized in Feinstein's notion of "paraclinical entity"—the physical reality of sickness that may or may not be manifested either in the symptoms experienced by patients or in the signs recognized by physicians (Feinstein 1967).

Illness accounts consider not only the body but also persons along with their bodies and their social environment as the source of sickness and the place of its occurrence. Illnesses are "experiences of disvalued changes in states of being and in social function; the human experience of sickness" (Kleinman, Eisenberg, and Good 1978). Relief of illness is thus likely to require attention to persons and their environments as the target of interventions. In traditional African settings, explanations of sickness as caused by grudges and witchcraft are examples of illness accounts (Evans-Pritchard 1936; Turner 1967). In Western society, the popular belief in "stress"—the pressures of the social environment—as a cause of sickness is another example of an illness account (Young 1980). Psychological and sociological theories of the effects of the social environment on sickness and healing are also illness accounts.

Disorder accounts regard the source and locus of sickness as lying not only in the bodies of patients or in their persons but in the universe at large. When the universe is unbalanced, sickness may be manifested in particular locales and individual patients. Relief of sickness may focus on the redress of cosmic imbalances. Traditional Chinese medicine, in its theory if not its practice, is an example of a disorder-oriented account of sickness (Unschuld 1985; Porkert 1974). (In contrast, much of contemporary Chinese medicine and psychiatry, like Western Biomedicine, is strongly inclined to disease accounts.)

Disease, illness, and disorder accounts are proposed here as "ideal types," guiding themes that may orient an understanding of sickness. They may not be found in pure form in any particular setting; though one of these account forms may be thematic and dominant, different societies and social strata may combine elements of differing accounts. The classification of account forms thus serves to distinguish divergent emphases rather than to provide clear-cut, exclusive categories.

Sickness Experiences

The sickness experience is the flow of sensations, beliefs, attitudes, and emotions that contribute to people's consciousness that something is wrong and undesirable in themselves. Symptoms are part of the experience of sickness; in Biomedicine, doctors often use them for medical diagnosis rather than to respond to the patient's experience itself.

Experiences of sickness may be more or less immediate. At a basic level are primary experiences—for example, "there is a sharp pain in my back." Primary experiences of sickness may be localized to parts of the body or they may be more general—for example, the patient may feel a vague uneasiness or anxiety. They may vary in modality—for example, discomfort, cold or heat, physical pressure or piercing; in intensity—sharp or dull; in severity—from minor and negligible, to moderate and debilitating, to excruciating and incapacitating; and in duration—brief, intermittent, or continuous. Such basic perceptions are not raw sense data, unaffected by the perceiver's expectations; but if they arise without reflection, they may be more direct than other perceptions.

Further removed from more immediate experiences are secondary reactions. Having a severe, sharp pain in one's back may evoke additional feelings, thoughts, associations, and interpretations—for example, memory of previous experiences, dread of immobility, or anticipation of care by someone else or of financial compensation. Sickness experiences may result from a dynamic interplay of unconscious as well as conscious memories and meanings—memories and forgotten events of sickness in oneself or others (Stein 1990).

Accounts of sickness and experiences of sickness may significantly affect one another. Accounts that become established in a society influence the experiences the members of society expect when they encounter sickness. Societal accounts give names and explanations to sensations. Patients who experience a particular symptom are likely to associate it with sicknesses recognized to manifest this symptom. They may then scrutinize themselves for other symptoms believed to be associated with the syndrome; and they may examine their past for recognized causes of this sickness. Experiences of sickness may affirm the accounts they are about, but they may lead to modification or rejection of accounts—for example, "my case of such and such was different."

Sickness-Related Roles, Actions, and Institutions

Societies respond to the experience of sickness with social roles (that is, prescribed and patterned forms of action) and organized institutions. Sickness-related actions, roles, and institutions are commonly justified by accounts of sickness; and the performance of these roles, in turn, may serve to affirm corresponding accounts. As I describe more fully in chapter 4, the social organization of roles, actions, and institutions powerfully shapes the way in which sickness is conceived of, distributed among individuals, and treated.

A "role" is a set of expectations of what incumbents of specific positions in society should do—how they should behave. Societies maintain rules about how roles come to be occupied, how they are maintained, and how vacated. Roles are deliberately designated positions and are thus named, for example, "patient," "healer," "physician," "shaman," "nurse," "therapist." Individuals who do not follow role expectations may be regarded as deviant; their deviance may be sanctioned. Patients may be expected to report their sickness experiences sincerely and then to try to find healing. When they fail to follow medical etiquette, patients are said to "abuse" the sick role; they may be described as "crocks." Healers are expected to pursue qualifying training and examinations and to follow community standards of practice. Persons who falsely assume the healing role are commonly described as "quacks"; those who fail to adhere to standards are said to be guilty of "malpractice."

An "institution" is a socially recognized and designated set of roles that is organized and conceptually, if not physically separate from the rest of society. In Western society, the most visible health-related institutions are medical settings, such as doctors' offices, clinics, and hospitals. But there are also organizations of professionals and of patients, insurance companies, drug and equipment manufacturers, medical schools, institutions of medical research, and governmental health agencies. In Western societies, institutions commonly occupy separate physical settings. In non-Western societies, healing institutions may be less readily distinguished from other social organizations—for example, religious or political institutions.

Causes of Sickness

The causes of sickness are the circumstances that precede and lead to it. A *necessary cause* is one that must be present in order for the sickness to occur, or to put it the other way around, the sickness cannot occur in its absence (though the sickness needn't necessarily occur in its presence). A *sufficient cause* is one that makes the occurrence of sickness inevitable; the sickness can occur in the absence of a sufficient cause, but in its presence the sickness inevitably occurs. In Biomedical nosology, sicknesses are often defined in a way (by their causes) that makes specific causes necessary; the cholera organism is a necessary cause of cholera, motor vehicles a necessary cause of motor vehicle fatalities. Isolated sufficient causes are rare, because 100 percent causal efficacy—independent of other circumstances—is unusual. Untreated exposure to the bite of a rabid animal may be an exception; it is both a sufficient and a necessary cause of rabies (unless one is infected in a rabies laboratory) and of rabies death (unless one is immunized).

A complex array of causes precedes most events of sickness. In the chain of causation, there are relatively *immediate* causes of sickness (for example, promoters that accelerate the growth of malignant tumors that have already begun to grow); relatively *remote* causes (for example, smoking or cigarette smoke as an initiating cause of a cancerous tumor). There are causes *within* causes (for example, the compounds of tobacco that cause the cancerous process), and the causes *of* causes (for example, the circumstances that lead to the habit of smoking).

It is critical to distinguish the causes of sickness from the sicknesses themselves. Some inherited conditions, such as Huntington's chorea, may not manifest themselves until decades following birth. Were we to equate the sickness with its cause, persons who inherit Huntington's chorea would be sick at birth, if not before.

Similarly, chronically elevated blood pressure levels may be lethal, but are often "silent," causing no pain or other sensation. High blood pressure is an important cause of sicknesses such as stroke and heart disease; high blood pressure may be a sickness itself only when recognized and unwanted by its bearers. And a cancerous tumor may originate with a malignant division of a single cell many years before it can be detected by patient, clinician, or laboratory. We would not want to describe a person as "sick" from the instant of this cell division, since the disease might never follow or might follow only decades later. Such events may be common, though they are also commonly aborted by immunological processes. With a definition including all first events in causal processes as sicknesses themselves, we would all be sick from birth, for it is likely that causal processes of sickness and aging are present from the outset.

When in the causal chain does a sickness begin? Sickness begins when the condition becomes unwanted. It may begin when the person has unwanted symptoms, or it may begin when he or she has no symptoms but is aware of an impending condition. Asymptomatic conditions may thus be included as sicknesses, insofar as they are recognized and unwanted by their bearers. In the case of persons infected with the human immunodeficiency virus that causes AIDS, sickness may begin when manifested in symptoms. When recognized, however, the sickness AIDS may begin when a person is infected with the human immunodeficiency virus, because currently AIDS is unavoidable at the time of this event. Sickness is in the mind and heart of the beholder—the patient.

Causes of sickness are common foci of accounts of sickness. For example, the Azande of the Sudan look to witchcraft for the cause of sickness and to oracles for diagnostic knowledge of specific causes (Evans-Pritchard 1937). In traditional Chinese medicine, causality is sought in the imbalance of cosmic forces (Porkert 1974). And in Biomedicine, causality is most often examined as an alteration of human physiology, as in cells (see chapters 6–7).

UNIVERSALITY, TRUTH, AND EFFICACY

The diversity of accounts, experiences, roles, institutions, and even of causal circumstances of sickness in different cultural settings raises serious doubt that a universal system for classifying sickness is possible. Can we define forms of sickness—for example, "diarrhea," "depression," "broken arm"—with criteria that can be assessed in any cultural setting? Or are nosological systems culture-bound, appropriate only to the setting in which they are formulated? In a more general form, this question arises throughout anthropological inquiry.

Biomedical physicians might respond that a universal nosology already exists, namely, the *International Classification of Diseases*. The ICD is a product of international collaboration, but collaborators have thus far all been trained in Biomedicine; traditional, non-Biomedical medicines have not been represented. Anthropologists are more likely to respond that a universal nosology, if at all possible, is highly problematic. Like all social phenomena, sickness is so affected by the social context in which it occurs that there will be no way to find commonalities across cultural boundaries.

Were a universal nosology *not* possible, then such labels as "diarrhea," "depression," and "broken arm" would be narrow in meaning and very different from current conceptions. They could not be appropriately used to refer to human sicknesses found anywhere, except, in this case, the societies where Biomedicine is the principal medical system. "Diarrhea" would more accurately be "diarrhea—implicitly Western," "depression" would be "depression—implicitly Western," and so on. The labels for sickness we commonly use and those in use within Biomedicine would no longer refer to generic human conditions. Moreover, there would be no language to talk about the sicknesses of one culture in the language of another. The practice of international health and of medical anthropology would be difficult, if possible.

I believe that a universal cross-cultural nosology is possible, but only if it takes cultural setting into account. By this standard, the ICD has thus far failed. If the object of a nosological system is ultimately to study, diagnose, and treat the diverse forms of human sickness; and if, to do so, the specific goal of a nosology is to group and distinguish conditions by basic features of etiology, diagnosis, manifestations, and treatment, then an effective nosological system must recognize the sociocultural environment in which sicknesses occur.

A universal nosology would have an appearance very different from those currently in use. Two alternative versions seem plausible. In one version, current entries in the ICD would be amended to describe the variability found in diverse cultural settings. However, since there is likely to be much commonality within each culture regarding multiple sickness categories, this version of a universal nosology would be repetitive and unnecessarily cumbersome.

In a more concise version, the standard ICD would be modified. It would be expanded to include conditions reported in other cultural settings, but apparently not included within current ICD categories. The so-called culture-bound syndromes (considered in chapter 2) would be added. The universal nosology would also have a companion volume reviewing the ethnomedical systems found in each culture around the world, cross-referenced to corresponding sickness categories.

Clearly, the preparation of such a universal nosology would be a major enterprise. It would, however, bring enormous benefits. By adding currently unrecognized sicknesses, it would make the ICD more comprehensive, exhaustive, and relevant in diverse settings; it would become the *Intercultural Classification of Diseases.* By describing the varying contexts of sickness conditions, the ethnomedical encyclopedia would allow users to understand how the range of conditions found in the ICD are modified and manifested in particular cultural settings. It would thus sharpen etiological analysis and diagnosis, enhance relations with patients, and improve treatments and outcomes.

In addition to the question of a universal nosology, a second question arises: how can we compare conditions described in one system with conditions described in another? When are two conditions found in different cultural settings equivalent—for example, susto and depression, pora-keri dohari and breech position birth? This question is closely related to the first question, since we must presumably know how to compare sicknesses across cultural boundaries in order to classify them as similar or not and to distinguish them from other conditions.

An extreme example of the difficulties of translation is illustrated in attempts to translate conditions described as psychiatric in Biomedicine. Problems in the comparison of depression across cultural boundaries have been pondered by anthropologists and colleagues (Kleinman and Good 1985). In Biomedical thinking, depression is an affective disorder, an emotional problem within the individual's psyche. To begin, many non-Western cultures do not attribute sickness to internal states of the mind. For example, on the half-square-mile island of Ifaluk in the South Pacific, people who mourn for extended periods are not thought to suffer an internal, emotional problem—such states are not even considered; rather, mourners are believed to have not yet found an appropriate replacement for the person they have lost (Lutz 1985a). The problem is not intrapersonal or psychiatric, but social, interpersonal.

Another issue in the cross-cultural comparison of depression is the value attached to perceived symptoms. Thus, for example, Sri Lankan anthropologist Gananath Obeyesekere finds strange the conclusion of an epidemiologic study that "*generalization* of hopelessness . . . forms the central core of depressive disorder" (Brown and Harris 1978:235). A Sri Lankan described in such terms should be thought of not as a depressive but as a good Buddhist

(Obeyesekere 1985). The Buddhist seeks the acceptance of the hopelessness of the world as a step in the path of salvation. Obeyesekere describes the Buddhist "meditation on revulsion" in which laymen deliberately contemplate death, decay, and filth in order to recognize the "transitoriness of the body and the world" and to develop a contempt for bodily pleasures. Given their willing participation in an accepted practice at the heart of Buddhist ways of thought, it would be perverse to describe successful practitioners as sick or, more particularly, depressed. (Perhaps the Buddhist feels depressed when failing to overcome a contentment in daily life.)

In seeking comparisons of sickness concepts across cultural boundaries, I recommend use of the four dimensions described earlier. Strict equivalence is improbable, even between two patients within a single cultural setting. Cross-cultural approximations may be found and differences noted, however. Regarding the translation of depression, for example, Lutz argues that we should examine "indigenous definitions of situations of loss and the blocking of goals, and the social organization of responses to them" (1985a:92). I suggest that such comparison on broad dimensions will improve our understanding of sickness and our ability to treat it.

We want not only to be able to classify and distinguish the diversity of human sicknesses and to find approximate equivalents (and differences) from one system to another but also to compare medical systems and ask whether one is closer to "the truth" than another and whether one "works" better than another. These questions are independent, since one medical system may be knowledgeable, but unable to put its knowledge into effect, whereas another's techniques work, despite relative ignorance. The questions may be asked of medical systems as wholes or of their parts.

Westerners may take it for granted that their system, Biomedicine, is both closer to the truth and more efficacious than other medical systems. But there are several difficulties with this assumption. First, cultures may share many goals of medical practice—healing a broken arm or stopping diarrhea—but other goals may differ. The good Buddhist pursues experiences of generalized hopelessness for which the Westerner seeks treatment. Second, standards of truth may differ from one system to another, so that comparison is difficult. Part of what makes a belief true is its accordance with other beliefs and basic premises; another part of truth is correspondence with observations, but observations, too, are shaped by the perspective of the observer. Third, as I describe more fully in chapter 4, the efficacy of an intervention may be powerfully affected by cultural setting; thus, efficacy is not a fixed characteristic independent of context.

Finally, all cultural systems of beliefs are at best *approximations* of the truth. The wide variety of accounts and their historical evolution suggest a persistent separation between accounts and their referents. Some may be closer than others—in whole or in part—but none are "there," or likely to get "there." As noted, single beliefs about the world, such as ethnomedical beliefs, are elements in much larger systems of belief; the single belief makes sense only as part of the system. When a single belief improves, for example, by explaining more observations, it may drag the rest of the belief system along, forcing revision. Scientists are commonly impressed by what their predecessors, or they themselves, did not know or (erroneously) thought they knew even a decade before; they may also discover that new ideas have historical precedents. Ongoing revision may be an essential characteristic in the production of knowledge. Accounts are imperfect maps—perhaps inevitably so.

In recent decades, philosophers, historians, and social scientists, reacting to positivist and empiricist movements of earlier decades, have questioned the efficacy and superiority of scientific approaches to knowledge. They have challenged the notion of progress in scientific knowledge, arguing, like anthropologists, that what is known is relative to a given set of premises and that absolute criteria for the comparison of systems of belief have not been demonstrated and may not be possible (Richards 1987). This extreme relativism has been resisted by others (for example, Laudan 1977, 1990). But while objective reality is recognized to constrain the enterprise of human knowledge, the force of historical and cultural setting in the foundation and growth of knowledge is also widely accepted.

Even accepting the relative merits and progress of Western science, it is doubtful that Biomedicine, despite frequent professions of commitment of scientific foundations, is consistently scientific in practice. As described more fully in chapter 6, Biomedical practices are not always based on the best available scientific evidence. Practices may be adopted before evidence is available; they may be not adopted when evidence is available; and they may persist following evidence of inefficacy and even harm. We may believe in the relative merits of Biomedicine compared with most other systems for the understanding and treatment of many conditions, but scientific evaluation is not a consistent standard of practice.

For many, but not all conditions, Biomedicine appears closer to the truth and more efficacious than many non-Western ethnomedicines. Take the case of diarrheal diseases, estimated to cause between 5 and 7 million deaths per year around the world (Weiss 1988). In Western society, despite the demonstration a century earlier of the beneficial effect of intravenous rehydration, physicians continued their practices of bloodletting and fluid restriction; the use of purgatives and emetics continued as late as the mid-twentieth century (Weiss 1988). It is estimated that in the 1980s approximately five hundred U.S. infants died each year from diarrheal diseases, mostly preventable (Ho et al. 1988).

The Biomedical perspective currently claims that diarrheal deaths are most often the consequence of the severe dehydration associated with diarrhea. The principal Biomedical prescription is administration of oral rehydration therapy, commonly known as ORT, consisting of a solution of glucose and salts in clean water. The World Health Organization (1985) estimates that 60 to 70 percent of deaths from diarrhea, more than 3 million per year, could be prevented by proper use of ORT.

But the medical traditions of many regions of the world differ from the current Biomedical perspective and approach. In some settings, traditional approaches to diarrhea are not contrary to Biomedical practice. In rural northern India, mothers continue to breast-feed infants with diarrhea, they do not reduce fluids, and they alter, rather than restrict, the foods they give (Bentley 1988).

In other settings, however, traditional beliefs and practices may exacerbate diarrheal sickness. In Swaziland, most contagious diseases are thought to be airborne; diseases are not associated with feces, and, except for schistosomiasis, few are associated with water (Green 1985). Several forms of diarrhea are distinguished by their symptoms; dehydration is not regarded as a symptom of diarrhea. Some forms of diarrhea are thought to be associated with improper food or drink. Older patients may be given purgatives, younger patients enemas, both of which exacerbate dehydration.

In rural Honduras, the more severe forms of diarrhea are thought to be caused by improper foods, by worms, or by the malicious, penetrating glances of others—"the evil eye" (Kendall, Foote, and Martorell 1984). Rural Hondurans believe that most severe diarrheal conditions are beyond the powers of Biomedical treatment. Fallen fontanelle, recognized by Biomedicine as a sign of dehydration, is regarded as a condition unrelated to diarrhea, requiring separate treatment. Purgatives are given to cleanse the digestive tract.

It is likely that in most or all settings, patients want to avoid diarrhea and to cure it when it occurs. Where traditional beliefs and practices hinder effective treatment of diarrhea, knowledge of ORT and its efficacy are not sufficient by themselves. There is a vital difference between having an effective technique and having it adopted in a given setting. As I argue more fully in chapter 10, international public health efforts have often failed because they assumed that they were introducing their lifesaving knowledge and techniques into an "empty vessel"—a setting without established beliefs or techniques—so that the new approach would be rationally adopted. Public health practitioners have failed to consider local knowledge, practice, and social environment; potential recipients thus have often rejected the new approach.

To make ORT acceptable and practical in those settings requires an understanding of local thought and practice. For example, Kendall has recommended that ORT be offered as a purgative in the Honduran setting where purgatives are thought efficacious. Honduran physicians have resisted this approach because it misrepresents ORT as a purgative and appears to recommend the use of purgatives. In rural northern India, ORT was used but subsequently rejected by mothers who were little concerned with dehydration and who claimed that ORT did not cure diarrhea. The translation of ideas about dehydration and its association with diarrhea is essential (Bentley 1988). We cannot dispense with knowledge of *non-Biomedical* theories and practices if Biomedical practices are to be introduced into settings where most needed.

There are other conditions in which traditional non-Western approaches may be more effective than Biomedical treatments. The World Health Organization's International Pilot Study of Schizophrenia (1973) compared the occurrence and course of schizophrenia in nine centers around the world. As in the case of depression, the comparison of schizophrenia across cultures is problematic because it is a condition that involves delusions, disturbances of affect, thought, volition, and sense of self; since what counts as normal varies from setting to setting, comparison of disturbance—that is, variations from normal—will also vary. In the diagnosis of individual patients, the study found substantially less agreement among diagnosticians in *different* settings than among diagnosticians in *the patient's own* setting. The study made extensive efforts to establish comparability and to recognize differences.

Assuming the comparability of diagnoses, several studies have reported similar rates of the occurrence of schizophrenia in different cultural settings. What was discovered in the International Pilot Study was that rates of relapse from schizophrenia varied substantially. Good outcomes (such as lack of relapse) were more common in the two developing country sites—Ibadan, Nigeria, and Agra, India—and least common in developed countries— Aarhus, Denmark, London, England, and Prague, Czechoslovakia (World Health Organization 1979). Persons initially diagnosed as schizophrenic in Ibadan had the lowest rates of social impairment when assessed in follow-up visits. It is hypothesized that differences in outcome were associated with differences in the social environments and expectations of patients in these settings—for example, the strong family bonds and supportive social environments of developing countries versus the urbanized stresses of life in industrialized countries. These hypotheses were not tested in the International Pilot Study.

Other examples of relatively efficacious approaches in non-Western settings can be found in the arena of obstetrics. Maternal and infant mortality in the Western world have declined dramatically since the beginning of the twentieth century to levels far below those of the developing world. Nevertheless, a number of common practices are followed in Biomedical obstetrics despite evidence that they are not beneficial and may be harmful (Chalmers, Enkin, and Keirse 1989; Davis-Floyd 1992; Jordan 1993). For example, a review of studies of electronic fetal monitoring concludes that routine monitoring is expensive and commonly does not produce useful information beyond that available by traditional auscultation; in addition, electronic monitoring leads to higher rates of cesarean section and may cause infection and other damage to the infant (Banta and Thacker 1979). Routine episi-

otomy—the cutting of the vaginal entry to prevent tears from birth—has
also been found to have few benefits and many risks, including blood loss,
pain, swelling, anatomical damage, and infection (Thacker and Banta 1983).
Questions about the benefits and costs of cesarean sections, the use of the
supine lithotomy position for delivery, and routine induced labor have also
been raised (Marieskind 1980, Davis-Floyd 1992).

Abandonment of "external cephalic version," used extensively until the
late 1960s both in the United States and in non-Western settings to turn
fetuses from the breech position to normal position, has also been questioned
(Jordan 1993). Moreover, the supportive social environment common in
many non-Western birth systems seems to be beneficial to mothers and has
been recently readmitted into Western settings as part of the so-called natural
childbirth movement (Leavitt 1987). (Since humans are creatures of cultures
that profoundly shape the way they practice childbirth, there is no "natural
childbirth" [Jordan 1993].)

SICKNESS IN BIOMEDICINE

A recent Biomedical textbook of pathology begins, "Pathology is
the study of disease by scientific methods. Disease may, in turn, be defined as
an abnormal variation in the structure or function of any part of the body"
(Anderson 1985:1). A similar perspective is reflected in the notion of disease
proposed by Biomedical theorist Alvan Feinstein: " 'disease' refers to a structural or chemical lesion (or derangement) in the human body" (1964:759). In
Feinstein's scheme, some events of sickness may be experienced by patients in
the form of symptoms, regarded as subjective; other events of sickness can be
detected at the bedside by physicians in the form of signs, regarded as
objective. Objectivity and subjectivity are thus determined by the role of the
observer rather than by what is observed. But sickness may not be detectable
at the bedside by normal perception. The absence of clinical evidence of
sickness implies the detectability of sickness in only its more fundamental
form—"paraclinical abnormality" (Feinstein 1967). Paraclinical phenomena
are the essence of sickness; evidence from paraclinical colleagues—radiologists, pathologists, laboratory workers—provides direct knowledge of sickness. Corresponding to this hierarchy of sickness phenomena, physicians
have exclusive access to fundamental knowledge, and patients have at best
occasional access to subjective experience of their own conditions.

In the framework I propose, the Biomedical hierarchy of patient and
healer is turned upside down. I begin not with "underlying biological disturbance" but with the panhuman, though variable, biographical experience of
sickness. While biological disease processes may play a role in the *causation* of
sickness, it is the *unwantedness* of sickness *by its patients* that is primary and
that dictates what is to be causally explained and therapeutically encoun-

tered. In contrast to the *paraclinical* entities posited by Feinstein as the atoms of disease, I have proposed as the essence of sickness the *preclinical* experience of an unwanted state in one's person. The soul of sickness is closer to the self than to the cell.

The etymology of *pathology* suggests a view in which pathology is the science of "pathos," or suffering. This vision is obscured in contemporary Biomedicine. I am recommending that we take this etymology seriously— not that we reject the vast discoveries and lifesaving tools of pathology as practiced in contemporary Biomedicine but that we regard this practice from a different, perhaps ancient, vantage point in which the medical enterprise is driven not by cellular abnormalities but by the experience of human suffering.

Contemporary Biomedical pathology marks its progress in terms of smaller and smaller units of observation, but I am recommending a complementary move in the opposite direction to include the mind, human relations and society, and the broader environment. Let us critically expand our theory of sickness and our practice of healing to allow the diversity of its forms, its contexts, its interpretations.

2 CULTURE-BOUND SYNDROMES UNBOUND

One of the jumpers while sitting in his chair with a knife in his hand was told to throw it, and he threw it quickly, so that it stuck in a beam opposite; at the same time he repeated the order to throw it, with cry or utterance of alarm resembling that of hysteria or epilepsy. He also threw away his pipe when filling it with tobacco when he was slapped upon the shoulder. . . . They [the jumpers] could not help repeating the word or sound that came from the person that ordered them any more than they could help striking, dropping, throwing, jumping, or starting; all of these phenomena were indeed but parts of the general condition known as jumping. . . . All of the jumpers agree that it tires them to be jumped and they dread it, but they were constantly annoyed by their companions.

—"*Jumpers," Moosehead Lake, Maine, described by Beard 1880:487–88*

E. A. B. at the time of the event was 20 years old, unmarried, the third of four siblings and an Iban. At the time he ran *amok* he had been uprooted from his normal surrounding, a longhouse in one of the upper reaches of the Batang Lupar river. He was working in an oil drilling camp, approximately 200 miles from home with no direct communication. One night, while living on a barge near the camp, he grabbed a knife and slashed five of his fellow workers, three Malay and two Chinese.

—*A man with* amok *in Malaysia, described in Schmidt 1977:270*

A man, about age 45, with wife and children, took a second wife. Afraid of the first wife's jealousy, he tried to keep the new relationship secret, but in time the second marriage became known. One evening, he came home tired and fatigued. He got the shivers, broke out in a cold sweat, and felt that his penis was shrinking. At his cry for help, the neighbors came running. Only men helped him. One man tightly held the patient's penis while another went for a *sanro,* a native healer. The *sanro* performed one ritual and after a while the anxiety disappeared, ending the day's attack.

—*An Indonesian man with* koro, *reported in Chabot 1950:165, referred to in Edwards 1985*

Observers of seemingly strange behavior have distinguished a variety of behavioral syndromes that, because of their apparent uniqueness and fit to local cultural conditions, are described as culture-bound. The observers of such behavior have most often been from Western settings, the behavior observed principally in non-Western ones. In this chapter, I examine the logic by which the generic diagnostic label "culture-bound syndrome" is ascribed to some conditions and not to others. I claim that the idea of culture-bound syndromes is a conceptual mistake, confusing rather than clarifying our understanding of the role of culture in sickness and fostering a false dichotomy of events and the disciplines in which they are studied. All conditions of sickness are affected in many ways, and none is exhaustively determined by its cultural setting. Physiology, medicine, psychology, and anthropology are complementary rather than contrary and exclusive; all are relevant and necessary to the comprehensive understanding of human phenomena of sickness and healing.

Simons and Hughes (1985) have recently provided a survey and classification of culture-bound syndromes; they note the importance of a multidisciplinary approach to these conditions. Perhaps paradoxically, Hughes (1985) argues that the label "culture-bound syndrome" is misleading and should be abandoned in the development of a universal theory of sickness and its classification.

The very notion of a culture-bound syndrome indicates a form of reductionism—the explanation of a given phenomenon by a single principle or body of knowledge. Other explanatory principles are thus denied relevance. Reductionists may claim that they have fully explained a culture-bound syndrome and that, in consequence, this phenomenon falls exclusively within their domain of inquiry. This mistaken effort is apparent in versions of anthropology as well as in Western medicine, psychiatry, psychoanalysis, and psychology. I argue that such claims fragment human function and its study into falsely opposed divisions.

Although anthropologists may believe that they have established a firm position by appropriating culture-bound syndromes to their own domain of explanation, their claims are at once excessive and too modest, claiming too much for culture-bound syndromes and too little for the diseases staked out by Biomedicine. I argue that full explanation requires an opening of the inner sanctum of Biomedicine to anthropological review and a concomitant recognition of pervasive physiological constraint in the workings of culture. Humans are bound by their cultures—but not rigidly. Nor is culture the only binding principle; body, mind, society, and the broader environment also bind. An exploration of culture-bound syndromes thus reaches the variety of forms of sickness and the range of human disciplinary approaches.

To assess the notion of culture-bound syndrome, I briefly define *syndrome* and *culture* and suggest how syndromes might be *bound* by culture. I distinguish three ways in which culture-bound syndromes have been understood. I then speculate about how some behavioral event sequences have come to be labeled culture-bound syndromes. I investigate the logic of this label and examine some broader implications, recommending a framework close to those proposed by Simons (1980, 1985) and others (Brody and Sobel 1979; Lehrman 1970). I propose that we discard the misleading concept of culture-bound syndrome in favor of a broader study of the role of human mind, physiology, culture, and society in pathology and its relief.

SYNDROMES, CULTURES, AND BINDS

A *syndrome* (from the Latin "things that run together") is a group of conditions, generally pathological, that may be physical and/or mental, signs and/or symptoms, and that is thought to constitute a discrete entity. One syndrome, AIDS (acquired immunodeficiency syndrome), has gained recent attention; it is defined by a complex set of signs and symptoms that has evolved with changing knowledge as well as political-economic circumstances. Numerous other syndromes are named in Biomedicine, some after their discoverer, others after their symptoms. Syndromes are distinguished from other events that co-occur in that their co-occurrence is thought to be not simply coincidental; a syndrome is a part of a unifying phenomenon—for example, a recognized biological process. The constituents of a syndrome may reflect a group of similar causes. What makes AIDS a syndrome is the acquisition of a specific virus, the human immunodeficiency virus, which causes a range of outcomes constituting AIDS.

The specificity with which a syndrome is defined will substantially affect what can validly be said about it—its distribution by nation and ethnic group, and other characteristics. The more of the surrounding context that is included in the definition of a syndrome, the more restricted its distribution is likely to be. If the assault of multiple persons is a criterion of amok, the condition will be more widespread than if the outburst of violence is restricted to homicide, to any type of stabbing, to stabbing only with knives, or to stabbing with certain kinds of knives. The more culturally specific details a syndrome includes, the more likely it is to be a culture-bound syndrome. In the extreme, comprehensive description of a syndrome may pinpoint a single occurrence.

A culture, in the anthropological sense, is the set of beliefs, rules of behavior, and customary behaviors maintained, practiced, and transmitted in a given society. Different cultures may be found in a society as a whole or in its segments—for example, in its ethnic groups or social classes.

A syndrome may be regarded as culture-bound if particular cultural conditions are *necessary* for the occurrence of that syndrome; thus the culture-bound syndrome is thought not to occur in the absence of these cultural conditions. Some analysts of culture-bound syndromes may regard specific cultural conditions as *sufficient* for the syndrome's occurrence; in this view, no conditions other than these cultural ones (for example, other cultural conditions or noncultural ones) are necessary to provoke the occurrence of the culture-bound syndrome.

A HYPOTHETICAL ETHNOGRAPHY OF THE DIAGNOSIS CULTURE-BOUND SYNDROME

Some of the dilemmas inherent in the notion of culture-bound syndrome are apparent in the ethnographic sources of this diagnosis. The history of specific terms and interpretations of these conditions is most often lost in the memories and notes of colonial settlers. Winzeler (1984) provides a rare historical account of the development of notions of latah. Edwards (1985) formulates the history of another condition, koro, its multiple names, and purported cases; as in the example of koro described at the outset of this chapter, a person who experiences koro is usually under great stress or anxiety, suffers a retraction of the genitals, and may fear death.

In general, we may guess that the application of the generic label culture-bound syndrome and of terms for specific conditions, such as latah (Simons 1980; Kenny 1978), amok (Carr 1978), and "wildman behavior" (Salisbury 1966, 1967; Langness 1967), occurs in a sequence approximating the following:

1. Observers, most often trained in Western medicine, psychiatry, or psychoanalysis, or in anthropology or psychology, visit a foreign setting or an ethnic setting at home. Most often, ethnic settings are those that differ in their culture from the observers' own. Most often, though not always, the observers are white Americans or Europeans.

2. The observers notice behavior that seems strange (that is, unusual by their standards of normality) and indicative of deviance and disturbance. According to their interpretive bent, the observers are likely to take the observed behavior as pathological in some way—medically, psychiatrically, psychodynamically, behaviorally, and so on. Yet they may not know how to diagnose this pathology since it does not fit the familiar criteria of Western nosology. The culture-bound syndromes were early described as "exotic" (referred to in Yap 1962), a term that may tell us more about its users than about its intended referent.

3. The people among whom the strange behavior occurs may offer a solution to the diagnostic dilemma. They may distinguish and label the observed behavior, although recognition of such labels in an unfamiliar setting is problematic. A response to an observer's question (such as, "What am I observing, and what is it called?"), which perhaps is not well understood, may not truly indicate what nevertheless comes to be accepted as an indigenous label for the observed condition. Vallee, for example, suggests that the term for one such condition, *pibloqtoq* (also referred to as "Arctic hysteria"), is the fabrication of early explorers rather than a usual term of Eskimo usage (1966).

The local people may also manifest a broader classification, that is, a nosology, into which their diagnostic label fits, accompanied by a theory and a value system that account for their response to this condition. They themselves may or may not regard the condition as pathological, offensive, and worthy of treatment. Observers of an anthropological persuasion may take the indigenous cultural scheme as relevant if not definitive of the condition (but see Hughes 1985); others may ignore the indigenous perspective as local color, tangential to basic pathology.

4. The observers return home with their prized possession: a new syndrome that, because it seems to be found only in the cultural setting from which they have returned, is labeled culture-bound. Culture-bound syndromes are residual; they are conditions that do not fit the nosological scheme of a Western observer. Rather than questioning the completeness or validity of the Western nosology, the new syndrome is set apart as an oddity from another culture.

5. The observers now face the ambiguous challenge of showing how this culture-bound syndrome actually fits into their own explanatory paradigm. The dilemma here is that, as the phenomenon is encompassed by the observers' explanatory system, it may lose its uniqueness and become a version of the broader phenomenon. Explanatory gain may be culture-specific loss. Analysts of culture-bound syndromes have attempted to keep their syndrome while reducing it also, by showing how social, cultural, and psychological conditions—general elements of their own scheme—are so distinctively configured in the local scene as to make this particular syndrome unlikely to occur elsewhere. Their reductions combine the universal principles of their own discipline—for example, the learning theories of psychology—with the unique cultural peculiarities of the local setting—for example, the specifics of who teaches, what is taught, and how. The local fit and indigenous label appear to give these conditions an immunity from spreading elsewhere; they may *look* like the "xyz" syndrome found elsewhere, but they are really different.

6. Having established a new condition, often distinguished by an ascribed indigenous term, the "discoverer" of this syndrome (or other observers) may then find further instances of similar conditions in new settings, applying the established term, but now crossing cultural boundaries. Amok is the most notorious condition to be exported. Edwards (1985) argues that the Indonesian term koro has been (mis-) applied to conditions found among some Chinese populations (*suoyang*) and other groups as well, misguiding searches for an understanding of these events. Edwards claims that the association of koro and suoyang is superficial, and that influence is more likely to have been that of early Chinese over other indigenous groups. He believes the pseudo-association of koro and suoyang to be the product of the observer's theories, a narrow psychoanalytic view that latched onto the central and most frequent symptom of these conditions, the extreme retraction of the penis. He argues that there are two distinct syndromes, each more culture-bound than a psychoanalytic account would suggest.

UNDERSTANDING CULTURE-BOUND SYNDROMES

Three alternative understandings of culture-bound phenomena are plausible. One may be described as "exclusionist," the other two as "inclusionist." I refer to one inclusionist position as "nature-culture continuum," to the second as "multiple-aspect."

The exclusionist interpretation of culture-bound syndromes is suggested by the phrase "culture-bound syndrome" itself. The phrase implies or assumes that some conditions are culture-bound and others are not. Conditions that are not culture-bound may be regarded as culture-free, culture-blind; perhaps they are thought of as nature-, physiology-, or materiality-bound. In the exclusionist view, that a condition falls in one-half of this divide implies that it does not fall in the other, and vice versa. Latah and amok are culture-bound syndromes; measles and lung cancer are not. This division is held to correspond to disciplinary divisions as well, so that culture-bound syndromes are the concern of anthropological and/or psychological or psychiatric expertise and culture-free syndromes are the subject of medical or physiological examination.

Kenny (1978, 1983) provides an excellent example of the exclusionist position in his analysis of latah. In Kenny's work, some conditions are regarded as clearly culture-bound and others as clearly universal (though universal conditions may be differently interpreted in different settings).

> Measles or smallpox, for example, are clearly identifiable disease entities, but receive very different cultural interpretations. Is this also true for "latah," "amok," and other ostensibly culture-bound syndromes? In short, are latah-like startle responses better considered [quoting Simons 1980] as the "exploitation of a neurophysiological potential," *or* are they themselves more plausibly considered as the outcome of social *rather than* biological factors?   (Kenny 1983:161; emphasis added)

Kenny's "or" and "rather than" are exclusive connections. "Disease entities" are regarded as universal phenomena, the results of biological factors; culture-bound syndromes, in contrast, are not diseaselike and result from social factors. Kenny claims (1983:160) that cultural patterns "fully explain" latah; it would thus seem that biological explanation has no room.

Kenny claims (personal communication, 1983) not to assume a strictly exclusionist position. He has argued only that, on the ground of empirical fact rather than on general principle, the cultural context of latah provides its "best" explanation. This claim is inconsistent with many of Kenny's published remarks, an interpretation of Kenny's writings with which Simons (1983) concurs. Though Kenny's published remarks focus on latah, the understanding of disciplines (for example, anthropology, medicine, and psychology) in his writings strongly suggests a division of human phenomena into those that are "fully" or "best" accounted for by one discipline, and those by different disciplines. Again, if a phenomenon is fully accounted for, further accounts are unnecessary, if not false. When Kenny writes, "there is no purely psychogenic latah," he suggests that other conditions may be "purely psychogenic," or at least that someone believes so (1978:216). He also writes: "I suggested above that depth psychology is unlikely to be able to fully explain this fact, since latah is a well-known and role-like condition which can be imitated and which appears to occur in certain definite contexts. Sociological analysis cannot explain it either, but merely predicts that phenomena like it will occur elsewhere in similar conditions" (1978:218).

Kenny believes the "true" nature of latah to be dramaturgic, an arena he believes unrelated or exclusive of human biology. (For similar dramaturgic visions of culture-bound syndromes, see Karp 1985; Lee 1981; Salisbury 1966, 1967; Langness 1965.) Kenny writes: "If this is the case, then the latah performance is taken out of the province of biomedical reductionism and is seen in what I take to be its true light—as theater" (1983:166). Kenny here replaces biomedical reductionism with theatrical reductionism.

Psychologist John Carr's (1978) interpretation of another Southeast Asian condition, amok, represents a version of the exclusionist position distinct from Kenny's. Though Carr writes that some syndromes are culture-bound, he goes on to formulate a plausible interpretation of amok behavior based on a theory of learning from Western psychology. Carr applies universal principles to the Malay setting, asserting that amok is a learned behavioral response to a highly ambiguous yet demanding cultural situation. Langness (1965) claims that similar cultural conditions—"contradictory demands and discontinuities"—account for "wildman behavior" in New Guinea.

Yet although Carr relates this culture-bound syndrome to universal principles of learning, like Kenny, he explicitly dissociates it from universal processes of disease, as formulated in Biomedicine: "The notion that culture-bound syndromes share underlying common disease forms is rejected. Instead, the ethno-behavioral model postulates that culture-bound syndromes consist of culturally specific behavioral repertoires legitimated by culturally sanctioned norms and concepts, but with both behavior and norms acquired in accordance with basic principles of human learning universal to all cultures" (1978:269).

Using notions of disease and illness developed by Kleinman, Carr associates culture-bound syndromes with illness behavior, which, "as distinct from the disease process, is always culturally determined." He concludes that a culture-bound syndrome is "a distinct repertoire of behaviors that (1) have evolved as the result of a social learning process in which the conceptual and value systems, and the social structural forms that mediate their effects, have served to define the conditions under which such behavior is an appropriate response, and (2) have been legitimated within the indigenous system as *illness* primarily in terms of extreme deviation from the behavioral norm as defined by preeminent culturally-specified conceptual dimensions governing social behavior" (1978:289).

This description of culture-bound syndromes parallels Kleinman's distinction between disease and illness and corresponds to disciplines appropriate to each:

	EXPLANATORY PRINCIPLE	
	Culture	Nature
Condition	Culture-bound	Culture-free
	syndrome	syndrome
	Illness	Disease
Discipline	Psychology	Physiology
	Anthropology	Medicine
		Psychiatry

Carr notes, however, that culture-bound syndromes "may be precipitated by any number of etiological factors, among them physical, as well as socio-cultural determinants" (1978:273). Thus, the basic cause of amok is thought to be psychological; the particular elements that are psychologically incorporated are culturally specific, and given this established syndrome, a number of precipitants, including physical ones, may elicit this behavior. Carr regards diseases as phenomena that appear universally, in "inviolate" form, and that are the legitimate concern of medicine and psychiatry, whereas illnesses are "always culturally determined" and are thus the legitimate concern of psychology and anthropology.

More recently, Carr (Carr and Vitaliano 1982) has modified his earlier analysis, maintaining a position defined below as inclusionist; he refers, for example, to biological, cultural, and environmental influences and mechanisms in learning itself. Here illnesses also are said to have biological determinants. Carr reconceptualizes culture-bound syndromes as follows:

> The phenomenon of *amok,* like depression, is one of several alternative *distress* responses to aversive or stressful conditions—the specific behavioral response representing a final common pathway of multiple etiological determinants, among them environmental, biological, psychological, cognitive, and socio-cultural factors. Further we would hypothesize that so-called "culture-bound syndromes" are in fact by-products of this process; that they are clinical manifestations of the "final common pathway" distress response in which socio-cultural variables especially have played a prominent role in determining the idiosyncratic nature of the response.   (Carr and Vitaliano 1982:17)

The inclusionist nature-culture continuum position maintains that all human events, including the supposed culture-bound ones, have cultural *and* biological *and* cognitive *and* psychodynamic aspects, though some events are more profoundly shaped by one of these aspects than by others. Thus, although no conditions are exclusively culture-bound or culture-free, some may be largely culturally shaped and others principally determined by universal physiology. In this conception, the notion of culture-bound syndrome remains a valid one. An example of the nature-culture continuum position is the work of Leighton and Murphy:

> So far as the total process in the development of psychiatric disorder is concerned, it would seem best to assume that heredity, biological, and psychological factors are all three engaged. To claim dominance for one, or for any subarea within one, *as a matter of general theory,* is to express a linear conception of cause and effect which is out of keeping with what we know about all the processes in the world around us. More germane is an approach to the topic that aims to discover and map out the interrelated factors and the nature of their interrelationships.   (1965:11)

The recommendation that the relative importance of heredity, biology, and psychology cannot be theoretically determined in advance but must be empirically analyzed suggests that these factors may have more or less weight for different sicknesses.

The continuum understanding would make the extent to which a condition is culture-bound a matter of degree. It might be possible, at least theoretically, to quantify the proportions in which different factors contribute to given outcome conditions. Measles might occupy the natural, physiological end of this spectrum, the culture-bound syndromes the other; it is not clear what sorts of conditions might fall between—perhaps depression and alcoholism.

Yap (for example, 1969; see also Linton 1956) seems to have maintained a continuum position, claiming that culture-bound syndromes fit into a universal psychiatric nosology but take unusual shape because of distinctive local cultural conditions. Although Yap made a sharp division between "organic" and "functional" conditions, he discerned biologic as well as cultural effects in both. He rejected the phrase "exotic psychoses," recommending "culture-bound reactive syndrome" (Yap 1962). He offered a scheme from the psychiatric nosology of Biomedicine, which he believed encompassed both recognized culture-bound reactive syndromes and those not yet known. In medicine, kindred approaches have been termed "biopsychosocial" (Engel 1977), "systems" (Brody and Sobel 1979), and "multi-aspect" (Hahn and Kleinman 1983a). (See chapter 3; Landy 1983, 1985; Low 1985.)

Simons's (1980, 1983) explanation of latah exemplifies the inclusionist stance. (Simons refers to prototypical latah as found in Malaysia with an uppercase "L" ["Latah"] and to latah-like conditions with a lower case "l".) Simons calls latah and other conditions culture-bound syndromes, yet he explains latah as a cultural elaboration of a universal behavioral and physiologic complex, the "startle reflex," shared by humans and other mammals. In some societies, such as the United States, the reflex is little elaborated, whereas in Malaysia and Indonesia it is the object of terminologic distinction, folk-medical treatment, and an explicit and detailed social response. The power of such societal elaborations is suggested by Simons's (1983a:201) footnote about three Westerners (at least one anthropologist among them) living in regions of latah elaboration who began, against their wills, to show mild forms of latah behavior.

Simons distinguishes three types of latah. The first two are in part involuntary responses to startling events; these he calls "authentic" (1980:200). In the strongest authentic response, "Attention-Capture Latah," the subject completes actions initiated by someone else and, less often, follows commands. In a second authentic form of latah, "Immediate-Response Latah," the subject responds markedly to a stimulus, for example, a sudden noise. Finally, in "Role Latah," the subject chooses to perform behaviors observed in immediate-response or attention-capture Latah, yet without the stimulus that provokes these. Role Latah performers may use behavior not usually part of startle-stimulated latah. Role Latah would be found in societies that elaborate the social significance of such behavior. Role Latah (which in Simons's conception is not "authentic") resembles Kenny's conception of all latah as theater.

That Simons maintains that the "Continuum" variant of the inclusionist position is suggested by his assertion: "I believe that in at least some of the syndromes the effects of psychological, social, and cultural factors are mingled with the effects of biological factors in an intricate way. . . . It is possible, and I believe in some instances necessary, to consider factors in many disciplines simultaneously" (1985:26).

The inclusionist multiple-aspect position takes a stance distinct from the nature-culture continuum position, asserting that all human conditions are *equally* biologic *and* cultural *and* social, cognitive, psychologic, *and* psychodynamic, and so on. Biology, anthropology, and psychology do not have more or less weight in given conditions, for each considers a distinctive aspect of a common phenomenon. The multiple-aspect position thus makes the same claims for measles and tuberculosis as for depression and culture-bound syndromes. In the multiple-aspect position, all syndromes are regarded as equally culture-bound, so that the concept of "culture-bound syndrome" is itself not a useful distinction.

I am not aware of analysts of culture-bound syndromes who have adopted a multiple-aspect position; indeed, such analysts would argue that syndromes taken by others as "culture-bound" were the product of many effects, only some of which were cultural. The work of Lehrman (1970), a physiologic psychologist, illustrates a kindred position (see Simons 1985). Although he does not refer to pathologic states in particular, Lehrman insists that all behavior is at once 100 percent determined by its biology and 100 percent determined by its experiential history. As he writes, "The ontogenetic development of species-specific behavior patterns may often depend upon influences from the environment which interact with processes internal to the organism at all stages of development, in such a way that it is misleading to label those behavior patterns that seem to depend upon ordinary learning, and those that do not, as 'learned' and 'innate,' with the implication that they have dichotomously different developmental origins" (1970:19–20).

ANTHROPOLOGICAL QUERIES AND LOGICAL DOUBTS
The Source and Location of Cultural Binds

The distribution of culture-bound syndromes around the world might make us suspicious of this label. With the possible exception of the marginal jumpers of Maine (Beard 1880), associated by some researchers with the latahs of Southeast Asia (Simons 1983), culture-bound syndromes characteristically have been found in societies other than our own. Despite Yap's suggestion (1969) that "atypical" conditions such as depression, mass excitement, and anorexia were found in Western, industrialized societies as well as elsewhere, domestic culture-bound syndromes have only very recently been explored. Like the popular understanding of accents in speech, culture-bound syndromes are what other people have. The increased application of an analytic category at greater distances from the home of its progenitor parallels the definition of ethnomedicine as the theories and practices of non-Western, nonscientific systems (Hughes 1968; Foster and Anderson 1978), a usage that distorts the comparison of medical systems.

To demonstrate a more evenhanded conception of culture-bound syndromes, Cassidy (1982a) and Ritenbaugh (1982) have reformulated the concept in a discussion of protein energy malnutrition (PEM) and obesity. The first is a condition that affects 400 million people in a great variety of cultural settings. The argument of Cassidy and Ritenbaugh has some strange consequences, however, for they define culture-bound syndromes not as specific conditions bound to the cultures in which they are found but as uniquely appropriate to the culture that diagnoses them. They write:

A culture-bound syndrome is a constellation of symptoms which has been categorized as a dysfunction or disease. It is characterized by one or more of the following:
1. It cannot be understood apart from its specific cultural or subcultural context.
2. The etiology summarizes and symbolizes core meanings and behavioral norms of that culture.
3. Diagnosis relies on culture-specific technology as well as ideology.
4. Successful treatment is accomplished only by participants in that culture.   (Cassidy 1982a:326)

Although this definition appears to accord with the usual understanding of culture-bound syndromes, the "specific cultural or subcultural context" to which they refer is not that of the setting where the condition is found but rather that of the setting in which the diagnosis is formulated. This interpretation becomes clear when Cassidy discusses the "specific cultural or subcultural context" of PEM, which is twentieth-century Biomedicine rather than the third world where the condition is prevalent. According to Cassidy, PEM is a culture-bound syndrome because the concept is bound up in Western scientific ideologies. She shows how the Biomedical etiology ascribed to the condition has hindered efforts to alleviate this widespread ill.

Ritenbaugh's treatment of obesity differs logically from Cassidy's analysis of PEM, because the former condition is found among those who apply the label. Ritenbaugh's analysis here accords with usual usage. But, rather than using the indigenous definition, Ritenbaugh considers as obesity only mild to moderate forms of this condition. This definition cuts the ordinary American use of this term too thinly and, in doing so, misses the essence of the popular understanding of obesity.

Perhaps Ritenbaugh assumes that extreme obesity is "real" disease, pathological in terms of universalistic, biological criteria, whereas less extreme cases represent "role obesity" in Simons's terminology. Role obesity would be a performance enacted in response to scientific and public knowledge of real obesity. Yet the entire range of this condition is culturally affected, so that Ritenbaugh's formulation neglects the cultural premises underlying and connecting all the forms of "fatness" or "overweight."

Cassidy and Ritenbaugh explore homegrown culture-bound syndromes and indicate the cultural bases of Biomedical thought. Yet their definition turns the usual division of culture-bound syndrome/non-culture-bound syndrome upside down, with confusing results. If amok, latah, susto, and pibloqtoq are culture-bound, are they culture-bound only when they are applied to settings other than those in which they are conceived? If PEM is culture-bound, is it a culture-bound condition because it is misconceived by Biomedical practitioners, and because it does not take local culture and sociocultural etiological factors into account? It is essential to acknowledge the cultural roots of a diagnosis, but it is important also not to conflate this cultural connection with the connection between a condition and the context in which it is found.

Defining Syndromes: Category and Context

The prevailing view of culture-bound syndromes is that these behaviors are distinctive of their cultural circumstances. Taken to its extreme, this view has implications that make scientific comparison impossible. All phenomena and events are unique, each differentiable from all others by some or, more likely, by many characteristics: each screw produced in a factory,

every case of depression and tuberculosis, every episode of latah. The variations of each occurrence of a phenomenon are explicable, though perhaps not
by current knowledge, in terms of the context of that occurrence. Indeed,
such explanation is what we mean by "context"—a phenomenon's context is
its circumstance, its environment. It is the explanatory power of a phenomenon rather than its simple physical contiguity that constitutes the context of
something to be explained. Because one phenomenon is significant in the
explanation of another, however, does not bind the two to the exclusion of
other explanatory principles. Occurrences of latah may well be different in
large and small communities, as manifested by older and younger performers, by one person and another, even by an individual person at different
times or in different circumstances. Do we then talk of community-bound,
age-bound, person-bound, person-time-circumstance-bound syndromes?

By contextualizing in this way, we end up with a list of occurrences-for-
persons-at-times-in-circumstances, and so on, ad infinitum. Then, since
each instance is unique, we could not compare; there would be no two
instances of any "thing" to compare. In such a perspective it is not even clear
how we talk of events in the first place, other than by specifically naming each
one. Kenny (1983) writes of the problem of including too little in defining a
category so that we ignore its local fit. I am arguing that we may run into the
opposite bind of including so much context in category definitions that we
will have no comparative categories at all. Although each differentiated
individual is unique and necessarily appropriate to its historical circumstances, the assumption that general principles consequently do not apply is
illogical. If we cannot compare apples and oranges (because they are too
different?), can we compare Valencias with navels, one navel with another,
one navel with itself at some other time or circumstance?

On latah, for example, Kenny writes, "Simons is working within a Biomedical paradigm which stresses human biological and ethological universals and which requires concepts which are cross-culturally applicable"
(1983:161). Kenny asserts that such comparative categories are inappropriate. The label "latah," as he claims to use it, fits only conditions and circumstances found in Malaysia. Whereas for Kenny, latah includes a complex of
ideology, values, and practices that accompany the behavioral response, for
Simons, latah is a sequence of behaviors in response to an environmental
stimulus. Kenny characterizes Simons's definition of latah behavior as "im-
possibly superficial," claiming that each definitional element "would ideally
have to be understood in its cultural and social context before any claim could
be made to truly comprehend the whole" (1983:161). Thus, he does not
distinguish the phenomenon from its explanation. He goes on to claim that
by discovering "the whole" he has dissolved the paradox that latah-like
phenomena are widely distributed yet locally determined; he asserts that
these phenomena are entirely distinct wholes, only superficially comparable
(Kenny 1983). In contrast, Simons resolves the paradox by assuming that

cultural differences affect variations in the presentation of a universal human behavioral sequence.

In Search of the Whole: Interpretive and Causal Explanation

The exclusionist claim that some behavioral complexes are culture-bound and that others are not, and that the latter fit into some universal scheme, suggests that the culture-bound phenomena are so distinctive that they are beyond comparison. The explanation of such phenomena, exclusionists assume, connects them with other local phenomena and patterns of meaning, rather than with phenomena and patterns elsewhere. This perspective parallels one of two radically different positions that divide anthropology as well as literary studies, historiography (Weber 1984), and psychology: interpretive and causal. Culture-bound syndromes provide a perfect example of the interpretive school, since they are thought to be explicable only by their local context.

According to the interpretive understanding, a position also called hermeneutic and phenomenological and sometimes associated with the philosopher Ludwig Wittgenstein (Winch 1958), social and cultural phenomena are fully explained when they are shown to fit with other local phenomena in a system that "makes sense." In this view, questions about the causes of the phenomena of interest are regarded as misconceived or tangential. Thus, Kenny objects to attempts to explain culture-bound syndromes by universal, causal principles: "These medical or pseudo-medical labels evoke the notion that there is some kind of causal process underlying *latah*. The interpreters of *latah* seek to identify factors in the life experience of the victim which make her condition inevitable" (1978:214). It is implied that no kind of causality underlies latah. In a more general vein, Geertz writes, "Believing, with Max Weber, that man is an animal suspended in webs of significance he himself has spun, I take culture to be those webs, and the analysis of it to be therefore not an experimental science in search of law but an interpretive one in search of meaning" (1973:5).

Although it is obvious that anthropology is not an experimental science, Geertz goes further to assert that a search for law, presumably causal, excludes a search for interpretation. Interpretation is deemed appropriate only in the study of the workings of culture. Thus Geertz distinguishes blinks, which may be causally analyzed by science, from winks, which are intentional acts shaped by cultural systems to be analyzed by an interpretation of meaning in society and the circumstances of the winker. Yet, at some level, human biology is the mechanism of winks and may be involved in their motivation as well, and blinks, too, may express a symbolic meaning; these two forms of eye movement are not as distinctive as Geertz claims them to be.

By seeking out and respecting the systems of meaning of others, the interpretive stance has served to moderate the ethnocentrism of our civilization. But, at least in some versions, it has gone too far. It might be described as "xenocentric," positing that what other people believe about their circumstances fully accounts for these circumstances. Thus, for example, Kenny seems to adopt the theory of disease causation reported among the Koryak people of Siberia in the early part of the twentieth century when he writes, "Given this theory, it may be seen that special conditions involving mimesis and obscenity are parts of a much more inclusive whole in which 'startle' only ambiguously figures as causal agent. Illness is considered due to the departure of something—the soul; but the cause of its departure must be construed as 'fear' not 'startle'" (1983:162). Kenny maintains that if startle is not part of the indigenous explanation for a behavior, then it is, in fact, not a true or valid explanation; local understandings provide sufficient explanation for local action. The role of outside observers is not to analyze or to compare but to translate and represent the indigenous interpretation and context.

Several difficulties are implicit in the xenocentric stance. First, not one, but many differing and inconsistent beliefs exist in every society. Indeed, single persons often produce great inconsistent tangles of belief. Which belief predominates, and what criteria make sense of contrary beliefs or practices? Moreover, we know that intentions often do not lead to action or to the action intended; beliefs are not sufficient explanation for the actions they are said to explain. The world constrains our actions in many ways. The assumption that cultural and mental principles and the thoughts they generate alone account for human behavior is erroneous.

Finally, if comprehensive explanation rests with those who perform an action, we become ensnared in webs of meaning that lead logically to solipsism. If local phenomena and labels for them can be understood only in terms of other local phenomena and their labels, then research across localities, as in much of anthropology, becomes impossible. Anthropologists may pursue their own tales, but not those of others.

ANTHROPOLOGY, SIBLING DISCIPLINES, AND THE SPECTRUM OF SICKNESS

A conceptual and theoretical solution to the troubles of the exclusionist position might be founded in four principles:

1. A cross-cultural theory of sickness should begin, though not necessarily end, with the indigenous and personal understandings of the sufferer. Forms of suffering that do not fit the Biomedical mold will not be excluded as culture-bound. Patients at home will not be rejected as superstitious or as "crocks" because they fail to fall into Biomedical diagnostics. Pathology would be defined by the experience of the patient rather than by principles that seem a priori universal because they work fairly well among some groups at home and because they can be significantly explained by physiology, also

apparently universal. Although a person may be (asymptomatically) unaware of the conditions that might later affect his or her well-being, still the state of well-being itself, and thus the sources of threat to it, are defined by the thought world of the patient him- or herself.

2. Interpreting a human act or syndrome—that is, showing its fit to the understandings and to the local circumstances in which it occurs—may be necessary, but it is not sufficient for full understanding. Minimally, an explanation that some phenomenon occurs in one place because of such-and-such conditions must also show that it does not occur elsewhere, where these conditions are not met. Comparison is a necessity and requires the development of comparative categories so that we may say that this is found here but not there, and that that is found there but not here. Even interpretation itself requires comparative categories; without them, the terms of one language and culture (say, the interpreter's) could not apply to those of another; translation would be impossible, and interpretation could thus be made only in local terms and only for local consumption. Exclusionism, by insisting on the exclusive local fit of all cultural phenomena, thereby precludes comparison; indeed it precludes communication across cultural boundaries.

The difficulties of causal explanation are notorious, though perhaps better recognized than the hazards of interpretation. Nevertheless causal explanation, however systematic and nonlinear, must be pursued. In this way a universal scheme will come to take local meaning into account.

3. The course of human events is inevitably many-leveled, so that neither our disciplines—such as anthropology, physiology, psychology—nor their central concepts—culture, biochemical exchanges, human experience—can exclusively appropriate any event. That is, human events are not simply cultural or psychological, but inevitably bear these aspects and others.

4. As described more fully in chapter 4, there are several ways in which the organization and culture of societies affect their processes of pathogenesis and healing. Societies inform their members about how the world is divided up and put together. With regard to pathogenic and healthful processes I have recommended three forms of understanding: *disease* models, *illness* models, and *disorder* models. Societies also engage in the production of sickness because of the ways in which they organize cultural beliefs and social relations. Carr's psychosocial analysis of amok illustrates the pathogenic powers of the social environment.

Such a sociocultural framework applies not only to conditions that are obviously affected, but to the purportedly hard-core diseases as well. The Biomedical model has obscured rather than enlightened such effects. Yet the history of tuberculosis, as brilliantly portrayed by René and Jean Dubos forty years ago (1952), illustrates sociocultural effects in this condition whose biological characteristics appear to be clearly defined. The variety and power of ideology in tuberculosis-like conditions in European society are visible in a great range of attitudes toward this former (and reemerging) "captain of the men of death," its victims sometimes believed to manifest intensified creative powers as they were "consumed." Ideologies continue to be modified. The Duboses suggest that the term *tuberculosis,* already bearing a denotation not directly indicative of contemporary etiological conceptions, could be modified to fit current knowledge. The bacterium itself was then being shown to be neither necessary nor sufficient to the symptomatic complex that we call tuberculosis. The Duboses insisted on the causative importance of the host's sociocultural and natural environment. They also noted that though psychological factors were likely to be of importance, their extent and workings were unknown. A great variety of remedial efforts have also followed beliefs about this condition and about the broader order of social life. Tubercular patients have been revered and isolated, placed in dry climates and wet ones, required to rest and to exercise exhaustively.

Culture, nature, and the human mind between play central roles in diseases commonly thought of in terms of microorganisms and toxins as well as in apparently strange behavioral complexes. Only an inclusionist framework can encompass the range of pathological (and healthy) forms.

Culture-bound syndromes constitute an important frontier between anthropology, Biomedicine, and the medical systems of other societies. Built in premises different from our own, they challenge our standard divisions of things. In striking fashion they have reminded us that our own forms of sickness and of reacting to events do not cover the spectrum of the humanly possible. A comprehensive theory of human reactions and pathology must take them into account.

I have argued that the exclusionist understanding of culture-bound syndromes, implicit in the term, yet not intended by early proponents, distorts the role of culture and of physiology in human affairs. It claims too much of culture at the margin of our nosological scheme and too little of culture at medicine's core. Medical professionals, anthropologists, and others have conspired in a false division of labor. False divisions obstruct understanding. The abandonment of the erroneous category, culture-bound syndrome, might serve to redirect our attention to the formulation of a theory of human sickness in which culture, psychology, and physiology were regarded as mutually relevant across cultural and nosological boundaries.

3

THREE THEORIES OF
SICKNESS AND HEALING

The price of metaphor is eternal vigilance.

—Lewontin 1983:36

Scholars have proposed a wide range of explanations for the forms of human sickness and healing found in different cultural and historical settings. In this chapter, I review three basic theories underlying a variety of explanations: an *environmental/evolutionary theory*, which argues that the physical environment and human adaptations to it are the principal determinants of sickness and healing; a *cultural theory*, which posits cultural systems of beliefs, values, and customs as basic determinants; and a *political/economic theory*, which proposes that economic organization and contending relationships of power are the principal forces controlling human sickness and healing. Some of the examples I examine are not directly concerned with sickness and healing, but nevertheless have profound implications for an understanding of these matters. Several of the scholars I discuss are anthropologists, and others are sociologists, biologists, physicians, and geographers.

The explanations I review differ not only in what they consider the determinants of sickness and healing but also in the nature of this determination. Three alternative positions, reductionism, emergentism, and interactionism, may be found in versions of the major theories I examine. Each posits a different basic relationship between phenomena of different "levels"—for example, molecules, cells, tissues, organs, organisms, persons, societies, and ecosystems.

Reductionism: Explanations that assert that one phenomenon (for example, social behavior) is entirely explained by another phenomenon (for example, human biology or genetics) are reductionist—they *reduce* phenomena of one kind to phenomena of another kind.

Emergentism: Other explanations assert that the phenomena of interest are autonomous, independent of phenomena at lower levels of organization. Because higher-level phenomena (such as human behavior) are said to have distinctive properties that *emerge* from the combination of lower-level phenomena (such as genes), these explanations are described as emergent; the emergentist position is captured by the epigram, "The whole is greater than the sum of its parts." For example, Emile Durkheim, a father of twentieth-century sociology, regarded social phenomena as inherently unpredictable from psychological states. He wrote, "There is between psychology and sociology the same break in continuity as between biology and the physiochemical sciences. Consequently, every time that a social phenomenon is directly explained by a psychological phenomenon, we may be sure that the explanation is false" (1966/1895:104). Emergentist explanations are the opposite of reductionist explanations; what one claims the other denies.

Interactionism: Finally, interactionist explanations assert that phenomena at different levels—for example, human social behavior and genes—are separate but mutually influential or *interacting*. Genes constrain behavior; behavior modifies the distribution of genes in populations.

Proponents of different theories commonly think about reality in a variety of ways. They may maintain variant ideas about the grounds of knowledge—how we justify our claims—and about "human nature" and its features. They may define "sickness" and "healing" differently. They may differ as well about the goals of their research (for example, knowledge and/or intervention and social change) and the implications of the research for human well-being. Insofar as these differences are discernible in the theorists' writings, I attempt to describe them.

Theories of sickness and healing may be arrayed on a continuum according to their principal determinants (Hahn and Kleinman 1983a). At one end of the continuum are theories that focus on the environment and human biology; at the other end are theories that focus on cultural beliefs and social relationships. In the middle are theories that recognize roles for biology, the environment, and human society and culture. In my review of alternative theories, I first analyze environmental/evolutionary theories, next consider cultural theories, and conclude by examining political/economic theories.

ENVIRONMENTAL/EVOLUTIONARY THEORIES

In *Adaptation in Cultural Evolution: An Approach to Medical Anthropology,* Alexander Alland (1970) outlined the importance of principles of evolution for an understanding of medical systems found in different cultural and historical settings. Alland claimed that a society's environment and its medical system influenced each other in powerful ways: "My theoretical bias is tied to the biological theory of evolution. It is my strong conviction that the evolution of human behavior, including what has come to be called culture history, can best be understood in terms of such a theory" (1970:5). Alland, however, was not a reductionist but adopted an interactionist position; he believed that the effects of evolution on human culture were limited: "The role of the environment must not be exaggerated in explanations of cultural development. Environment is a selecting agent and not an active force itself capable of producing change" (1970:34).

Like species, human cultures and their medical systems evolve over time. Although Alland did not believe that environmental circumstances determined the specifics of cultures, he asserted that the environment might constrain cultural development, since cultural practices affected the success of a population in reproduction and survival in its environment. "Man changes his environment, often drastically, through the adaptive mechanism of culture, and this changed environment then acts as a selective agent on man's physical structure as well as on his behavior" (34). "I would expect that much (certainly not all) of what appears to be irrational behavior will turn out to fit the prevailing ecological conditions and demonstrate that much of behavior is either health oriented or produces maximization in some other way" (129). The "carrying capacity" is a measure of a population's successful adaptation and ability to maintain or increase its size in given ecological circumstances.

Alland defined disease and health in terms of the observable physical conditions of people in societies rather than in terms of the people's own experiences of unwanted states. For example, he reports that, though the Mano people of Liberia do not consider malaria to be a disease, malaria is widespread among them, significantly affecting their well-being and ability to survive and reproduce in their environment. (Perhaps because it is so common, the Mano take malaria for granted, the way things are, natural.) Thus, contrary to Mano thought, by Alland's definition, the Mano have a substantial disease burden in their endemic malaria. Alland believes that consideration of sickness as what people themselves report—the approach of cultural analyses—will be blind to much suffering. "An ethnoscientific analysis [that is, one that focuses on the native point of view] of medically oriented behavior will miss much of this material because it restricts itself to what the natives themselves define as medicine" (1970:129).

Alland cited the remarkable and well-documented association between sickle cell anemia, malaria, and human behavior in West Africa. Sickle cell anemia (named for the effect of the disease in creating a sickle-shaped red blood cell) is an inherited condition. If inherited from both parents—that is, homozygously—this form of anemia is most often fatal; but if inherited from only one parent, heterozygously, it may cause nonlethal symptoms but also reduce susceptibility to the effects of malaria. Thus, in this case a relatively mild pathology (sickle cell anemia) protects its patients from another more serious one (malaria).

In 1958, Frank B. Livingstone published a breathtaking study demonstrating that in regions of Africa where malaria was most prevalent, sickle cell anemia was also more common, and vice versa. Since the homozygous sickle cell condition is fatal at young ages, Livingstone assumed that reported sickle cell prevalence rates were essentially rates of the heterozygous, nonlethal, antimalarial form.

Livingstone then gave evidence that the historical appearance of malaria in certain regions of Africa was associated with the introduction of agriculture. *Anopheles gambiae,* the mosquito vector of malaria in West Africa, cannot live in dark, shaded areas or areas with quickly running water; in addition, the mosquito requires a "blood meal" from another animal in order to reproduce, and it reproduces most effectively with larger and more concentrated host populations. Thus African people who live in wooded regions, most often nonagricultural hunter-foragers, suffer little malaria. But when hunters become agriculturalists, clearing land, living in larger communities, and leaving standing water (for example, in pools or refuse piles), they provide more hospitable breeding grounds for the mosquito. The shift to agriculture thus fosters the introduction of malaria, which in turn increases the likelihood that populations with high frequencies of heterozygous sickle cell trait will survive. In this interactionist view, human culture leads to environmental change that then alters population biology and patterns of sickness.

The environmental/evolutionary theory has much in common with the field of medical geography, "that discipline that describes spatial patterns of health and disease and explains those spatial patterns by concentrating on the underlying processes that generate identifiable spatial forms" (Mayer 1984:2680). A basic theme of medical geography is that health characteristics of populations are significantly associated with patterns of human interaction with the physical environment. Melinda Meade suggests that thinking in geography has evolved through several stages, from " 'environmental determinism' (hot wet climates cause lethargy and poor health) to 'possibilism,' in which the environment sets the ultimate constraints (one cannot get mosquito-transmitted diseases at 15000 feet elevation) but interacting cultural forms are varied, to a 'cultural ecology' in which human existence is inextricably interwoven with the biosphere" (1986:314).

Some geographic patterns are explained by the distribution of risk factors—the behaviors that cause a disease. For example, the highest mortality rates of chronic obstructive pulmonary disease, caused principally by a history of cigarette smoking, occur in western states (Centers for Disease Control 1989a); it is likely that this concentration is explained by geographic patterns of smoking (Centers for Disease Control 1989b), possibly also by the migration of people with lung disease to western states where air is believed to be healthier (Lebowitz and Burrows 1975). Similarly, the highest rates of stroke mortality are concentrated in southeastern states, possibly corresponding to greater rates of untreated hypertension, particularly among blacks (Centers for Disease Control 1989c). Knowledge of the spatial distribution of disease rates has been used to plan the location of medical facilities and emergency vehicles (Mayer 1984).

Biologists also have proposed accounts of human social life, including patterns of sickness and healing. Perhaps the most extreme environmental/biological explanation developed in recent years is sociobiology, "the scientific study of the biological basis of all forms of social behavior in all kinds of organisms, including man" (Wilson 1979:230). Edward O. Wilson, sociobiology's foremost proponent, argues that early in the growth of disciplines there is a more established "antidiscipline," a devil's advocate that seeks to reduce the phenomena of the new discipline, say, human social and cultural life, to lower-level phenomena such as human biology. Wilson believes that biology is the antidiscipline of the social sciences. "Biology is the key to human nature, and social scientists cannot afford to ignore its rapidly tightening principles" (Wilson 1979:14). In addition to evolutionary and genetic principles, the other discipline that Wilson believes underlies, reductionistically, sociology and human social behavior is brain biology. As this discipline develops, Wilson predicts, "cognition will be translated into circuitry. Learning and creativeness will be defined as the alteration of specific portions of the cognitive machinery regulated by input from the emotive centers" (1975a:575).

Wilson claims that there is a "human nature" fundamentally determined by human genetics and Darwinian natural selection. Genetics explains the reproduction and variation of population characteristics from generation to generation, and natural selection accounts for the perpetuation of populations whose characteristics allow them to best procreate and survive in their environments. Humans are primates who left their relatives in the trees and began to walk on their lower limbs, freeing their hands for other purposes and accelerating the growth of tool use. At the same time, increasing human brain capacity facilitated the growth of culture, communication, and society. These developments have enhanced the ability of humans to survive in their environments.

Wilson believes that genetic and evolutionary principles have determined fundamental features not only of human biology but of human social life as well, both prior to and following the advent of culture. He has argued, for example, that incest rules found in different forms in all societies prevent the hazards of inbreeding and thus strengthen the ability of populations to survive and reproduce. He has also claimed that warfare serves adaptational needs of protecting and expanding the society's territory for its survival.

Wilson asserts that evolutionary principles explain the overall shape of human society and culture, but not its specifics. He refers to variant cultural forms as "accidental details," minimizing their significance. "Most kinds of human social behavior are hypertrophic [greatly elaborated] forms of original, simpler responses that were of more direct adaptive advantage in hunter-gatherer and primitively agricultural societies" (1979:226).

He draws conservative political conclusions from his research by arguing that social movements directed against purportedly overwhelming biological imperatives will exact great costs in energy and social functioning and are likely to fail. For example, he recommends that genetic differences in human nature, such as those that supposedly exist among "races," should be investigated, perhaps with the rationale of justifying and accepting the differential distribution of resources and opportunities. Wilson also believes that affirmative action to achieve equality of employment for men and women contradicts human nature and evolutionary principle and should thus be avoided. He has argued that ethics should be founded on biology rather than philosophy: "Scientists and humanists should consider together the possibility that the time has come for ethics to be removed from the hands of the philosophers and biologicized" (1975a:562). The role of sociobiology, Wilson believes, is to assess the best way to live, given the underlying biological principles of human social life.

Sociobiology has been widely criticized both as scientific theory and as political agenda. For one, biologist Richard Lewontin has argued that most sociobiological explanations are "imaginative reconstructions" for which evidence is not produced, perhaps because it cannot be produced (Lewontin 1983). For example, Wilson makes no attempt to demonstrate a genetic basis for aggressiveness or xenophobia in "human nature." Nor does he present evidence for the universality of these traits—in fact, he ignores anthropological evidence to the contrary.

Lewontin also claims that sociobiological arguments for the necessity of existing forms of social organization, such as male domination, are illogical. They assume that, because group averages—say, in the capacity for analytic reasoning—differ among men and women, therefore there is an inherent, categorical difference between all men and all women. To the contrary, Lewontin argues, population averages are not inherited and cannot justify current arrangements of power. Sociobiology is seen as a misleading rationalization of the status quo.

In contrast to theories focused on the determining influences of genetics, evolution, and adaptation on human society and culture, Marvin Harris has proposed a theory of "cultural materialism" (Harris 1968, 1974, 1977,

1979). Harris claims that sociobiologists have ignored the great range of societal and cultural patterns, providing speculative explanations for human social life without evidence. "Our primary mode of biological adaptation," Harris writes (1974:85), "is culture, not anatomy." He argues that social organization and culture are fundamentally determined by the way in which human societies satisfy the basic needs of their members—nutrition, shelter, conservation of energy, sex, and love and affection.

Building on his interpretation of the ideas of Karl Marx, Harris distinguishes three levels in the organization of a society: the infrastructure, the structure, and the superstructure. A society's *infrastructure* includes a "mode of production," the technology and activity directed toward the production of food and energy, and a "mode of reproduction," the means of sustaining and reproducing the population. Included in the infrastructure's mode of reproduction are patterns of birth, disease, and death. Infrastructure "is the principal interface between culture and nature, the boundary across which the ecological, chemical, and physical restraints to which human action is subject interact with the principal sociocultural practices aimed at overcoming or modifying those restraints" (Harris 1979:57). A society's *structure* consists of its "domestic economy," its way of organizing home life, and its "political economy," its way of organizing the segments of society or the nation as a whole. Finally, the *superstructure* consists of religion, music, literature, other arts, and sports; included also is science, thus presumably medicine as well.

Harris summarizes the thesis of cultural materialism as follows: "The . . . behavioral modes of production and reproduction probabilistically determine the . . . behavioral domestic and political economy, which in turn probabilistically determine the . . . superstructures. For brevity's sake, this principle can be referred to as the principle of infrastructural determinism" (1979:55–56).

Among Marxist scholars who interpret Marx as taking what they call "dialectical" and what I have called an "interactionist" position, Harris has been accused (by Sahlins 1978, for example) of practicing a form of "vulgar Marxism," that is, "a form of economic reductionism that locates all forms of human consciousness, knowledge, and cultural expression as determined by the mode of economic production and the social relations that this engenders. . . . Disease, illness, depression, and the pain of day-to-day living are no more than the inevitable consequence of a capitalist and patriarchal social order. The only 'science' is economics" (Lewontin, Rose, and Kamin 1985:76). In his defense, however, by describing the determining power of infrastructure as probabilistic, Harris allows for the possibility that superstructure may influence structure and infrastructure.

In contrast to many other anthropologists, Harris is explicit about the methodology he believes underlies his research strategy. Others may (and do) disagree with his position, but at least they know what it is. Harris believes that anthropology should be a science in which theory, hypothesis, and inductive inference (from elementary fact to theory) are balanced.

> The aim of scientific research strategies in general is to account for observable entities and events and their relationships by means of powerful, interrelated parsimonious theories subject to correction and improvement through empirical testing. The aim of cultural materialism in particular is to account for the origin, maintenance, and change of the global inventory of sociocultural differences and similarities. Thus cultural materialism shares with other scientific strategies an epistemology which seeks to restrict by means of explicit, logico-empirical, inductive-deductive, quantifiable public procedures or "operations" subject to replication by independent observers. (1979:26–27)

Although Harris does not directly address matters of sickness and healing, his theory and analyses touch on matters of health, such as nutrition. For example, he has examined the role of cattle in Indian society (Harris 1974). While Hindus say they do not eat beef because the cow is a sacred animal— Harris refers to this reverence as "cow love"—Western agronomists proclaim that malnourished Indians are wasting a valuable food resource by not fattening and slaughtering the "excess" animals that wander freely in the cities and countryside. In contrast, Harris shows how Hindu beliefs rationalize an effective and balanced use of cattle in their ecological setting and how Westerners are mistaken about the case of India and are themselves relatively inefficient.

In India, the population of cows is approximately two-thirds that of oxen, suggesting systematic elimination by some unspoken means. But there is also more direct evidence that, in addition to the consumption of cows' milk, cattle themselves are eaten—by Muslims and Christians, by Hindus of the untouchable caste, and, under conditions of famine, even by Hindus of other castes.

Cattle also fulfill many needs other than the provision of meat. Perhaps most important, oxen are needed as draft animals for cultivation—a possible explanation of their greater survival than cows. In addition, cattle dung provides fertilizer, cooking fuel, and material for covering dirt floors. Leather is used as well. Moreover, Indian cattle consume few resources of direct use to humans. Harris suggests that the Indian arrangement with cattle provides a near-optimal use of local resources. "Cow love mobilizes the latent capacity of human beings to persevere in a low-energy ecosystem in which there is little room for waste or indolence" (1974:30). Hindu superstructural beliefs about the sanctity of cattle are explained by the Indian infrastructure of agriculture, technology, and demographics.

Harris finds further support for the theory of "probabilistic infrastructural determination" of ritual, medicine, and religious ideas in the cultural distribution of attitudes about pig flesh. While among some Oriental and Western societies, pork is a prized dish, pig meat is abhorrent—an abomination—to "pig-hating" Jews and Muslims and is sacred to "pig-loving" societies in New Guinea. Harris rejects the explanation of pig hating as the tacit recognition of disease (now known to be trichinosis) transmitted by consumption of insufficiently cooked (infected) pork. Diseases transmitted by consumption of undercooked beef, goat, and mutton, such as brucellosis and anthrax, are far more serious than trichinosis. In addition, if undercooking were the problem, the respective gods of the Hebrews and the Muslims could simply have mandated thorough cooking instead of abstinence.

As an alternative to the explanation in terms of disease risks, Harris proposes a broader public health perspective that considers the organization of Hebrew and Muslim economic and social life and its ecological setting: "The Bible and the Koran condemned the pig because pig farming was a threat to the integrity of the basic cultural and natural ecosystems of the Middle East" (1974:40). Early Hebrews inhabited arid lands and were "nomadic pastoralists, living almost entirely from herds of sheep, goats, and cattle." In contrast to these animals, pigs do best with low cellulose diets, preferably of grains, nuts, fruits, and tubers, which generally require cultivation and a sedentary way of life; in addition, pigs have a low tolerance for heat and cover themselves with their dung when overheated, thus increasing the likelihood of disease transmission in inhospitable porcine environments. Consumption of pork would thus have required the abandonment of nomadic pastoralism—highly suited to arid Middle Eastern environments. In addition, the raising of pigs would have required supplementary agriculture for production of food for pigs that was also edible by humans themselves. Harris argues that Hebrew and Muslim gods forbade the consumption of tasty pork to eliminate a temptation ecologically inefficient and harmful to their followers. Again, religious beliefs are maintained because they are ecologically sound.

Based on the research of Roy Rappaport (1967), Harris describes the contrasting situation of the pig-loving Maring people of New Guinea. The Maring are a sedentary people who inhabit a forested mountain environment well suited for pig raising. Unlike cow love among Hindus, among the Maring, "the climax of pig love is the incorporation of the pig as flesh into the flesh of the human host and of the pig as spirit into the spirit of the ancestors. Pig love is honoring your dead father by clubbing a beloved sow to death on his grave site and roasting it in an earth oven dug on the spot" (1974:46). Most of the time, the Maring abstain from the consumption of pork. But about every twelve years, Rappaport estimates, Maring clans have massive pig feasts in which large portions of their herds are slaughtered. They invite their allies and "pig out" over the course of a year. During a festival witnessed by Rappaport, about seven-eighths (by weight) of the pig population was slaughtered. The Maring then take to war with their enemy in order to defend or expand their territory; during war, they continue to consume their pigs. Their protein nutrition is thus greatest, Harris argues, during a period when it is most likely to be needed. Eventually, the Maring declare the war ended and return to nurse their sacred, though depleted pig stock.

Among the Maring, care of pigs is women's work. Along with their infants, women carry piglets around and are responsible for the gardening that provides food for their families as well as their pigs. Rappaport calculates that, as the herd matures, a woman may spend half of her energy providing for her pigs. New gardens may be needed, requiring longer walks and more carrying. Mature pigs invade fenced gardens, destroying crops. In addition to normal women's work of child care, cooking, and the manufacture of artifacts, the burdens of piggery may lead to increasing tensions within families and among neighbors. Thus, as the local herd grows following feasts, social relations may be strained. The Maring come to decide it is time to feast again.

Harris proposes that the ecology of the Maring setting, along with their technology and basic social organization, makes their practice of cyclical pig raising and pig slaughter an efficient way to live; Maring ideas about pigs and ancestors make local sense of a highly rational process.

CULTURAL THEORIES

In contrast to proponents of environmental and evolutionary theories, many anthropologists have focused on cultural systems as basic determinants of sickness and healing in societies. A cultural system is a more or less coherent set of values, concepts, beliefs, and rules that guide and rationalize people's behavior in society. Cultural anthropologists who adopt this perspective examine the elements of cultural systems in order to portray the interconnections among elements and to explain the behavior of persons inhabiting these settings.

Marshall Sahlins is a cultural anthropologist who has reacted strongly and articulately to environmental and materialist theories such as those of Wilson and Harris (Sahlins 1976, 1978). Harris, for example, in a manner similar to his explanations of human arrangements with cows and pigs, has proposed an explanation of human sacrifice among the Aztecs as a means of satisfying nutritional needs. "The Aztec priests can legitimately be described as ritual slaughterers in a state-sponsored system geared to the production and redistribution of substantial amounts of animal protein in the form of human flesh" (1977:164).

Against this explanation, Sahlins contends that the nutritional argument is inadequate for a variety of reasons: there are reliable historical records of abundannt alternative sources of protein in the Aztec environment; the food and care lavished on sacrificial candidates would have made sacrifice a highly inefficient source of nutrition; sacrifice was commonly preceded by self-initiated ritual bleeding by the sacrificial consumers; and the amount of flesh provided to Aztec citizens, on the average, was negligible—less than a pound each year. To Harris's suggestion that human flesh went mostly to the nobility, Sahlins replies that the nobility in particular had many other sources of protein.

Sahlins sketches an alternative, cultural theory of Aztec sacrifice. Sacrifices were held regularly in the Aztec calendar. They involved highly elaborate, interrelated beliefs and practices—hardly worthwhile for an extra pound of meat a year. "In connection with various sacrifices, different categories of people would ritually fast, bleed themselves, paint themselves, climb mountains, go into and come out of seclusion, stage farces, drink pulque, eat earth, offer valuable gifts to the gods, take ceremonial baths, parade in the streets, play games, hold sham fights, practice chastity, hunt deer, sing and dance for days on end, beg alms, erect and adorn idols, prepare and eat special delicacies, and much else" (1978:45). For Aztecs themselves, sacrifice fit into a cosmological scheme in which sacrificial subjects—mostly captives and slaves—were "treated as if they had been gods"; gods were made offerings, and humans partook in the divine feast. Blood was associated with flowers and with the fertility of the land. Sacrifices were rituals for the renewal of society and of cosmological and earthly connections.

Sahlins comments on Harris's studies in cultural materialism: "What is truly at stake in these works is whether human culture is meaningful in its own right. . . . Do people employ customs and categories to organize their lives within local schemes of interpretation, thus giving uses to material circumstances which, cultural comparison will show, are never the only one possible?" (1978:49).

Sahlins argues that to explain elaborate cultural institutions in terms of their satisfaction of nutritional needs, Harris "abandons the possibility of understanding" and makes "some kind of bargain with ethnographic reality" (Sahlins 1976:47, 45). Sahlins remarks that Harris's approach, despite assertions to the contrary, "demands a heroic disregard of the appearances in favor of a theory of the realities"; that is, under the influence of his theory, Harris disregards empirical evidence. Sahlins refers to Harris's technique as "a kind of academic parlor game. . . . any sort of economic value that can plausibly be suggested for any cultural practice scores points—regardless of whether the same custom entails economic penalties or irrationalities in some other sector of the social order" (1978:52).

Harris describes his thesis as "cultural determinism," but Sahlins suggests that Harris's position is not truly cultural insofar as Harris, for the most part, looks at behavior as an outsider, ignoring its meaning to participants. Sahlins believes that cultural conditions—the indigenous worldview and symbolism—explain the way in which the material world is encountered rather than the reverse.

A cultural approach more focused on medical matters has been formulated by psychiatrist-anthropologist Arthur Kleinman (see chaps. 1 and 10, this book). In a classic paper, "Culture, Illness, and Care," Kleinman and his colleagues, Leon Eisenberg and Byron Good, note the popular perception of a crisis in medical care in the United States (Kleinman, Eisenberg, and Good 1978). They believe that effective response to this crisis requires attention to popular medical culture; they describe responses that do not address the concerns of popular culture as mere tinkering.

Kleinman and his colleagues outline for physicians the role that culture plays in medical settings. First they report that between 70 and 90 percent of episodes of sickness in the United States are not brought to medical attention. Based on their ideas about sickness and healing, people take care of most of their conditions themselves. Cultural ideas play a central role in determining who seeks medical attention, for what conditions, when, and with what results. Again based on their ideas, people may decide to seek medical help; they may also respond to clinical recommendations based on their own ideas. Thus, Kleinman and his colleagues argue, if people are to receive appropriate medical treatment (however "appropriate" treatment is determined), it is essential to understand their cultural ideas about sickness and healing.

Kleinman and his colleagues encapsulate their approach to "clinical social science" in the notion of "explanatory model," that is, a set of ideas about sickness. Both patients and healers have explanatory models. Patients have learned theirs in common cultural settings; healers have acquired additional training—overlapping their first cultural learning—in professional schools. An explanatory model (affectionately known as an "EM") is characterized by five elements: (1) an explanation of the cause(s) of a sickness, (2) a description of precipitating circumstances and first symptoms, (3) an explanation of the physiology of the sickness, (4) an outline of the course of the sickness and appropriate patient behavior, and (5) a formulation of available treatments. Explanatory models, particularly those of patients, may be only partially articulated and may be inconsistent or even self-contradictory. Kleinman and his colleagues recommend that clinicians include as an essential component of medical practice the elicitation of patients' explanatory models. They further recommend that physicians make their own explanatory models explicit and seek negotiated understandings with their patients.

Along similar lines, a colleague, Marjorie Muecke, and I have taken a cultural approach in preparing a guide for Biomedical clinicians to variations in birth practices in five U.S. ethnic populations—whites, blacks, Chinese, Mexican Americans, and Hmong (Hahn and Muecke 1987). We first describe the great variety of characteristics reported for these populations in prenatal care, fertility, low birthweight, and infant mortality. For example, three times as many blacks and Mexican Americans (10 percent) are reported to delay prenatal care (in Biomedical settings) as whites and Chinese (3–4 percent). On the other hand, blacks are reported to have twice the infant mortality of whites, and Mexican Americans and Chinese are reported to have lower rates of infant mortality than whites.

It is our premise that a large part of the differences in birth-related events among these populations can be explained by their cultural attitudes and practices regarding childbearing. We summarize published studies of the birth cultures of these populations and of Biomedicine as well. We then recommend to clinicians attending childbearing women and their families ways to understand and respond to the cultural variations among their patients. We recommend that childbearing women and their families be given orientations to the culture of Biomedical settings where they deliver, and that culture brokers, intermediaries between patient cultures and medical cultures, be available to translate the cultural differences between childbearing women and medical attendants.

Among cultural perspectives, an extreme, but currently fashionable version—one with which I disagree—leads to a paradoxical view of reality as fiction. In the classic study *The Social Construction of Reality,* for example, authors Berger and Luckmann describe the way in which persons in society collaborate in the formulation of the way the world is. Despite its centrality to their perspective, the notion of "reality" is dismissed in a sentence: "It will be enough, for our purposes, to define 'reality' as a quality appertaining to phenomena that we recognize as having a being independent of our own volition (we cannot 'wish them away')" (Berger and Luckmann 1966:1). It is as if reality exerted no constraint on the way in which humans come to view it. Berger and Luckmann go on to argue (contrary to such analysts as E. O. Wilson) that there is no human nature determined by "a biologically fixed substratum," but rather that "man constructs his own nature, or more simply, that man produces himself" (1966:49). It seems, according to this view, that human beliefs constrain nature rather than the reverse.

A view of reality as a human product rather than as "something out there" emerges from a fascinating study of the evolution of medical knowledge in *Laboratory Life* by Bruno Latour and Steve Woolgar. "Science," they write, "is entirely fabricated out of circumstance" (1986:239). And circumstance, they suggest, is the evolving product of human interaction.

Latour and Woolgar observed a setting of Nobel Prize–winning research on Thyrotropin Releasing Factor (Hormone), "TRF(H)," a compound now thought to play an important role in the control of thyroid and reproductive function. (It is found in such small quantities in research animals that purification of only 1/1,000th of a gram for laboratory analysis required extraction from the hypothalamus glands of a million sheep that had been slaughtered for meat.) Latour and Woolgar argue that TRF(H) was not *discovered,* but *created* in a social dialogue that depended in part on "facts" already established by similar processes and physically incorporated in laboratory equipment and techniques: "We do not wish to say that facts do not exist nor that there is no such thing as reality. In this simple sense our position is not relativist. Our point is that 'out-there-ness' is the *consequence* of scientific work rather than its *cause*" (1986:180–82).

Latour and Woolgar describe the development of facts such as TRF(H) in terms of five types of statements found in researchers' writings and dialogues: (1) statements of conjecture or speculation, (2) statements regarding the evidence for (or against) an association, (3) statements about associations embedded within other statements about the status of evidence for these associations, (4) statements of association that are deemed credible, but that still bear repetition, and (5) statements corresponding to acknowledged "facts." The work of science is the stabilization (or destabilization) of statements about matters of interest. "A laboratory is constantly performing operations on statements; adding modalities, citing, enhancing, diminishing, borrowing, and proposing new combinations. Each of these operations can result in a statement which is either different or merely qualified. Each statement, in turn, provides the focus for similar operations in other laboratories" (1986:86–87).

For example, prior to 1962, researchers had speculated that TRF(H) might exist. Culminating from the research of this lab in 1962, researchers came to believe in TRF(H) and now speculated whether it was or was not a peptide. Speculation continued until January 1969 when TRF(H) was confirmed as peptide and its chemical components analyzed. In April 1969, researchers proposed alternative structures of TRF(H), excluding others as implausible. And in November 1969, the structure was confirmed (from among structures previously judged implausible). Thus, though not always in linear sequence, new "things," such as TRF(H), are created from others already accepted as real.

> Scientific activity is not "about nature," it is a fierce fight to *construct* reality. The *laboratory* is the workplace and the set of productive forces, which makes construction possible. Every time a statement stabilises, it is reintroduced into the laboratory (in the guise of a machine, inscription device, skill, routine, prejudice, deduction, programme, and so on), and it is used to increase the difference between statements. The cost of challenging the reified statements is impossibly high. Reality is secreted.   (1986:243)

Latour and Woolgar claim that, once a new thing has been established as real, it is embodied in equipment and technique. It is taken for granted, difficult to dislodge from reality. And the social circumstances of its creation are forgotten.

With laudable consistency, Latour and Woolgar conclude by examining their own research activity by the same standards they use to examine the inventors of TRF(H). They conclude, "In a fundamental sense, our own account is no more than *fiction*" (1986:257; emphasis in original).

Although this cultural perspective illuminates the evolution of scientific knowledge, I believe that its proponents' ideas about reality are untenable. Moreover, these ideas are not only unnecessary for their analysis, but make the whole enterprise futile and vacuous. Like Berger and Luckmann, Latour and Woolgar appear to believe both that there are "facts" and "reality" independent of human knowledge and that facts and reality are human "constructions," "fictions." They concede to "facts" and "reality" parenthetically and apologetically, while insisting adamantly on the essence of human invention. They give minimal credence to the referents of these realities—what they are about—for example, sicknesses. They seem to assume that there is no physical and biological reality, independent of human ideas, from which cultural realities are constructed.

In my view, human knowledge is, perhaps inevitably, imperfect. Our knowledge is persistently based on interpretation, shaped by prior interpretations and by observations framed by interpretation. But our interpretations and observations are objectively constrained by the physical and other realities we observe. Misinterpretations and poor (unobjective) observations may lead to actions that indicate our error. Our knowledge evolves and may increasingly approximate truth. We propose principles and standards, themselves subject to examination and improvement, by which to judge and advance our knowledge. In contrast, the constructionist cultural perspective eliminates standards of evidence and standards of inference. There are no grounds to stand on, no grounds to judge our own work or the work of others. Indeed we have no reason to judge since all is interpretation.

POLITICAL/ECONOMIC THEORIES

Over the past decade, a movement referred to by its proponents as "critical medical anthropology" has grown in reaction to approaches described by proponents as "conventional"—that is, ecological and cultural theories. Although the specific referent of the "critical" perspective is not made explicit, the writings of proponents indicate several candidates: Biomedicine itself, the capitalist society whose interests Biomedicine is said to serve, and conventional forms of medical anthropology. Critical medical anthropologists have several specific complaints about conventional medical anthropology (Singer 1989; Morsy 1990).

They complain that the ecological approach to sickness and healing ignores the role of power in society in controlling factors such as "ownership of the means of production, export of capital, extraction of profit, and racial and sexual oppression that underlie and ultimately determine human response to the physical environment" (Singer 1989:1194). Human populations do not interact directly with their environments; rather, populations are organized by societal rules, backed by consensus and/or force, which differentially allocate control over material hazards and material resources. The human benefits (and harms) of interaction with the physical environment are unequally distributed in society. Societal changes that are adaptive for one societal segment may be detrimental for another segment.

Critical medical anthropologists also claim that, by focusing on isolated populations and circumscribed settings, for example, in medical clinics or so-called traditional societies, conventional, noncritical anthropologists have failed to consider the broader social forces that shape these settings and populations. Omafume Onoge describes this flawed approach as a "truncated sociology" (1975:221). Conventional anthropologists have ignored the influence of capitalist social organization (for example, the accumulation of corporate profit by entrepreneurs) on medical settings in Western societies; they have also ignored the forces of colonialism and the capitalist "world system" affecting sickness and healing in so-called traditional societies whose apparent isolation is illusory. With an emphatic political connotation, critical medical anthropologists define "health" as "access to and control over the basic material and non-material resources that sustain and promote life at a high level of satisfaction" (Baer, Singer, and Johnsen 1986:95). They argue that the economic forces of capitalism are manifest not only at international and national levels, but in local settings and local relationships as well, resulting in an unequal societal distribution of sickness and healing.

Several social scientists have explored effects of the international economic world system on the world distribution of sickness and healing (for example, Elling 1981; Onoge 1975). Onoge and others (such as Navarro 1976; Taussig 1978; Brown 1979) have argued that, rather than promoting the health of third world countries, colonialism and imperialism have served capitalist interests, while degrading the health status of its subjects, causing underdevelopment rather than alleviating it. Fertile land has been appropriated for the cultivation of crops to be exported to the colonists' home nations, thus reducing traditional sources of nutrition and trade; laborers have been forced to migrate to earn meager wages under minimal conditions, disrupting family and community connections; colonized people have been persuaded to consume goods from the colonists' home nations—at high cost and frequently little benefit, and resulting in dependency on the colonizers; and colonial medicine has served the exploitive goals of the colonists, assuring human capital for labor. Onoge argues that the systems of exploitation left by colonists have often been retained by new national governments.

Analysts of the capitalist world system have distinguished a core of entrepreneurial nations that direct the system and accumulate its profits from both a periphery of nations where natural resources are extracted and poorly paid laborers are employed in the production of goods and a semiperiphery of nations that occupy an intermediate position. Ray Elling has analyzed the effects of this system on the health and sickness of its participants (1981). To begin, there is a strong inverse correlation between per capita gross national product and national rates of infant mortality. Conversely, there is a direct correlation between per capita gross national product and life expectancy. There is also what Elling refers to as "comerciogenic malnutrition," that is, not only the restriction of traditional land use noted above, but also the export to peripheral nations of inappropriate dietary products—for example, baby formula for routine use. Elling also notes examples of the export of drugs that are either banned or whose use is highly restricted in core nations, but are freely, probably inappropriately, dispensed in peripheral nations. Elling notes a study of this phenomenon by Mintz (1979) entitled, "If There Are No Side-Effects, This Must Be Honduras." Hazardous industry—for example, the production of asbestos products—may also be exported to peripheral nations, a phenomenon known as "dumping." Critical theorists argue that the core nation programs for the accumulation of profit are often cloaked in ideologies of benevolent assistance and development.

Critical medical anthropologists call conventional colleagues to task for adopting an "ahistorical, apolitical, and cultural relativistic stance" (Morsy 1990:27). The relativistic stance assumes that societies are integrated systems of customs, values, roles, and institutions that all fit together and are comprehensible as a whole. This assumption has been pejoratively referred to as "socioculturalism" (Onoge 1975:221). The sociocultural position tends to place blame for poor health in impoverished and/or underdeveloped areas on the victims of those settings, insofar as their cultural beliefs and practices are regarded as obstacles to proper medical treatment. In addition, non-Western medical traditions are regarded as nonscientific, if not irrational. But, Onoge points out, "surely it must have required an exploratory scientific attitude toward the ecology to select out what was edible from the billions of weeds. It required an experimental attitude to achieve the feat of processing vegetables and tubers that are poisonous in their natural state into safe items for the palate" (1975:222).

In contrast to the sociocultural view, the critical perspective posits that societies, at least capitalist societies and societies under the influence of capitalism, are not harmonious, integrated wholes, but are riddled by conflicts and struggles among social classes—principally the classes that control resources and those whose labor produces wealth, but who do not benefit proportionately. When societies are examined in terms of their historical and political relations with other societies, critical medical anthropologists argue, conflict and struggle become apparent.

In the same way that early anthropologists who worked in colonial settings have been accused of having produced "colonialism's social science," so conventional medical anthropologists are accused of reinforcing "the medical monopoly on human suffering," the exclusive control by the Biomedical profession in defining sickness and treating it (Singer 1989:1194). Critical medical anthropologists fault their colleagues for not reflecting on their own perspective as the product of historical and political circumstances. They argue that the conventional discipline has been "a handmaiden of medical imperialism," serving the interests of Biomedicine by working to facilitate doctor-patient communication in clinical settings. They refer to the co-optation of medical anthropologists within Biomedicine as "the medical-ization of medical anthropology" (Singer 1989:1194). Traditional anthropol-ogists perpetuate the capitalist relations of oppression and exploitation, instead of working toward a radically new medical system and a radical transformation of existing social and economic relationships (Baer, Singer, and Johnsen 1986:97). What is regarded as revolutionary in the cultural perspective (for example, Kleinman, Eisenberg, and Good 1978) becomes complicit tinkering in the view of critical medical anthropologists.

Critical medical anthropologists have an explicit political agenda; consis-tent with their agenda, their writings read like political arguments as well as scientific analyses. The new order they envision is based in broad societal reform and the egalitarian social distribution of resources. They focus on prevention rather than on curative medicine and on primary rather than tertiary specialty care of patients in the later stages of sickness. They encour-age community participation in health decisions. Critical medical anthropol-ogists hope that in these transformations, their discipline will serve as "a vanguard of social liberation" (Baer, Singer, and Johnsen 1986:97).

A THEORY COMBINING
THE BEST OF OTHER THEORIES

I find much merit in each of the three basic theories I have re-viewed. I reject, however, both reductionist and emergentist claims that all matters of sickness and healing are explained either solely or not at all by other specific chosen phenomena. Instead, I maintain the interactionist posi-tion that the world consists of phenomena of different levels that are neither entirely determined by or entirely autonomous of each other. For example, lower-level physiological phenomena, such as genes, cells, and body organs, constrain the functioning of higher-level phenomena, such as thought, cul-ture, and society; but higher-level phenomena may affect lower-level ones as well. I thus consider theoretical principles insofar as they do not profess exclusivity. I suggest in chapter 4 that systems theory provides a useful framework in which to examine the interactions among levels of phenomena. Systems theory has been applied to matters of sickness and healing by How-ard Brody (Brody and Sobel 1979) and George Engel (Engel 1980).

Any theory, including a theory of sickness and healing, is itself part of a cultural system, namely the theorist's. It is an interpretation of observed events framed by particular concepts and values. Science is associated with particular kinds of theories characterized by adherence to basic principles, among them, the validity of concepts, the examination of hypotheses by systematic observation, and pursuit of consistency among theory, method, and observation. Speculation, intuition, and imagination are integral elements of the scientific process whose results should be rationally scrutinized and empirically tested before accepted as valid. I have suggested that several conceptual and speculative elements in sociobiology, cultural materialism, and the cultural perspective fail to meet rational or empirical standards.

Although I cannot here propose a detailed theory of sickness and healing, my theory would include principles of human evolution and human culture. Humans adapt to novel environmental events and commonly alter their environments in doing so. As evidenced by the evolution of humans, malaria, and the physical environment in Africa, cultural practices may affect an environment and, by doing so, subsequently modify the biological characteristics of the human population. Knowledge of the local culture allows prediction of its adherents' responses in new environmental circumstances.

While I believe that a comprehensive theory of sickness and healing must consider adaptation and culture, my own theory would begin with the position of critical medical anthropology, for several reasons. First, as critical medical anthropologists clearly recognize, events that occur in social settings are powerfully influenced by forces emanating from far beyond those settings; the understanding of local events must take wider forces into account. Second, power, including the control of exposures to sickness and resources for healing, is unevenly distributed in most societies; the understanding of sickness and healing must take into account the local and global maldistribution of power. Third, theories, including anthropological theories of sickness and healing, are themselves elements of a culture, principally a Western, developed-world culture; the roots and values of this culture must be acknowledged and made explicit. And fourth, research and theorizing are themselves social acts; they must be made ethical acts. Where injustice and inequity prevail, scholars must strive not to rationalize the system (which may support their work) but to unmask and remake it.

4

THE ROLE OF SOCIETY
AND CULTURE
IN SICKNESS AND HEALING

> In view of the history of infectious disease in the last 150 years, it is at least as sensible to say that unregulated capitalism causes bronchitis as it is to blame bacilli.
>
> —*Lewontin 1983:34*

Humans are born into societies that inform them how the world is and how to behave in it. People born into one society are likely to have views of the world and of proper behavior very different from the views of people born into another society. In part because they see the world differently, in part because what they see *is* different, they live in different worlds.

In this chapter, I analyze the ways the society in which people grow up affects their sickness and healing. The organization of societies affects not only what conditions people "get" and "have," but who gets which ones, how sick persons and their conditions are perceived, and what is done in response to sickness. I argue that the effects of societal organization and culture on sickness and healing are powerful and pervasive. Sociocultural effects are causal in the same way that environmental carcinogens, toxins, and bacterial and viral pathogens are. Sociocultural effects do not preclude but rather complement biological modes of causation in sickness and healing. They present a profound challenge to the underlying theory of Biomedicine, because in Biomedicine it is commonly assumed that sickness and healing are essentially biological events in which sociocultural phenomena play at most a secondary role.

In the sections that follow, I describe three distinctive but related forms of sociocultural influence on sickness and healing; I refer to these forms of influence as "construction," "mediation," and "production." I give examples, beginning with the effects of national and societal organization on the health of populations and ending with the effects of immediate social environments on the health of individuals. Finally, I review the place of sociocultural influences within Biomedicine and formulate an alternative, interdisciplinary approach in which sociocultural phenomena are central.

THREE MODES OF SOCIOCULTURAL INFLUENCE ON SICKNESS AND HEALING

The sickness and healing we experience are constrained but not determined by our biological makeup and the physical environment we inhabit. Within biological and physical limits, and perhaps stretching these limits, human societies and their cultures affect events of sickness and healing in three basic but related ways. Human biology and the physical environment, in turn, may also be modified by society and culture.

First, borrowing a concept from the phenomenological school of sociology (for example, Berger and Luckmann 1966), the culture of a society *constructs* the way societal members think and feel about sickness and healing. That is to say, the members of a society are taught by others about different sicknesses and their names, their characteristic symptoms and courses, their causes and mitigating circumstances, their cosmological and moral significance, and appropriate responses. What counts as sickness may differ from society to society, and given conditions of sickness are understood in very different ways. Anthropologists refer to the part of a society's cultural reality concerned with sickness and healing as its "ethnomedicine." The metaphor of construction suggests that reality is a structure of ideas built by society through social interaction that may include informal as well as formal education. The reality constructed by society makes sense of the experience of sickness and healing to its members.

Particularly in complex societies, differing medical realities may be constructed in different social sectors; professional healers often maintain one reality (or several), folk healers others, and laypersons still others (Kleinman 1980). All are first introduced to a shared, popular reality of sickness and healing; this orientation shapes the subsequent training of those who become professional healers. In turn, popular media may carry professional medical realities back to folk healers and the lay community. The members of a society may encounter multiple medical realities in the course of life. When sick, patients may resort to several different societal sectors for treatment.

The reality constructed by society also affects events of sickness and healing in two additional ways.

Mediation, a second mode of sociocultural influence on sickness and healing, is perhaps the best recognized of sociocultural effects. The concepts, ideas, and values of a society's culture guide the behavior of societal members, distributing them in time, space, and activity. The members of a society live in certain kinds of dwellings and certain kinds of communities; they pursue diverse occupations and social and recreational activities. By such guided movement, they are brought into greater or lesser contact with pathogenic sources; thus sickness may be fostered or prevented. In Western society, activity-specific types of medical practice—for example, occupational medicine and sports medicine—attest a partial recognition of the sociocultural mediation of sickness.

Sociocultural mediation brings the members of society into greater or lesser contact not only with causes of sickness but with therapeutic resources as well. Resources may be located in different places and institutions, and access to them may be determined by the patient's condition, characteristics, or circumstances. A society's sick roles also guide the activities of members by telling them what to do when sick—when to take to bed (or hammock, sleeping mat), to consult with family members or friends, to seek medical attention. The sociocultural mediation of sickness and healing may be regarded as a form of cultural transportation of persons, pathogens, and therapeutic agents.

Production is a third sociocultural effect on sickness and healing. A society's beliefs and patterned relationships produce events of sickness and healing not only by transporting persons, pathogens, or therapies—as in sociocultural mediation—but by more direct causation as well. Relationships and cultural beliefs may themselves be pathogenic or therapeutic, regardless of what they lead the members of society to do. Sickness or healing may result from beliefs and interpersonal relationships with regularity just as they result from better recognized biological pathogens and medicines.

Perhaps the most striking example of the production of pathological and therapeutic events is the placebo phenomenon, in which beliefs and expectations produce the reality to which they refer—belief in a pill fosters its efficacy. But beliefs may also have other effects that are seldom noted and perhaps not as spectacular: it is likely that beliefs of certain kinds affect not only the conditions they refer to but other, tangential conditions as well. For example, it may be that fear of cancer does not produce cancer but does produce some other condition, perhaps elevated blood pressure or compromised immune function. Such side effects of beliefs differ from the placebo phenomenon itself.

There is evidence that social relationships, as well as beliefs, produce sickness and healing not only because they guide people to sources of sickness and healing but because they are themselves more directly pathogenic and therapeutic, for example, in the death of one spouse shortly after the death of the other. These effects may seem puzzling if we think of relationships as being "out there," disconnected from physiological functioning. If, however, we acknowledge that relationships, and beliefs as well, are embodied within us as well as among us, then the sociocultural production of sickness and healing becomes more reasonable.

In characterizing the role of society and culture in the causal production of sickness and healing, it is important to recall several basic features of causality. First, events of sickness and healing are rarely, if ever, caused by a single event; more often, causation requires the concurrence of many circumstances. For example, exposure to *Mycobacterium tuberculosis* may be necessary but is not sufficient to cause tuberculosis; not all exposure leads to infection or disease (Dubos and Dubos 1952; Harris and McClement 1983). The amount and means of exposure to the organism affects the occurrence of infection; and characteristics of the host (for example, age, nutritional and immune status, and the presence of other diseases such as diabetes or alcoholism) affect the likelihood of contracting disease once a person is infected. Such conditions may not be necessary for the occurrence of tuberculosis, but in the presence of the *Mycobacterium* agent, they may be sufficient causes. Poverty and crowding are also known to increase the likelihood of tuberculosis transmission; and medical treatment for tuberculosis decreases the likelihood of transmission by reducing the number of infective transmitters.

In fact, *Mycobacterium tuberculosis* is not a necessary cause of tuberculosis; other mycobacteria also cause tuberculosis. The causation of tuberculosis by other mycobacteria points to an important characteristic of the causal process. If contact with one of several different organisms results in a common outcome, then it is likely that some feature shared by these organisms, rather than each organism as a whole, is causal. Experimental evidence indicates that several fragments of mycobacteria can cause tuberculosislike reactions in animals. Indeed, similar fragments have even been synthesized in the absence of mycobacterial organisms, so that mycobacteria themselves are no longer necessary causes, but rather the vehicles of causal fragments. Mycobacteria are regarded as "the cause" of tuberculosis because, in human environments, the causal fragment occurs most often in their company. Were the causal fragments more commonly attached to another entity in the human environment, this entity would more likely be regarded as the cause of tuberculosis.

The notion of causation I am presenting here might be couched in terms of *distal* and *proximal* causes, causes more or fewer steps removed from the outcome. For example, the *Mycobacterium* is a distal cause of tuberculosis in comparison with the fragments that are believed to be the more direct, real causes. It should be noted that distal and proximal causes are assessed relative to other causes. The fragments themselves may be shown to be distal to smaller bits that cause tuberculosis, whereas the *Mycobacterium* is proximal to the social conditions that promote its spread, subsequent infection, and disease.

When I claim that sociocultural conditions produce or cause sickness and healing, the sense of causation is the same as that in claims that *Mycobacterium tuberculosis* is the cause of tuberculosis. The difference may be one of proximity to the outcome in a causal chain. In sum, the presence of a pathogen alone is not sufficient to cause a pathological outcome; other conditions must also be met. Even given known pathogens, it may be some facet of the pathogen rather than the whole thing that, in conjunction with other causes, results in the outcome.

SICKNESS, HEALING, AND THE LIFE OF SOCIETY: BODY POLITIC AND BODY SOCIAL

In this section I illustrate the sociocultural effects of construction, mediation, and production at different levels of social life, from nations as wholes to the more intimate social environments of persons. I use examples from the developing as well as the developed world.

Example 1: National Economy and Individual Health

A society's economy is an index of the way in which it organizes its activity and exploits and distributes its resources. Thus, one way to assess the effects of societal organization on the health of a population is to examine the association of national economic conditions and trends and corresponding health rates. In general, we would expect that a lack of resources would lead both to increased exposure to the causes of disease and to a diminished ability to treat persons for disease once it has occurred. An uneven distribution of resources in society would lead to a parallel uneven distribution of sickness and healing.

M. Harvey Brenner has conducted studies to assess the association between economic events and mortality from different causes in nine industrialized nations: Australia, Canada, England and Wales, Denmark, the Federal Republic of Germany, Finland, France, Sweden, and the United States (Brenner 1973, 1981, 1983, 1987). Brenner draws two basic conclusions. First, he finds that long-term trends in per capita income are inversely associated with rates of mortality: as per capita income in a nation rises, the nation's mortality rates fall. Long-term increases in per capita income are associated with declines in infant mortality, mortality from coronary heart disease, and several types of cancer. This association is found in all of the nine nations except France (for reasons not clear).

Second, Brenner has also examined associations between mortality rates and short-term economic events—recession (as measured by unemployment), rates of business failure, and national welfare expenditures. He argues that, while unemployment rates are likely to affect mostly the lower socioeconomic classes of a population, business failures are more likely to affect other classes as well. He finds that short-term fluctuations in economic growth are associated with increasing rates of death from the same causes—infant mortality, coronary heart disease, and several types of cancer. The delay between economic event and changes in mortality rates varies by disease; effects appear to be rapid—within a year—for infant mortality, homicide, and suicide, and to peak after two to three years for coronary heart disease and cirrhosis.

Brenner explains the associations of long- and short-term economic conditions and mortality rates by the distribution of recognized risk factors—cigarette smoking, alcohol, and diets high in fat; these are examples of sociocultural effects I have referred to as "mediation." But Brenner also notes the increased disruption of social relationships that accompany economic change; he shows that, in many nations, rapid economic fluctuations are associated with increased mortality rates, independent of changes in risk-factor prevalences. Thus it seems that psychological reactions and social relationships may be more directly associated with mortality outcomes; these are sociocultural effects I have referred to as "production."

Although studies of this sort suggest a powerful connection between the economies and the health of nations, it is important to note crucial methodological limitations. Brenner's studies are based on separate information on the economic conditions of nations and on their mortality rates; thus, we cannot know that the individuals affected by economic fluctuations are the same ones who suffer adverse health events. In addition, long-term declines in mortality have coincided with many changes in addition to increases in per capita income—for example, improvements in sanitation and public health. These changes may also explain changing rates of mortality.

Information on the economic and health conditions of nations has also been interpreted in a different way. For example, Marxist researcher Joseph Eyer believes that capitalist societies exploit workers for the benefit of entrepreneurs (Eyer 1977). Eyer has claimed, to the contrary of Brenner's analysis, that economic prosperity is associated with *increasing* rates of mortality. While one segment of society prospers, another suffers. Eyer believes that, rather than unemployment, it is employment in capitalist society that is stressful for workers because they must be more mobile, thus disrupting their systems of social support.

Further evidence for Brenner's claim has been found in other studies, however. Kitagawa and Hauser (1973) have shown that low levels of education and income are both, independently, associated with high rates of infant mortality and overall mortality in individuals in the United States. Syme and Berkman (1976) and Kaplan and colleagues (1987) have shown that, for individuals, morbidity and mortality levels are inversely associated with income for a wide range of conditions; even when known risk factors—smoking and obesity, and lack of access to and utilization of medical care—are taken into account, differences in health status by income remain. Colleagues and I have recently estimated that poverty accounts for 6 percent of mortality among black and white adults in the United States (Hahn, Eaker, Barker, Teutsch, Sosniak, and Krieger in submission). Researchers hypothesize that poverty compromises resistance to a broad range of diseases by placing greater burdens on people and by taxing their capacities to respond (Kaplan et al. 1987).

Example 2: The Health of Blacks in South Africa and the United States

A comparison of the health conditions of blacks in South Africa and the United States provides another striking illustration of the effects of culture and societal organization on the health of populations. In South Africa, at least until recently, the dominant white regime succeeded in enforcing a comprehensive system of the oppression of blacks and other non-white populations. In the United States, a system of black slavery and formal segregation has been replaced by one more egalitarian in principle, but nevertheless one in which discrimination persists. (My evidence on South Africa is provided in reports by Anderson and Marks 1988; Jinabhai, Coovadia, and Abdool-Karim 1986; Nightingale, Hannibal, Geiger et al. 1990a, 1990b; and World Health Organization 1983. My evidence on the United States is provided by the Centers for Disease Control 1993b; U.S. Department of Commerce 1990; Thernstrom, ed., *The Harvard Encyclopedia of American Ethnic Groups;* and other individual researchers.)

In South Africa, race has been the most prominent theme of societal organization in recent decades. The white cultural system of apartheid constructed a rationale for white domination and maintained domination by law and by force. The 14 percent minority white population has controlled 74 percent of the disposable income and 82 percent of the land (and a greater proportion of the high-quality land). While Asian Indians and mixed-race "coloreds" had separate and proportionately small legislative representation compared with that for whites, until 1994, black South Africans had no representation at all. Yet, it was the white government that dictated the societal distribution of resources. (South Africa provides better evidence for Eyer's theory of national prosperity as a cause of death than the democratic industrialized nations studied by Brenner.)

Places of residence for blacks were determined by the apartheid government. Black communities were forcibly relocated; 74 percent of the black population was moved to "homelands" where there was little or no employment. Housing shortages were estimated to be thirteen times greater for blacks than for whites. Access to basic sanitation, water, and food have usually been inadequate in black settlements.

The movement of black individuals has also been strictly regulated. Laws provided for the legal detention of blacks, including children, without charge; torture of children as well as adults was reported to be common. Because they have owned most natural resources—principally gold and diamond mines—whites have also controlled labor opportunities. Many blacks have been forced to adopt a migratory life, disrupting family and other social connections. It is estimated that 80 percent of the male population has been involved in migratory labor. Unemployment among urban blacks was reported to be 88 percent, compared with 5 percent for whites.

Prevailing poverty and segregation have produced severe health problems for blacks (relative to Indians and coloreds as well as to whites). "Poverty remains the primary cause of the prevalence of many diseases and widespread hunger and malnutrition among black South Africans" (Nightingale et al. 1990a:2098).

In addition to substantial health problems, the quality of public health surveillance—the collection, analysis, and dissemination of health information—has also been less adequate for blacks than for whites, and least adequate for blacks in remote, rural regions where the burdens of sickness are greater. Thus, it is likely that available statistics understate health conditions of South African blacks. But they provide at least an indication of the health system of apartheid.

Life expectancy at birth for white South Africans was seventy-one years in 1985; that for blacks was sixty-two years. Infant mortality is another good indicator of a society's overall health; whites have a rate of infant mortality of 9/1,000 live births (comparable with U.S. whites); blacks have a rate of 61/1,000 (more than 6 percent, compared with less than 2 percent among U.S. blacks). Thus, black South African infants die at a rate 6.8 times that of white South African infants.

Among children who survive, malnutrition is common, leading to stunted growth. It is estimated that 2.9 million South African children—mostly black—are malnourished and that 15,000 to 30,000 die annually from malnutrition. Infectious diseases also occur at far higher rates among blacks than whites in South Africa; in 1979, for example, rates of tuberculosis were fifty-nine times greater among blacks than among whites. Black miners, mostly relatively healthy adult males, are estimated to have died at a rate of 390/100,000 per year between 1979 and 1983—a rate slightly less than that for black men 25–34 years of age in the United States.

Not only does the structure of South African society cause (that is, mediate) high rates of sickness in its black population; it has also withheld the means of treatment. The apartheid government had fourteen separate health ministries—one each for whites, blacks, coloreds, Indians, and all races combined, and one for each of the semi-autonomous homelands. Per capita health-care expenditures for blacks have been 25 percent and those for coloreds and Indians 55 percent of the expenditures for whites. Researchers estimate that there is one physician per 400–6,300 white patients and one black physician per 90,000–326,000 black patients—a ratio of 225:1, inversely proportional to medical need. Hospitals have commonly been segregated, and hospitals for whites may have empty beds, while hospitals for blacks (with half the number of beds per capita) are greatly overcrowded. Physicians who resist the oppressions of apartheid have been harassed and killed.

Finally, the society of apartheid also restricted access for blacks to general and medical education. Per capita expenditures on education for whites have been 10.2 times higher than expenditures on education for blacks, and though only 1 percent of whites cannot read, 33 percent of blacks are reported to be illiterate. Only 4 percent of a recent medical school class were blacks.

The socioeconomic and health conditions of blacks in the United States, though now generally better than conditions of blacks in South Africa, were perhaps worse (than those of South African blacks at the same time) until at least the end of the Civil War (Savitt 1978). Under slavery, U.S. blacks were treated as less than human; they were sold and traded, breaking family and community relations; they were forcibly subjected to arduous labor and given minimal food and quarters (Savitt 1978).

Although the figures may not be fully reliable, a report from the U.S. Bureau of the Census in 1850 indicates that, despite apparently higher rates of some diseases among whites (for example, malaria and tuberculosis), overall mortality in Virginia was 1.6 times greater among black slaves and 1.3 times greater among freed blacks than among whites (Savitt 1978). Most deaths were ascribed to tuberculosis, respiratory diseases, unspecified nervous system diseases, diarrhea, cholera, and "old age."

The Emancipation Proclamation and subsequent constitutional amendments and legislation formally ended slavery and gave black men the vote. Despite formal emancipation, however, the civil rights of blacks were obstructed in many regions of the country in an apartheid-like system that predominated until the second half of the twentieth century, when the civil rights movement and civil rights legislation more firmly established legal access for blacks in many arenas of U.S. life. Conflicting cultural ideologies in the United States have disputed appropriate approaches to equality—by redressive affirmative action, by antidiscrimination legislation, or by a more individualistic "freedom of choice."

With relatively greater civil rights in the United States, substantial inequities in well-being between blacks and much of the rest of society have been reduced but not eliminated. Socioeconomic opportunities and resources are unequally distributed in U.S. society, and efforts to create a balance are resisted. In 1988, more than a quarter of black families lived on incomes below the poverty level, a rate almost four times that of white families; even among black families in which the householder had some college education, 11.5 percent lived below the poverty level, a rate still more than four times that of white families. Unemployment in 1988 was also 2.5 times greater among blacks than among whites, independent of educational level.

Blacks have higher prevalences than whites of many risk factors for major causes of death—obesity (10 percent higher for black than white men, 83 percent higher for black than white women), hypertension (13 percent higher for black than white men, 48 percent higher for black than white women), and cigarette smoking (37 percent higher for black than white men, 6 percent higher for black than white women) (Centers for Disease Control 1990a). At all educational levels, blacks also suffer higher rates of occupational injury, suggesting assignment to positions with greater exposure to risk (Robinson 1989).

Access to and/or utilization of health care is also substantially lower among blacks than among whites in the United States. For example, 1.6 times as many blacks as whites under sixty-five years of age were without any type of health insurance in 1986. And for the same diagnoses, kidney disease and heart disease, blacks were less likely to receive medical procedures or surgery than whites (Kasiske et al. 1991; Ford et al. 1989). As an overall index of nonutilization of health care, blacks in the United States are 4.5 times more likely than whites to die of medically preventable conditions (Schwartz et al. 1990).

The health status of blacks persistently differs from that of whites, although the difference has diminished substantially since the beginning of the twentieth century. While in 1900, life expectancy of white newborns was 47.6 years, life expectancy for nonwhite newborns (including populations other than black) was only 33 years—an excess of 44 percent. In 1990, U.S. whites could expect to live 76.1 years and blacks 69.1 years—an excess of only 10 percent; however, life expectancy for blacks has recently declined for the first time this century. The proportion of blacks who assess their health as fair or poor is almost twice that of whites, and blacks are only 71 percent as likely as whites to rate their own health as excellent.

Infant mortality in 1987 was reported to be 2.1 times greater among blacks (18.7) than among whites (9.1), a difference present regardless of the mother's level of education. Emanuel (1986) has reviewed evidence that birthweight differences cannot be easily corrected from one generation to the next, because women who are small because of the small stature of their own mothers are themselves likely to bear low-weight infants. In a study of hospital deliveries in Seattle, the risk of abnormal births was 2.5 times greater for women who were themselves born with a low weight than among women whose birthweight was higher (Hackman et al. 1983). Poor health status is thus perpetuated from generation to generation, a cycle that may require more than routine prenatal care to interrupt.

In 1987, the age-adjusted death rate from all causes was 1.5 times greater among blacks than among whites. Rates of homicide (for victims) were 7 times greater among black than among white men and 4.2 times greater among black than among white women. Many infectious diseases—for example, acquired immunodeficiency syndrome, tuberculosis, syphilis, and hepatitis B—also occur at substantially higher rates among blacks than

Table 4.1   Health Conditions of Blacks and Whites in South Africa and the United States

	South Africa		United States	
	Black	White	Black	White
Life Expectancy (years)				
1900	NA	NA	33.0	47.6
1980s	62	71	69.4	75.6
Infant Mortality	61	9	18.7	9.1
(deaths/1,000 livebirths)				
Tuberculosis	170	15	21.9	6.1
(cases/100,000 population)				
Measles	71	24	0.4	0.5
(cases/100,000 population)				

Sources: Data from CDC 1990a, Buehler et al. 1989, Anderson and Marks 1988, and Nightengale et al. 1990b.

among whites (Buehler et al. 1989; Hahn et al. 1989; Selik et al. 1988; McQuillan et al. 1989). A recent study by Otten and colleagues (1990) indicates that 31 percent of the black adult excess in mortality in the United States reflects differences in the prevalence of known risk factors (for example, hypertension and alcohol consumption); another 38 percent is attributable to differences in family income; the remaining 31 percent is unexplained. Similarly, Navarro has recently presented evidence (1990) that much of the differences between the health status of blacks and whites in the United States are due to differences in socioeconomic status.

In 1986 U.S. blacks were only 54 percent as likely to have completed college as whites. In 1987–88 blacks represented 6 percent of medical school classes and approximately 12.2 percent of the U.S. population as a whole.

Comparison of South Africa and the United States (table 4.1) indicates that differences in the health conditions of blacks and whites are caused principally by the sociocultural and socioeconomic circumstances of these nations rather than by biological, "racial" differences between blacks and whites. Cultural systems have fostered forms of societal organization, which, in turn, through sociocultural mediation, have differentially distributed the causes of sickness and the resources for its remedy among blacks and whites. Cultural systems have also affected social relationships and expectations, which may in turn have affected the health conditions of blacks in the United States and South Africa.

During the slavery years and the period immediately thereafter, the health of blacks in the United States was apparently far worse than that of blacks in South Africa today and was certainly worse than that of U.S. whites at the time. Sociocultural movements, following emancipation in the United States, gradually reversed this difference in the status of South African and

U.S. blacks. We can hope that the emancipation of South African blacks will eventually improve their health status and that further efforts to create equality of opportunity in the United States, following generations of oppression, will reduce the remaining gap between the health of blacks and whites.

Example 3: Social Relationships and Health Status in the Local Environment

Having considered examples of the effects of national and societal organization, I now examine evidence for the effects of people's immediate social environments on the mediation and production of the sickness and health they experience.

A number of studies demonstrate that a person's connectedness with others is an important determinant of sickness and health (House, Landis, and Umberson 1988; Berkman 1984). In a study in Alameda County, California, almost 7,000 adults were first questioned in 1965 about their health status, behavior, and social contacts, including their marital status, relationships with other family members and close friends, and church and other group membership (Berkman and Syme 1979). A Social Network Index was used as an overall measure of connectedness. Over the next ten years, 682 of the persons first interviewed in 1965 died. Men with the lowest Social Network Index were 2.3 times as likely to have died as men with the highest Index; women with the lowest Index were 2.8 times as likely to have died as women with the highest Index. Among persons with a low Social Network Index, there was an excess mortality from heart disease, all types of cancer, stroke, and all other causes of death combined, suggesting that the effect of connectedness on mortality was associated not with the etiology of specific diseases but with some more general factor of resistance or susceptibility.

Since it is possible that the observed association between social connectedness and mortality might be explained by a lack of connectedness among people with poor health (that is, poor health causing fewer connections), researchers attempted to confirm their own explanation (that is, lack of connectedness as a cause of increased mortality) by examining the initial health status of the persons they studied. Even when factors such as health status in 1965, risk behavior (for example, smoking, hypertension, overweight, and heavy alcohol consumption), socioeconomic status, and preventive health-care practices were taken into account, persons least connected with others were still more than twice as likely to have died in the ten-year interval than persons who were more connected with others. The persistence of an association between social connectedness and mortality—having controlled for initial health status and risk factors—suggests both that social connectedness is a precursor rather than (or in addition to) a result of poor health and that the effect of connectedness is independent of other major risk factors for death.

Researchers have also focused more narrowly on the health effects of marital status (Helsing, Szklo, and Comstock 1981a; Koskenvuo et al. 1980). They have found that widows and widowers are more likely than comparable married persons to die from several causes, for example, coronary heart disease and all types of cancer. Most studies indicate that excess mortality is greater for men than for women. Several studies indicate that the excess peaks within several months following a spouse's death, but persists for years. A study comparing the prevalence of major risk factors for mortality among never-married, married, divorced, and widowed persons in the United States found no differences in risk factor prevalence that might account for higher mortality rates among widowed than among married persons (Weiss 1973); thus it seems that differential mortality by marital status is unlikely to be explained by corresponding differences in major risk factors. Some studies show more directly that the effect of marital status remains even when controlling for risk factors, preventive health care, and socioeconomic status (Helsing, Szklo, and Comstock 1981b).

Other research indicates that the effects of a person's social environment need not involve direct personal contact. An association has been found between traumatic death or violence in the community environment and subsequent suicide or suicide-like behavior. For example, when newspaper or television stories about a suicide are released, the rate of suicide increases in the following week; the greater the circulation of the newspaper, the greater the increase in suicides (Phillips 1974). When Marilyn Monroe killed herself in 1962, 197 suicides occurred during the following week— 12 percent more than the number expected on the basis of "normal" suicide patterns. A recent study indicates that teenagers are more susceptible to televised publicity about suicide and that increases in suicides are greater for girls than boys (Phillips and Carstensen 1986).

Although not commonly thought of as suicidal, motor vehicle crashes follow a similar pattern. The well-known Japanese writer, Mishima, committed ritual suicide (hara-kiri) on November 24, 1970; Phillips (1977) estimated that in California, 98 motor vehicle fatalities would have normally been expected in the following week, whereas 117 occurred. Phillips calculates that, on average, motor vehicle fatalities increase 9 percent above the expected rate in the week following front-page newspaper stories, and that, for newspapers with greater than average circulation, the increase is 19 percent.

Finally, though for ethical reasons, experiments are rarely conducted on human beings, the birthday lottery system deployed to select men for military service in the Vietnam War has been used in a clever study to examine the effects of selection for war on selectees (Hearst, Newman, and Hulley 1986). As if in a randomized experiment, the long-term health of men selected, more or less by chance, to serve in Vietnam was compared with the health of men not selected. Rates of suicide and motor vehicle fatalities were significantly greater among those selected than among those exempt. Only 28 percent of those selected actually served, however; assuming that all the excess deaths occurred among those who served, their rates of suicide would have to have been 86 percent greater and their rates of motor vehicle deaths 53 percent greater than those not selected. While selectees and nonselectees did not differ in rates of mortality from most other causes combined, mortality from cirrhosis of the liver was lower among selectees (for reasons not explained). We thus have evidence that selection for war, and most likely service in war, increases the susceptibility to subsequent suicide and motor vehicle fatality. A plausible explanation is that people internalize their social environments, and when these environments are violent, then self-destructive violent behavior may be expressed in response. It remains to determine factors or circumstances that distinguish persons who are so influenced from those who resist.

While in the language of Biomedicine, "communicable diseases" are sicknesses contracted by the spread of infectious microorganisms, the phrase may be more apt for conditions that work by means of human symbols and communication. When rates of suicide and motor vehicle fatalities increase following mass media events or profound interpersonal experiences, it seems that messages are communicated that trigger a vital (and mortal) response in a susceptible audience.

Example 4: Cultural Expectations, Sickness, and Healing

Perhaps the most famous of sociocultural phenomena is the placebo effect (from the Latin, *placere*, "to please"). Placebo medicines and procedures, even placebo surgery, are thought to produce desired effects because they are believed by patients to have these effects. Placebos (that is, the medicines and/or the procedures) are thought to work independently of specific pharmacological or physiological properties, such as those associated with other medical treatments. While, as I describe in more detail below, placebos play an ambiguous role in Biomedical practice and research, perhaps they pique public curiosity because their effects are so widespread yet apparently lacking explanation.

Shapiro (1960) has claimed that the placebo phenomenon has been the dominant mode of healing throughout human history. It might also be claimed that in the contemporary nonindustrial world, the placebo phenomenon persists as the major, most pervasive force in healing. Summarizing a large number of studies, Beecher concludes that, even in the industrial world, "physical" placebo therapies have "an average significant effectiveness of 35.2% +/− 2.2%," that is, the percentage of patients for whom there is satisfactory relief (Beecher 1955: 1603).

The placebo response parallels that of pharmacologically active drugs. In the course of an enlightening philosophical discussion of the placebo phenomenon, Howard Brody (1977) summarizes the parallels: placebo effects peak several hours following administration; there is a cumulative effect as the placebo is continued over time, a residual effect after the placebo is stopped, and a decreasing efficacy with increasing severity of symptoms. Placebo drugs can also have toxic "side effects," for example, somnolence, insomnia, palpitations, irritability, and rashes. In addition, placebos can be addictive, causing withdrawal symptoms when discontinued. There are reports that the colors of placebos moderate their effects: yellow and white capsules are said to be most effective, red and gray ones to have most side effects (Honzak, Horackova, and Culik 1972). One study suggests, paradoxically, that placebo pills may be effective even when patients are informed that the pills are thought to be pharmacologically inert (Park and Covi 1965).

A painful experiment shows how placebos work by ordinary pharmacological mechanisms. Levine, Gordon, and Fields (1978) studied patients whose teeth had been extracted and whose pain had been significantly diminished by placebo medications. The researchers gave these patients naloxone, a compound that blocks the effects of pain-killing opiates; they found that the patients' pain increased again, almost to the level of patients who had not initially responded to the placebo. The experiment suggests that the expectation of pain relief causes the release of opiates.

Placebo healing is a physiological effect of expectations—largely shaped by the patient's cultural setting (Hahn and Kleinman 1983b). Expectations are not simply logical propositions about future events; they are physically embedded in the brains of those who maintain them and they are thus associated with neurotransmitters and/or hormones that affect physiological functioning. Expectations are a bridge connecting our cultures and our bodies. Thus, it is reasonable that placebo effects should be found in all cultural settings, and that, with differing expectations in different cultures, specific placebo effects should vary substantially from one setting to another.

Evidence for cross-cultural variation in the placebo effect is found in Daniel Moerman's insightful reanalysis of thirty-one studies, carried out in sixteen nations, on the efficacy of cimetidine for relief of gastric and duodenal ulcers (Moerman 1983). All the studies that Moerman reviewed were conducted in a manner common to drug testing generally in Biomedical settings: study subjects were initially evaluated for the presence of ulcers and assigned to treatment or nontreatment control groups; while the treatment group was given cimetidine, the control group received a placebo, believed (by the investigators) to have no specific pharmacological effect on ulcers. To ensure that results of the study would not be influenced by either the patients' or the researchers' knowledge of who was receiving cimetidine and who the placebo, the studies were "double-blinded"—neither patients nor researchers knew which group the patients were in until after the patients had been assessed for final results.

Four to six weeks after the initiation of the studies, treatment and control patients were reexamined for the presence of ulcers. If the 1,692 patients from all thirty-one studies are added together, 76 percent of the experimental group and 48 percent of the control group were healed, indicating that cimetidine added 28 percent to the efficacy of the placebo alone, a result highly unlikely to have occurred by chance. Looking at the thirty-one studies separately, however, only thirteen showed a statistical difference in outcome between experimental and control groups, and eighteen showed no statistical difference.

Moerman compared the patients in studies showing cimetidine effective with the patients in studies showing cimetidine not significantly different from placebo. For patients treated with cimetidine, results were similar in both the statistically significant and the nonsignificant studies; 75 percent in the former group and 77 percent in the latter group were healed. But the proportion of patients healed by placebo in the significant studies was far lower (37 percent) than the proportion healed in the nonsignificant studies (58 percent). Thus, what made the significant studies significant was not the efficacy of cimetidine among those treated, but the relatively lower efficacy of the placebo in the control group.

In addition, one of the studies reviewed by Moerman (Sonnenberg, Keine, and Weber 1977) indicated a remarkable difference in the results of cimetidine and placebo healing. Ulcers recurred among 48 percent of patients treated with cimetidine, but they recurred among only 9 percent of patients treated with placebo, suggesting that "while cimetidine 'heals' ulcers, placebo treatment can 'cure' ulcer disease" (Moerman 1983:14). (However, unless pharmacologically active drugs *detract* from placebo effects, this result is puzzling, since neither patient nor physician knew who was receiving placebo treatment, so that whatever caused placebo curing should also have caused cimetidine curing. Treatments that are pharmacologically effective should always have efficacy beyond their own placebo effect.)

Among the thirty-one studies he reviewed, Moerman noted that the efficacy of the placebo varied greatly, from 10 percent in one study to 90 percent in another. He also noticed that there was a variation in placebo efficacy from country to country; the six studies conducted in Germany had a significantly higher rate of placebo healing (63 percent) than studies conducted in the other twenty-five countries combined (41 percent). One might speculate that international differences in placebo efficacy correspond to cultural differences in beliefs about the power of medicine and its administration.

The influence of cultural expectation is manifest also in the experience of pain—of which the pain of childbirth is said to be one of the most excruciating. Brigitte Jordan has studied beliefs and practices surrounding childbearing in the Yucatan, Mexico; Holland; Sweden; and the United States (Jordan 1993). From one setting to another, beliefs vary greatly about the nature of birth itself and, more specifically, about the pain associated with labor, the need for anaesthesia, and the role of childbearing women in controlling the administration of anaesthesia.

While the experience of pain may be impossible to compare from one person to another, Jordan observed marked cultural differences in the display and apparent experience of pain. Among women attended (in their own homes) by a local indigenous midwife in the Yucatan, pain is expected, accepted, and responded to with empathy by companions selected by the laboring women. In Holland, where births are thought of as essentially healthy, and where healthy births are also attended by midwives and a companion of the woman, it is believed that the woman's body "knows best"; anaesthesia is not used. In Sweden, where all births take place in technologically sophisticated hospitals, childbearing women expect anaesthesia, are informed of available anaesthetic options, and themselves select methods they deem appropriate, as needed.

Finally, in the United States, where birth is regarded as a medical event and therefore subject to control by physicians, childbearing women must demonstrate their pain in order to convince attending physicians of their need for anaesthesia. Lack of control in the obstetrical setting and anxiety about pain may heighten the experience of pain itself. Jordan notes that "the experience of pain is observationally more visible in U.S. obstetrical wards than in Holland, Sweden or Yucatan" (Jordan 1993:52). (For an analysis of the development of anaesthesia and its control in U.S. obstetrics, see chap. 8 in this book.)

Cultural expectations have also been shown to affect the timing of major health events; a remarkable example is the postponement of death. David Phillips has recently shown that deaths among the Chinese in the United States from 1960 through 1984 were 35 percent less likely to occur in the week before and 35 percent more likely to occur in the week after the Chinese Harvest Moon Festival (Phillips and Smith 1990). Phillips suggests that determination to see the holiday extends the life span. He has also found that death rates for Jews but not for other groups decline in the week preceding and rise in the week following Passover, again suggesting the postponement of death for celebration of an important cultural event (Phillips and King 1988).

At a more personal level, Phillips (1972) has also demonstrated that the time of year in which a person is born may be connected to the time of year of his or her death. A sample of 1,251 people in biographical dictionaries were 28 percent more likely to have died in the same month in which they were born or in the two following months than in the two months preceding the month of their birth. Again one may speculate that people postpone their deaths to witness an event important to them. (It would be interesting to compare this phenomenon in cultural settings where the uniqueness of individuals is less valued than the well-being of a social group, and where the events of an individual's life may not be celebrated as they are in the West [White and Kirkpatrick 1985].)

Evidence suggests that cultural expectations can lead not only to the postponement of major health events but, under different circumstances, to their acceleration. To distinguish salubrious placebo effects from noxious effects of cultural expectations, Kissel and Barrucand (1964) coined the term *nocebo* (from the Latin *nocere,* "to hurt"). Nocebos are expectations of harmful or painful events that lead to the fulfillment of those expectations.

The most infamous of nocebo effects is voodoo death. In 1942, the physiologist Walter Cannon, better known for his discovery of the "fight or flight response," surveyed the variety of voodoo death phenomena reported in so-called traditional societies (Cannon 1942): from Australia, where, among some aboriginal peoples, pointing a bone at someone was said to induce quick death of that person, to Latin America and Africa, where belief that one is bewitched was also said to lead to rapid death. Cannon explained this mortality as a result of prolonged and heightened emotional stress and activation of the sympathetic nervous system. He believed that the phenomenon was far more likely to be found among "primitive people, because of their profound ignorance and insecurity in a haunted world, than among educated people living in civilized and well-protected communities" (Cannon 1942:174). In contemporary Western societies, however, Engel (1968, 1971) has described and analyzed the similar phenomena of the "giving up–given up complex" and "sudden and rapid death during psychological stress." A review by Gomez (1982) indicates the breadth of such phenomena in industrialized society, from faith healing to medical rounds in hospitals.

It is unlikely that belief in the healing power of large doses of arsenic would transform this chemical into a healing agent: yet I submit, though I would not attempt to prove it, that such a belief would retard its lethal effects. Likewise, lack of faith in antibiotics may diminish the potency of these drugs, and faith or skepticism about materials or practices thought of (in Biomedicine) as pharmacologically inert may shift the results in expected directions.

Placebos are the self-fulfilling prophecies of healing, nocebos the self-fulfilling prophecies of sickness. The hypothetical effect is illustrated in figure 4.1. Expectations are represented on the vertical axis, outcomes on the horizontal axis. Expectations that healing will occur are represented above the horizontal axis, the stronger the higher; expectations that sickness will occur are represented below the horizontal axis, the stronger the lower. Similarly, healing outcomes are represented to the right of the vertical axis, the more powerful the further to the right; and pathological outcomes are represented to the left of the vertical axis, the more powerful the further to the left. The placebo/nocebo phenomenon predicts that, because outcome events are affected by expectations in the expected direction, events of sickness and healing in human life will concentrate in the upper right and lower

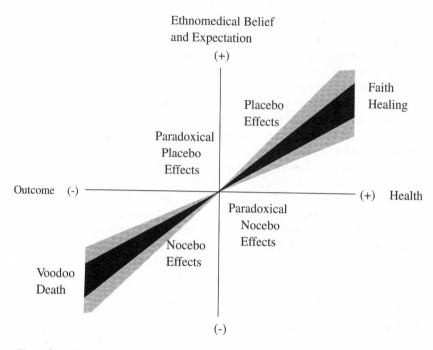

Figure 4.1   The placebo thesis: Relations between expectation and outcome (From Hahn and Kleinman 1983b. Reprinted by permission.)

left quadrants of this graph. Events in the other two quadrants might be regarded as placebo/nocebo side effects.

BIOMEDICINE AND THE CONSTRUCTION, MEDIATION AND PRODUCTION OF SICKNESS AND HEALING

A central tenet of Biomedicine is that human sickness is, in theory, if not in practice, essentially reducible to disturbances in human biology and that healing is reducible to the correction of biological disturbance: "The dominant model . . . assumes disease to be fully accounted for by deviations from the norm of measurable biological (somatic) variables" (Engel 1977:130). Sociocultural effects on sickness and healing, if considered, are regarded as peripheral and secondary—perhaps caused by but without important causal role in human biology.

Of the three sociocultural effects on sickness and healing I have described—construction, mediation, and production—only mediation is accepted in Biomedicine. Patterns of human interaction and social organization are acknowledged to play a part in outbreaks of infectious disease, in diseases associated with "life-style," in clusters of environmental disease, in intentional and unintentional injuries, and in differential access to and utilization of health care within segments of the population. Marcia Angell, a physician and an editor of the prestigious *New England Journal of Medicine,* writes, "There is overwhelming evidence that certain personal habits, such as smoking cigarettes, drinking alcohol, and eating a diet rich in cholesterol and saturated fats, can have great impact on health, and changing our thinking affects these habits" (1985:1572).

Beyond recognized risk factors, such as smoking and cholesterol, however, mediational effects of human behavior and social organization may be subjected to mockery and to unusual scrutiny in Biomedicine. Physician and author Lewis Thomas comments in the *New England Journal of Medicine* (1978) on an early analysis of the Alameda study described above. The researchers (Belloc and Breslow 1972; Belloc 1973) found that seven factors—eating breakfast; not snacking, smoking, or drinking excessively; exercising regularly; maintaining normal weight; and regularly sleeping eight hours a night—each predicted enhanced longevity. Of these factors, Thomas accepts only not smoking or drinking excessively, because they fit what he knows contribute to several diseases and to automobile crashes. He ridicules the other risk factors indicated in the study (which he refers to as "playing tennis" and "going off on family picnics") as well as "the science that produced this illumination."

Thomas asserts that the Alameda study fails to control for the participants' initial health status, which might account not only for the differential mortality but also for the distribution of risk factors in the study population; for example, people sick when initially interviewed might not eat well, sleep well, or exercise *because* they are sick. But Thomas does not consider whether the initial health of the study population might affect the habits he believes detrimental as well as those he questions. Moreover, the researchers do in fact control for the initial health status of study subjects, at least insofar as reported by the subjects themselves. The seven behaviors are still associated with lower mortality rates for all age groups; and the greater the number of these behaviors a person has, the longer he or she is likely to live.

The mockery of non-Biomedical beliefs is common. An editorial in the *New England Journal of Medicine* asserts that "holistic" approaches to healing "can be divided into those that are adaptations of traditional medical practices in other societies—Chinese, Navaho, and so forth—and those that were invented, so to speak, the week before last by some relatively successful crank." In contrast, "medicine in industrialized nations is scientific medicine" (Glymour and Stalker 1983:960).

It is what I have referred to as the sociocultural production of sickness and healing, a more direct causal effect of social relationships and beliefs, that incurs the greatest skepticism in Biomedicine. Angell writes, "it is time to acknowledge that our belief in disease as a direct reflection of mental state is largely folklore (1985:1572).

Attitudes toward and uses of placebos in Biomedicine are indicative of Biomedical disdain. Moerman points out (1983) that, if, as he found for placebo efficacy studies, a drug were discovered to have an efficacy ranging from 10 percent to 90 percent, Biomedical researchers would rush to discover what accounted for this range and, in particular, for the 90 percent success. However, Moerman points out, placebo responses are examined in order to control or minimize their effect in research settings; medical research focuses on efficacy beyond the placebo effect. Placebos are a nuisance.

The Biomedical attitude toward placebos is also notable in clinical practice. A study of placebo use by physicians and nurses in a teaching hospital shows that the placebo phenomenon is commonly misunderstood, its powers underestimated (Goodwin, Goodwin, and Vogel 1979). Placebos are often administered to show that a patient's pain is "all in his (or her) head" and that there is nothing "really" wrong. Sixty percent of physicians report giving placebos to ascertain whether the patient's pain is "real." Placebos may also be given to patients for whom standard treatments are not working or to patients thought undeserving of pharmacologically active drugs.

It may be the combined power of the placebo phenomenon and its anomalous position in Biomedical theory that make it a highly charged matter. Physician and philosopher Howard Brody goes so far as to define the placebo phenomenon as an anomaly for the Biomedical perspective. In formal fashion, he proposes, for example, that "the change in C [patient's condition] is attributable to I [active intervention], but not to any specific therapeutic effect of I or to any known pharmacologic or physiologic property of I" (1977:41). The paradoxical consequence of this definition is to make the placebo phenomenon forever incompatible with known pharmacological or physiological properties. As the phenomenon is recognized within pharmacological or physiological science, so it disappears; as it is known, it ceases to exist. It seems strange to define a phenomenon in terms of current ignorance, and more reasonable to regard placebo (and nocebo) phenomena as inexplicable by contemporary physiological and pharmacological knowledge, yet necessarily compatible and requiring revision of current physiological and pharmacological thought.

A SOCIOCULTURAL PERSPECTIVE ON SICKNESS AND HEALING

The sociocultural perspective on sickness and healing suggests an understanding very different from that of Biomedicine, different also from Western thought in general. Nevertheless, even within Biomedicine, there is a range of views, some of which are much closer than others to the sociocultural perspective. The specialty of family medicine, for example, recognizes the importance of interpersonal relationships in pathology and healing; some forms of psychiatry similarly recognize and treat patients for interpersonal relationships; and the fields of epidemiology and public health also consider effects in the distribution of sickness and health in populations.

Approaches similar to the one I propose have also been formulated by Biomedical physicians in response to their own tradition. Brody and Sobel (1979) have applied systems theory to the understanding of sickness and healing. They distinguish hierarchical levels of interacting phenomena, including not only molecules, cells, organs, and human bodies, but persons, families, societies, and the biosphere. The elements within each of these levels interact; different levels also interact with one another. Brody and Sobel define "disease" as "a failure to respond adaptively to environmental challenges resulting in a disruption of the overall equilibrium of the system" (1979:93). They define "health" as "the ability of a system (for example, cell, organism, family, society) to respond adaptively to a wide variety of environmental challenges (for example, physical, chemical, infectious, psychological, social)" (1979:92–93). Brody and Sobel do not explain what they mean by adaptation—adaptation to what end, defined by whose goals? But, they note the importance of cultural values and personal judgment in determining what counts as health.

The systems approach has also been adopted by physician George Engel in a landmark article, "The Need for a New Medical Model: A Challenge for Biomedicine" (1977). Engel outlined the fundamental assumptions of Biomedicine and noted that, though the Biomedical model has yielded enormous benefits, it is inadequate and has become a dogma in Western society. "We are now faced," Engel wrote, "with the necessity and the challenge to broaden the approach to disease to include the psychosocial without sacrificing the enormous advantages of the biomedical approach" (1977:131). In response to this challenge, he proposed an alternative, "biopsychosocial" model: "To provide a basis for understanding the determinants of disease and arriving at rational treatments and patterns of health care, a medical model must also take into account the patient, the social context in which he lives, and the complementary system devised by society to deal with the disruptive effects of illness, that is, the physician role and the health care system" (1977:132). Engel's model included psychosocial effects on susceptibility to sickness, its timing, severity, and course, as well as the patient's experience and reporting of symptoms. Medicine, Engel recommended, had to take these effects into account.

Engel has illustrated the biopsychosocial model with the case of a patient, "Mr. Glover," who suffers a myocardial infarction (Engel 1980). Engel examined the multiple events occurring inside and around Mr. Glover on chemical, physiological, psychological, social, and symbolic levels. He demonstrated how Mr. Glover's personal qualities—he was a hardworking, driven man—affected his own response to early symptoms as well as the responses of those around him, including his supportive employer. Mr. Glover's own response may have worsened his condition, while his employer's response led Mr. Glover to seek medical help. Engel also described how the behavior of the physicians in training who treated Mr. Glover exacerbated Mr. Glover's condition by not listening to him or responding to his anxiety. Engel then showed how the biopsychosocial approach, in addition to responding to Mr. Glover's physical condition, would make use of information about his personal characteristics and his social circumstances to minimize his symptoms, respond to his personal concerns, and enhance his recovery.

In this chapter, I have displayed a range of sociocultural effects on sickness and healing. I have not presented a comprehensive review (which would require several volumes) but rather have focused on evidence from diverse studies. The evidence indicates the power of cultural constructions in mediating the social distribution of both exposures to sickness and resources for its relief. Evidence also indicates the more direct power of social relationships and cultural expectations in the production of events of sickness and healing. Societies and their relationships and beliefs sicken, kill, and heal as well.

The sociocultural perspective suggests that human societies, interpersonal relationships, and cultural beliefs are not simply outside of and in the space surrounding us, but rather are embodied, literally, as a part of our anatomy and physiology (Hahn and Kleinman 1983b). There is a physiology of belief and of interpersonal relationships. Similarly, sociocultural phenomena suggest that the body is literally mindful, moving and functioning not only from biological but from cultural and social imperatives as well.

5 | ANTHROPOLOGY AND EPIDEMIOLOGY: ONE LOGIC OR TWO?

Most olfaction researchers agree that smells are detected when "odorants" (small, volatile, lipid-soluble molecules) bind to receptor proteins on the surface of nerve cells in the nose's olfactory epithelium, triggering electrical signals to the brain.

—Barinaga 1991:209

Nobody combines facts or features to identify the smell of coffee.

—Dreyfus and Dreyfus 1986:23

How do we justify our claims to knowledge about events of sickness and healing in society? And how do we achieve and verify new knowledge? Epidemiology is one approach to such knowledge—widely respected, though less well understood; anthropology is another—unfamiliar as an approach to sickness and healing. Among practitioners of both disciplines, as well as among their audiences, the two may be regarded as tangential if not antithetical. Epidemiology is seen as an objective science focused on the assessment of clearly specified associations among precisely defined variables through measurement, counting, and statistical analysis. Anthropologists have accused epidemiologists of "scientism" (Rubinstein 1984) and rigor to the point of "rigor mortis" (Nations 1986). In contrast, anthropology is thought of as a subjective discipline devoted to understanding the inner worlds of others by means of close, empathic encounters. The two disciplines seem to share little.

To the contrary, I believe that the underlying logics of anthropology and epidemiology have much in common and that practices developed in each discipline are necessary complements to practices in the other. In this chapter I outline their common foundations and complementary practices. I then illustrate their complementarity with an example of how they might collabo-

99

rate in the understanding and resolution of a persistent puzzle and dismal failure of public health—the large gap in rates of infant mortality between U.S. whites and blacks.

I am impelled to explore connections between anthropology and epidemiology not only because I believe their combination provides key solutions to major challenges in the study of sickness and healing but also because I practice both disciplines. Most often, when I do one, I am not aware of doing the other; yet, the principles of the other echo in the back of my mind, constraining my methods and my results. I look for unity in my work.

ANTHROPOLOGY AND EPIDEMIOLOGY: ONE LOGIC OR TWO?

The principles of knowledge that underlie a discipline are referred to as its "logic of inquiry" or "epistemology" (from the Greek, "to stand upon"—an epistemology examines the foundations of knowledge). The epistemology of a discipline describes how practitioners know what they know; it justifies the methods they use in designing studies, making observations, analyzing findings, and drawing inferences. In this section, I ask, "Do anthropology and epidemiology have radically different, even contradictory epistemologies, as I believe many practitioners of both disciplines would claim? Or are their epistemologies similar or complementary?"

In understanding the logic of a discipline, one must look beyond the explicit statements of its practitioners. The process of scientific research and discovery discernible in published scientific papers bears little evidence of what scientists actually do. Unspoken assumptions, complex personal motivations, intuitions and hunches, false starts, frustrations and satisfactions, and the personal relationships of collegiality and competition—these rarely, if ever, appear in descriptions of research results. (Not that we would want biographies or detailed logs of personal interaction appended to scientific papers; but more information about fundamental assumptions, ongoing puzzles, dead ends and hesitant conclusions might be useful in understanding the product.)

In addition, scientists may be unaware of the logic underlying their work. They may believe that they do something they do not do or that they don't do something they do; they may misperceive connections among parts of their work. Thus, to understand the logic of a discipline, it is important to examine not only what practitioners say about the foundations of their work but also what they actually do in practice.

It is also important to recall that there are many versions of anthropology (see chap. 3), some more obviously compatible with epidemiology, others seemingly incompatible; each version may have a different underlying logic.

For purposes of this chapter, I focus on a central tradition of anthropological thought, cultural anthropology. Epidemiology also has diverse approaches, though perhaps not as varied as anthropology.

I am by no means the first to propose close connections between anthropology and epidemiology (Trostle 1986a, 1986b). Pioneering efforts began in this arena more than thirty years ago with the work of John Cassel (1964), Frederick Dunn (1979), and others. Several scholars (for example, Dunn 1979; Janes, Stall, and Gifford 1986; Nations 1986) have pointed out the need and utility of incorporating anthropological methods and theory into epidemiology; others (such as True 1990) have proposed the inclusion of epidemiological methods in anthropology. Arthur Rubel and his colleagues applied epidemiological methods to the study of a folk illness, susto, in a Mexican village (Rubel 1964; Rubel, O'Nell, and Collado-Ardon 1984).

The comparison of disciplinary logics may indicate basic research strategies. If the two disciplines have separate logics, critical decisions would follow. If their logics are contradictory, then both cannot be true. We must decide which, if either, is correct; to do so, we must first choose criteria for such a judgment. If their epistemologies are distinct but not contradictory, the two should proceed on separate tracks, reasonably ignoring each other. If, on the other hand, their epistemologies are complementary or ultimately unified, practitioners should further explore common interests and methods; they should pursue the synthesis of both disciplines toward the enhanced achievement of shared goals.

The epistemology of a discipline may be characterized by three elements: (1) *a problematic*—a way of conceiving problems; (2) *sources* of evidence; and (3) *methods* of analysis and inference. In describing the epistemologies of anthropology and epidemiology, I examine these elements and describe what practitioners in both fields think they are doing in their work—their explicit epistemologies—as well as the logic I believe underlies their practices.

Because I contradict some of the explicit epistemological beliefs of practitioners of both disciplines, my answer to the question I pose—two logics or one?—is unlikely to satisfy practitioners of either discipline. "Positivist," the anthropologists may cry; "soft-headed," the epidemiologists may counter. Perhaps the descriptions "soft-headed positivist" or "positivist of the soft" are apt. Practitioners in both disciplines fail to recognize basic assumptions underlying their own disciplines. Some anthropologists neglect the objective world or would wish it away. Most epidemiologists would dispense with subjectivity entirely if they could. I argue that these disciplines have essentially common grounds, some ignored by one, some by the other. I show that anthropologists are unwitting epidemiologists in their work and that epidemiologists practice anthropology unawares. The elaboration of common foundations will enlighten both practices.

Problematics in Anthropology and Epidemiology

Practitioners of different disciplines have characteristic ways of looking at problems; like societies, they see the world differently. A problematic addresses the questions, "What kinds of things or events in the world constitute a problem to be solved by this discipline?" and "What about these things or events is problematic?"

In anthropology, a principal problematic is the understanding of the inner worlds of members of particular societies. Many anthropologists describe the concerns of their discipline as (a) representation of "the native point of view"—most often the point of view of the members of foreign societies, but, more recently, also the members of their own society, and (b) the analysis of patterns of interaction and social organization that accompany the native point of view. The local point of view and social organization are often referred to as the "culture" of these people and the description of a culture as "ethnography." The anthropologist shows how elements in the foreign setting—for example, categories and theories of sickness, and the behavior of sick persons, their kin, and healers—all fit together, giving coherence to the whole scene. The complex of associations among the elements of a cultural setting is said to "explain" or "make sense of" the elements. Elements of a culture are also thought to derive meaning from their context, so that to remove an element from its setting and compare it with elements from other settings is to violate its essence.

A secondary problematic in anthropology is the discovery of "human nature"—characteristics shared by human beings and social life everywhere. In their descriptions of different cultural settings, anthropologists employ abstract concepts, such as "symbol," "ritual," "role," "social structure," and "culture" itself, at the same time using their observations in particular settings to refine the same concepts.

In epidemiology, the dominant problematic is the determination of the causes of health-related events—sickness and death, but also health-care practices and risk behaviors (such as smoking and nonuse of seat belts). Epidemiologists devote much attention to factors that might obscure the process of causal assessment; they attempt to ensure that, as much as possible, when they say that "x causes y," or, more cautiously, that "x is a risk factor for y," other known plausible explanations for the association of x and y have been eliminated. Epidemiologists search for universal laws, invariant from setting to setting. In order to do so, elements from the setting where information is collected are deliberately stripped of all but essential connections with other elements. A basic characteristic of the "variables" that epidemiologists measure and compare is that they may be assessed in any setting.

Anthropology and epidemiology appear to differ radically in their problematics. Anthropologists focus on the uniqueness of particular settings and on meaning determined by the interconnections of local details. Once they have achieved understanding of the local framework, anthropologists strive to dispense with the universal one. In contrast, epidemiologists focus on causality, on the universality of human processes, and on the interconnections of universal phenomena. Epidemiologists strive to eliminate local detail in order to achieve universal principles. Thus, where anthropologists deploy universals to arrive at particulars, epidemiologists tolerate particulars in their quest for universals. Anthropologists paint pictures rich in color, shading, shapes, and detail; epidemiologists sketch without shading—they are minimalists.

Sources of Evidence in Anthropology and Epidemiology

Anthropologists speak of the source of their evidence as "the field"; they go to and live in "the field," they conduct "fieldwork," they keep "field notes." The field is a particular social setting, often circumscribed by cultural, if not physical boundaries. Anthropologists immerse themselves in the social life of the setting they seek to understand. They refer to the people they select to interview (or who select them), particularly those who give them the information they need, as "informants." Anthropologists may note how the informant's social position affects the information provided; but anthropologists seldom draw systematic samples of informants to interview, and they rarely assess the representativeness of the information they collect.

Anthropologists seek to describe the world of others as the world appears to them—the others—without interjecting their own, anthropological viewpoint. They avoid "ethnocentrism," that is, looking at the world from the point of view of their own culture. Sometimes anthropologists seem to believe they have achieved the "true" native point of view—that they have in essence become native, without accent—free from their culture of origin.

The avoidance of ethnocentrism has powerful implications for the way in which anthropological research is conducted. Anthropologists seldom use questionnaires because questionnaires presume that what is relevant to ask about in the local setting can be known in advance. Anthropologists never quite know what to expect; ideally, they remain open to new ideas emerging from the novel setting. They must even learn how one asks questions in this society and how one learns. Some of what they record in field notes may make no sense to them initially, but later will fall into place with other puzzling pieces.

In describing their work of cultural description and analysis, anthropologists use an analogy from linguistics. Linguists begin analyses of foreign languages by using a set of all sounds thought possible in human speech. With this universal phonetics, they are able to transcribe speech found in any language. In any particular language, however, only a selected set of sounds is relevant. The significant units of sound in a language are called phonemes.

Phonemes are minimal features of speech sounds that allow the distinction of one word from another in a given language. For example, the English phonemes "a," "e," "i," "o," and "u" allow the distinction of "bat" from "bet" from "bit" from "bought" from "but." Different pronunciations of "a" or "e" may produce dialectal accents, idiosyncratic variations, or nuances of meaning, but all variants still count as "a" and "e" and allow distinction among words that contain them.

Anthropologists speak of *etics* (from "phonetics"), a universal grid that allows them to record their observations in different cultural settings in a search for the *emics* (from "phonemics")—the set of distinctions that make a difference to people in those settings. Etics is an external framework applicable anywhere; emics an internal, local one. The anthropological task is to use the universal framework of observation in order to achieve an understanding of the local framework. Anthropologists regard themselves as translators.

Anthropologists observe and record what the people they study do and say. Initially they may describe actions as physical motions and speech as phonetic sequences. Ultimately, they are not interested in uninterpreted sounds or movements—subject S moved her left hand upward ten inches and three inches to the right—but rather in underlying meanings and intentional acts—she waved. Some anthropologists believe that even the elementary observations on which they base their subsequent analyses are not physical movements or sounds but interpreted actions and utterances of participants in the local scene: "*We begin with our own interpretations of what our informants are up to, or think they are up to, and then systematize those*" (Geertz, 1973:15; emphasis in original).

Anthropological interpretations of events in the foreign scene are sometimes acknowledged to depend on a vast array of implicit assumptions and background interpretations on the part of the observer:

> This fact—that what we call our data are really our own constructions of other people's constructions of what they and their compatriots are up to—is obscured because most of what we need to comprehend a particular event, ritual, custom, idea, or whatever is insinuated as background information before the thing itself is directly examined. . . . Right down at the factual base, the hard rock, insofar as there is any, of the whole enterprise, we are already explicating: and worse, explicating explications. (Geertz 1973:9)

Some anthropologists have gone so far—much too far, I believe—as to assert that there is no objectivity in anthropology and worse, that lack of objectivity is not a shortcoming. "The data which derive from fieldwork are subjective and not objective. . . . So what should be done? Nothing. Anthropological texts are interesting in themselves and not because they tell us something about the external world" (Leach 1984:22).

For an epidemiologist, the world of evidence has a very different appearance. Epidemiologists speak of "measuring variables" and "gathering data." Variables are comparable to the elements of the anthropologist's etic framework; data, however, bear little resemblance to the anthropologist's final goal—the local, inside, emic perspective. The notion of "data" (singular, *datum,* from the Latin, "a thing given") corresponds to a concept of information as discrete things in the world—bundles of fact—independent of the observer and undistorted by the observer's cultural beliefs or psychological processes of inference; data can be "collected"—picked up as units, "edited," and "cleaned"; they can then be combined with other data to draw logical conclusions. Although epidemiologists gather information from humans in societal settings, they examine settings not for their uniqueness but, to the contrary, for their representativeness and indication of universal processes.

Things in the world have different properties that allow their assessment or measurement by different means. Epidemiology requires that the characteristics of subjects, their environments, and pathological agents should be appropriately assessed—categorized, measured, and counted. Pulses are measured in frequency by touch and a clock, weight in kilograms on a scale, age in years by questioning or from records; we categorize occupations and ethnicities also by questioning or, indirectly, by examining records. Epidemiologists try to ensure that they are measuring what they want to measure and that the means and the units of measurement fit the thing measured. They are persistently concerned with "misclassification," erroneously classifying a phenomenon as something it is not; misclassification leads to distorted results, masking true relationships or creating false ones.

Epidemiologists are interested in the reproducibility of their work because research methods are supposed to work regardless of who follows them, and because repeated observation of a phenomenon adds credibility. They develop "instruments" and seek data that are "reliable." Instruments, such as questionnaires, are the standard procedural means by which information on subjects and their environments is collected. Reliability is the constancy of results on repeated examination of the "same" phenomenon or event. Standardization is intended to ensure that information on all subjects and environments is collected in the same way. For example, questionnaires are designed to be asked in specified settings, say, in homes, with subject alone, and following specified rules. Epidemiologists assume that, because a question is always asked in the "same" way, it will be identically interpreted and responses to it will be comparable.

To ensure that they are measuring what they think they are measuring and that they are doing so accurately and reliably, epidemiologists are careful to characterize their informational sources and procedures. They undertake research to compare different methods of measurement—for example, the assessment of medical histories from hospital records versus those from patient interviews. Thus they conduct epidemiological studies of epidemiological sources and methods.

Analysis and Inference

Some anthropologists think that the description of the inner worlds of persons and societies radically distinguishes anthropology from the natural sciences. Anthropology studies systems of meaning and rules, whereas the natural sciences test hypotheses about causation. The basic method of the natural sciences is causal analysis; the method of anthropology is interpretation. Causal methods are described as "empirical," "objective," "quantitative"; interpretive methods as "subjective" and "qualitative." Some anthropologists assert that causal analysis and interpretation are mutually exclusive approaches, not both appropriate for the same questions, or at best appropriate to different aspects of the same question (Geertz 1973).

Anthropologists commonly claim detailed familiarity as the basis of their knowledge. The basic anthropological method is cryptically referred to as "participant observation," suggesting that anthropologists observe foreign scenes while also participating in them. The extent of participation and the procedures of observation are rarely discussed. It is recognized that the observer may affect the scene that provides information; however, this presence is most often assumed not to greatly distort anthropological analyses. Most anthropologists agree that a good interpretation is one that is both internally consistent—the pieces of interpretation fit together—and consistent with the events it is supposed to interpret.

In the epidemiological assessment of causality, two different measures of association between exposures and outcomes are pursued, depending on the way a study is designed. The "relative risk" compares rates of an outcome among populations exposed and unexposed to a risk factor; the "odds ratio" begins with populations with and without the outcome, such as a disease, and looks backward to compare the proportions of exposed and unexposed persons among those with and without the outcome. By both measures, a result of 1 indicates no association—no difference in disease rates by prior exposure, or no difference in likelihood of prior exposure among persons with and without the disease. Results greater than 1 indicate excess risk among persons exposed, and results less than 1 indicate a protective effect of exposure.

Epidemiologists sometimes write (mistakenly) as though they were assessing the "true" relative risk or odds ratio between given exposures and outcomes, adjusted for all distorting variables and independent of setting. Relative risks, however, are dependent on the particulars of social and historical settings and will vary when background rates of disease differ across time and/or space.

Epidemiological investigations are generally thought to follow a sequence of steps, so that, with a list of study subjects and relevant characteristics, colleagues would recognize how the researchers drew their conclusions. The steps include the following:

(1) *Problem description and hypothesis formulation:* Like the practitioners of other disciplines, epidemiologists respond to problematics of their field. They review the state of knowledge on a topic to ascertain unanswered questions of interest to them or to challenge or verify questionable "answers" that may already have been given.

(2) *Research design:* The investigation of epidemiological questions or hypotheses is thought to require certain steps: formulation of a hypothesis, definition of variables and specification of procedures for their collection, description of procedures to avoid distortion or "bias," and description of methods for determining associations among variables.

(3) *Data collection:* Operational definitions are set so that data collection will produce unbiased data.

(4) *Data analysis:* Assessment of epidemiological hypotheses is thought to require description of the data (for example, by age, sex, and race), followed by explicit examination of the hypothesis according to stated methods. The goal is to determine whether there is a causal relationship between specific variables, unbiased by other variables. Epidemiologists have explicit principles and criteria for the assessment of these relationships.

Epidemiologists seek to minimize bias—the distortion of true associations by extraneous factors. In "recall bias," for example, persons with a disease may be more likely to recall a suspected exposure event than persons without the disease, producing an appearance of association between exposure and outcome simply because of differences in recall, but independent of real differences in exposure. In "selection bias," the way in which subjects are selected for participation in the study makes it more likely that an association will be found, even though there is in fact no association. The randomized experiment is the methodological ideal in epidemiology and one approach to minimizing bias; epidemiologists conduct experiments when ethically feasible—for example, in clinical trials of new immunizations. Experiments, however, are rarely feasible, ethically or otherwise.

Epidemiologists seek elimination of bias by several means referred to as "adjustment" or "control." Control is intended to ensure that in comparison of persons exposed and not exposed, "all other conditions are the same"—an assumption sometimes referred to with the Latin phrase, "ceteris paribus." Control is ideally achieved by ensuring *not only* that a posited "outcome" does occur, or occurs more frequently in the presence of a "cause," *but also* that it does not occur or occurs less frequently in the absence of this "cause," all else being equal. Control is achieved when factors that might distort a true, underlying association of interest have been determined and taken into account.

Epidemiologists commonly attempt to demonstrate that their findings are not coincidental by use of statistical methods. Most often these methods are designed to show that, if there is no relationship between exposure and outcome, then the association actually observed between the two would be unlikely to occur; if the association has occurred, it it unlikely that there is no relationship. The more unlikely the occurrence observed, the greater epidemiologists have statistical "significance" or "confidence," qualities for which numerical values are calculated. Epidemiologists also attempt to be certain that, if a posited association is false, they will know it; this ability is described as statistical "power" and is also given a numerical value.

Epidemiologists have proposed (and debated) a variety of criteria, including statistical ones, by which to assess causal relationships between variables:

(1) *Temporal sequence:* A cause must precede its consequence.
(2) *Biological plausibility:* There should be some pathway of biological causation that makes sense of the association of risk factor and outcome in terms of accepted knowledge.
(3) *Strength of association:* The stronger the association and the more (statistically) unlikely it has occurred by chance, the more likely it is true.
(4) *Specificity:* The fewer other known causes of this outcome there are, the more likely this is the cause.
(5) *Consistency of association:* Associations are more likely if corroborated by other, independent evidence.
(6) *Coherence:* There should exist an internal logic of evidence and theory.
(7) *Experimental evidence:* Where it exists, it confirms an association.
(8) *Analogy:* Parallel associations in similar phenomena add credibility.

These criteria are accepted as guidelines rather than absolute prerequisites for true associations.

Epidemiologists sometimes distinguish "risk factors" from "risk markers." A risk factor is the true cause of an outcome, whereas a risk marker is only an indicator of the true cause. For example, an association between race and health status is commonly reported—not in the belief that some biological characteristic is directly related to the outcome, but rather on the assumption that racial groups behave and are treated in ways that are likely to affect the outcome. Race is thus a risk marker, and the behavior of the racial group or of others in response to them is the risk factor.

HOW DIFFERENT ARE THE LOGICS
OF ANTHROPOLOGY AND EPIDEMIOLOGY?

I shall now argue that, despite appearances of substantial divergence in problematics, sources, and methods, anthropology and epidemiology have a common underlying logic. Failing to recognize commonality, each discipline has developed particular methodological skills, although implicitly relying upon and taking for granted principles of knowledge akin to those developed in the other discipline.

To begin, though anthropology and epidemiology have differing intellectual goals—respectively, the analysis of meaning in particular settings and the discovery of universal causal processes—knowledge of particulars and knowledge of universals are inextricably linked in the means by which this knowledge is achieved.

To clarify the epidemiology-like logic of anthropological methods, consider the case of an anthropologist arriving in a strange setting, ignorant of the local environment and unacquainted with the language, beliefs, and customs (Hahn 1973; Quine 1960). How does this anthropologist come to understand what the people say and do, what a word means, or how behavior and social life are organized?

The interpretation of foreign utterances and actions is in essence a process of hypothesis testing, most often intuitive and tacit, about specific observations of the foreign scene. Interpretation of a native utterance depends on the interpreter's assumptions about the rationality and motivations of the local population and about the way the world works—what is "really" going on about which the native may be commenting. Such assumptions, seldom explicit, derive from the observer's own cultural tradition.

In Quine's (1960) anthro-fiction example, to understand the native meaning of *gavagai*, a phrase seemingly (that is, hypothetically) uttered when rabbits hop by, we must assume that what we and the native witness are rabbits hopping by and that the native is being rational and sincere in his utterances. Different assumptions will lead to different conclusions about what our informant is saying. Because of the assumptions required on the part of the observer in translation, what comes to be described as a foreign culture is a complex transformation of the observer's own culture (Hahn 1973).

I suggest that the method by which hypothesized translations and interpretations are assessed is a complex form of epidemiology. Though anthropologists may not think of themselves as investigating hypotheses, at root, they must assess associations among different aspects of the local scene, controlling for conditions regarded as extraneous. For example, in the relatively simple case of utterances about present events, the anthropologist must correlate native utterances with scenes with and without the hypothesized referent, while attempting to elicit the native's assent to proposed interpretations. The details of this anthropological epidemiology have not been worked out, though a foundation is provided in the classic work of philosopher W. V. O. Quine (1960). I wish simply to indicate the presence of such a logic underlying anthropological claims to knowledge.

Finally, while the imagined setting foreign to the observer's own may clarify the nature of translation and interpretation, similar issues arise in research in familiar settings. The assumption that we understand what some-one says because he or she uses the "same language" we do should be questioned and validated.

Anthropology is also involved in essential ways in the logic and methods of epidemiology. To begin, the goal of assessing and explaining the distribution of diseases in human populations is an inherently anthropological task. The distinction of populations and of population segments such as classes and ethnic groups and the recognition of patterns of behavior and social interaction associated with sickness are anthropological issues, resting on anthropological assumptions. Such assumptions may be based on systematic study or on unexamined common sense.

Failure by epidemiologists to acknowledge fully the role of social factors in epidemiological method is evident also in epidemiological criteria or the assessment of associations between risk factors and outcomes. While biological plausibility is a recognized criterion, psychological and social plausibility are ignored. It is as if only biology provided plausible connections between risk factors and health outcomes.

Epidemiologists seek universal variables and associations, independent of the context or setting in which they are found. But context may be stripped off only with knowledge of both what there is to be stripped off and how the embedding context is connected to the variables of interest. The ascertainment of epidemiological information therefore rests upon anthropology-like assumptions of the way in which human society works.

In most instances, epidemiologists derive the information on which they base their inferences from interactions, such as interviews, with other humans, their study subjects. To know how best to ascertain desired information in the first place and then to ensure that the information collected is the information desired, the interacting observer must know (or make assumptions about) the way in which information is produced, distributed, and communicated in that setting. The distribution of knowledge, values, and rules of communication vary widely from society to society—again inherently an anthropological matter.

Epidemiologists attempt to control their data through standardization of the instruments with which they collect their information—for example, questionnaires. The assumption that justifies standard data collection is that, insofar as all respondents answering the same question will be responding to a common stimulus, their answers will be comparable. This assumption, however, ignores the cultural variations in the meaning of things.

Common epidemiological assumptions about the way human interaction works in the communication of information are misleading. Suchman and Jordan have recently argued (1990) that the standardized interview violates common rules of conversation that allow participants to clarify parts of a conversation they do not understand. The rules by which standardized interviews are conducted may explicitly deny an opportunity of clarification.

Since researchers are never sure that a question has been understood, they are consequently unsure of the meaning of responses. Validity is undermined in the pursuit of reliability.

The assumption of ceteris paribus is never precisely true, but serves as a holding pattern that facilitates research by incorporating the best of current knowledge. Were *all* other factors controlled, associations between exposures and outcomes would be complete (odds ratios or relative risks of 0 or infinity) or completely absent (an odds ratio or relative risk of 1).

The matter goes deeper. The social processes of knowledge production and the interaction inherent in research suggest that the notion of "data" as discrete bits of knowledge simply collected and combined is misleading and masks the social nature of scientific knowledge. Epidemiological research and its findings are the product of a social institution whose practitioners are trained to think in a characteristic way and who are judged by these standards. The discipline has its own cultural conventions—for example, a definition of true associations with a standard statistical cutoff point of less than a one-in-twenty chance of error.

My answer to the question posed in this section, "One Logic or Two?" is *"more than one, but considerably less than two."* To the contrary of many practitioners, I have argued that several of the explicit principles of practitioners are false, and that their underlying epistemologies are fundamentally complementary. There is no contradiction and much common ground. Practitioners have doubted that a marriage is possible. I propose that a separation is inadvisable.

In express goals, these disciplines differ substantially. Anthropology seeks analyses rich in context, showing how many of the local details hang together to form a unique picture. Epidemiology, in contrast, seeks analyses linking universal facts, free from context. The discipline of anthropology is fat and soft, that of epidemiology lean and hard—"thick" and "thin," in the metaphor of Geertz (1973). While a basic methodological principle of epidemiology is the elimination of extraneous difference to achieve ceteris paribus, a basic premise of anthropology might be summarized as ceteris numquam paribus—all else never the same. Anthropologists seek to characterize the ways in which "all else" fits together to make unique sense of a given social setting.

Although anthropology and epidemiology differ greatly in explicit goals and products, these differences are often mutually relevant. Epidemiological method may illuminate the processes of hypothesis testing that underlie the anthropological attribution of beliefs and practices. In turn, anthropological method may provide for epidemiology a sense of the meaning of events to participants. If the epidemiologist has found that a certain behavior is associated with some disease, knowledge of the meaning of this behavior to those who do it may be a prerequisite to understanding the means and the effect of modifying it.

ANTHROPOLOGY AND EPIDEMIOLOGY AS KEY TO THE BLACK/WHITE GAP IN INFANT MORTALITY

In the United States in the 1980s, approximately 1 percent of newborns died within the first year of life. Of these infant deaths, 64 percent occurred in the twenty-eight-day neonatal period following birth, the remaining 36 percent in the postneonatal period from the twenty-ninth day up to one year of age. Over the human life span, infants died at the highest rate for any age until about sixty years. In 1988, despite spending by far the greatest amount per capita and the greatest proportion of gross domestic product on health care, the United States ranked only twenty-third on a list of infant mortality rates in developed nations (Centers for Disease Control 1992a).

The rate of infant mortality in the United States is currently more than twice as high among blacks as among whites. (For all ages combined, including infants, U.S. blacks die at an age-adjusted rate 1.5 times that of whites.) Despite a 66 percent overall decline in infant mortality from 1950 to 1989, the ratio of infant mortality among blacks compared with whites increased during this period by more than 30 percent, from 1.6 to 2.2. Blacks achieved the infant mortality rate that whites had in 1950 by 1975 (twenty-five years later) and the rate that whites had in 1970 in 1987 (seventeen years later). The fact that blacks eventually "catch up" to whites suggests that the differences in infant mortality rates are largely determined by social and environmental conditions.

Rates of infant mortality differ among blacks of different ancestries— U.S.-born, West Indian, Haitian (Centers for Disease Control 1991a). Overall, infants born to foreign-born black mothers suffer 67 percent the rate of low birthweight (a major risk factor for infant mortality) and 72 percent of rate of death as infants born to native-born black mothers (Taffel 1980; Kleinman, Fingerhut, and Prager 1991). These differences may be explained at least in part by differences in the prevalences of known risk factors, such as higher rates of birth to teenage and unmarried women among U.S.-born blacks (Centers for Disease Control 1991a).

While we have learned much about the causes of infant mortality, we do not have a good explanation for the large and persistent black/white gap. We know that rates of infant mortality are higher among infants born to mothers who are younger, unmarried, less educated, poorer, and who delay or forgo prenatal care (Taffel 1978). But, in general, rates of infant mortality are higher among black than among white women who are younger, unmarried, uneducated, poorer, and who delay or forgo prenatal care (Carlson 1984). Thus, while each of these factors contributes to infant mortality, none is sufficient to explain the black/white gap.

The Gray of "Black" and "White"

First, it is important to decipher what it means to refer to someone as "black" or "white." We commonly think of these designations as "racial" categories denoting biological differences, but I believe this conception is incorrect. There are few if any genetic or other biological markers that distinguish all persons referred to as "black" from all persons referred to as "white." To begin, it is estimated that humans are identical in approximately 75 percent of their genes; of the remaining variable, polymorphic genes, 93 percent of the variability (approximately 0.93×0.25, that is, 23.3 percent of all human genetic matter) lies within "racial" groups, and only 7 percent (approximately 0.07×0.25, that is, 1.7 percent of all human genetic matter) lies among them (Lewontin 1982). If there were no variability within races—that is, all members were identical—and great variation among races, we would have grounds to believe that there are true races. But with relatively small variation overall and far more variability within than among races, there appears to be little justification for classification of persons into races of *genetically* related persons: "To put the matter crudely, if, after a great cataclysm, only Africans were left alive, the human species would have retained 93% of its total genetic variation, although the species as a whole would be darker. If the cataclysm were even more extreme and only the Xhosa people of the southern tip of Africa survived, the human species would still retain 80% of its genetic variation. Considered in the context of the evolution of our species, this would be a trivial reduction" (Lewontin 1982:123).

Lack of clarity about what "race" is may have hindered the collection of statistics on "race" groups. To assess the consistency of racial classification in vital records and national health statistics, colleagues and I have compared the classification of race on the birth and death certificates of all U.S. infants born from 1983 through 1985 who died within a year (Hahn, Mulinare, and Teutsch 1992). Although only 1.2 percent of infants classified as white at birth were classified with a different race at death, 4.3 percent of infants black at birth had a different race at death, and a striking 43.2 percent of infants classified as of other races at birth (American Indian, Chinese, Japanese, and Filipino) were assigned a different race at death. While at birth, race is determined by questioning the mother, at death race is determined by a funeral director who may judge from personal observation rather than querying the next of kin. Most infants who "changed" their race from birth to death (87 percent) became white. This suggests that statistics such as infant mortality rates that use information from both birth and death certificates are problematic. The root of the problem may be uncertainty about just what race is.

Rather than thinking of black and white as races, it may be more accurate to think of them as ethnicities, that is, ways in which people classify themselves socially, culturally, and historically. They are also ways in which people classify each other. Insiders and outsiders may *believe* this classification is based on physical characteristics and biological differences, but this belief is only partially correct. It is likely that all humans have common origins and that relatively isolated groups have intermarried during their histories. With the biological notion of race, we have selected a few obvious, visible physical features—like the features that distinguish each person from all others except, perhaps, identical twins—and we have given these features inordinate social weight—weight far beyond any likely physical significance.

If black and white are ethnicities rather than races, then the black/white gap in infant mortality is more likely to be associated with learned cultural and behavioral differences and with discrimination than with innate biological ones. For example, there may be differences in diet, formal as well as informal education, occupation, physical activity, and beliefs and practices regarding childbirth that affect birth events and infant health. It is also notorious that blacks and whites have unequal access to benefits and bear unequal burdens in U.S. society.

What Epidemiologists Know about Black/White Differences in Infant Mortality.

(1) *Causes of death among black and white infants:* Overall, in 1987, black infants died at 2.1 times the rate of white infants (table 5.1, Iyasu 1992). Among specific causes of death listed, only rates for birth defects were similar among blacks and whites (with a relatively small black excess of 10 percent). Respiratory conditions originating around the time of birth constitute 18.3 percent of infant deaths among blacks and contribute a large portion to the black excess in deaths. Infectious and parasitic diseases occur three times more frequently among blacks than among whites. Remarkably, though rates of homicide are not a major cause of infant mortality, they are reported to occur at more than three times the rate among black as among white infants. The greatest rate ratio of blacks compared with whites is for deaths attributed to prematurity and low birthweight—blacks dying at almost four times the rate of whites. More broadly, conditions originating in the perinatal period (including respiratory diseases) account for 55.3 percent of black infant deaths and occur 2.6 times mores frequently than among whites.

(2) *Birthweight differences between blacks and whites:* Further indication of the importance of birthweight in black/white infant mortality differences is the distribution of birthweights among black and white newborns and the differences in mortality of blacks and whites in each birthweight range. First, birthweight between 1500 and 2500 grams is associated with from 4 to 8 times the rate of infant mortality as birthweight ≥2500 grams (that is, 5.5 pounds); and birthweight less than 1500 grams is associated with from 57 to 99 times the infant mortality as birthweight equal to or greater than 2500

Table 5.1 Causes of Mortality among Black and White Infants, United States, 1987 (Rates per 100,000 infants)

	Blacks	Whites	Ratio
All Causes Combined	1,786.4	862.5	2.1
Perinatal Conditions	987.6	377.6	2.6
Prematurity and low birthweight	233.2	59.4	3.9
Respiratory conditions	326.9	153.6	2.1
Birth defects	226.5	206.2	1.1
Sudden Infant Death	225.5	120.5	1.9
Parasitic/Infectious Diseases	44.2	14.8	3.0
Unintended Injuries	42.4	21.7	2.0
Homicide	17.0	5.2	3.3
Other Causes	246.2	116.5	2.1

Source: CDC 1989d.

grams (table 5.2). Second, blacks are born 2 to 3 times more commonly than whites in low birthweight categories (less than 2500 grams; table 5.3). Within each of these low birthweight categories, however, white infants die at a somewhat greater rate than black infants, while in the "normal" birthweight category (≥2500 grams), blacks die at 1.65 times the rate of whites. It can be shown that, if blacks and whites had the same distribution of birthweights, say that of all U.S. infants, the excess black mortality would drop by 83 percent, substantially below rather than above the black/white mortality ratio for causes of death at all ages. This suggests that, if not a direct cause of infant mortality, low birthweight is closely associated with an important cause.

The distribution of birthweights and mortality rates indicates two crucial facts about the black/white gap. *First,* reduction of the black/white difference may require reduction of the large proportion of blacks bearing children at low birthweights. At these low birthweights, the problem is not that blacks die at a higher rate than whites—they do not—but that *all* infants at this weight die at a far higher rate than normal birthweight infants, and there are many more blacks than whites born at these low weights. Very low birthweights among blacks increased more than 20 percent from 1960 to 1985 (National Academy of Sciences 1990) and by 9 percent from 1985 to 1989 (Centers for Disease Control 1992a). Reduction of the high proportion of low birthweight blacks requires assessment of the causes of low birthweight among blacks. *Second,* reduction of the black/white gap may also require reduction of the black excess mortality even at normal birthweights, here requiring an understanding of this excess.

(3) *Risk factors for low birthweight and prematurity:* Numerous studies have indicated a wide range of risk factors for low birthweight and prematurity.

Table 5.2   Mortality Rates (per 1,000 Livebirths) at Different Birthweights,
United States, 1987

Race	<1500 gm	1500–2499 gm	>2499 gm
Black	375.6	25.5	6.6
White	395.9	31.0	4.0
Ratio (B/W)	0.9	0.8	1.7

Source: CDC 1993b.

Prominent factors include, first, income, socioeconomic status, and education. Though dated, a study by MacMahon, Kovar, and Feldman (1972)
indicates that both income and parental education are risk factors for infant
mortality; further, though income and education are correlated (parents with
higher incomes are likely to have higher educational levels, and vice versa),
both independently affect infant mortality. (Such studies are difficult to
conduct in the United States, and thus rare, because government health
documents rarely record income.) In 1965, infants born to families with
incomes less than $3,000 were almost 17 times more likely to die within a
year as infants born to parents with incomes greater than $10,000. An infant
born to a father with no more than eight years of education was 1.9 times
more likely to die within a year as an infant born to a father with sixteen years
of education. The relationship among income, education, and infant mortality was true for several specific causes of infant death as well, for example,
asphyxia, congenital malformations, birth injury, respiratory diseases, digestive diseases, and traumatic injury. Social class differences in infant mortality
have been found in many countries where data are available (Antonovsky
1977). Socioeconomic factors affect infant mortality in the postneonatal but
not the neonatal period (World Health Organization 1987).

MacMahon and colleagues also found that, even at the same income and
educational levels, black infants generally died at a higher rate than white
infants; and far fewer blacks were found in the higher educational and income
levels. A study of risk factors for infant mortality in New York City in the late
1960s found that blacks had 3.4 times the sociodemographic risk as did
whites (Institute of Medicine 1973). Based on such studies, one analysis has
concluded: "The strong correlation between social class and low birthweight
suggested that social changes abolishing social inequities would be most
efficient in preventing low birthweight and preterm birth" (Hemminki and
Starfield 1978).

More recent studies have confirmed the effects of education on infant
mortality. Schoendorf and colleagues (1992) examined rates of black and
white infant mortality when both parents were college-educated. Even at this
higher socioeconomic status, black infants died at a rate 1.9 times that of

Table 5.3 The Distribution of Birthweights among Black and White Newborns, United States, 1987

Race	<1500 gm	1500–2499 gm	>2500 gm
Black	2.7	10.0	87.3
White	0.9	4.7	94.3
Ratio (B/W)	2.9	2.1	0.9

Source: CDC 1990a.

white infants. As among infants at all educational levels combined, the reason for greater death rates among black infants was the greater proportions of black infants at low birthweights. At lower birthweights, white infants died at slightly higher rates than did black infants—similar to what happened among infants in all educational levels combined. Among normal-weight infants, however, there was little difference in mortality outcomes between blacks and whites—unlike infants at all levels of parental education combined. Moreover, educational level did not seem to affect mortality rates for low-weight infants—rates were similar at higher and all educational levels, but substantially lowered mortality rates for normal-weight infants. Even among highly educated parents, twice as many blacks as whites received late or no prenatal care, and in this highly educated population, the risk of infant death was 38 percent higher among infants whose parents received late or no prenatal care. Educational level thus did not affect the rate of mortality among low-weight infants, but did affect that among normal-weight infants.

Blacks in the United States remain at greater risk of low socioeconomic status than whites. In 1989, 3.1 times as many blacks as whites were covered by public assistance, and 1.6 times as many blacks as whites had no health insurance (Centers for Disease Control 1992a). In 1988, 30.5 percent of black households and 9.2 percent of white households were reported to be headed by a female with no male present; white female-headed households had a median income of $18,700; black female-headed households, $11,000 (Bureau of the Census 1989). More than two-thirds of the black female household heads were younger than forty-five, and a fourth of these women had less than a high school education (Bureau of the Census 1989). A study in California indicates growing proportions of uninsured persons during the 1980s, particularly among blacks and Hispanics; for uninsured black infants, the risk of adverse health outcomes (prolonged hospital stay, transfer to another hospital, or death) is 4.3 times greater than for insured white infants (Braveman et al. 1989). Unfortunately, there is also evidence that provision of prenatal services may be ineffective; a study in Tennessee shows that, despite increased enrollment following expanded Medicaid services in 1985, there was no increase in first trimester utilization of prenatal care and no significant change in the incidence of low-birthweight or neonatal mortality (Piper, Ray, and Griffin 1990).

Another set of risk factors for low birthweight and prematurity includes age, marital status, violence, and reproductive control. Rates of low birthweight are highest among teenagers, decrease to a low among mothers twenty-five to twenty-nine years of age, and increase in the later reproductive ages (Taffel 1980). In 1989, 10.8 percent of white infants and 23.4 percent of black infants were born to mothers younger than twenty (Centers for Disease Control 1992a). Except among mothers younger than eighteen, infants born to married mothers are less likely to die than infants born to unmarried mothers. In 1983, white infants born to unmarried mothers were 1.7 times and black infants 1.3 times as likely to die before their first birthday than, respectively, white and black infants born to married mothers (Centers for Disease Control 1990). In 1989, 19.2 percent of white births and a remarkable 65.7 percent of black births were to unmarried mothers; one can calculate that 16 percent of black infant deaths are attributable to their being born to unmarried mothers (Centers for Disease Control 1992a). Among ten other developed countries in the 1980s, the United States had almost twice the rate of teenage childbearing compared with the next highest rate (in the United Kingdom). Sex education was less frequently available as was access to contraception (Miller 1988).

There appears to be a complex of demographic and reproductive characteristics affecting childbirth outcomes. Poverty and lack of education may be associated with lack of knowledge of contraception; unwanted pregnancy leads to inability to pursue further education, in turn associated with poverty; poverty and lack of education may also be associated with lack of ability or perceived need to pursue prenatal care. A nationally representative survey conducted in 1982 indicates that 54.1 percent of black infants and 35.4 percent of white infants born to currently or previously married mothers (ages fifteen to forty-four) were "unwanted" or "mistimed" at conception; among unmarried mothers, 71.2 percent of black infants and 60.8 percent of white infants were either unwanted or mistimed at conception (Pratt and Horn 1985). In 1988, rates of abortion (nationally, 35.1 per 100 live births) were 11.3 times higher among unmarried than among married mothers and 1.9 times higher among nonwhite races than among whites (Centers for Disease Control 1992a). Collaborators at the World Health Organization (1987:131) conclude, "Intuitively, we link unintended pregnancy and infant mortality." They also point out that, at least in the mid-1970s, U.S. federal programs spent thirty times more on Aid to Families with Dependent Children than on family planning services (1987).

The hazards of childbearing are increased not only by poverty and lack of reproductive control but by overt violence from men. A recent study of women receiving prenatal care in two public hospitals (in Houston and

Baltimore) found that 29 percent of both black and white women reported physical or sexual abuse during the past year and 19 percent of both black and white women reported additional abuse during their pregnancy (McFarlane et al. 1992). Among 60 percent of the women, the abuse was recurrent. Abused women were 1.9 times as likely to begin prenatal care during their third trimester as women not abused. (Abuse among women not seeking any prenatal care could not be assessed in this study.)

A third risk factor for low birthweight and prematurity is maternal health. Numerous studies indicate that various maternal health conditions, such as hypertension, sexually transmitted diseases, and urinary tract infections, affect the prematurity, birthweight, and mortality of the infant (Hemminki and Starfield 1978; Hardy and Mellits 1972; Lieberman et al. 1987). Lieberman et al. demonstrate that the rate of prematurity accelerates with declining hematocrit (an indicator of oxygen-carrying capacity); in this study, hematocrit level accounts for 60 percent of the excess of prematurity of blacks compared with whites. Hemminki and Starfield (1987:347) report that an estimated 4 percent of low birthweight among black infants is attributable to maternal health conditions not directly related to pregnancy (Hemminki and Starfield 1987:347).

Maternal cigarette smoking is another well-documented risk factor for both prematurity and low birthweight, as well as for spontaneous abortions, stillbirths, and poor health among infant survivors (Myer and Comstock 1972; Myer, Jonas, and Tonascia 1976; Surgeon General 1989). The mean birthweight of infants born to smokers is 150–250 grams less than the birthweight of infants born to nonsmokers. Myer and Comstock (1972) estimated that 31 percent of low birthweight is attributable to smoking during pregnancy. Premature births (less than 38 weeks gestation) are increased by 20 percent among women who smoke less than a pack a day, and by 50 percent among smokers of more than a pack a day (Myer, Jonas, and Tonascia 1976). Controlling for other risk factors, Kleinman and Madans (1985) found that the black infants of mothers who smoked less than a pack a day were 25 percent more likely to die during their first year than infants of nonsmoking mothers; infants born to mothers who smoked more than a pack a day were 53 percent more likely to die. They estimated that an increase of five cigarettes smoked per day increased the likelihood of low birthweight by 26 percent. Surveys of the U.S. population indicate that the same proportion of black and white infants (28 to 29 percent) were exposed perinatally to cigarette smoke (Overpeck 1991).

Meyer (1977) compares the effect of cigarette smoking with the effect of high altitude: both deprive the fetus of oxygen essential for nutrition and growth. The placenta of smokers (and of residents of high places, such as Denver) have been found to be larger than the placenta of nonsmokers, presumably a physiological response that compensates for deficient oxygen supply.

Maternal nutrition and weight gain during pregnancy have been shown to have a powerful effect on prematurity, birthweight, and fetal mortality (the ratio of stillbirths and early infant deaths to live births). The prevalence of low-birthweight infants among women who gain less than sixteen pounds during pregnancy is 13.9 percent; among women who gain twenty-one to twenty-five pounds, the prevalence of low-birthweight infants is 6.1 percent (Taffel 1986). These effects are greatest in women with lower prepregnancy weights. Similarly, the fetal death ratio (fetal deaths/[live births + fetal deaths]) among women who gain less than sixteen pounds is 10.5 percent, while the fetal death ratio among women who gain twenty-six to thirty-five pounds is 3.8 percent. In 1980, a fifth of white mothers and a fourth of black mothers whose pregnancies extended to at least forty weeks gained less than twenty-one pounds (Taffel 1986). A study of mothers in 1988 indicates that 12.4 percent of white women and 32.5 percent of black women are advised by their physicians to gain less than twenty-two pounds; reasons for this large discrepancy in medical advice are unknown (Taffel and Keppel 1993).

An association between maternal weight gain and infant birthweight seems logical; fetal weight is a portion of maternal weight gain. Studies indicate that "the products of conception," including the fetus itself, account for an increasing proportion of maternal weight gain during pregnancy— approximately 20 percent at twenty weeks, 30 percent at thirty weeks, and 40 percent at forty weeks (Myer and Comstock 1972).

There are many risk factors for low weight gain during pregnancy: "Women who have a high prepregnancy weight, who smoke during pregnancy, who have a low family income, who are 35 years of age or older or in their teens, who have less than 9 years of schooling, who are having a fourth or higher order birth, or who are unmarried are all more likely to gain less than 16 pounds and less likely to gain 26 pounds or more during their pregnancy" (Taffel 1986:2).

Nutrition is an obvious source of weight gain, though its precise effects on birth have been difficult to demonstrate (Bergner and Susser 1970). Susser and Stein (1972) used the results of a precisely dated disaster, the Dutch famine during World War II, which lasted from October 1944 to May 1945, to examine the role of severe nutritional deprivation on subsequent infant and later mortality. The greatest rate of low birthweight and early infant mortality occurred among infants exposed to the famine during their third trimesters of gestation. Hemminki and Starfield (1978) have estimated that 57 percent of low-birthweight infants born to black women is attributable to poor nutrition during pregnancy.

An association between prenatal care and other health-care utilization and birthweight has been extensively documented, though the contents of care are seldom examined. For example, Taffel (1980) reports that, controlling for maternal educational level, U.S. whites in 1976 who had no prenatal care were 3.1 times more likely to bear low-birthweight infants than white women who began care in the first two months of pregnancy; and U.S. blacks who had no prenatal care were 2.3 times more likely to bear low-birthweight infants as black women who began care in the first two months of pregnancy. Quick, Greenlick, and Roghmann (1981) controlled for obstetric as well as demographic risk factors and still found increased risk of low birthweight and infant mortality associated with decreasing levels of prenatal care.

Care currently classified as "adequate" begins in the first trimester and continues regularly; "inadequate" care is none at all or care beginning only in the third trimester; "intermediate" care begins in the second trimester or includes an insufficient number of visits. In 1989, 31 percent more whites than blacks began their prenatal care in the first trimester, and 129 percent more blacks than whites began care in the third trimester or had no prenatal care at all (Centers for Disease Control 1992a). Even with the same prenatal care, however, blacks have poorer birth outcomes than whites; a study conducted in New York City in 1968 found that, controlling for differences in prenatal care visits, U.S.-born blacks had 2.3 times the rate of infant deaths as U.S.-born whites (Institute of Medicine 1973).

In contrast, Lieberman et al. (1987) examined the role of different risk factors in accounting for black/white differences in prematurity. As noted earlier, differences in hematocrit levels accounts for 60 percent of the difference between blacks and whites; addition of four sociodemographic factors—age, marital status, education, and welfare status—reduced to only 3 percent the difference between blacks and whites in rates of prematurity. It is thus possible that massive social interventions to alter the age, marital status, education, and income of childbearing women might enhance the likelihood of normal birthweight and infant health.

What Epidemiologists Don't Know about Black/White Differences in Infant Mortality

(1) *The big picture—a system, a framework, a context:* Epidemiologists have analyzed the associations of many variables with prematurity, low birthweight, and infant mortality. They have isolated the influence of particular variables by controlling for other variables; to the extent they have done so, they know that the effect of each variable is not an artifact of its association with other variables. What they do not know is how all these factors work together to produce the outcomes we observe. With rare exceptions (Gortmaker 1979; Sheehan 1991; National Academy of Sciences 1990), epidemiological studies have not systematically analyzed how all the elements fit together.

(2) *The smaller, detailed picture—the meaning and context of perinatal events in the lives of participants:* We know that teenage childbearing, lack of education, and lack of weight gain are risk factors for low birthweight and infant mortality. We know far less about why education is associated with poor

outcomes, why so many black teenagers bear children, and why women fail to gain weight during pregnancy. Education does not lead directly to greater birthweight; so how does education, independent of income, affect birth outcomes—is it by means of knowledge and healthy behavior, by increased utilization of health services, or what? We do not know. Why do twice as many blacks as whites seek late or no prenatal care? Epidemiologists have paid little attention to the social context of black life that leads to early childbearing and poor birth outcomes.

Thus, the epidemiological approach to the analysis of demographic variables misses two crucial facets of phenomena: *the bigger picture*—the broader context that connects phenomena to one another—and the *smaller, detailed picture*—the inner workings of phenomena—their cultural meaning.

What Anthropologists Know about Black/White Differences in Childbearing

Anthropologists and other social science researchers are trained to address both of these matters—broad sociocultural contexts and detailed systems of meaning. Here I examine examples of investigations by anthropologists and other social scientists on three issues related to black/white differences in infant mortality: (1) black family life and social relationships, (2) the quality of basic statistical knowledge of black communities, and (3) black diet and the history of nutritional recommendations to pregnant women.

Black Family Life and Social Relationships. In the late 1960s, anthropologist Carol Stack and her young son moved into a poor black neighborhood to study community life from the perspective of its participants (Stack 1974a). She called this setting "The Flats." Many residents of The Flats were caught in a system that perpetuated their poverty from generation to generation. Stack came to focus her research on community strategies for coping with poverty; though some of her conclusions may be dated, basic themes probably persist and are relevant to an understanding of infant mortality among blacks today.

Stack found that, instead of the nuclear family and household, the principal unit of social life in The Flats was a network of kin and friends who constantly exchanged money, food, caretaking, and residence; people referred to this network as "all our kin." "Kin and friends in domestic networks establish mutual ties of obligation as they bestow rights and responsibilities upon one another. As these responsibilities are met with satisfaction, the depth of the involvement between kinsmen and between friends increases" (Stack 1974a:87). "An individual may eat in one household, sleep in another, contribute resources and services to yet another, and consider himself or herself a member of all three households" (1974b:116).

Several factors mitigated against stable marital unions. Men commonly faced unemployment and could not assure the support of their partners or children; mothers were not eligible for welfare if they lived with a partner; and, because the network of kin relied on members, including mothers, for assistance, husbands and steady partners were often regarded as competitors for attention and resources. "When a mother in The Flats has a relationship with an economically nonproductive man, the relationship saps the resources of others in her domestic network" (1974b: 124–25). Thus, poverty contributed to the instability of marital units in several ways. Nevertheless, there were most often men present in households, and these men played important roles in the support and care of children.

In The Flats, the role of childbearing was clearly distinguished from that of mothering. Marriage was not regarded as a prerequisite for childbearing. Young males were encouraged and praised by their kin for the number of children they had fathered, regardless of their subsequent relationship with the children's mother. And young women were rewarded both socially and financially for bearing children. "People show pride in all their kin, and particularly new babies born into their kinship networks. Mothers encourage sons to have babies, and even more important, men coax their 'old ladies' to have their baby" (1974a: 121). At least in retrospect, mothers recognized that they were immature when they began having children. And biological parents—fathers in particular—were not necessarily expected to rear the offspring. "Mothers generally regard their children's fathers as friends of the family—people they can recruit for help—rather than as fathers failing in their parental duties" (1974a: 119). Child rearing was shared among "all our kin," particularly among female kin on either the mother's or the father's side. "Children born to the poor in The Flats are highly valued, and rights in these children belong to the networks of cooperating kinsmen" (1974a: 89).

In a more recent study, *Capital Crime* (Boone 1989), anthropologist Margaret Boone combines statistical analyses with in-depth interviews to examine the context of very low birthweights and high rates of infant mortality among blacks in Washington, D.C. From 1987 to 1989 Washington had the highest rates of very low birthweight and infant mortality among blacks in any region of the United States: very low birthweight among blacks were 53 percent higher than the average rate for U.S. blacks, and infant mortality rates were 35 percent higher than the mean U.S. rate for blacks (Centers for Disease Control 1992a). By interviewing mothers in an inner-city hospital and comparing black mothers who gave birth to very-low-birthweight infants with those bearing normal-birthweight infants, Boone sought an understanding of the meaning of childbearing, social relationships, and poverty among these women, and the role of these factors in birth events.

Like Stack, Boone reports that childbearing plays an important role in the way young black women define themselves, serving both to enhance their status and to gain social and financial support. She also finds that young black women have little control of their reproductive lives—they are uninformed about contraception and inconsistent in its use, and they are subject to abuse and violence by men. Sexually transmitted diseases are common, as are abortions. Alcoholism and drug abuse are also common in this population, though less among teens than among older women; alcohol and drugs serve to blunt or escape the persistent problems. Rates of alcoholism and nonuse of prenatal care are substantially greater among women bearing very-low-birthweight infants than among women bearing normal-birthweight infants.

Boone also reports that infant mortality rates do not differ among women living in conjugal relationships and in the matrifocal families in which they are heads of the household and no regular male partner is present. Boone finds that matrifocal living arrangements are adaptive for many women, because their male partners are often unreliable and/or abusive. Contrary to common assumptions, Boone reports that many women receive their principal support from other women rather than from their mothers.

Studies such as those of Stack and Boone illuminate the multiple ways in which poverty, lack of education, and discrimination interplay and affect low birthweight and infant mortality. These studies illuminate the attitudes of black communities toward children and parents, suggesting reasons for teenage and unmarried childbearing. They also demonstrate the stressful role of violence and abuse, and, at the same time, the powerful place of social networks in the support of procreation and childcare. By analyzing the context of childbirth and the details of attitudes and relationships surrounding it, such studies suggest the broad changes that may be required to reduce the risk of poor birth outcomes among blacks.

The Quality of Statistical Information on Black Communities. Charles and Betty Lou Valentine began conducting anthropological research in a black inner-city community (which they called "Blackston") in 1968. In 1969, the Bureau of the Census sent teams of interviewers to evaluate the population census that had been conducted in the same area. The Valentines compared what they knew through close contact with the community with what was reported in the census itself and in census evaluation research (Valentine and Valentine 1974).

The Valentines found that one residence (out of thirty-three) was incorrectly classified as a household and that, overall, the census evaluation undercounted the population by 17 percent. Most remarkable were the findings that men nineteen years and older were undercounted by 61 percent and that, though 72 percent of Blackston households were reported to be headed by women, anthropological evidence indicated only 12 percent of the households were. The large discrepancies were the result of different definitions of "household" and the reluctance of interviewees to report the income contributions of resident men. Residents associated census interviewers with government agents who threatened to cut off support services and funds; moreover, some of the men in the community were involved in illegal activities.

Lack of close contact with the community and unawareness of motivations for the divulgence of information produced highly misleading results by census interviewers. A close understanding of the community is critical in eliciting even basic information such as how many people live in a given place. The Valentines assert that there is no way to improve census techniques without close community contact. Their study indicates an inherent fault of the survey methods on which most epidemiological research relies.

Black Diet and the History of Nutritional Recommendations to Pregnant Women. Claire Cassidy (1982b) has reviewed studies of cultural differences in diet among U.S. ethnic populations that are relevant for maternal and infant health. To begin, she notes that "the orthodox middle-class American diet, which is the model upon which nutritionists have designed scientific dietary recommendations, is as much a product of history and culture as is any other diet" (1982b:27). She reports that observers of diets among U.S. blacks have found much regional variation.

Beliefs about the contributions of different foods to "hot" and "cold" blood are reported to be common in black communities. Since pregnant women are thought to be in a hot condition, it is believed that their diet should be controlled to avoid "high blood"; meat is also regarded as a virile food, too strong to be eaten by children and during pregnancy. Thus, foods high in protein and calories may be avoided in a diet that may already be inadequate in these nutrients (Snow 1983). In addition, a remedy for "high blood," associated with high blood pressure, is sodium-rich or astringent foods such as brine or pickles (Snow and Johnson 1978). Caloric restrictions would reduce weight gain, and sodium-rich foods would actually promote the high blood pressures they are believed to treat. Both dietary beliefs would thus be associated with poor birth outcomes. Finally, milk is an important element of diets recommended for pregnant women. Yet many blacks are physiologically intolerant of milk; in some regions of the country, blacks are reported to consume far less milk than whites.

The history of intertwined scientific and popular beliefs about diet and childbearing also indicates a possible source of current ideas about weight restrictions during pregnancy. During the nineteenth and early twentieth centuries, maternal mortality during vaginal childbirth was common, and the alternative, cesarean delivery, was treacherous (Leavitt 1987). Restrictions of diet for pregnant women may thus have been recommended to produce smaller babies and easier deliveries (National Academy of Sciences 1990). During the early decades of the twentieth century, excessive weight gain was also associated with edema (pathological swelling) and with toxemia (a poisoning of the blood); restrictions of weight gain were also prescribed for this reason.

During the last fifty years, recommended weight gains have almost doubled. It is important to know how such knowledge spreads to different populations, for it may be that popular knowledge about appropriate restrictions of weight correspond to historical rather than recent recommendations. As noted, 2.6 times as many black as white women have been recently recommended to gain less than twenty-two pounds during pregnancy.

THREE PROJECTS OF ANTHROPOLOGICAL/ EPIDEMIOLOGICAL COLLABORATION

(1) *Community-based studies of the social conditions of childbearing:* Given the magnitude of the problem of high infant mortality rates among blacks in the United States (and of the United States among the developed nations of the world), anthropologists have directed little attention to this matter. With several exceptions (Boone 1989; Davis-Floyd 1992; Ginsburg 1989; Hahn, ed. 1987; Hahn and Muecke 1987; Jordan 1993), few anthropological studies have focused on reproductive issues—a traditional subject of anthropological investigation in non-Western settings. We know very little about the conditions of reproduction in white, black, and other communities in the United States. We know little about social conditions and social relationships, attitudes and values, behaviors, or attitudes toward and the use of health-care facilities. Anthropologists could usefully conduct community studies to understand what childbearing means in different segments of U.S. society and how people conduct their lives around reproduction.

(2) *Studies of prenatal care practices:* We have reports of the proportions of black and white women who seek prenatal care at different phases of their pregnancies. We also know basic consequences of these events. We know little, however, about what happens during prenatal care visits, about how physicians and others treat black and white pregnant women and how black and white women respond to prenatal care. It would be useful to videotape prenatal visits and to interview participants to better understand these events. Video equipment can be used in ways that are unobtrusive and inoffensive and even helpful to patients and clinicians. Analysis of patient-clinician interaction might provide valuable insights about why black women—even college-educated black women—delay or do not use prenatal care at higher rates than college-educated white women. (Obviously, such studies would not reach women not receiving prenatal care at all.)

In 1988, the Institute of Medicine reviewed current knowledge of prenatal care, including studies of women's perceptions of barriers to prenatal care among those who either did not use prenatal care or delayed their use. The most common barriers mentioned were lack of finances, lack of recognition of the value of prenatal care, lack of transportation, lack of knowledge of their pregnancy, fear of prenatal care, and "negative institutional practices" (Brown 1988). These findings suggest critical topics for further investigation—means of financial assistance, experiences in and attitudes toward medical settings.

(3) *Qualitative case-control studies of women with good and with poor birth outcomes:* The quantitative case-control method of epidemiology could be usefully combined with the in-depth, qualitative methods of anthropology to compare black and white women with successful outcomes with black and white women with poor birth outcomes. I refer to this method (for example, Boone 1989) as the "qualitative case-control design." Such a study might begin with groups of black and white women who had recently given birth to normal- and to low- or very-low-birthweight infants. These women could be interviewed in an open-ended fashion about their attitudes toward childbearing, their economic conditions, their home and social environments, the circumstances and courses of their pregnancies, their diets and behavior, their attitudes toward medical institutions, and their contacts in prenatal care settings. This approach might produce rich portraits of the events of birth for whites and blacks with poor and good outcomes. Comparison of subjects in such a study might also suggest hypotheses for further investigation.

The comparison of epistemologies is a fertile, but little cultivated field. It is important because it surveys the grounds on which seemingly diverse approaches to knowledge are based. An exploration of epistemological links and gaps between anthropology and epidemiology is a step in that direction.

My argument for basic epistemological commonalities between anthropology and epidemiology is twofold: first, that the anthropological construction of context—a network of interrelated details—requires inferences that are essentially epidemiological, and the epidemiological stripping away of context in the search for universal laws requires anthropological assumptions about the context stripped away. Anthropologists test hypotheses and count; epidemiologists interpret local practices. Anthropologists have ignored the means by which their basic knowledge is acquired—through controlled inferences about observed associations, based on numerous assumptions from their own culture about the reality they observe. Epidemiologists have neglected some of their sources and methods as well—the cultural rules that allow the eliciting of information and the extraction of variables from their social context. Like Molière's bourgeois gentleman who had been speaking prose for forty years without knowing it, anthropologists have been doing epidemiology without knowing it, and epidemiologists have been anthropologists unawares. Unlike many contemporary anthropologists and epidemiologists, Molière's gentleman discovered his prose and was pleased.

Although anthropologists and epidemiologists have been unwittingly and inevitably engaged in each other's disciplines, they may not have been doing so effectively. Practitioners of both disciplines may benefit from exploration of common roots and from explicit synthesis of methods.

part
two BIOMEDICINE OBSERVED

6

BIOMEDICINE AS
A CULTURAL SYSTEM

> Begging the forgiveness of the clergy and the poets let us begin this
> consideration of pathology with the observation that man is basically a
> complex aggregation of highly specialized cells. The health of the indi-
> vidual has its origin in healthy cells. It is necessary then to begin our
> consideration of pathology with an examination of disease at the cellular
> and, indeed, subcellular levels.
>
> —*Robbins, Angell, and Kumar, 1981:3*

Over the last century and for the first time in human history,
one medical system—Biomedicine—the medicine of the twentieth-century
Western world, has come to influence the health and healing practices of
human societies worldwide. In Western societies, where it originated, Biomedicine is the dominant medicine; it embraces the complex social and
cultural arrangements not only of physicians who diagnose and treat disease
but also of diverse personnel and institutions of care, extensive industries,
programs of health insurance, research, and multiple government and private agencies. In the United States, health care occupies more than 8 percent
of the civilian work force and consumes more than 14 percent of the gross
domestic product. The practices of Biomedicine have penetrated the developing world as well, commonly playing a prominent role in conjunction
with traditional forms of healing. In this chapter, I characterize Biomedicine
as a cultural system by focusing on physicians, its preeminent practitioners.

A society's culture tells its members how the world is divided, interconnected, and known; it specifies what is valued and what is not, what is good,
beautiful, right, wrong, and indifferent; it provides rules of conduct whereby
the society's members know how to behave and how to judge the behavior of
others. The elements of a culture—its beliefs, values, and rules—may be

131

consistent, inconsistent, or even contradictory. The more or less coherent organization of cultural elements makes them a system.

Subcultures within a society's culture may be distinguished by their differing beliefs, values, and behavioral rules. The medical subculture informs participants what conditions of sickness and health there are, how these are caused and treated, and how to behave while in them (Kleinman 1980). Anthropologists have coined the term *ethnomedicine* to refer to the variant medical subcultures found in different societies, in the same way that *ethnobotany* refers to cultural versions of botany, and *ethnophilosophy* to versions of philosophy.

Cultural and subcultural systems have four components: (1) a *domain of knowledge or belief,* that is, a definition of what this cultural system or subsystem is about, (2) a *system of values and ideals of behavior,* (3) an *organized means for teaching this domain and its cultural values to recruits and other participants,* and (4) a *setting and norms of behavior and practice* in which these beliefs, values, and teachings are enacted. In describing the cultural system of Biomedicine, I begin by analyzing the domain of Biomedicine and its division into specialties. I describe the central values of Biomedicine. I then review the process of medical education as a phase in the professional life cycle of physicians. Finally, I examine the nature of medical work and the norms, or rules of behavior, that guide it; I focus on physicians' relations with their patients.

In describing Biomedicine as a cultural system, I do not deny the knowledge or efficacy of this system. Biomedicine has made revolutionary discoveries and created powerful inventions. Rather, I claim that Biomedicine is one ethnomedicine among many others, and that, like all ethnomedicines, it is rooted in cultural presuppositions and values, associated with rules of conduct, and embedded in a larger societal and historical context.

THE DOMAIN OF BIOMEDICINE AND ITS SPECIALTY DIVISIONS

The Domain of Biomedicine

Although anthropological and other observers use the prefix *bio-* to highlight the biological focus of Western medicine, practitioners refer to their work simply as "medicine." In order to examine the defining characteristics of the domain of Biomedicine, I refer to *Stedman's Medical Dictionary,* compiled by the medical community as a guide to medical concepts and terminology. The dictionary may not represent conceptions embodied in medical practice, but it does convey conscious concepts of the medical community.

"Medicine" is defined in *Stedman's* as:

1. A drug.
2. The art of preventing or curing diseases; the science that treats of disease in all its relations.

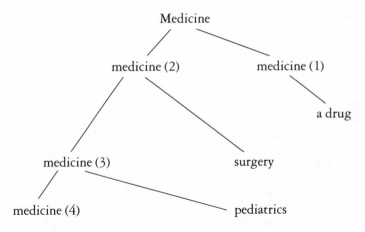

Figure 6.1   Definitions of "medicine."

3. The study and treatment of general diseases or those affecting the
    internal parts of the body, distinguished from surgery. (1976:836)

The domain of medicine can be seen to include four distinct, increasingly
specific forms (see figure 6.1). First, the "art" and "science" of medicine (2),
that is, the practice of medicine—the prevention, cure, and study of disease—is distinguished from the concrete, physical medicine (1)—a drug.
Then the treatment of general diseases, medicine (3), is distinguished from
surgery. Finally, although not explicitly noted here, in its focus on adults,
medicine (4), that is, internal medicine, is distinguished from pediatrics.
The specialty of "internal medicine" is also referred to simply as "medicine."
Internal medicine is "the branch of medicine dealing with non-surgical
diseases of a constitutional nature in adults"—"constitutional" referring to
the physical system of the body as a whole (*Stedman's* 1976:837).

A prominent feature of *Stedman's* definition of the domain of medicine is
the designated subject of medical work: medicine prevents and cures, studies
and treats, not persons, nor their bodies, but the diseases of bodies. In
describing the domain of medicine, there is no mention of persons. As
characterized in *Stedman's,* persons who are diseased are peripheral to the
work of medicine. There is a striking contrast (described in chap. 1) with
many non-Western medical systems, in which the healer treats disorder that
is not only corporeal but personal, social, and even cosmological.

Within Biomedicine, pathology is the specialty that addresses the basic
nature of disease. Pathology is "the medical science, and specialty practice,
that deals with all aspects of disease, but with special reference to the essential
nature, the causes, and development of abnormal conditions, as well as the

structural and functional changes that result from the disease processes"
(*Stedman's* 1976:1041).

The Biomedical focus on bodily pathology is again clear in *Stedman's*
definition of "disease":

1. Morbus; illness, sickness; an interruption, cessation, or disorder of
   body functions, systems, or organs.
2. A disease entity, characterized usually by at least two of these criteria: a recognized etiologic agent (or agents); an identifiable group
   of signs and symptoms; consistent anatomical alterations.
   (1976:401)

The body and its parts are thought to have normal tasks or functions. Disease
is the disturbance of normal function. The notion of normal function is taken
for granted, perhaps equated with what occurs most frequently in a population—a view that becomes problematic when disease conditions are widespread. Physicians speak of such alterations as physical "lesions." A "lesion,"
in turn, is

1. A wound or injury.
2. A more or less circumscribed pathologic change in the tissues.
3. One of the individual points or patches of a multifocal disease.
   (1976:774).

The elementary unit of disease is the "entity"; ideally, all disease events can
be classified into this, that, or the other entity, "an independent thing; that
which contains in itself all the conditions essential to individuality; that
which forms of itself a complete whole; denoting a separate and distinct
disease or condition" (1976:467).

Finally, diseases are conceived of as natural phenomena. There is talk in
Biomedicine of "natural course" and "natural" or "spontaneous remission"—
that is, relief from disease without medical intervention. It is implied that
what is not treated medically is natural or even spontaneous (without cause).
It is further suggested that the "natural" and the "medical" are complementary and mutually exclusive domains. A role for human societies and human
minds in the conception, production, and response to disease is not noted.

"Health" is defined as "the state of the organism when it functions op-
timally without evidence of disease or abnormality" (*Stedman's* 1976:467).
Like disease, health also is a characteristic not of persons but of physical
beings—organisms.

Specialties: The Biomedical Division of Labor

Although the domain of Biomedicine is unified by underlying
themes, its practice is divided into many specialties. Biomedicine is many
medicines. At the end of the nineteenth century, over 90 percent of American

physicians were "generalists"; 74 percent were "generalists" by 1928. By 1990, fewer than 4 percent of the 600,000 physicians listed in the American Medical Association's Master File identified themselves as general practitioners, with an additional 8 percent identifying themselves with the relatively new specialty, "family practice" (Luce and Byyny 1979; Roback, Randolph, and Seidman 1992). From 1965 to 1990, the ratio of persons in the population to physicians in clinical care increased by 50 percent—the increase owing entirely to the greater number of specialists. The twenty-four boards of the American Board of Medical Specialties grant forty-one specialty certificates and an additional twenty-five subspecialty certificates, ranging from allergy and immunology to blood banking to reproductive endocrinology to urology (American Board of Medical Specialists 1992).

The emergence of a specialty signifies a recognized field of knowledge about distinctive phenomena, thought to be separately treatable and worthy of such treatment (see Luce and Byyny 1979). The history of specialty divisions, however, is evidence that Biomedicine has not simply divided its work on human pathology on the basis of systematic theory and empirical evidence. Specialties have resulted not only from technical advances and new knowledge but from intense struggles for recognition by practitioners. Specialty divisions attest to the interplay of political, economic, technical, and social forces (Stevens 1971). In a discussion of the productivity and counterproductivity of specialization, Chase describes steps in the historical development of medical specialties:

1. As a result of advances in a field or development of new technology, a new group develops special expertise in this area.
2. An organization or society is formed for an exchange of ideas and to display advances to one another.
3. Membership in the organization becomes a mark of distinction in the field, and, in an effort to externalize that recognition, certification of excellence in the field becomes established.
4. Institutions with responsibility for quality of health càre soon accept certification as evidence of competence and limit care within that field to those certified. (1976:497–98)

Thus, for example, the separation of ophthalmology from a practice that treated both eye and ear followed the invention of the ophthalmoscope by von Helmholtz in 1850 and of the otoscope and the laryngoscope in the late 1850s (Stevens 1971). Establishment of the American Ophthalmological Society (1864) was followed by publication of the *American Journal of Ophthalmology*. After prolonged political struggles, principally directed at the exclusion of optometrists, ophthalmology became the nation's first specialty board in 1916. The establishment of otolaryngology as a specialty followed in 1924.

Other specialties have been proposed and have gone unrecognized. A century ago, urologists attempted, but failed to establish a male counterpart to gynecology, andrology (Stevens 1971). More recently, in the late 1950s, a small movement among surgeons to establish a subspecialty in abdominal surgery met vigorous opposition from the larger organization of surgeons, on the grounds that abdominal surgery had no special technique or knowledge; abdominal surgery thus remained the work of general surgeons (Stevens 1971). The human body, its function, and its pathology have been partitioned into zones of problems and expertise. In recognized specialties, some physicians have been certified as experts, and others have been excluded from specialty practice.

The predominant thrust of Biomedical specialization is curative, directed toward the control or elimination of pathological conditions that have already occurred. Although many physicians are also concerned with preventing pathology in their patients, only 0.3 percent of physicians surveyed by the AMA in 1989 reported a practice devoted to preventive medicine or public health.

Specialty divisions are based on a wide range of dimensions: sex, age, patient circumstances, occupations, body parts, organs, and organ systems treated, stages of medical intervention, etiological agents or symptoms of diseases, and techniques of treatment. Some specialties are distinguished by the circumstance in which pathology occurs. There are occupational and industrial medicines, aerospace medicine, and tropical medicine. Emergency medicine was designed to treat problems arising suddenly and requiring urgent care. Forensic medicine addresses pathology in which legal issues arise. Other specialties are distinguished on the basis of causative agents or subsequent symptomatology, for example, the specialties of infectious disease, oncology, and allergy and immunology.

Dividing the human life cycle, obstetricians deliver and pediatricians treat infants and children; internists treat adults, and family practitioners and primary care physicians treat both children and adults. Within pediatrics, specialization has grown not only along criteria of age (for example, neonatology and adolescent medicine), but also in the forms of pathology treated (pediatric cardiology, nephrology, surgery, child psychiatry). Within internal medicine, there is a growing subspecialty concentration on geriatrics. Specialization also occurs on other demographic dimensions. Gynecologists treat women only, supposedly for reproductive problems, but commonly for other medical problems as well (Marieskind 1980).

Many specialties are distinguished by the body part they treat and the technique of treatment. Take, for example, the alimentary canal, from mouth to anus. In the former Soviet Union, the mouth was the medical realm of stomatology, but in the United States teeth are relegated to dentists, separately trained and licensed, and, on certain occasions, such as oral cancers, the mouth comes to the attention of medical specialists in head and neck surgery. Otolaryngology, another surgical specialty, also treats the mouth, throat, and adjacent regions and passages. From the esophagus to the rectum, the alimentary tract is the territory of the gastroenterologist, a subspecialist in internal medicine. Finally, the rectum and anus are also claimed by the surgical specialty, proctology.

Several body parts are divided between surgery and medicine. Ophthalmology is a surgical specialty, and endocrinology and hematology are specialties of medicine. Other body parts, including the kidneys and urinary system, the joints, the chest, and the heart and circulatory system may be treated by both medical and surgical specialists. Treatments recommended for a given problem by surgical and medical specialists may be complementary; but appropriate treatment may also be a contested matter.

Medical specialties are accorded different status both within and beyond the Biomedical profession. At the top of the hierarchy are specialties such as thoracic surgery, neurosurgery, cardiology, and internal medicine; at the bottom are general practice, allergy medicine, dermatology, and preventive medicine (Shortell 1974). Shortell argues that status corresponds to the degree of control the specialty is thought to have in the lives of its patients. Status may also correspond to the symbolic value ascribed to the treated body part and function: the heart and brain are regarded as central organs—used to define the boundary of life and death (Fox 1979)—the skin, allergies, and "minor problems" treated by general practitioners are seen as relatively unimportant.

The medical specialties divide patients, pathologies, and personnel in complex ways, but these divisions are also bridged by several means. Early medical training is shared by all specialists, and later training may involve study in several specialties. In addition, not only do practitioners use the knowledge and techniques developed in other specialties, they often consult or "refer out," sending patients to other specialists when their own abilities are limited. Thus, there are basic and ongoing interconnections among Biomedical specialties. Nevertheless, substantial differences in understanding, values, and even language and communicational habits persist (Hahn and Gaines 1985; Lock and Gordon 1988).

VALUES AND PRACTICE IN BIOMEDICINE

What are the values that motivate practitioners of Biomedicine? In what conditions, relationships, attitudes, and practices do they find merit? How do physicians rationalize their actions to themselves and to others? What are they seeking to achieve?

It is difficult to describe basic values in Biomedicine (or in any discipline) because values may not be visible, because they vary substantially among practitioners, and because expressed values may be inconsistent with themselves and may contradict unspoken values manifest in action. I begin by briefly summarizing the principles underlying professional oaths and codes that are a public expression of professional values in Biomedicine. But oaths are guides and ideals; they may be visionary. They are not descriptions of what adherents *actually do,* but prescriptions for what they believe they *should do.*

I then review values discernible in Biomedical thought and practice as well as in professional codes. I distinguish values concerned with *conditions of patients, relations with patients and colleagues, the physician him- or herself, the sources and distribution of medical knowledge,* and *medical action.* I describe professed values as well as evidence that these values are (or are not) enacted in practice. There is much idealism and dedication in the practice of Biomedicine; there is also substantial deviation from expressed ideals among a significant minority of Biomedical practitioners.

Although not widely representative of medical practice in its day (Carrick 1985), the Hippocratic Oath is regarded as the source of contemporary Biomedical codes of practice and has still been administered in medical schools in recent times—some twenty-three centuries later (Irish and Mc-Murry 1965). The Hippocratic Oath is expressly religious: practitioners swear "by Apollo Physician and Asclepius and Hygeia and Panaceia and all the gods and goddesses." In the oath itself, the adherents assert their expectation of a good life and fame if they follow its prescriptions, and "the opposite of all this" if they violate them.

The first and most detailed principle in the Hippocratic Oath is its reverential commitment to the medical fraternity itself—to the practitioner's teacher and the teacher's sons, to the practitioner's own sons, and to other practitioners—"to hold him who has taught me this art as equal to my parents." In his commitment to patients, the practitioner promises to benefit the sick, to protect from harm and injustice, not to practice surgery (left to other specialists), to forbear from personal abuse—sexual or other, and to maintain in confidence all that is learned from and about patients. The practitioner also promises never to provide the means of abortion or to give deadly drugs (presumably to assist in suicide). The implicit goal of medical practice is the maintenance of life in the sense of biological survival and well-being.

The American Medical Association first formulated a Code of Ethics at the time of its founding in 1847. Its Principles of Medical Ethics, substantially revised in 1957 and updated in 1980 and again in 1992, are not explicitly religious and are acknowledged to have no legal force (AMA Council on Ethical and Judicial Affairs 1992a). They are offered as a standard to guide and assess medical practice in relations with patients, other medical personnel, and the public. The 1992 revision avoids the generic male pronoun *he* in reference to physicians; it suggests that patients should be informed participants in their own care.

The American College of Physicians (ACP), the national organization of practitioners of internal medicine, has also formulated an Ethics Manual, first published in 1984 and already in its third edition (ACP 1992). This visionary document explicitly recognizes the roots of contemporary medical (Western) ethics in the moral and religious values of the society in which it participates; the ACP code has been developed with substantial contributions from current philosophical medical ethics.

In contrast to the Hippocratic Oath, the focus of AMA Principles and the ACP Manual for physicians is the patient "entrusted to their care" (AMA 1957). Further, physicians are recommended to attend to the needs not only of individual patients but of community, society, and humanity more broadly. Regarding other physicians, both the AMA Principles and the ACP Manual advise the protection of the public and the profession itself against immoral, unethical, or incompetent practitioners; physicians are exhorted to cease practice when they themselves are "impaired" and to "expose, without fear or favor, incompetent or corrupt, dishonest or unethical conduct on the part of members of the profession" (AMA 1992).

In the AMA oath, physicians are told to base their practice in science and to avoid professional association with nonscientific practitioners. They are asked to improve their knowledge and skills continually, but to recognize their limitations, not to compromise their practice, and to seek the help of colleagues when it may benefit the patient. Though they are told to maintain the confidentiality of their patients, they are also advised to compromise confidentiality when required by law or to protect the patient or the community. Physicians are asked to limit their income to medical services rendered to patients for the benefit of patients, and to charge patients according to their ability to pay.

Values Regarding Conditions of Patients

Although it may seem a cliché to note the Biomedical focus on the *promotion and maintenance of life* as a principal value, it is critical to clarify "the meaning of life" that prevails in Biomedicine. In Biomedical practice, despite the finding of some researchers (such as, Crane 1975; Muller and Koenig 1988) that physicians consider the interactive capacities of patients in addition to their physiological functioning in choosing interventions near the end of life, life is most often regarded essentially as physiological function—the effective working of the body. Although the legal criterion for death in Biomedicine has shifted from the cessation of heart function to irreversible brain states, the criterion remains a physiological one (Fox 1979).

Death is commonly experienced as a failure of medicine and the practitioner. "Modern medicine has come to see a patient's death as a failure, and the unavoidable approach of death as a reason to back off rather than as a call for even more intensive medical engagement (albeit palliative rather than curative)" (Brody 1992:1385). "For the physician . . . the fear of death may reflect a sense of impotence, a defeat as a physician" (Seravalli 1988:1728). An intense concern or fear of death may be a motive for pursuit of a medical career, and the death of patients may involve deep personal meaning for the patient's physician (Stein 1985b).

Regarding the participation of physicians in the death of patients, a distinction is often made between "active" and "passive" euthanasia: in active euthanasia, the physician (or someone else, other than the patient) deliberately commits an act that accelerates and/or "causes" the patient's death, say by injection of a lethal substance. In passive euthanasia, the physician (or other) either forbears from an action that would prolong the patient's life (withholding resuscitative procedures or life-sustaining nutrition) or withdraws a prolonging life support therapy such as oxygen.

Passive euthanasia has been regarded as legitimate in Biomedicine, though withdrawal is felt to be more problematic than withholding. In 1982, a Louis Harris poll found that 46 percent of the public supported the ethical propriety of active termination by physicians of a patient's life at the patient's considered request, but only 4 percent of physicians supported this position and only 2 percent said they would comply with such a request (though 26 percent of physicians also said they would support legislation to legalize such actions). In acts of omission, since the physician does not "do" anything, he or she is thought not to be responsible for the ensuing death. (In other circumstances, omission may be neglect.)

The AMA's Council on Ethical and Judicial Affairs has recently published a position paper titled "Decisions Near the End of Life," arguing that "passive euthanasia" may not be a reasonable concept. The position paper is profoundly ambivalent, acknowledging the right of patients to control their own treatment, but opposing active euthanasia and physician-assisted suicide. Ambivalence is suggested by the non sequitur: "Rather than condoning physician-provided euthanasia, medicine must first respond by striving to identify and address the concerns and needs of dying patients" (AMA Council on Ethical and Judicial Affairs 1992b:2232–33). *First* responding to patient concerns does not imply not *then* condoning euthanasia; indeed, responding to patient concerns may call for euthanasia or assisted suicide. The council finds no ethical distinction between the withholding and the withdrawal of treatment. The closest it comes to condoning medical participation in the acceleration of death is in the use of palliative treatments, such as morphine, with fatal side effects. (Presumably, then, if palliative treatments without such side effects were found, they would be deemed more desirable and ethical, regardless of patients' wishes.) The council describes risks in the use of euthanasia, such as the undermining of patient trust that physicians, as Brody puts it (1992:1387), "never say die."

The AMA has consistently opposed active euthanasia: "The intentional termination of the life of one human being by another—mercy killing—is contrary to that for which the medical profession stands and is contrary to the policy of the American Medical Association" (1973). And "The physician should not intentionally cause death" (AMA Council 1992a:14). Active euthanasia is held to be fundamentally inconsistent with the healing mandate—the promotion of life. "Medical education and socialization and the business of health all focus on offering and providing treatment, not on facilitating death" (Dubler 1993:23).

Perhaps for related reasons, the medical profession has explicitly condemned the administration of lethal injection to individuals judged by the state to be criminal and sentenced to death (AMA 1992a; ACP 1992). Some physicians have objected to capital punishment itself, others only to lethal injection or to physician participation (Bolsen 1982). Thus also, the solitary physician, Jack Kevorkian, who has recently assisted the considered suicides of patients suffering from painful and/or terminal sicknesses is thought to violate the principles of medical practice and is prosecuted as a criminal for violation of the law.

A notion of life as determined by the values and interests of the body's "occupant"—the person—is recent and uncommon in Biomedical ideology and practice. Referring to the paternalism common in medical practice, the ACP Ethics Manual notes that "the convergence of many forces—scientific advances, public education, the rise of participatory democracy, the civil rights and consumer movements, the effects of law and economics on medicine, and the moral heterogeneity of our society—poses serious challenges to the long-held, noble vision of Hippocratic ethics" (1992:247). Although the ACP recognizes a yearning in the profession to "return to the simplicity of the past," it concludes that such a return is impossible. The ACP presents its vision of the patient-physician relationship as follows:

> Whatever the treatment setting, at the beginning of a relationship the physician must understand the patient's complaints and underlying feelings and expectations. After they agree on the problem before them, the physician presents one or more courses of action. If both parties agree, the patient may then authorize the physician to initiate a course of action, and the physician accepts this responsibility. The relationship has mutual obligations.   (1992:948)

Given this perspective, the ACP, unlike the AMA, does not categorically oppose physicians' assistance of considered suicide. "Physicians and patients must continue to search together for answers to these problems without violating the physician's personal and professional values and without abandoning the patient to struggle alone" (1992:955).

Among developed nations the Netherlands is unique in condoning the practice of euthanasia. Nevertheless, the Dutch legal code also reflects an ambivalence toward the practice. Euthanasia remains illegal in the Netherlands, but at the same time Parliament has formulated procedures that physicians can follow in order not to be prosecuted. It is estimated that one-fourth of patient requests for euthanasia are honored by physicians and that physician-assisted deaths, including assisted suicides, account for 2 percent of deaths in the Netherlands (*New York Times*, Feb. 9, 1993).

Finally, there is another matter of controlling processes of life—that of abortion. The AMA has not morally condemned abortions as does the Hippocratic Oath, but it has not positively supported the right of physicians to perform abortions either (AMA Council on Scientific Affairs 1992): "The principles of Medical Ethics of the AMA do not prohibit a physician from performing an abortion in accordance with good medical practice and under circumstances that do not violate the law" (1992:2). The AMA as well as the ACP leave decisions regarding abortion to the individual physician. The ACP, however, insists that physicians who do not themselves perform abortions should refer women who seek them to settings where abortion services are available.

In addition to its physiological criterion of life, the Biomedical focus in the United States is *individualistic* rather than utilitarian; that is, practitioners direct attention to the promotion and maintenance of life in patients one at a time rather than to the distribution of well-being in society as a whole: "It seems fair to say that while physicians do not lack a service or collectivity orientation, it does not seem to be a very prominent value compared to others. Furthermore, the value is addressed to concern for helping individuals rather than to serving society or mankind" (Freidson 1970:178).

Responding to concerns about the societal allocation of scarce health resources, the AMA Council recommends a defensive position: "Physicians have a responsibility to participate and to contribute their professional expertise in order to safeguard the interests of patients in decisions made at the societal level regarding the allocation or rationing of health resources" (1992a:3).

When Marcia Angell, an editor of the *New England Journal of Medicine*, writes of "Medicine: The Endangered Patient-Centered Ethic" (1987), she is not advocating a medicine that addresses the patient's perspective or the societal distribution of health benefits but rather one that focuses on individual patients one at a time. With a focus on individual patients, physicians can do their utmost for the welfare of individual patients; they need not take into account the implications of this use of resources for the well-being of others. Suggestive of the individualistic focus, I have noted that only 0.3 percent of physicians in the United States in 1989 characterized their own practice specialty as public health.

The ACP Manual is again exceptional, indicating a need for physicians to be constantly concerned with *justice* and the *distribution of health care resources* as well as with the administration of the best available care for each of their patients. But the ACP position also indicates ambivalence and conflicting values: "In the final analysis, no external factors should interfere with the dedication of the physician to provide optimal care for his patient" (1984b:266).

Values Regarding Relations with Patients

Biomedical pronouncements, such as the AMA Principles and the ACP Manual, express a *universalistic ideal*—that physicians should treat (or be willing to treat) all of humanity without distinction by race, gender, age, religion, socioeconomic status, or sickness condition. Both the AMA Principles and the ACP Manual, however, also recognize a right of physicians to "choose whom they will serve." There is substantial evidence of discrimination within Biomedical institutions against minority patients, women, the elderly, and the poor (AMA Council on Ethical and Judicial Affairs 1990, 1991a, 1993; Brooks, Smith, and Anderson 1991; Kellerman 1991; Baker, Stevens, and Brook 1991). Though physicians alone may not be responsible for this discrimination, it is likely that they play a role. Recognizing the potential for discrimination, the AMA Council recommends that "physicians should examine their own practice to ensure that racial prejudice does not affect clinical judgment in medical care" (1992a:47). In another form of discrimination, patients with certain kinds of sicknesses—alcoholism, AIDS, mental disorder—may be judged morally "guilty" or "tainted" and receive inadequate treatment. And patients who do not follow medical etiquette—"health care abusers" or "crocks"—may also be treated with less than standard care.

Once having chosen to care for a patient, physicians are sworn to *fidelity*— ongoing attention and commitment to the medical welfare of this patient. In their relations with patients, physicians value *privacy;* they may regard their professional standing and the oversight of the medical community as sufficient public guarantee of their competence, so that routine review by others is unnecessary. Physicians also promise their patients *confidentiality,* though suspension of this principle is advised to comply with the law or for the protection of the patient or others. Perhaps to protect their patients from stigmatization or reprisal, however, physicians have not routinely complied with legal (but seldom enforced) requirements—for example, to inform public health officials of infectious diseases, such as syphilis or AIDS, among their patients.

That, according to earlier AMA Ethical Principles (1957), patients are "entrusted to" the care of physicians and that physicians may abrogate confidentiality to protect the patient indicates a *paternalism* in which the physician, better than the patient, may be thought to know and judge what is best for the patient. In 1980, at his retirement address as editor of the *New England Journal of Medicine,* Franz Ingelfinger argued that "if you agree that the physician's primary function is to make the patient feel better, a certain amount of authoritarianism, paternalism, and domination are the essence of the physician's effectiveness" (1980:1507).

In its 1980 revision of its 1957 Ethical Principles, the AMA noted that "the traditional paternalism of the profession is in conflict with society," implying that public opposition was forcing the profession to modify this traditional principle (Veatch 1980). The ACP Manual refers to "the benign paternalism that has characterized much of Western medicine up to our own times" (1989a:246). Though attitudes may have changed in recent decades, the relationship between physician and patient has not generally been regarded as a collaboration in which the patient's perspective is a guiding principle. As the ACP remarks, "it is often difficult for them [physicians] to accept the fact that what is the 'best' decision for a particular patient (in the opinion of the patient) may not be the 'right' decision for that patient (in the opinion of the physician)" (1984a:264).

Values Regarding Relations with Colleagues

The AMA Principles require physicians to practice *collegial vigilance* (my phrase), guarding against incompetence and moral impropriety among colleagues. Such vigilance is noted to protect the profession as well as the public.

But, perhaps more in keeping with the Hippocratic reverence for professional colleagues, the reporting of incompetence and immorality by fellow professionals appears to be relatively rare in Biomedicine in comparison with the frequency of such occurrences. *Collegial protection* is a value visible in the practice of Biomedical physicians. Observers of Biomedicine have noted a "conspiracy of silence" in which practitioners report only the gross failures of other physicians (Freidson 1970; Reuben 1990; Scheiber and Doyle 1983). A study of the response to error among surgical residents indicates that, though "moral errors"—violations of etiquette within the medical community, such as reporting problems to superiors, are strictly sanctioned, "technical errors"—medical mistakes—are corrected, but regarded as a normal part of medical practice (Bosk 1979).

One may explore values regarding professional self-regulation within Biomedicine by comparing rates of various forms of incompetence and malpractice with the frequencies of sanction. The AMA estimated in 1973 that 4.1 to 6.5 percent of physicians were "impaired," that is, hindered in effective medical practice because of a personal problem, such as alcoholism or drug dependence (AMA Council on Mental Health 1973; Pfifferling 1980). This estimate is likely to be low because of underreporting; moreover, it does not include diminished competence, such as losses in dexterity or perception owing to sickness or aging. Other estimates of physician impairment range between 5 and 15 percent—more than twice as high as the AMA estimate (Scheiber and Doyle 1983). There is evidence of rates of alcohol consumption and prescription drug abuse among physicians greatly in excess of rates in the general population (Scheiber 1983). Although all states are said to have programs to address the problem of "impaired physicians," it is unclear how many seek help, either voluntarily or in response to a mandate. Recent information is hard to find; however, earlier studies suggest that at most one physician in four hundred per year is disciplined for alcohol or drug abuse (Brewster 1986).

Incapacities and moral errors may result in malpractice and negligence. Malpractice is a broad concept defined as "any professional misconduct, unreasonable lack of skill or fidelity in professional or fiduciary duties, evil practice, or illegal or immoral conduct" (*Black's Legal Dictionary*, 5th ed.). It may cover a broad range of acts and omissions, including

> abandonment; failure to continue to provide needed service in the absence of proper relief from responsibility; assault and battery; use of procedures, often surgical, not consented to by the patient; breach of express contract, when the physician fails to fulfill an express agreement, for example, to provide certain services for a stated sum or to effect a cure or specified result; deceit or fraud, when, for example, a physician conceals facts giving rise to a negligence action, fraudulently secures consent to a medical procedure, or otherwise falsely misrepresents a material fact as to diagnosis or treatment; willful misconduct such as drunkenness during surgery; and miscellaneous tortious wrongs such as false imprisonment, defamation, invasion of privacy, breach of confidential communications, and injuries to third parties (for example, through failure to warn of a patient's danger to others).   (Hauck and Louisell 1978:1020)

Malpractice may be unintentional or intentional; it may or may not have harmful consequences for a given patient. For example, sexual relations with patients are considered malpractice, regardless of consequences (AMA 1991b; ACP 1992). Studies indicate that 5 to 10 percent of psychiatrists have had sexual contact with patients, and it is assumed that the same holds true for other physicians (AMA 1991b; Gartrell et al. 1992). A survey indicates, however, that while 65 percent of psychiatrists have treated patients who claimed to have had sexual relations with previous therapists, only 12 percent of these psychiatrists reported this information to professional organizations or legal authorities (Gartrell et al. 1987). Legal proceedings for malpractice require proof of negligence—of practice *both* with harmful consequences and below community standards. Though not directly indicative of negligence, in 1990, there were 7.7 legal claims of negligence per 100 physicians, down from a peak of 10.2 in 1985; the rate of claims was lowest among pathologists (1.5 claims/100 physicians) and psychiatrists (2.4 claims/100) and highest among surgeons (11.5 claims/100) and obstetrician/gynecologists (11.9 claims/100) (Gonzalez 1992).

A palpable result of incompetence or improper practice may be inappropriate medical care or error in diagnosis or treatment. A recent survey of hospitalizations in different sites around the country found that 23 percent of hospitalizations were inappropriate (Siu, Manning, and Benjamin 1990).

Within medical settings, it is difficult to determine the frequency of negligent practice because of both underreporting and false claims. An intensive study of hospitalizations in New York State (Brennan et al. 1991; Leape et al. 1991; Localio et al. 1991) found that 3.7 percent of hospitalizations ended in "adverse events"—that is, in injuries "caused by medical management (rather than the underlying disease) and that prolonged the hospitalization, produced a disability at the time of discharge, or both." Such outcomes are referred to as "iatrogenic" (from the Greek, *iatros,* "physician") or "noso-comial" (from the Greek, *nosokomeian,* "hospital"). Among adverse events, 2.6 percent led to long-term disability and 13.6 percent to death. Of hospitalizations with adverse events, 28 percent (thus almost 1 percent of *all* hospitalizations) were due to medical negligence; an additional 30 percent were errors not judged to be negligent—because they did not fall below community norms. A greater proportion of negligent adverse events occurred among elderly patients, but the proportion was similar for men and women. Although not strictly comparable because of methodological differences, other studies have reported higher proportions of adverse outcomes attributable to negligence (for example, Lakshmanan, Hershey, and Breslau 1986; Steel et al. 1981; Justiniani 1984).

The New York study also found that *claims* of negligence were made in only 16.8 percent of negligent incidents (Localio et al. 1991). Thus, in 83.2 percent of negligence cases, the responsible physician was not held accountable. (Note that these statistics refer to hospitalizations and adverse events rather than to the physicians who are responsible; since physicians may be responsible for multiple hospitalizations during a year, the proportion of physicians involved is likely to be smaller than the proportion of hospitalizations.)

In his study of self-regulation in the medical profession, Freidson (1970) found that physicians reported that they most often would do nothing in response to an observed error on the part of a colleague. Physicians reasoned that mistakes are inevitable in medical practice and that they themselves could be subject to the same critical response and social control; they also feared law suits brought by accused colleagues. They were thus extremely restrained in responding to an error. In cases of severe error, they might "talk to" the colleague or engage in a "personal boycott" by not referring patients to this physician.

At a formal level, all states have boards responsible for the granting of licenses and the sanctioning of improper and incompetent practice. This system, however, has been described as "a disjointed, unwieldy and loophole ridden system of medical peer review . . . plagued by flawed laws, feuding officials, underfinanced agencies and a fear among many physicians that actions against incompetent colleagues will prompt expensive lawsuits" (*New York Times,* Sept. 3, 1985). In New York State in 1985, there were said to be 1,800 complaints awaiting review; of complaints received, only 11 percent were initiated by the medical community—physicians, hospitals, and medical societies.

The Federation of State Medical Boards reports a wide range in rates of "prejudicial actions" taken nationwide in 1991; some states (Maine, Pennsylvania, and New York) took fewer than one action per 1,000 licensed physicians in the state; others (Alaska, North Dakota, and Oklahoma) took more than ten per 1,000. In 1991, altogether 2,804 physicians in the United States were disciplined—one-half of 1 percent of the physician population reported by the AMA (Roback, Randolph, and Seidman 1992); 34 percent of the actions were license revocations, 40 percent were probations or restrictions, and 26 percent were other actions such as penalties or reprimands (Federation 1992). Sanctioned physicians are reported to move to other locations and freely continue to practice (*New York Times,* Sept. 3, 1985).

Thus, while perhaps 10 percent of physicians are impaired, almost a fourth of hospital admissions are inappropriate, and a minimum of 1 percent of hospitalizations end in negligent adverse outcomes, only one-half of 1 percent of practicing physicians are reported to be formally sanctioned by licensing boards annually, and it is likely that the overwhelming majority of such actions are not initiated by colleague physicians. In practice, the norm of silence clearly dominates that of collegial vigilance.

Values Regarding Self

The training and work of Biomedical practice involve intensive *commitment* and *self-sacrifice.* In 1990, physicians worked a median of 59.1 hours a week, almost 1.5 times the standard workweek; hours at work ranged from a median of 50.1 for pathologists and 50.4 for psychiatrists to 63.9 for obstetrician/gynecologists and 66.1 for anesthesiologists (Gonzalez 1992). At the same time, the medical career is recognized to bring great personal rewards and satisfaction to practitioners. Physicians may participate in the intimate lives of their patients; they may positively affect their patients and be deeply respected and appreciated for doing so. Paradoxically, the "demands" of Biomedical practice may also lead to inattention to the practitioner's own well-being and to that of his or her family (Gerber 1983). "Medicine is a jealous mistress," writes physician-observer George Vaillant (Vaillant, Sobowale, and McArthur 1972:372). Physicians "tend to take care of everyone and everything before themselves," writes an obstetrics resident of her own pregnancy (Trupin 1986:131).

Conflicts of interest also arise between the welfare of patients and the benefit to physicians themselves; conflicts indicate a strong value placed on the *accumulation of wealth.* "Physicians emphasize the value of the income and prestige connected with their occupation" (Freidson 1970:178). In 1990 the median income (after expenses, but before taxes) of physicians was reported to be $130,000, ranging from $93,000 for general and family practitioners to $200,000 for surgeons, radiologists, and anesthesiologists (Gonzalez 1992). It is estimated that approximately 10 percent of physicians in the

United States have ownership in medical facilities to which they refer their patients (AMA Council on Ethical and Judicial Affairs 1992a). Though some patient referrals to facilities owned by the referring physicians may be medically justified, there is evidence that patients are far more likely to be referred for medical services when the referring physician owns the facility than when he or she does not; further, the cost of such self-referrals generally exceeds that of the same services provided by others. The AMA Council on Ethical and Judicial Affairs (1992c), like the ACP, has recommended, in general, against such self-referral.

There are further indications that physicians may act in their own interest rather than that of their patients. For example, while a part of the wide regional variation in rates of medical care, such as surgical procedures, may result from regional differences in the need for such procedures, a substantial part of the difference has been attributed to the number of available hospital beds, the number of physicians available to perform these procedures, and differences in "style" of medical practice from region to region (Wennberg and Gittelsohn 1982; Lewis 1969). Other studies have produced evidence against these explanations (LoGerfo 1977). Roos, Roos, and Henteleff (1977) demonstrate that in Manitoba, though there is a remarkably low compliance (14–17 percent) with recommended surgical standards for tonsilectomy and adenoidectomy, there is no association between rates of these surgeries and rates of respiratory illness, the availability of surgeons in the area, or noncompliance with surgical standards.

Professional autonomy is a prominent value in Biomedicine—indeed a value associated with the notion of profession itself. A profession is an occupation that, because of its expertise, moral standing, and societal importance, is thought of as capable of self-government. Autonomy refers both to the control of the profession by its own members—collective autonomy—and the self-control of each physician in his or her own work—individual autonomy (Light 1979). In the twentieth century, Western society has, in essence, granted to Biomedical physicians the right to define sickness, to designate and control legitimate therapies, to define and license medical training, and to regulate many aspects of practice. Physicians and their principal professional organization, the American Medical Association, have resisted attempts to restrict their professional autonomy.

Another value discernible in Biomedical practice is *personal convenience*. The timing of childbirth is a striking example. Births in the United States are 26 percent more likely to occur on a Friday than on a Saturday and 24 percent less likely to occur on a Sunday than on a Monday; other births are evenly distributed during the week (Centers for Disease Control 1993c). The difference is greater for cesarean than for vaginal deliveries, but true for both. Some births appear to be timed to fit the physicians' schedule. Similar effects have been shown for time of day during which the deliveries occur (Fraser et al. 1987). The scheduling may well be done with the consent of patients and perhaps for their convenience as well, but it is likely that the patient is following the physician's advice. In any case, in a substantial number of instances, the normal event of birth is not allowed to take its course. Such alteration is not designed for the medical benefit of either mother or infant. The effect is greater for white than for black women, probably because white women are likely to be better insured than black women and can thus pay for the time-adjusting procedures (CDC 1993c).

Values Regarding Knowledge

Prominent values in Biomedicine are an insistence on the foundation of medical practice in *science* and a strong preference for *objective evidence, logical inference,* and *rationality.* It is unclear, however, how much of actual medical practice is, in fact, based on science and how aware practicing physicians are of the existing scientific foundations of medicine.

A historical study of "discarded operations" between 1880 and 1942— surgical procedures used but later rejected as harmful or ineffective—indicates the prominent role of inadequate evidence and of the recommendations of influential colleagues in the selection of procedures used during this period (Barnes 1977). The author of the study acknowledges improvements in methods to evaluate medical techniques, but he suggests that medical practice does not always avail itself of these methods (Barnes 1977).

More recently (beginning in the late 1950s) a surgical procedure of tying off a blood vessel supplying blood to the heart—"mammary artery ligation"—was recommended and used to reduce angina pectoris; the operation gained wide attention and was featured in *Reader's Digest* (Barsamian 1977). To determine the efficacy of the procedure, two independent researchers performed placebo surgery experiments, in which some of the randomly assigned patients had the standard procedure, including the opening of the chest cavity, except that the blood vessel of the heart was not tied; other patients underwent the standard, full procedure. The placebo patients in both studies fared as well as (actually slightly better than) patients with the standard procedure, suggesting that it was the surgical procedure per se rather than the ligated artery that effected relief from angina. Although these experiments would be regarded as unethical today, they effectively ended the use of the mammary artery ligation procedure and indicated a critical need for "control"—that is, randomized comparison of the procedure in question either with the standard procedure of the day or with a placebo, in the evaluation of medical interventions (Barsamian 1977).

McKinlay (1981) has claimed that medical innovations generally pass through several stages as they become "standard procedures." First, a "promising report" leads, most often without critical evidence, to professional and organizational adoption, followed by public acceptance and state (third-party endorsement)—still without essential experimental evidence. The status of the innovation as "standard procedure" is then established, attested by (uncontrolled) observational reports. A randomized controlled trial is conducted, followed by professional denunciation and discreditation. McKinlay argues that many medical interventions are accepted, adopted, and widely used in practice without valid evidence, sometimes with detrimental effects and often at enormous expense. He believes that randomized controlled trials should routinely be performed *before* new procedures are adopted.

A particularly tragic case was the use of diethylstilbesterol (DES) to prevent spontaneous abortions. By 1955, no controlled studies had shown DES to be effective for this purpose, and six controlled studies had shown it ineffective (Chalmers 1974). Nevertheless, it is estimated that physicians prescribed DES to approximately fifty thousand women each year for the next fifteen years. In 1971, it was discovered that DES was the cause of specific forms of vaginal and cervical cancer in the daughters of women who had taken DES while pregnant. It is estimated that approximately 1/1,000 of the exposed daughters developed one of these otherwise rare cancers (Herbst et al. 1977).

Thomas Chalmers (1974) has examined the scientific status of diverse medical techniques and found many wanting, particularly techniques used in obstetrics and gynecology (see also I. Chalmers, Enkin, and Keirse 1989; Davis-Floyd 1992). Cardiologist David Spodick reviewed sixteen journals reporting the results of treatments for heart disease interventions in 1971; he found that, while nine of twenty-one medical intervention studies were "controlled," none of the forty-nine surgical studies were (Spodick 1973). Chalmers and colleagues have recently reviewed several therapies used for heart attack patients; they found that several procedures persisted despite evidence of their harmful effects and lack of benefits, and that other therapies were not adopted in practice for more than a decade despite solid evidence in their favor (Antman et al. 1992). Chalmers remarks of cancer therapies, "There is little information in the literature on the degree to which the practice of medicine in the community is a reflection of the results of controlled clinical trials" (Chalmers 1974:753). He estimates that perhaps 5 percent of procedures currently in use in medical practice are supported by solid evidence such as randomized clinical trials (Chalmers, personal communication, 1993). Clearly, reliance on the best scientific principles has not determined the selection of many standard practices of Biomedicine. Fineberg concludes, "we have failed to evaluate what we do to the extent that we can and should" (Fineberg and Hiatt 1979).

Some analysts (such as Freidson 1970) have argued that the clinical frame of mind associated with Biomedical practice is not compatible with the standards of scientific investigation: "One whose work requires practical application to concrete cases simply cannot maintain the same frame of mind as the scholar or scientist; he cannot suspend action in the absence of incontrovertible evidence or be skeptical of himself, his experience, his work and its fruit" (Freidson 1970:169).

Physicians highly value *their own experience* as a source of knowledge in medicine—what has happened to them personally in their dealings with patients. "In having to rely so heavily upon his personal, clinical experience with concrete, individual cases, however, the practitioner comes essentially to rely on the authority of his own senses, independently of the general authority of tradition or science" (Freidson 1970:170). Similarly, Bosk has written "By basing decisions on personal clinical experience the attending physician now demonstrates that the documented scientific and clinical experience of others is not relevant to the case at hand" (1980a:74).

In the conflict of personal experience and science, the personal experience of the physician comes to dominate scientific findings in his or her own thought and the teaching of others. This value is inconsistent with scientific principles thought to benefit from the comparison of events in diverse settings. Bosk tells of a surgeon who assuages the concerns of residents unable to perform a procedure by saying that "the problem is in Mr. Eckhardt's [the patient's] anatomy and not in their skills" (1979:44).

There is a strong value placed on *certainty* and *the control of uncertainty*. Uncertainty either about a patient's condition or about effective response may severely hinder medical practice. Fox has described "training for uncertainty," by which student physicians learn to balance the uncertainty of their own knowledge with the uncertainty of the field of medicine itself (Fox 1957). They also learn to adopt "a *manner* of certitude." Katz argues that, though physicians may be theoretically aware of the uncertainties of their medical practice, in the course of treatment, they commonly suppress uncertainty both in their own thought and in what they communicate to patients (Katz 1984).

The practices of Biomedical physicians (and of many patients as well) suggest belief in a *hierarchy of authoritative knowledge;* different sources of knowledge are ascribed distinctive values and different personnel are thought to have privileged and exclusive access to "better" sources (Jordan 1992). Fundamental and essential knowledge in Biomedicine is thought to be produced by and shared among physicians. In contrast, the value of information provided by other medical personnel, such as nurses, and by patients is ascribed lesser validity, reliability, and value. The "signs" that physicians determine from their own observation of patients are regarded as objective evidence to which they have exclusive access, whereas the "symptoms" reported by patients of their own conditions are thought of as subjective. In addition, physicians have ascribed special status to the procedures and equipment used to measure and monitor the conditions of patients: "Many modern physicians thus seem to order the value of medical evidence in a hierarchy: facts obtained through complex scientific procedures they regard as more accurate and germane to diagnosis than facts they detect with their senses, which, in turn, they value more than facts disclosed by the patient's statement" (Reiser 1978:171).

Regarding the dissemination of information by physicians, although guidelines such as the ACP Manual insist on the importance of providing extensive and appropriate information to patients, physicians in practice do not commonly regard the provision of information as critical and overestimate the information they provide. Intensive analysis of 336 physician-patient encounters in a variety of medical settings indicates that, whereas physicians believe that they spend about 9 minutes of a 20-minute interaction giving information to patients, they actually spend a median of 1.3 minutes per patient (Waitzkin 1985). Moreover, information is often provided for the patient's awareness rather than for his or her participation in decisions; physicians are reported to have often already determined the best course (Lidz et al. 1983).

Values Regarding Action

Patients commonly go to physicians for resolution of a problem of sickness. There is a strong value among Biomedical physicians to respond to the patient's problem. "The central task," writes sociologist Donald Light (1979:313), "is to *act* in the face of various uncertainties." Observers of Biomedicine have described this value as "meliorism" (Fox 1989), "instrumental activism," (Parsons 1967), and "therapeutic activism" (Stein 1990). Though constrained by the principle ascribed to Hippocrates, "First, do no harm," physicians have a strong urge to "do something." "First the aim of the practitioner is not knowledge but *action*. Successful action is preferred, but action with very little chance for success is to be preferred over no action at all. There is a tendency for the practitioner to take action for its own sake on the spurious assumption that doing something is better than doing nothing" (Freidson 1970:168).

A study of surgical errors of treatment resulting in adverse outcomes indicates that errors of commission are three times as likely as errors of omission (Couch et al. 1981). The authors (themselves surgeons) attribute the errors to "misplaced optimism," "unwarranted urgency," the "urge for perfection," "vogue therapy," and "insufficient restraint and deliberation." Another commentator notes, "Physicians generally receive satisfaction from performing procedures that they can do well, which can lead to an overutilization of diagnostic or therapeutic procedures and to overestimation of the applicability and effectiveness of the procedures for the problem at hand" (Myers 1981:665).

Mold and Stein (1986) have described "the cascade effect in the clinical care of patients," akin to cascade effects in biological processes such as blood clotting. They argue that the presence of a patient with a seemingly urgent problem arouses anxiety in the attending physician. The physician's anxiety promotes a hasty and inappropriate response that is followed by an exacerbation of the patient's initial problems and additional anxiety-driven responses on the part of the physician. Elements in the clinical cascade may include "an incomplete or inaccurate data base," "an error in data analysis," "underestimation of the risks of evaluation or treatment," and "unwillingness on the part of the physician to risk a bad outcome" (Mold and Stein 1986:512). The urge to act overwhelms rationality.

In Biomedicine, *technological means* of diagnosis and intervention are greatly preferred over interpersonal and social means. Nontechnological activities, such as talk with patients, may not be considered part of treatment at all. The value attributed to technology also corresponds to the social status and relative incomes of medical specialties that employ these technologies— surgery, radiology, and anesthesia at the "top," family and general medicine, pediatrics, and psychiatry at the "bottom" (Shortell 1974; AMA 1992).

Finally, Biomedical practice values *curative interventions* above preventive ones, although the curative approach is often not the most effective or efficient available means for promoting patients' health. It is recognized that much sickness and death could be prevented by the reduction or elimination of major risk factors, such as cigarette smoking, hypertension, and obesity (Fielding 1978; Hahn et al. 1990). In comparison with cure and rehabilitation, prevention is a relatively inexpensive method of disease control. Nevertheless, surveys indicate that fewer than half of primary care physicians ask their patients about high-risk behavior; fewer than half believe that reduction of risk factors, such as high levels of alcohol, salt, and fat consumption, is "very important"; and even smaller percentages believe they could succeed in encouraging risk reduction among their patients (Wechsler et al. 1983, Becker and Janz 1990). Nor, except in health maintenance organizations, has the system of financial rewards favored a preventive approach to medicine; in general, physicians are paid far more for technological procedures than for counseling their patients about unhealthy habits.

Physicians commonly claim that they do not advise risk reduction because evidence for the effect of risk factors is preliminary; yet they are often willing to prescribe drugs the evidence for whose efficacy is also preliminary (Dismuke and Miller 1983). Moreover, since surveys of physician health indicate a lower prevalence of risk factors and better health status than found among persons with similar sociodemographic standing (such as lawyers), it appears that physicians do give some credence to preventive measures (Wyshak et al. 1980).

BIOMEDICAL SOCIALIZATION

In many non-Western societies, healers are believed to acquire their abilities through the intercession of cosmic powers. In some societies, following a "calling," recruits experience dream visitations or engage in vision quests to encounter the spiritual beings that guide their healing.

During healing sessions, healers may be possessed and instructed by a spirit guardian. In other societies, persons who have had a certain sickness are called to become specialists in the treatment of that sickness. In many non-Western ethnomedicines, disease and healing are explicitly linked to the balance and restoration of cosmological relations and moral order.

In contrast, in Biomedicine, the pursuit of a healing career is commonly regarded as a voluntary choice of individuals. While a review of medical autobiographies (over several centuries) indicates that some physicians report a spiritual motivation or "an inexplicable desire to become doctors," and others report pursuit of a medical career following an influential sickness during their childhood, the medical vocation is most often regarded as a personal choice rather than a spiritual calling (Brody 1955).

The training of Biomedical physicians, from medical school through residency, must be among the most intensive ordeals found in human societies anywhere; Bosk (1980b) compares medical education with military training and seminary. In this section, I examine the characteristics of young adults selected for medical careers and the contents and process of their transformation into physicians. Medical education—of approximately 1/250 persons in the current adult U.S. population, 15,000 students per year during the 1980s—has been closely scrutinized since the middle of the twentieth century by sociologists, psychologists, and anthropologists, as well as by the medical profession itself.

The median age of physicians currently in practice is the early forties; these physicians were thus born around 1950, attended medical school in the early 1970s, and undertook their residency training in the mid-1970s. Insofar as information is available, I focus on these modal physicians, while briefly noting the twentieth-century evolution of Biomedical education as well.

Despite extensive efforts in recent decades to recruit minority, women, and lower-income students into medical careers, the demographic characteristics of physicians in practice differ strikingly from those of the population at large. For example, though 10 percent of the U.S. population in 1950 was black, only 2.1 percent of physicians were black. By 1980, despite national efforts in minority recruitment, the disparity had changed little; 11.7 percent of the U.S. population was black, but only between 2.6 percent and 3.1 percent of practicing physicians, and 1.7 percent of medical school faculty were black (Sullivan 1983; Lanphear 1986). By 1990, the gap had lessened: 12.3 percent of the population and 6.5 percent of medical students were black (Centers for Disease Control 1993b).

Though women have also been greatly underrepresented in Biomedicine, change in recent decades has been dramatic. Only 8 percent of graduates from medical school prior to 1960 and currently in practice are women. By 1990, however, women constituted 16.4 percent of physicians in practice and 38.8 percent of medical students (Centers for Disease Control 1993b).

The Biomedical profession has also been unrepresentative of the socio-economic characteristics of the nation. In 1968, 57 percent of U.S. workers were skilled or unskilled laborers, but only 17 percent of physicians had parents from this class; in contrast, professionals were only 4.9 percent of the population, yet 31 percent of physicians had professionals as parents (Lyden, Geiger, and Peterson 1968). In the 1960s, 12 percent of medical students were from families with median or lower income levels, the same as in 1920 (Kleinbach 1974). Differences in socioeconomic status among physicians in training overlap with racial differences. A national survey in 1982 found that black medical residents were half as likely to have a college-educated parent as white residents (Bazzoli, Adams, and Thran 1983). Navarro (1976) has claimed that the capitalist class perpetuates its wealth and power within medical institutions and the medical profession.

Nor do physicians mirror the nation in terms of cultural or religious background. A representative survey of physicians in New York State in the mid-1960s found that approximately 50 percent came from Jewish backgrounds, and 25 percent each had been raised Protestant and Catholic (Colombotos 1969). The Protestants were largely from higher socioeconomic strata, the Jews from middle strata, and the Catholics from lower strata. Jews were more likely than Protestants to consider themselves Democrats and to favor "liberal" policies regarding medical care and welfare; Catholics fell between the Jews and the Protestants in their political attitudes (Colombotos 1969).

Finally, the personal characteristics of physicians-to-be have also been found to differ from those of the population at large. A study of a class of Harvard undergraduates compared physician and nonphysician alumni, matched for socioeconomic status, and found that the physicians were 60 percent more likely to have come from families with significant interpersonal problems; physicians were twice as likely themselves to be hypochondriacal and freely expressive of their problems, but at the same time twice as likely to be self-denying and altruistic as their nonphysician classmates (Vaillant, Sobowale, and McArthur 1972). In their adult lives, the physicians were more likely than classmates to have marital problems, to abuse drugs, and to seek psychiatric help (Vaillant, Sobowale, and McArthur 1972; Scheiber 1983).

Among the medical students observed in the classic study of medical education, Merton and his colleagues' *The Student Physician,* 45.3 percent had either a father or another relative who was a physician (Rogoff 1957). Thielens's observation that law students had similar proportions of family members in the law (51 percent) as medical students had physician family members (50 percent) suggests the importance of parental (in this case, paternal) modeling in the adoption of these professions (Thielens 1957). Fifty-one percent of medical students reported first considering a medical career before the age of fourteen; 74 percent of these students had physician fathers (compared with 40 percent of students who considered a medical career before the age of fourteen who had no relative in medicine). Most students, especially those who decided early to pursue a medical career, also report being strongly influenced by their fathers (whether physicians or not); mothers' influence was not examined (Rogoff 1957).

The organization of contemporary Biomedical education is the result of the turn-of-the-century forces that established Biomedicine as the dominant ethnomedicine of Western society, greatly reducing the medical pluralism that characterized the nineteenth century (Starr 1982). In 1910, Abraham Flexner published a landmark analysis of medical education in the United States and Canada, recommending the restructuring of medical education based in scientific knowledge and training. As the Biomedical perspective increasingly controlled medicine, its education and certification, non-Biomedical medicines (such as osteopathy, chiropractic, midwifery, and naturopathy) survived in marginal positions only through persistent battle (Baer 1981). Freidson (1970) has referred to Biomedicine as a monopoly.

While basic features of medical training were established in the early decades of the twentieth century, both the content of medical training and the characteristics of trainees have evolved substantially. Funkenstein (1979) has discerned six periods in the evolution of contemporary medical education from its establishment with the Flexner Report until the late 1970s:

1. "The General Practice Era: 1910–1939" during which medical education focused on the training of general practitioners and research and specialty practice were relatively uncommon. The first two years of medical education were devoted to basic sciences related to medical practice, the second two years to training in clinical work. Licensure required an additional year of "internship"—an intensive practice of clinical medicine under the guidance of experienced physicians.
2. "The Specialty Era: 1940–1958" during which specialty medical knowledge and technique evolved rapidly and the proportion of physicians devoted to general practice declined from 70 percent to 20 percent. Graduates of medical school increasingly began to pursue specialty "residencies" following their internships.
3. "The Scientific Era: 1959–1968" during which federal funding for basic research and medical education was established, the number of medical schools and their graduates grew rapidly, and "the social responsibility of the physician was considered to be research, first, and patient care, second" (Funkenstein 1979:55).
4. "The Student Activism Era: 1969–1970" during which medical students became more interested in resolving the maldistribution of

medical care than in basic research. There was little agreement among
students and faculty on the primary responsibility of physicians.

5. "The Doldrums Era: 1971–1974" during which funding for research
   and training had declined, and there was uncertainty about the basic
   goals of medicine and appropriate medical education.

6. "The Primary Care and Increasing Governmental Control Era: 1975–
   1979" during which federal funding has been directed to the training
   of primary care physicians and the supply of medical personnel to
   underserved areas.

To understand the social and psychological processes by which physicians
were created, two pioneering studies were conducted during the 1950s. One
group of researchers observed medical students at several universities and
collaborated in *The Student Physician* (Merton, Reader, and Kendall 1957).
Another group of researchers studied medical students at the University of
Kansas and wrote *Boys in White* (Becker et al. 1961). Many subsequent
studies of medical education and the training during internship and residency have followed the models set by these early studies.

The authors of *Boys in White,* Becker and colleagues, recognized that
"medical students acquire two cultures during their years in school: student
culture and the rudiments of the culture of the medical profession" (Becker
and Geer 1958:71). In *Boys in White,* the researchers were interested principally in describing "student culture, . . . the collective understandings
among students about matters related to their roles as students" (Becker et al.
1961:46). (The authors note that approximately 10 percent of the medical
school class are "girls," but they make little further reference to student
gender in medical education.) The researchers followed a theoretical perspective referred to as "symbolic interactionism" in which individuals' ways of
thinking and acting are seen as largely determined by their interactions with
other persons in the same environment.

Becker and colleagues report that medical students begin their studies
with the idealistic goal of acquiring all there is to know in order to suc-
cessfully treat their future patients. They quickly learn that there is a seemingly endless amount of information to learn. In order to succeed in medical
school, they must figure out how to choose among all that they can possibly
learn and how to deal effectively with the faculty members who teach them
and judge their work. Student culture is the product of collaboration among
medical students as they solve these immediate problems of adaptation to the
medical school environment. "Intensive interaction in an isolated group produces the understandings and agreements we call student culture—a set of
provisional solutions and guidelines for activity" (Becker and Geer 1958:72).
For example, in their basic science courses, the students come to value
information that they need for their exams and for later practice; they want
the faculty to "give it to us straight." They avoid learning anything extra.

Similarly, in their clinical years, the students want experience with techniques and conditions they will encounter in their careers. The students' perspectives evolve as they meet new challenges and work together in their solution.

In contrast, the authors of *The Student Physician* were interested in how medical students learn underlying elements of "the professional culture of medicine"—the values, knowledge, and techniques they will later apply in their medical careers (Merton, Bloom, and Rogoff 1956:555). A member of the *Student Physician* team, Renee Fox, examined the "sociological calendar," the unfolding sequence of events through which medical students pass as they learn firsthand and up close about patients, life, death, birth, sexuality, sickness, bodies, and the role of physicians in dealing with these matters (in Merton, Reader, and Kendall, eds. 1957). Fox described how students learn to deal with their personal uncertainties of knowledge, the uncertainties of medicine itself, and the boundary between these two. She described how physicians in training adopt a posture of "detached concern," balancing compassion for their patients and the distance necessary to respond objectively and effectively to the patient's condition and to protect themselves from emotional involvement. Though the explicit goals of medical education are the learning of pathophysiology and technique, there is an essential undercurrent of values and behavioral norms that accompany the explicit agenda.

Researchers in each of these projects and others as well (such as Levinson 1967) have argued that, beyond possible differences in the student bodies and medical school settings that may account for some differences in findings in the two projects, the perspectives and findings of other research team are misleading, if not erroneous. I suggest that each project looked at a different facet of a common phenomenon—Becker and colleagues at conscious strategies of adaptation to the immediate environment of medical school, Merton and colleagues at the partially unconscious socialization of long-term understandings for a medical career. The perspectives are not exclusive. Moreover, researchers in each project made at least a passing reference to learning of "the other" sort. For example, Becker and colleagues examined the long-term learning of "responsibility" and the role of personal "experience" in medical practice. They described how the initial idealism regarding the work of medicine was tempered by the realities of medical practice. Fox described how medical students collaborated in a "little society" to solve the immediate problems of being a medical student; and she noted that, in addition to learning how to think about and inwardly respond to uncertainty, a medical student learns to adopt a *"manner* of certitude . . . even when he does not actually feel sure" (Fox 1957:227).

A more recent study of medical education combines the approaches of Becker and Merton and their colleagues, albeit at a medical school—McMaster University in Ontario—with an unusual, community, practice–based training (Haas and Shaffir 1987). These researchers examine commonalities of short- and long-term and surface and deeper learning during medical training. Akin to the "manner of certitude," they demonstrate that students adopt "a cloak of competence," in which they act as if they were proficient in diverse tasks. The "cloak"—perhaps symbolized by the white coat—serves three functions: to convince the students themselves that they are competent, to convince their mentors, and to convince their patients. Thus, a habit they adopt in training serves them as practitioners as well. Anthropologists have described similar experiences among non-Western healers, for example, a Kwakiutl shaman famous in early decades of the twentieth century in the coastal region of British Columbia, who, initially skeptical of shamanic powers, becomes a renowned shaman himself as he experiences his own influence and the responses of others (Lévi-Strauss 1963).

Other researchers have expanded the findings from earlier studies. Based on Fox's analysis, for example, Donald Light elaborates the diverse forms of uncertainty faced by Biomedical trainees (1979). He notes uncertainties regarding instructors ("What do they want?"); professional knowledge ("What are the limits of knowledge in medicine?"); diagnosis ("What does the patient really have?"); treatment ("What, if any, is the best treatment?"); and client response ("What does the patient really want, and is he or she satisfied?"). For each form of uncertainty, Light describes the means by which trainees attempt to gain control. For example, to counter the uncertainties resulting from extensive knowledge in the field of medicine, trainees specialize, so that they can familiarize themselves with a smaller body of knowledge; they also adopt a school of thought, its rationale and its practice, so that they need not repeatedly consider alternatives. To respond to uncertainties of treatment, they focus on routines based in clinical experience and judgment, and they emphasize technique (over which they have some control) rather than results (over which they have less control).

During medical school, students form images of the personal characteristics of specialists—images that may influence their own specialty choices. The surgeon is regarded as "a decisive *and efficient* man of action driving forcefully to achieve his goals in an impersonal and autocratic manner" (Zimny and Thale 1970). The pediatrician is regarded as responsible and as having "warm, friendly interpersonal relationships." Internists are thought of as intelligent and responsible, and psychiatrists as retiring and self-concerned (Zimny and Thale 1970). Students also acquire attitudes about the kind of patients they seek to treat. For example, observers of *The Student Physician* report that 49.4 percent of students prefer patients whose conditions are "entirely physical"; 2.4 percent prefer those whose illness is "chiefly emotional"; the remaining 48.2 percent have no strong preference (Martin 1957).

Following medical education—referred to as "undergraduate" education—an additional "internship" is required for medical licensure, and two or more years of "residency" are required for specialty certification. Internship and residency training are notorious as the most intense phase of training in Biomedicine. In 1983, interns in the United States were reported to work a mean of 85.6 hours per week, not including hours "on call"; residents worked between 66.5 and 73.4 hours per week (Hough and Bazzoli 1985). Commonly, residents are on night duty every third or fourth night—a mean of eight nights per month—working with no sleep for as many as thirty-six hours. High rates of depression are reported, along with fatigue; and relationships with spouse and others suffer from lack of time, energy, and attention.

A matter of intense concern to trainees as well as educators, internship and residency training have been referred to as "hazing" (Cousins 1981), and many observers, including physicians, have argued that there is substantial evidence of short- and long-term detrimental effects of the deprivations of this training and little evidence of any beneficial effects (Asken and Raham 1983; McCue 1985). Many residency programs offer support groups, professional counselors, or part-time residencies to reduce the stresses of residency training. In the late 1970s, residency programs in family medicine and psychiatry were most likely to offer such support; programs in surgery were the least likely (Berg and Garrard 1980).

Studies of medical internship parallel the Becker and Merton studies on undergraduate medical education. Miller (1970) approximates the former as he describes the ways in which interns in a city hospital program associated with a university expend much effort learning the ropes in addition to developing skills for later medical practice and research. Miller describes the major activity of the "elite intern" to be coping with competing demands in an institution not designed to suit his purposes of further training.

In contrast, Mumford (1970), a researcher in *The Student Physician* project, compares the experience of residency in a community hospital setting and a university hospital and finds that the community hospital inculcates enduring understandings, values, and habits in its interns very different from what is taught in the university hospital, with its focus on research, teaching, and specialization. Community hospital interns encounter the more common problems of patients; they believe that rapport with patients is an essential part of their practice; and they intend to establish private medical practice following their internships. University hospital residents seek out complex patient problems; they give little importance to their rapport with patients; and they anticipate careers in medical research and hospital practice. These institutions are themselves culturally distinct.

It is during residency training that individual patterns of practice are formed. A resident in orthopedic surgery comments, "This is the thing about being a resident. It is a time to decide what you are going to do in the real practice" (Knafl and Burkett 1975). Even within specialties such as surgery, residents learn that decisions are often not "clear-cut." They must develop

"treatment philosophies." Orthopedic surgeons, for example, choose between "conservative" philosophies that favor restricting invasive surgery
when less invasive approaches may work or "liberal" philosophies that favor
surgical approaches over others. Choice of philosophy is often guided by
personal experience and by the practices of mentors rather than by systematic
review of scientific foundations (Knafl and Burkett 1975).

While most studies of medical education have focused on the contents
of medical culture and specialty subcultures, the research of Bucher and
Stelling 1977; Stelling and Bucher 1979) has examined the processes by
which this learning takes place. Bucher and Stelling asked (my phrasing),
"What is it about the social environment of graduate education that leads
professionals-in-the-making to adopt their basic orientations, values, and
habits?" The researchers compare the training of psychiatrists in psychoanalytic programs, psychiatrists in public hospital settings, internists, and
Ph.D. candidates in biochemistry; they conclude, "It is primarily through
their role playing activities that trainees derive their sense of mastery, their
definitions of what constitutes the really interesting and important work of
the profession, and their perceptions of their own future professional roles"
(1979:148–49). Stelling and Bucher also claim (1979:153) that "the residents learned to size up their supposed mentors and to manage the interaction
so as to maximize their own learning and minimize interference." Residents
do not directly model their own behavior on that of their mentors, but choose
those characteristics of selected mentors to combine in their own ideal.

RELATIONS BETWEEN PHYSICIANS AND
THEIR PATIENTS

In this section, I examine the work of medicine by exploring
relations between physicians and their patients. Social science research on the
patient-physician relationship has deployed a rich diversity of quantitative
and qualitative methods (Roter and Frankel 1992). I first outline the scope
and magnitude of patient and physician populations and their contacts in
contemporary U.S. society. Next I review patterns of patient-physician communication—the observable *text* of this relationship. I analyze the underlying psychodynamics of this relationship—its *subtext*—as well as the broader
social environment within which patients and physicians interact—its *context*. The work of medicine includes far more than the diagnosis and treatment of patients—for example, relations with medical colleagues and others, administrative and financial relations with institutions, interactions
with settings and equipment, and research and continuing learning. I focus
on relations between physician and patient as the principal object of the
broader enterprise.

Patients

In 1990, 8.9 percent of persons in the United States assessed their own health as "fair" or "poor" (CDC 1992a). The prevalence of fair or poor health was slightly higher for women than for men, almost twice as high for blacks as for whites, lower with higher family income, and greater at older ages— almost a third of persons seventy-five years or older assessed their health as fair or poor, compared with less than 6 percent of persons between the ages of fifteen and forty-four. Also in 1990, almost 9 percent of the U.S. population reported being restricted or unable to carry out "major activity" because of a chronic condition, such as arthritis or asthma. Men and women were similarly restricted, but again rates were higher among blacks than whites, lower with higher family incomes, and greater at older ages (CDC 1992a).

In 1990, U.S. residents spent approximately $2,566 per person on health care; only 18.9 percent of this amount went directly to physician services, but an additional 61.5 percent was spent on services and supplies prescribed by physicians (Levit et al. 1991). The ability to pay for health care differed widely among segments of the population. In 1989, 15.7 percent of the population under sixty-five years of age—more than 34 million persons— were not covered by any health insurance (CDC 1992a). A greater proportion of men (16.4 percent) than women (14.9 percent) were uninsured, more blacks (22.0 percent) than whites (14.5 percent), and a far greater number of persons with low than with higher family incomes (3.2 percent among persons with incomes of $50,000 and above, and 37.3 percent among persons with incomes less than $14,000); there was no clear association between age and lack of insurance. At ages sixty-five and older, all were covered, in theory, by Medicare.

In 1990, U.S. residents had approximately 1,375 million contacts with physicians—about 5.5 per person; 60 percent were visits to physicians' offices, the remainder to hospital outpatient departments, clinics, or contacts such as home visits or phone consultations (CDC 1992a). The number of contacts was greater for women (6.1) than for men (4.7), slightly higher for whites (5.3) than for blacks (4.9); contact frequency varied little by income, but increased with age. Patients reported that 41.3 percent of visits to physicians' offices lasted no more than ten minutes.

The number of persons in the population per physician has declined substantially in recent decades—from approximately 700:1 in 1950 to approximately 500:1 in 1990. All of this decline, however, is due to the increase in specialists. In 1989, there were approximately 1,800 patients for each physician in primary care practice—family medicine, internal medicine, or pediatrics.

In the U.S. population overall in 1990, there were approximately 9.1 hospital discharges per 100 persons—for a national total of approximately 22.7 million hospitalizations. The rate was similar for men and women, higher for blacks (11.2) than for whites (9.0), declined with increasing income, and increased rapidly with age (CDC 1992a). Males of all ages combined underwent 8.5 million operations in 1990, females 14.5 million. Many operations on males were for conditions of the heart or the musculoskeletal system; 40 percent of operations on females were for obstetrical or gynecological events—principally birth—approximately 4 million per year (CDC 1992a).

It should be noted that by no means do all persons who regard themselves as sick seek care from physicians; nor—from the Biomedical perspective— are all persons who seek medical care sick. The classic study by White, Williams, and Greenberg (1961), though perhaps dated in detail, indicates the role of Biomedicine within the broader picture of the experience of sickness. Based on various surveys, White and colleagues estimated that of 1,000 adults, as many as 750 experienced an illness or an injury during any given month. Of these, 250 consulted a physician, 9 were hospitalized, 5 were referred to another physician for further consultation, and 1 was referred to a university medical center for specialty, "tertiary" care. Thus, only one-third of sickness episodes were brought to medical attention.

The use of medical care varies substantially by sickness condition. According to the current National Health Interview Survey, which interviews a sample of almost 50,000 U.S. residents a year, approximately one-third of persons who experience headache or influenza seek medical care, whereas all persons with conditions of the skin or eyes or, for women, the genital tract, seek medical attention (CDC 1992c). Anthropologist Noel Chrisman has described the "health seeking process" by which individuals from different cultural backgrounds who experience sickness decide what to do, often in consultation with their families (Chrisman 1977).

Beyond contacts with Biomedicine, an estimated third of the U.S. population reports consulting with one or more non-Biomedical practitioner (such as acupuncturists, chiropractors, and massage therapists) during the course of a year (Eisenberg et al. 1993). Perhaps contrary to expectation, use of such therapies is more common among persons with college education and higher income than among persons with less formal education and lower income. Patients using alternative therapies make an average of nineteen visits per year for a national annual total of approximately 425 million visits. Those who consult with physicians as well as non-Biomedical healers often do not inform their physicians of their alternative treatment. Patients with conditions regarded as severe commonly consult Biomedical practitioners in addition to alternative therapists; 3 percent of persons see only alternative healers; 33 percent consult neither Biomedical nor alternative healers. (The estimate of proportions of the population who do not consult physicians differs from that of White and colleagues [1961], perhaps because White used information about conditions during the preceding month rather than the preceding year, perhaps because he considered different sorts of conditions.) Overall, patients spend $13.7 billion annually on alternative healing services in addition to the costs of prescribed treatments.

These alternative therapies are referred to as "unconventional medicine" because they are not commonly taught during medical training; from the perspective of patients, however, they are far from unconventional, accounting for an equivalent of more than a third of the number of visits to Biomedical physicians.

Physicians and Patients

Why do people go to see physicians? What happens during the encounters of patients and physicians? How is information exchanged? What else is exchanged? How do exchanges differ in different settings and among patients and physicians with distinctive characteristics? What are the effects of these exchanges on subsequent patient attitudes and behavior? What cultural rules govern the encounter of patient and physician?

First, what do patients want? Oddly enough, it is difficult to ascertain just what patients want from their physicians. Mary-Jo and Byron Good provide insight on this critical question in their study of what patients say they want as they attend one of several primary care settings—a private rural clinic, a university medical center family practice, a free clinic for women, and a holistic health clinic (staffed by two Biomedical physicians as well as an acupuncturist, a nutritionist, and a Feldenkreis "body worker") (Good and Good 1982). The Goods conducted in-depth interviews to develop a questionnaire and a list of thirteen distinctive patient concerns, including explanation, diagnosis, test results, treatment requests, medications, and so on. In each setting, patients ranked the relative importance of each concern.

Test results ranked as the first concern in two settings (the family practice clinic and the women's clinic), treatment requests in one setting (the rural clinic), and the sharing of perspectives in one setting (the holistic health clinic); explanation ranked second in all settings except the holistic health clinic. The Goods concluded that "information seeking is a foremost goal of patients in primary care settings" (1982:287). Proportions of patients interested in information ranged from 61 percent in the rural clinic to 96 percent in the free clinic for women. In contrast, the desire for tests ranged from 33 percent in both the rural and the university clinics to 46 percent in the free clinic (principally for pregnancy tests). And requests for medication ranged from 7 percent in the holistic health center to 49 percent in the free women's clinic (principally for contraceptives).

Other researchers have focused more narrowly on what patients want in terms of information and participation in decision making. In a national survey, Harris and Associates report that 94 percent of the public wants to be told "everything" about their medical care and 72 percent prefer to participate jointly with their physicians in decision making (Harris and Assoc.

1982). Other studies have examined attitudes and practices in local or regional areas of the country. In a survey of metropolitan and rural areas in a midwestern state, 60 percent of patients were found to desire an active role in medical decision making; however, only 47 percent of patients had ever challenged their physicians' explanations or recommendations (Haug and Lavin 1981). Younger patients and patients who had experienced a significant error on the part of their physicians were more likely to adopt the "consumerist" position. (The 1982 Harris poll of U.S. adults found that 21 percent had refused a recommended treatment and 36 percent had changed physician because of disagreement.) In the same study, 81 percent of physicians supported a strong role for patients; however, few physicians accepted patient challenges to their explanations and recommendations. (The 1982 Harris poll of U.S. physicians found that 75 percent believed it was their responsibility to persuade patients of the best course of action.)

Similarly, a 1979 study of cancer patients found that between 80 percent and 96 percent of patients preferred to be given "bad" as well as "good" information, and most preferred a maximum rather than a minimum of information (Cassileth et al. 1980). Between 51 percent and 87 percent of patients preferred active participation in their medical decisions. Desire for information and participation was greater among younger than among older patients. And a study of patients in hypertension treatment programs found that the desire for participation in medical decision making varied by treatment setting: it was lowest (39 percent) for patients in a VA hospital, higher for patients in a community hospital (54 percent), and highest in an HMO (63 percent) (Strull, Lo, and Charles 1984). It may be that patients with particular attitudes and behaviors are more likely to attend one of these facilities than another; but it is also possible that the facility fosters an environment in which preferences for participation differ. These researchers found that, though physicians *underestimated* the amount of information wanted by patients, they *overestimated* the desire of patients to participate in medical decisions.

What do patients get? A study of the communication behavior of patients and physicians in a university primary care internal medicine clinic indicates that the concerns patients bring to their physicians are not well heard (Beckman and Frankel 1984). Beckman and Frankel scrutinized seventy-four tape-recorded interviews and found that only in 23 percent did the physician provide the opportunity for patients to fully describe their concerns; when patients succeeded in presenting their concerns, most of their presentations lasted less than a minute, and the longest took two and a half minutes. On the average, physicians interrupted patients eighteen seconds after they had begun to describe their concerns, by which time patients had usually expressed only one matter. The physicians may have assumed that patients had only one concern or that they were presenting their principal concern first. Once having interrupted, physicians invited completion of the patient's description in only one case out of fifty-two. Beckman and Frankel found that physician's paraphrasings and requests for elaboration derailed patients' completion of their lists, whereas expressions such as "go on" and "I see" encouraged completion.

In the late 1970s, in order to study medical communication skills, Duffy and colleagues observed a group of interns and residents in sixty patient interviews (Duffy, Hamerman, and Cohen 1980). Of ten skills examined, five were observed not to be practiced in 25 percent or more of patient encounters. In three-fourths of the encounters, the physicians allowed their patients to ask questions; in only 62 percent did physicians explain to patients their conditions, while patients were asked what they understood of their conditions in only 27 percent of interviews; patients' recent social histories were elicited in only 59 percent of interviews and their emotional responses were ascertained in only 35 percent. The residents commented that

1. The role of the internist is to care for "medical" problems, not "psychosocial" problems.
2. The internist has insufficient time to deal with the social and psychological problems of his or her patients.
3. Talking with a patient about his or her emotional distress is too painful for the patient and is best not done.
4. It is a waste of time to address a patient's psychosocial problems because these problems are beyond the internist's capacity to solve. (1980:356)

During the 1970s, physician-sociologist Howard Waitzkin and colleagues tape-recorded and closely analyzed the sequence of events in 336 patient-physician interactions randomly selected among physicians in three settings—the practices of internists in a Massachusetts county, an outpatient clinic and private practices in two counties in California, and a large hospital in Boston (Waitzkin 1985). The diversity of these settings suggests that Waitzkin's sample is indicative of the range of patient-physician interactions in the United States. Waitzkin investigated the hypothesis that physicians withheld information and maintained uncertainty in order to preserve their power over patients. He was also interested in barriers to physician-patient communication that might be associated with differences in communicational styles among socioeconomic classes.

Waitzkin focused on the exchange of information in the patient-physician encounter, which lasted an average of 16.5 minutes. Over the course of the encounter, patients spent an average of 8 seconds asking questions of their physicians. Physicians *believed* they spent an average of almost 9 minutes providing information to patients; however, they actually spent less than 40 seconds. Patients were asked how much information they wanted; physicians were also asked how much information their patients wanted. Physicians overestimated the information wanted by patients in 6 percent of encounters and underestimated the amount of information wanted in 65 percent of encounters.

The amount of explanation and the appropriateness of information that physicians gave (in language corresponding to the patient's background) was affected by the characteristics of patients, physicians themselves, and setting. Physicians with higher incomes gave fewer and less appropriate explanations—probably because they saw patients more quickly, the source of their greater incomes. Physicians with liberal values gave more explanations and explanations appropriate to the patient's knowledge. Physicians with a greater "need for power" (as assessed in a questionnaire) gave less appropriate information. Older patients, women, long-standing patients, and patients from higher socioeconomic classes were provided with more information that was also more appropriate. Waitzkin reports that patients of the working class as well as middle and upper classes desire information.

Waitzkin's hypothesis that physicians maintain their power by controlling information and uncertainty was not confirmed in this study. His analysis suggested, however, that though middle-class patients communicate directly and verbally, working-class patients tend to communicate nonverbally, using tone and gesture to indicate their concerns; this difference creates a potential barrier in patient-physician communication when patients are from the working class and, as is often the case, physicians are from the middle or upper class.

The Harris poll of U.S. adults (1982) also found a substantial discrepancy between the perspectives of patients and physicians regarding events that occurred when they met. Ninety-eight percent of physicians reported that they discussed the prognosis of patients' conditions with their patients, but only 78 percent of patients reported that they were informed of their prognoses. Ninety-six percent of physicians reported that they discussed the nature and purpose of recommended treatments with their patients, but again, only 78 percent of patients reported that they were informed about recommended treatments. Eighty-four percent of physicians said they informed patients about the pros and cons of alternative treatments and 93 percent said they told patients about side effects, but only 68 percent of patients reported being informed about pros and cons and side effects. Assuming that both parties are accurately reporting their behavior, there are obvious gaps in communication between patients and their physicians. When physicians withheld information, they said they did so because patients could not cope with the information (34 percent), or they would not understand it (28 percent); some withheld information by request of the patient's family (21 percent) or of the patient (16 percent).

Since the 1960s, beginning with the study of pediatric clinics by Korsch and colleagues (1972), many researchers have systematically analyzed the interactions between patients and physicians by direct observation or by audio or video recording. Roter and Hall have synthesized the results of more than forty studies of patient-physician interactions, their circumstances, and their outcomes (Roter, Hall, and Katz 1988; Roter and Hall 1989; Hall, Roter, and Katz 1988). The separate studies examined almost 250 characteristics of the interaction process, and Roter and Hall then summarized these characteristics into six aspects of the interaction—information-giving, information-seeking, social talk, positive talk, negative talk, and partnership building. They assessed the association of interaction with three characteristics of patients (gender, age, and class) and three outcomes (patient satisfaction, recall and understanding of information, and patient "compliance" with the physician's recommendation).

Like Waitzkin, Roter and Hall find that patient-physician interactions (in the United States) last a median of 16.5 minutes; patients produce less than 40 percent of the dialogue—mostly providing information—while physicians produce the rest. Overall, Roter and Hall report, "the minority of patients are given adequate information about the drugs they take or their medical condition. What is worse, patients forget a great deal of what they are told; in fact, on average most estimates of patient recall are only about 50% of the facts communicated by the physician" (1989:167).

Also like Waitzkin, Roter and Hall find that older patients, females, and middle- and upper-class patients are likely to receive more information than younger, male, and working-class patients. Summarizing many studies, they conclude that patients who receive more information are much more likely to be satisfied with the encounter, much more likely to understand and recall the information received, and more likely to comply with the physician's recommendations. They note that the more questions physicians ask, the less likely patients are to comply with physician recommendations. Patients who hear more "negative," hostile talk from their physicians are also less likely to comply with the physician's recommendations, whereas those who hear more "positive," supportive, and pleasant talk are more likely to be satisfied.

In diverse settings, social scientists have examined the organization of "discourse"—normal conversation, interviews, classroom instruction, and other forms of verbal interaction—in order to formulate what rules are followed about who goes first, who chooses and changes topics, who interrupts, how misunderstandings are corrected, and how the interaction is closed. Analysts of medical discourse have formulated some rules thought to underlie the observed patterns of verbal exchange between patients and physicians. Though the relationship is sometimes described as physician domination, analysts point out the consensual basis of the exchange (West 1984).

One rule commonly noted is the "dispreference for patient-initiated questions." "Overwhelmingly it has been shown that physicians ask and patients answer questions" (Beckman and Frankel 1984:694). For example, observers in a study of a family practice setting noted that 91 percent of questions were initiated by the physician and only 9 percent by the patient; of twenty-one interactions observed, the greatest proportion of questions initiated by any patient was 50 percent and 19 percent of patients did not ask a single question (West 1984). Patient acceptance of the question initiation rule is suggested by the high frequency (46 percent) of verbal disturbances, such as stuttering, recorded in patient speech (West 1984). Analysts have also noted that physicians control the flow and content of dialogue by interrupting, restricting patient responses with "closed-ended" questions, using jargon, changing topics, and not responding. In one study, 2 percent of physician-initiated and 13 percent of patient-initiated questions were unanswered (West 1984).

Observers have also examined the emotional exchanges between patients and physicians. Hall, Roter, and Rand (1981) analyzed fifty interactions and assessed the anger, sympathy, and anxiety manifested by patients and physicians; they also examined the assertiveness and satisfaction of patients and the dominance and businesslike manner of physicians. The researchers compared assessments of audiotaped interactions with written transcripts and with audiorecordings in which the words were made uninterpretable by electronic manipulation, but emotional tone was still recognizable. (It is notable that there was little correspondence between the emotions judged from nonverbal recordings and those from transcript or full recording.)

The researchers found that patients and physicians tended to match each other in terms of emotions as judged by the analysts; when the physician was perceived as sympathetic, so was the patient (and vice versa), and when the physician was perceived as angry, so was the patient (and vice versa). They also found that verbally expressed anxiety on the part of physicians was associated with lower satisfaction, but greater subsequent compliance on the part of patients. Surprisingly, nonverbal physician anger predicted greater patient satisfaction. A businesslike verbal manner on the part of physicians was also associated with greater patient satisfaction.

Physical contact and examination is another essential component of many medical encounters. An extreme example, the vaginal examination, illustrates the separation of the culture of Biomedicine from the culture of daily life in the United States and the elaborate rules required to maintain this separation. In ordinary life, the touching of genitalia is deemed legitimate and not abusive only between consenting intimates and, with restrictions, between parent and child. Among adults, public exposure of the genitalia is most often regarded as illegal if not immoral, prurient, and obscene. Children are taught to hide their genitals by dress and by behavior. Inadvertent exposure commonly evokes embarrassment on the part of both parties—the exposed and the witness.

On the other hand, in Biomedicine, the touching and examination of the genitals is regarded (at least by physicians) as essential both for routine disease prevention and for the treatment of specific conditions. Ritualistic procedures have evolved to clarify the separation of daily life and Biomedical practice in the touching of genitalia. Emerson (1970) describes the delicate performances required on the part of (mostly male) physicians to balance a demonstration of care and concern for the patient with a definition of nonsexuality and distance in the vaginal exam. Henslin and Biggs (1971) describe a process of depersonalization and desexualization as the woman patient moves from the waiting room to the physician's office and then the examination room. In the examination room, the woman exposes herself below the waist; her legs are covered with a sheet that visually isolates her from the physician and from her pelvic area; the physician wears a glove, symbolizing his distance, as well as reducing possible contamination. Henslin and Biggs argue that, during the exam, the woman has become "a pelvic." Emerson notes additional gestures of separation and distance from daily life and personal involvement as the physician avoids reference to the vulgar expression, "spread your legs," and says instead, "let your knees fall apart," and as he refers to "*the* vagina" instead of "*your* vagina." The woman is restored to a patient as she dresses and consults with the physician in his office; she fully becomes a person again when she returns to the reception room.

Subtext: Unconscious Foundations of Patient-Physician Relations

Most often hidden from human consciousness is a dense web of feelings that accompanies and underlies thought and action. People interact with others not simply on the basis of their own immediate and current interests and the perceptible features of others, but also of long-standing personal desires and the features that others represent of significant persons from the past. What is perceived as the "outside" world is to a significant extent the world of internal images "projected" outward; actions that appear to respond to current circumstances may be the acting out of unfinished dramas from one's past.

The persistent and pervasive unconscious presence is important in multiple ways in patient-physician relations. It affects the patient's perception of his or her condition and may affect the way in which conditions are acquired; it may also affect the patient's presentation of conditions in medical settings and his or her perception of the physician—as a parent figure, for example, a protector, savior, or threat. The multiple effects of unconscious processes in the patient's situation—referred to as "transference"—are increasingly recognized in Biomedicine, particularly within some specialties, such as family medicine and psychiatry.

The reciprocal process is also crucial and was early recognized by Freud, principally for the purposes of psychoanalysis. It has been elucidated by medical anthropologist Howard Stein, who has worked extensively in the training of family practice residents and other medical personnel (Stein 1985b). Physicians may come to their medical career because of powerful and most often unrecognized psychodynamic processes; facets of their medical work may represent and play out personal issues from their own past. Manifestations of these processes are referred to as "countertransference"—transference on the part of healers. With the exception of psychoanalysis—a therapeutic practice most often requiring prior Biomedical training—the relevance if not the existence of countertransference is ignored in Biomedicine. Countertransference conflicts with the Biomedical values of objectivity, rationality, certainty, and, it is believed, science. Acknowledgment of countertransference might constrain action (which may be acting-out) and diminish control (because events may be affected by unacknowledged forces).

Context: Social Foundations of Patient-Physician Relations

Interactions between patients and their physicians are shaped not only by the unconscious personal histories that both bring to the clinical setting but also by the powerful forces of the surrounding society (see chapter 4). The influences of societal forces on medical practice have been perhaps most carefully examined in sociologist-physician Howard Waitzkin's studies of the "micropolitics" of clinical settings (for example, Waitzkin 1979). Social forces affect medical encounters by (1) causing the conditions of sickness that patients bring to the clinic, (2) mirroring societal organization in the clinic itself, (3) fostering forms of interaction between patient and physician that ignore the social roots of sickness, and (4) thereby reproducing the social order. Like unconscious personal influences, social forces are often invisible to participants; these forces may thus be reenacted and reinforced in the medical arena.

As described in greater detail in chapter 4, many of the conditions that patients bring to medical settings have their origins in the way in which society is organized—in socially arranged work and leisure activities and their distribution among persons of different "races," genders, social classes, and religious and cultural backgrounds; I refer to these powerful effects as the "social production of sickness." Because of their social circumstances, individuals with differing characteristics have different exposures to the hazards (and the protections) associated with particular settings. Also associated with their social characteristics, they are more or less likely to have resources that provide them (or fail to provide them) with different forms of care. In sum, social organization significantly affects events of sickness and healing.

I have also presented evidence earlier in this chapter that the hierarchy of society is mirrored in the organization of medicine. The physicians who, at least until recently, have been the dominant force in the organization of Biomedicine and its clinical settings largely come from the upper classes of society. As Waitzkin's studies indicate, reinforced by the Biomedical theory of disease causation that focuses on biological processes, the control of talk within medical encounters by physicians minimizes recognition of the social origins of patients' conditions (Waitzkin 1985, 1989a). By a process described as "medicalization," conditions whose origins are in part social, such as job stress, marital problems, and abuse, are increasingly treated as medical conditions so that their social origins are not addressed. Moreover, physician control reinforces societal ideas about the distribution of knowledge and authority. Sicknesses are cast as problems of the body and its immediate environment. They are conceived of as the problems of individuals rather than groups of persons in certain social positions: "Management of contextual difficulties takes place in several ways: through subtle ideological messages that reinforce adherence to mainstream expectations, through systematic in-attention to the possibility of social reform or collective action, and through therapeutic actions that provide personal gratification while enhancing social control and encouraging consent" (Waitzkin 1989:436).

Because the Biomedical setting reproduces the social order and its relationships, and because, in doing so, it masks its own social context, it effectively perpetuates that social order rather than changing it and rather than addressing the deeper societal roots of sickness.

7
A WORLD OF INTERNAL MEDICINE: PORTRAIT OF AN INTERNIST

> Nothing is black or white. I'm beginning to think there's no such things as black or white. When they're dead, they're white.
> —*Barry Siegler, M.D., 1979*

In the late 1970s, I spent five months observing a practitioner of general internal medicine in his daily work. Here I portray the thought world of this practitioner, sketching the premises, attitudes, and values that guide, express, and rationalize his experience of medicine, its troubles and its pleasures. I formulate the coherence and incoherence of his thought, its dominant metaphors. I explore the ways in which general internal medicine corresponds to this practitioner's consciousness, action, and environment. I refer to him as "Barry Siegler," though this is not his name.

The development of internal medicine in the United States followed the attention of late-nineteenth-century physicians to the scientific medicine of Germany (Bloomfield 1979). The first German congress of internists was held in 1882, followed by publication of a journal *Centralblatt für Innere Medizin*—inner medicine. Internists became recognized as "distinguished from general practitioners by their investigative spirit and their deeper knowledge of pathophysiology" (Luce and Byyny 1979:384).

At the 1916 American Congress on Internal Medicine, First Scientific Session, in New York, President Reynold Webb Wilcox defined "The Field of Internal Medicine," listing twelve topics of the field: parasitic, infectious, and "constitutional" diseases, intoxications, digestive diseases, diseases of blood and ductless glands, circulatory system, respiratory system, mediastinum, urinary system, and muscular system (Wilcox 1916). In retrospect, it is surprising that "diseases of the nervous system, including those of the mind" were also on this list. Wilcox and his colleagues, however, maintained a reductionist view of mental phenomena, insisting on the dependence of internal medicine on the natural sciences and their "legitimate applications to that complex category of physio-chemical relationships, which we call life" (Stern and Cornwall 1916:11). "Medicine," he said, "is a brand of physical science" (p. 20). Wilcox's materialist stance was echoed by his colleague, Francis X. Dercum of Philadelphia: "the closer psychiatry is brought to internal medicine, the better both for the patient and the psychiatrist. A patient is a patient; he is sick in a material way" (1916:70).

Journals of internal medicine were established and the specialty achieved board certification in 1936. Internal medicine has assumed a central position in Biomedical practice, itself the parent of more subspecialties (twelve) than any other specialty.

Internal medicine is the mind, if not the heart, of Western medicine— Biomedicine. It is called simply "medicine." It is medicine's medicine, the generic and central specialty to which other specialties refer for the last word on our underlying ills, our "diseases." Internal medicine is perhaps the most rational among Biomedical specialties, advocating action by systematic calculation of the patient's pathophysiology in preference to more direct, surgical penetration for unobstructed vision and local intervention. Internists are inclined to favor reason over force and integral strategy over topical action.

Although its techniques are often vitally and lethally powerful, medicine is known among fellow specialties as "conservative." To "go medically" is purportedly to intervene more cautiously, to act mainly from outside the body's boundaries, "noninvasively." Perhaps it is to respect more fully the body's systemic, physiological process. Yet even noninvasive medicine can be more or less "aggressive," actively intervening or forbearing entirely—"doing nothing"—to allow a so-called natural course.

The work of general internal medicine was succinctly defined by another internist I observed as "physiological integrity." In this case study of Barry Siegler, I explore implications of the division implied by this definition. The division of the world into bodies and the nonbodily environment is closely allied with principles deeply embedded within our culture—mindbody dualism, individualism, and logical materialism (Dumont 1965; Fox 1979; Tocqueville 1969). These notions are manifest in my analysis of Barry Siegler.

I met Barry Siegler through a colleague and asked him if I might follow him in his work to learn what he did and how he thought. He consented. I accompanied him on daily hospital rounds, consultations at a hypertension clinic, office visits, and night and weekend call. Most often, Barry introduced me as "Dr. Hahn," as if I were a member of the medical team. I suspect

that even when he introduced me as an anthropologist, some patients believed me to be a medical specialist, another ———-ist, like a cardiologist or a
nephrologist. Barry would occasionally introduce me as a researcher observing the practice of medicine in the United States.

My participation in the scene I observed was minimal. I attempted not to
interrupt the press of medical work, the work of doctors and patients. As we
moved between medical events, Barry would often share with me his reactions to the events and persons he encountered; perhaps he did so to get his
thoughts off his chest, perhaps to inform me, perhaps for other reasons.
When the pace permitted, I would ask questions; or Barry might offer
unsolicited explanations. In minimal reciprocity, I took phone messages,
recalled phone numbers, and reminded Barry that he had been paged on the
loudspeaker system. Barry would sometimes call me as a witness to others in
the rounds team that he had said or done something. Some of the residents
were novices, and by the end of my study, I would occasionally watch them
make what I knew was, by Barry's standards, a mistake.

My ignorance of medicine proved both a handicap and an asset. Though I
learned some medicine on the job, I was never sufficiently well versed in its
principles to be able to evaluate or even to understand decisions made, to
assess intentions, alternatives, or consequences. But my ignorance gave me
the pleasure of encountering a new language—the dialect of medicine—rich
in its own forms and vocabulary. Medical talk maintains a separation from
patients and a distance from their suffering. Referring to cancer as "CA" and
to an amputation as "BK"—below the knee—may afford this double defense. I attempted to see the profusion of color in this language and to understand its medicalized interpretations—elevated, cut and cleaned, antiseptic.
Barry spoke this dialect with grace. He, too, seemed aware of its poetry.

I have paid close attention to the idioms and epithets that Barry repeats in
many settings. I analyze the life of his metaphors to discover how close a literal interpretation accompanies metaphorical allusion. In Barry's talk, references to God, sex, and excrement are more than simple metaphors. When
literal referents are nearby in time, the idiom is not simply "dead" metaphor.

The majority of the information I analyze is verbal, consisting of hundreds
of hours of Barry's talk with patients, residents, nurses, colleagues, and me.
The talk I recorded is principally "meta-medical"—in addition to being *a
part of* medical work, it is talk *about* medical work. I have explored the
interstices of Barry's medicine in the interludes between calculations of how
much medicine is required for this or that condition, between the gathering
and giving of more narrowly medical information, between visits with different patients. I have been less concerned with the details of medical logic
than with the framework in which this logic is set—its goals, its assumptions, and its uncertainties.

My own feelings about Barry will be apparent in my portrait. I was and
remain ambivalent, admiring his medical competence, his social and politi-

cal agility, yet disagreeing with his medicalized vision that ignored what I take to be the essence of persons, disliking also his vulgar and abusive remarks directed especially to women and to persons he held in moral contempt. Perhaps I have been insufficiently compassionate with the plight of his work, overwhelmed by his harsh expressions of suffering.

Little of Barry's dark side did I suspect as I began my work. From other work in the hospital, I knew of him only as a physician repeatedly paged on the hospital loudspeaker. I knew that he was highly respected and sought after. He was the first physician I approached for my study, and I was delighted that he accepted my request without hesitation. Several readers of this portrait, physicians among them, have commented that Barry is representative of many internists they have known.

Despite what I believe is my penetration of Barry's cosmological framework, I do not feel that I have shared Barry's more intimate feelings about his medical practice. He was guarded, defensive, and not highly introspective.

As with other internists I have followed, I believe that Barry derived some personal satisfaction in being thought sufficiently interesting to be closely observed by a serious anthropologist. But, thoroughly practical, Barry had little regard for "academics." I believe he was as often irked as stimulated by my probing and by some of the "liberal" values that may have been hidden or explicit in my questions, my beard, and my casual dress (though still within the mode of jacket and tie). Though I did not ask him, I believe that Barry also had mixed feelings about me.

Although Barry warmly accepted my request to accompany him in his work, he was cautious about my joining him in office visits, because, he said, it would slow him down too much, and he already "ran behind." In the hospital and clinic—his more public work—Barry was quite receptive. I believe that my presence affected his performance only a little, though people who worked with him told me he was gentler than usual in my company. While at some level highly self-aware, he did not seem inhibited. Only once or twice did he ask me not to repeat something he had said—his right, my obligation.

I do not think that Barry understood my search for his cosmic framework—a notion he might deny understanding or considering worthy. I believe he accepted my company as another contribution to the circummedical world. Highly competent in his work, he had nothing to hide. Perhaps through my work, he might serve as a model in the community, as he already does in his teaching.

I doubt that Barry would like my portrait. I was unable to arrange time in his schedule to talk with him about my findings. Yet, perhaps perversely, I take this avoidance as further evidence for my representation. Barry avoids the personal, the obscure corners, the psychiatric facets of others and himself. Medicine is a practice in which suffering and the self may be reduced to pathophysiological process, allowing the practitioner a more distant contact.

Internal medicine is not always approached in this way, but does provide such a path, well marked and well worn. Barry follows this path, though not with full success. However indirect, his language is fully passionate.

BARRY SIEGLER, PERSON AND WORK

Barry Siegler, in his early fifties when I studied him, has practiced general internal medicine in "Cartown," an American city of 200,000 people, for more than twenty years. "Call me Barry, Barry is fine," he said when I asked how I should address him.

Barry is of average height and medium build. Sometime before I met him, he had begun jogging and had lost twenty pounds—so he told one of his patients. He runs regularly in the evening or on weekends, sometimes for more than an hour. Occasionally he runs outside, but says he finds this boring; he prefers to run in his basement while listening to cassette tapes of talks on current medical topics.

Barry dresses neatly, without flamboyance. He wears a sports jacket and tie, occasionally a suit. He rarely wears a white coat on hospital rounds, but he often wears one in his office. He always carries his stethoscope, draped around his neck; he uses it frequently.

Barry was born, raised, and educated in a large midwestern city. He is married and has a close family with several grown children. Several of his children are studying in medical-related fields. When home from medical school, Barry's daughter joins him in hospital rounds. His influence on his children is strong; he remarks ironically, "They did not learn." Barry's wife is not employed. He says of her jokingly, "She was the only smart one; she married me."

Barry was raised as an Orthodox Jew, and though he rejected Orthodox practices when beginning college, he maintains a strong Jewish identity. It troubles him to eat ham, and he is acutely aware of who among his patients and his co-workers is Jewish and who Middle Eastern or German and thus, he suspects, possibly anti-Semitic. On one occasion, he was especially concerned that a Jewish patient be quickly treated so that she could be home for religious holidays.

Following a college premedical education, Barry served in the army as a medical aide and technician. He remarked to me of this experience, "When I was a lab technician in the army, I could deal with anything but snot." Bodily effluents are powerful symbols in Barry's corporeal world.

Barry completed medical school in Chicago, moved away for his internship and residency in internal medicine, and settled in Cartown. While many of the specifics of medical practice—knowledge of pathophysiology and therapeutic techniques—have changed since the time of his medical training, several general principles from that period remain firmly rooted in his thought. His insistence on the diagnostic "listening to the patient," his use of direct, firsthand observation rather than technologically mediated means of knowledge, his emphasis in diagnosis on considering multiple rather than single patient characteristics and on deductive rather than inductive explorations—all derive from his own medical education and are now prominent in his teaching.

Barry recalls also principles he was taught that did not make sense at the time, but that he came to understand through practice: "This is what they used to describe in medical school all the time as 'sixth sense.' . . . Never knew what the hell that was. And it finally dawned on me after being in practice that there is nothing like a sixth sense; it's just your experience, what you've seen. You can draw upon what you've heard other people describe, what you've seen yourself, what you've read, and your different approaches to putting things together."

Barry is the senior partner in a three-man group of general internists. The membership of the group has changed over the years. Recently, a fourth partner was asked to leave. I asked Barry what had happened, whether there had been a difference of policy. He reluctantly said only, "No, there was a difference of habit." Characteristically, he did not want to elaborate the conflict any further.

With his current partners, relations seem amicable. Barry says he is pleased by their cooperation; beyond their division of work, they voluntarily help each other. I asked Barry about the similarities and differences between his younger partners' medical practices and his own. "I think they're pretty close," he said. "By and large they are. We differ in some areas. They are more aggressive, freer with meds, faster to discharge, too fast labeling people as 'crocks,' taking a stance and not backing off. I think that's just. . . . I was exactly like that, and maybe I still am."

The three partners share an office suite and nursing and administrative staff. In order to use the office effectively, they divide their hours, so that one, or at most two, are there at a time. They overlap briefly each afternoon, when they meet for a review of hospitalized patients, administrative matters, and other news.

Since the three partners alternate in visiting the same patients in hospital rounds, they are continually aware of each other's assessments and responses. Most often they agree. Occasionally, Barry will note that a partner has failed to treat a patient as he would. For example, when a resident informs him that a partner has recommended surgery for an older patient with circulatory problems, he replies, "I go medically on them regardless."

On another occasion, when a resident tells him that a partner has not "put a patient on" an anticoagulant, Barry is troubled and irritated, and exclaims, "Ah, shit!" I believe he is annoyed both by the partner's failure in treatment of his patient, and by a more persistent difference in practice. Many of Barry's patients have cardiac or circulatory problems. He is thus highly sensitive to the unobstructed flow of their blood, and he believes that anticoagulants are used insufficiently, with potentially fatal results. "I run scared of pulmonary emboli," he says of blood clots that lodge in vessels of the lung, obstructing oxygen uptake and damaging lung tissue.

In the group practice, each partner has his own patients for whom he is primarily responsible; each also may consult on the patients of other physicians. Barry has treated some of his patients since he began his practice. He notes that his patients grow older as he does. Each partner not only does rounds on the others' hospitalized patients, but takes night and weekend call for the others and sees the others' patients when their primary physician is away. Patients are thus given both the long-term continuing care of one physician and the "coverage" by this physician's partners during his absence.

Although the ultimate goal of Barry's work is the physiological well-being of his patients, actions toward this goal are surrounded by a much broader field of acts, relations, and institutions. This "circum-medical" field (the term is mine, not Barry's) includes the institutions within which medicine is practiced, their physical settings and equipment, their personnel, and the still larger societal organizations of which medicine is a part. Each has its properties and rules of interaction; each constrains and/or facilitates Barry's more medical work. A large part of his thought and energy is directed toward circum-medical arrangements, and Barry is as agile here as he is within the field of medicine itself. He notes that work in the circum-medical field is "a part of medicine that people don't appreciate."

Barry participates extensively in the administrative and political activities of the medical community. He was recently president of the county medical society. He founded and now directs the local PSRO (Professional Standards Review Organization), which surveys the hospital stays of all federally funded patients in order to ensure proper but not excessive treatment. Barry believes that physicians can best control the inevitable government encroachment on medicine by early participation in the process. Participation, he knows, runs against the grain of many of his colleagues—his own too. As he says, "Physicians like to be their own *macher*" (Yiddish for "agent").

Barry has served as chief-of-medicine at one of the hospitals in Cartown, and during my stay with him, he was asked to serve as chief at another hospital. He declined, he told me, because of personality conflicts with the administrator. He participates on Cartown University and community committees concerned with medical matters—the selection of faculty in the university Department of Medicine, the opening of a local HMO (health maintenance organization), and the purchase of an expensive CAT (computerized axial tomography) scanner by a second Cartown hospital.

Barry did not support the purchase of a second CAT scanner. Although he believed this machine to be "a tremendous instrument, and the information is really, really, really excellent," he felt that, given its great expense, one machine in the community was enough. The members of the county medical society did not agree, and their delegate voted for purchase. The machine was procured and is widely used, by Barry as well as others.

Although he served on a committee to consider and plan the development of an HMO for Cartown, Barry has doubts about this form of medical practice. He would not want to practice in one. He feels the HMO salary system undermines motivation and would undermine his own: "I think I'd be much less efficient, because . . . I would probably, if I were human, over a period of time, begin to slacken off and work at the same pace as the slowest person in that group, because I've seen that happen. . . . Why the hell don't I just do what he does, get the same thing?" He adds that in HMOs, patients don't always see the same doctor, "and the satisfaction, a lot of personal satisfaction in contact diminishes."

Barry's life is scheduled far in advance. He knows when he will take his vacation next year, which weekends and nights he is on call, which mornings he will make rounds in which hospital, and the hourly contours of each day. These plans are generally changed only for emergencies. Patient emergencies are the business of being on call, but these and other emergencies may interrupt the remainder of the schedule as well.

Barry's time is structured by degrees of medical engagement—of access by patients and of his reciprocal obligation to respond. Each partner has intense time "on" but certain time "off" as well. When off, each is covered by his partners. Barry once referred to periods spent in the hospital as "clump time" and to periods at home waiting to be called as "scattered time." While medical work in the hospital is continuous, call at home leaves him always susceptible to interruption. Emergency calls reach the office as well. When I first went to meet Barry in his office to explain my study and to ask to observe him, he had rushed off to see a patient just hospitalized with an "MI" (myocardial infarction, or heart attack). I left to return another time; patients were delayed.

Barry's schedule marks out his location and the general scope of his work at different times, but not which patients he will see or what specific problems he will treat. The schedule provides slots for work whose size is limited in several dimensions. Certain problems can be dealt with in the hospital, but not in the office; or in afternoon working visits, but not in hospital rounds; or in the intensive care unit, but not on the floor, and so on. Barry tries to fit the work into his schedule. If parts do not fit, they are abandoned or postponed, or the schedule expands, extending Barry's day, delaying other appointments. He "runs behind."

Barry is oppressed by two sorts of temporal constraints: too much to do in the allotted time and the urgency of action imposed by what are too often literal "deadlines." Time is differently shaped accordingly: excess draws it out, imminence intensifies each moment.

Barry's day begins before rounds at one of two hospitals. He often has breakfast before rounds in the hospital cafeteria with residents, students on his service, and another physician colleague. Talk at breakfast is often about recent leisure activity, sports, or food. Sometimes Barry will be in the hospital before breakfast to read his patients' electrocardiograms and other laboratory reports.

During rounds, Barry walks through the busy hospital floors on which his patients are staying. He is accompanied by the rounds team—from three to eight people, possibly including pharmacists, pharmacy students, nurses, and social workers, in addition to the residents and medical students. Barry often has patients on medical, surgical, and obstetrical wards, the ICU (intensive care unit), and the CCU (cardiac care unit); occasionally he has a patient on the psychiatric ward. On each ward, the team stops at the nursing station to collect the patients' charts from a central rack. Before each patient visit, the resident assigned to the patient presents or updates the case, referring especially to recent clinical observations and the latest laboratory results. The resident also reviews or modifies the diagnosis and therapeutic recommendations or notes problems in their formulation.

Most of Barry's hospital medicine, including diagnosis and therapy, is conducted with residents in rounds and follow-up visits. Often it is on hospital rounds that appropriate information is elicited and evaluated, that false or irrelevant information is sought out and discarded, and that decisions regarding therapy and its termination are made and revised. Much of Barry's medicine is thought rather than action.

In the hospital, the residents and medical students are perhaps the most important persons among his circum-medical relations. Though they are on his service (and on their training clerkship in medicine) for only periods of several weeks, perhaps months, it is they who spend most medical time with hospital patients. Nurses spend much more time with Barry's patients than he does; beyond their nursing care, however, they are acting on medical decisions made by Barry, his partners, and the residents. In this capacity, their role is assistant and advisory.

The residents pass their days, often nights, in the hospital gathering information from patients, analyzing, and initiating or altering therapies. While Barry and his partners are the attending physicians for these patients, the residents carry out much of the diagnosis and therapy. (The "attending" is ultimately responsible for the care of a patient or a patient ward.)

Barry claims that 90 percent of medical practice is learned after medical school. In accordance with his thorough pragmatism, he believes in learning by doing and by being held responsible. He tells the residents that the patients are not his, but theirs: "You are the attending on all these. I'm just a bystander."

This authorization is rhetorical. Barry maintains a close watch over his apprentices. He questions them socratically, but he corrects them definitively. He is visibly disturbed when he thinks they have made a false diagnosis or initiated a harmful "therapy." During the course of my study, one resident especially irritated him. He was Middle Eastern, and I do not know whether Barry was irritated simply by the resident's errors, or whether his medical errors were judged by his foreign origins, more specifically, his Muslim background. Barry is generally suspicious of foreign practitioners as well as minority medical students and residents recruited through affirmative action. Of this resident, he commented, "The first rule of medicine is 'Do no harm.' His rule is 'Do something.'"

In the teaching rounds, Barry does not hesitate to support a resident's plausible or correct assertion. Nor does he hesitate to express his own uncertainty or ignorance on any matter. Uncertainty is a central, though dreadful part of the work. He uses it to teach; he urges backing off when uncertain, and he recommends holding alternative hypotheses.

Barry's teaching is conveyed in two verbal genres: *within-medicine* citations of knowledge about physiology and pathology, and *meta-medical* principles, that is, general principles about medicine, its reasoning, and its values. *Within-medicine* talk—the majority of his discourse—includes specific discussion of the characteristics of patients—for example, blood chemistry, temperature, radiological findings—and general reports from population studies—about pathophysiology, the efficacy of certain drugs, and so on. *Meta-medical* talk includes a variety of remarks about how medicine is and should be done. Much of this talk consists of epithets—verbal formulae repeated, with variant versions, in many circumstances. The epithetical status of this talk is attested by Barry's quotation of it—for example, "That's why we say, ' . . . '"—and by its frequent repetition. Barry's epithets may be common in the medical community. In both genres of medical talk, Barry shows considerable verbal agility, using strong language, while remaining attuned to nuances, undertones, and shades of meaning.

Following the resident's presentation of each patient and Barry's response, the rounds team enters the patient's room. In a room of several patients, one of the team members may draw a curtain to visually and symbolically separate this patient's space. Barry or the resident will greet the patient and may introduce others in the team to the patient, either as "the other doctors who work with us," or as "Dr. So-and-So."

Barry often greets familiar patients by first name, regardless of age. A few reciprocate, calling him "Barry"; most address him as "Doctor" or "Doctor Siegler." He will call female patients "Hun" (Honey) or "Sweetie," and encourage them, "That a gal." Male patients he often calls "Guy." He will address new or consult patients by their family names, but may still comment, "That a gal," "That a guy." In their absence, for example, in corridor talks with the residents, beyond the patient's earshot, he also refers to patients as "this guy," "this gal."

In Barry's work with patients, touch is important in many ways. He often shakes hands with new or old patients. During the rounds visit, he may put his hand on the patient's shoulder, or hold a hand, particularly with a female patient, and especially if the patient seems upset. Almost always, as he leaves a patient, he will again shake hands, touch the patient's shoulder, or gently squeeze the patient's foot. Sometimes he simply holds up his open hand, palm toward the patient, and says, "Take care." These are touches and gestures of greeting and reassurance. I believe they are symbolic for him as they are for patients, recalling a connection and a power to heal.

There is another kind of touching, a medical one. In knowing about patients and their conditions, Barry relies heavily upon his senses. He resists the distortion and distance fostered by high-technology medicine. Touch is essential. He applies his stethoscope to the patient's body to hear blood flow and heart sounds, bowel sounds, and respiration. He also percusses—to evaluate pulmonary and bowel function, and liver and heart location and size. He palpates bowel, liver, neck, armpits, and many pulses. With a tongue depressor, he examines mouth and throat; he "does" "pelvics" and "rectals." He feels the skin, and flexes joints to assess mobility and neurological condition. He may also dress and undress wounds and remove dead tissue. Less often his contact is invasive; he may draw blood or other fluids by syringe, or he may inject medicines.

The boundaries between social and medical touching are unclear. In the patient's response to greetings, Barry may discern diagnostic signs. Medical touchings may disturb, expose, and penetrate, but they may also reassure.

By the patient's bedside, the prototypical "clinical" setting, the contrast between talk directed to the patient and talk about the patient is striking. If the patient is comatose, little or nothing may be said to him or her. If stuporous or somnolent, for example from medications, simple greetings may pass. If asleep, the patient is often awakened. Barry asks patients who are awake and alert how they feel, and he may probe them on particular symptoms. In turn he may inform them in a brief, straightforward fashion of his current diagnosis, prognosis, or recommendations. In doing so, he uses little medical terminology and explains terms simply when he does. He gears his talk to what he takes to be the alertness, the intelligence, and the interests of the patient. He seldom presents sufficient information to allow the patient to evaluate alternatives or to consent well informed.

He has doubts about the abilities of some patients. When I say to him that a patient we have just seen did not seem very intelligent, he replies: "Well, that's what you say when you're talking to patients, you know. How do you know? [laughs] How do they understand what you're saying? It's so hard. God!"

Barry believes that patients should be informed of their conditions only to the extent they wish to know. He objects to the contemporary insistence on full disclosure: "That's inhumane. A lot of people don't want to know. A lot of people go to their graves hoping they're going to make it."

In contrast to talk to patients, talk among the medical team is more quiet, sometimes whispered; the number of syllables per word increases and the rate of speech accelerates. Occasionally, when the patient is familiar and alert, Barry may ask for a characteristic of the patient, using the patient's name and everyday language, "Mr. Jones's blood pressure." More often, he asks for the patient's vital signs by saying, for example, "What's the blood pressure?" in an impersonal manner. He may say of a somnolent patient, "Look at the sensorium." In the following interaction, most of Barry's talk is directed to his nurse rather than to the patient:

Barry: "What's the height?"

Nurse: "59 inches, 213 [pounds]."

Barry (to patient, a Native American): "You ought to grow an inch or so more. This way (gestures upward), not this (gestures sideways)."

To nurse: "Femoral pulses are of good quality. Testes are normal. There is a small cyst at the inferior pole to the left, of the right . . . of the right testis, about a half centimeter."

To the patient, much louder: "Cough please. . . . Cough again. Cough again. . . . Looks good. Looks good, sir. A little too much beer, but otherwise OK. . . . Take care now."

The patient's talk is not taken at face value—as an expression of his or her thoughts and feelings—but rather, diagnostically, as an index of bodily functions. Talk with patients is translated into the language of medicine and examined for medical indications—coherence, affective tone, correspondence to reality, and alteration from normal. Interest in the patient's world is suspended if not lost in an exploration of physiological disturbance.

In the halls, Barry greets other physicians, nurses, and hospital staff. At one hospital he warmly chats with an older cleaning woman, "Bessie," a Jew, who, he tells me, fled from Germany during the war. With nurses, Barry will sometimes request information about patients or additional equipment for some procedure; he may ask them to make certain observations about a patient or to change the patient's diet. He often makes flirtatious remarks to the nurses.

Among medical colleagues, the principal relations are relations of referral and consultation. A physician who consults with a colleague retains responsibility for the patient's treatment and may or may not follow the consultant's advice. When a physician refers a patient, treatment responsibility shifts temporarily to the second physician. Barry both makes and receives referrals and consults. He may refer a patient for a specific procedure—for example, surgery—expecting the patient to return for his long-term care. Or he may refer a patient to another physician's long-term care, if either he or the patient finds incompatible the other's interests or practices. Some patients remain despite the trouble they may make for him. Half jokingly, Barry comments on one patient and the physician who referred her: "He referred her to me twenty years ago, and I've never gotten even with him."

Barry is attempting to limit new patients in his practice and so is reluctant to accept new referrals. He accepts many of the frequent consults made to him. In these exchange relations, he is sometimes disturbed, as when the consulting physician requests the consultation too late or immediately before discharging the patient; the consulting physician may be more concerned with legal threats than with helping the patient. Barry is irritated also when the attending physician has made mistakes or continues to do so by not following Barry's recommendations. He complains, for example, of an old community physician who, he says, "treats symptoms." He asks himself sarcastically, "Why doesn't he retire?" He complains also that the surgeons, for whom he frequently consults, do not use anticoagulants sufficiently, leading to life-threatening blood clots. He complains, too, of obstetricians who fail to consider systemic problems. "You can't treat a woman like a pregnant uterus."

Difficulties also arise with patients who present diagnostic or therapeutic dilemmas. Physicians generally consult in areas beyond their expertise, on matters outside the scope of general medical practice. The intensity of some consultations became clear to me one morning when Barry remarked to the rounds team, "We were asked to see him when his heart stopped."

Barry himself also consults other physicians—surgeons, neurologists, psychiatrists, anaesthetists, obstetricians, pathologists, radiologists, and others—about his own patients. He is unsure in these specialty areas and is glad not to work there. He says of one patient, "I think this guy, if he's not psychotic, is severely neurotic. I'm the poorest psychiatrist. I am as poor a psychiatrist as I am a dermatologist." And of oncology, "It's a horrible specialty. I can't imagine doing that. But thank God some people are willing to do that. . . . Cancer is a big ball game. You've got to treat it with big guns on day one."

Barry relies on these experts, yet he is often troubled by two aspects of relations with them: the medical content or rationale of their advice and their violations of etiquette in the medical community. Delayed responses frustrate him particularly in critical situations. "That's communication again with surgeons. We just don't get it. I get very irritated by that—not knowing what's going on with patients." If dissatisfied with a consultant's response (or nonresponse), Barry may override the recommendations. "Screw him. Fuck the anaesthesiologist. He can call us! That frosts me. . . . He didn't call. He just wrote the order. That's not the way it's done. . . . I had a run in once with an anaesthesiologist." Violation of these social norms in the circum-medical arena multiplies the problems that haunt Barry's more medical work.

Occasionally Barry is disturbed with a consultant's response to nonmedical constraints. He believes, for example, that radiologists sometimes fail to commit themselves in reading an X-ray film because they do not wish to be held legally responsible. "They hedge. It's very difficult for them to say it's black or white. They say it's gray." Here legal fears are rationalized in terms of the nature of the work itself, that is, unclear pictures. Barry is annoyed by the recent legal preoccupation of physicians: "If you have to treat the lawyer, then get out of medicine."

Barry is most often friendly with colleagues, patting them on the back, joking with them, and exchanging news and information about patients. To patients and subordinates, as well as to colleagues, Barry most often presents a gentle manner, soft speech, and frequent smiles. Gentleness, however, may give way to controlled, sharp-tongued anger when, for example, a resident begins an ineffective or harmful treatment with only a vague rationale. Sometimes a deeper rage seems to lurk behind his gentleness, as when he makes an angry remark following a seemingly calm phone conversation or, on rounds, when he appears friendly and reassuring to a patient and then complains angrily about the patient afterward. I believe that Barry's anger is partially rooted in the persistent threats of impotence in his medicine. Barry is aware of anger, but uncertain of its object. "I'm a terror sometimes. I get very angry sometimes. I like to think my anger is directed at shitty nurses and shitty doctors."

At the same time Barry has a persistent and characteristic sense of humor that manifests itself not only in the instructive remarks he makes to residents, nurses, and fellow doctors, but also in the stories he repeats, for example:

"Tell you the story about how doctors never change their minds once they've made a decision? Did I tell you this?"

"No," I say.

"And they tell a story in one of the southern medical schools about a kid who saw a patient in the hospital, ill, and the guy said, 'Well, I know what your problem is, sir. You've got locked bowels.' And the guy said, 'But I got diarrhea all the time.' He said, 'That's right. They're locked in the open position.' "

Sexuality and excretion are common idioms in both his humor and his anger. They appear frequently in Barry's circum-medical relations and in his practice of medicine.

Barry tries to finish hospital rounds by 9:00 A.M. so that office patients do not wait. He rushes impatiently, often postponing until the afternoon what he planned for the morning. Still, patients at the office sometimes wait as long as two hours to see him. Most are scheduled far in advance; others, "squeeze-ins," call with problems felt to be urgent and are seen if the partners or staff concur on the urgency. Barry says that he himself waits about five minutes every five years, when patients do not show up for appointments.

Barry's patients are scheduled between 9:00 A.M. and the early afternoon. One day when I accompanied him, he saw twenty-eight patients between 9 and 2:45 P.M., 12.3 minutes per patient. Some of this time was spent other

than in the patients' presence. He completes and signs forms, talks with his
staff and partners, goes to the bathroom, and makes phone calls. Barry takes
no break; he eats no lunch.

Barry's office visits with patients differ from his hospital rounds. In the
office most patients are familiar, most of their problems routine. Office visits
often concern matters for which responses are standard and uncomplicated
and outcomes predictable—that is, mild acute diseases or chronic ones
not requiring hospitalization. "These are the 'simples,'" he says, "routine
chronic disease and things like that." "That's all we do in the office, take the
stitches out that someone else put in." In office visits, Barry may check that a
patient is taking a medicine as prescribed and that there are no new side
effects. He may inquire also about the patient's personal life. Barry seems to
enjoy these visits, as do his patients.

The office provides Barry relief from the too-regular "tragedies" of hospital
work. On several occasions of great frustration in hospital rounds—moments
in which he is unable to relieve a "disaster"—Barry half humorously expresses a wish for more "juicy pneumonias," that is, for patients with significant diseases that are easily and effectively treated. He balances the high
tension and excitement of hospital work with the more certain and comfortable, but less "interesting" success of office work.

The office staff is familiar with Barry's routines. Procedures run smoothly,
with minimal need for communication. When doing pelvic exams, Barry has
a nurse chaperone, telling the patient, "Let's have a gal give us a hand."
Nurses also show the patients to examination rooms, take their vital signs,
and later may give the injections Barry prescribes. They and other office staff
will also prepare much of the paper work and patient records. Before Barry
sees each patient, the nurses often brief him on particular problems the
patient has mentioned, or on some other condition of the patient she thinks
pertinent.

Barry is visibly affected by his patients and their conditions. He is greatly
troubled by some, exclaiming to me, "Boy, a lot of these people look great,
but Jeez, they've got their problems." He winces when a patient tells him he
is short of breath, indicating circulatory problems. He is angered when a
patient with "essential hypertension," now short of breath, admits he is not
restricting the salt in his diet: "Why don't you knock it off? You got to make
some judgment whether you want the difficulty breathing, or whether you
want the salt." He expresses to me his anger also at another patient's husband
who left her for another woman, upon which the patient's disease worsened,
leading to hospitalization. "Her husband—I could wring his balls off, if I
could get a hold of him."

After office hours, Barry returns to the hospital to visit patients, work
with residents, review laboratory results, and write medical notes and orders.
One afternoon a week he is attending physician at the local hypertension
clinic. In addition, he has meetings to attend. Barry often gets home only at

9 or 10 at night, and then may still be called, requiring that he return to the hospital if he cannot handle the problem over the phone.

Barry alternates call with his partners, so that he is "on" every third night and every third weekend. Call is more frequent when one of the partners is on vacation. On weekend call, Barry makes Saturday and Sunday morning rounds in both hospitals on all of the group's private and consult patients. He will most often spend the whole morning in the hospitals, and again he may be called back later if problems arise that he, the resident, or a nurse feels require his presence. The office is closed on weekends, but the partner on call will be available to patients by phone through an answering service, and patients will be admitted to the hospital if necessary.

Barry looks forward to time off. "Any time I'm off is good," he said when I asked if he had enjoyed a free weekend. He sometimes expresses a need for time off when none is scheduled. He notes the difficulty of getting back to work after he has been away; the momentum has been lost. On longer vacations, he drives with his family to a cottage up north, where he hunts and jogs. He enjoys the peace and relaxation they bring him.

GOD, NATURE, AND MORAL CERTAINTY

Barry is a religious man—not in detailed conviction or extensive practice, but in deep personal identity. His world is anchored in a distant and overarching order, at once natural, God-given, and largely unknown. When I asked him at breakfast one morning what remained from his Orthodox upbringing, he replied: "Intellectually it doesn't make any sense to me; emotionally it does. I don't believe in the image of God, I believe in something—Nature. If you let things alone, don't screw around, Nature takes care of them."

Here, Barry's description of his religion is a literal one. Often, however, his religious allusions appear to be metaphorical expressions of anger or frustration at his inability to achieve some end. Idioms of heaven and hell, blessing and damnation, and God or the Good Lord, permeate his speech in a manner that seems to hover between metaphorical and literal reference. Barry also makes religious allusions in talk with patients—for example, "The Good Lord doesn't want you yet." In making these remarks, he may laugh or smile or raise his hands upward. For someone raised in Orthodoxy who professes residual religious belief, allusions are likely to be more than casual idioms. Although perhaps not intended literally, the frequency and intensity of Barry's religious expressions hint at an underlying religious stance. But the interpretation of Barry's religious (and blasphemous) remarks is not straightforward.

The Nature to which Barry refers is distinct from the nature of science—devoid of spirit, disenchanted. Nature is essentially purposeful and often benign. It takes care of things, if only too mortal humans do not interfere. Barry says he believes in Nature; he professes faith beyond knowledge. Barry's world is one of a deified Nature.

In deified Nature lies the ultimate fund of knowledge and the control of human access to knowledge. To Barry's deep frustration, human access is severely limited. "We're really so damned limited. There ought to be a lot more we can do for these old people besides give them a place to sleep and eat."

Barry's God is distant, inaccessible. Barry expresses anger toward an oncologist who delays responding to his consultation, comparing the oncologist to an unreachable God: "I said, 'Shit, trying to call you is like trying to call God.' "

While remote, God is yet provident. At least metaphorically, the Good Lord is said to provide not only life itself but also healing "mechanisms" and relief from suffering. "The Good Lord provides for some good mechanisms to heal, if you just don't screw around too much. Who the hell knows why. If you just let him [holds up his hands] do his work, and don't try to prevent him [laughs]. . . . He [the patient] had about a hundred things wrong with him. And by the grace of God, he got better." My field notes on Barry begin with his remark at morning rounds, "Williams expired through the night. That's a blessing!"

Barry curses his ignorance, his inability to diagnose, to know what to do once a diagnosis has been reached, and to predict with certainty: "The goddamn medication and their side effects."

Disease itself is a curse—hellish—some deaths—those of seemingly healthy and young people—a "goddamn waste." [A patient has died.] "What a goddamn waste. Only thirty-four years old. He had a hyperthermic reaction in surgery." [Barry is informed that the patient's family refuses to donate the patient's organs.] "That's a waste. That makes it a bigger waste."

God's work does not seem to be consistently good. Too often God does not seem to provide the relief that patients and their conditions call for—relief, perhaps found only in death. "He's so sick, that poor guy. Why the hell doesn't the Good Lord take him?" There is tension here between Barry's conception of "the Good Lord" and this God's seeming inaction and his tolerance of suffering. Barry suggests that the Good Lord may not be so good.

There are a number of tensions among Barry's beliefs. While he sharply distinguishes emotion and judgment from science in medicine, he justifies his belief in Nature—the source of healing and medical practice—on emotional grounds. That is, emotion and faith here justify the principle of science and medical practice that Barry more often regards as their opposite.

Barry is by no means a theologian. Theology itself lies in the domain of judgment, and Barry mocks what he calls philosophical issues, quoting the medieval question, "How many angels are there on the head of a pin?" as an example of irrelevance and insolubility. Though the tension between science and judgment/emotion can be seen to run through his thought and his work, this is an "issue" without interest to him.

I cite further paradoxes to suggest an implicit principle that makes fuller sense of his beliefs than does deified Nature alone. If Nature provides healing, and if this is the goal of Nature, why, then, is there disease and suffering? Are they somehow good—to be left alone? If not, when is interference appropriate, and when does interference become "screwing around," a promiscuity disrupting Natural events? And, if human healing powers are limited in a Natural fashion, why should Barry be so frustrated? Barry's religious ideas do not fully explain his thought and action.

Barry's religious view stands alongside, and sometimes is opposed to, another principle implicit in his discourse; I refer to this principle as "Moral Certainty." By Moral Certainty, some events and acts are clearly right, others clearly wrong. Disease and suffering are clear evils; efforts to remedy and relieve them are certain obligations; and failures to act are certain wrongs. I believe that Moral Certainty is an unspoken principle that justifies, indeed compels, much of his medical and circum-medical action. It is a foundation of his commitment to his work.

Moral Certainty accounts for Barry's moralism—his ambivalence toward the treatment of an alcoholic and his reluctance to treat a "promiscuous," poor, single mother. Moral Certainty accounts for a significant facet of Barry's relations with his patients—that is, his presumption of their interests, his apparent knowledge of what is best for them. Most often he need not ask the patient because he knows. And he informs patients about their conditions and therapeutic options in a manner likely to elicit consent to what he, Barry, thinks best.

Finally, Moral Certainty makes sense of Barry's puzzlement at Natural tragedies. It provides firm grounds for questioning Natural events. Moral Certainty justifies intervention itself, for there seems to be little other reason to intervene if all that is Natural is good.

In sum, Barry's universe can be regarded as supported by two sets of principles: his Jewish upbringing which persists in a deified Nature, and a deep moral sense by which he knows what is right, what is evil. The two structures often coincide in Barry's work. On some issues, however, Moral Certainty contends directly with the deified Nature. The "Good Lord" does not always act in a manner that Barry knows to be good. At such times he comes to doubt the wisdom and powers of God's Nature itself. Here his moral sense prevails. He knows the proper course of action.

KNOWLEDGE IN MEDICINE

A focal objective of Barry's work is the correction of systemic physiological disturbance in his patients and the relief of concomitant suffering. Often he succeeds. It is his knowledge—general knowledge of the principles of physiology and pathophysiology and particular knowledge of individual patients—that allows him to affect and to predict the course of patients' conditions. It is the faults in his knowledge that lead him to fail when he fails, and the gaps and limits of his knowledge that often lead him not to act at all. These limits are of profound and perpetual significance to Barry. Faults and gaps demarcate his powers; they foreshadow health and disease, life and death, in his patients. Well within these limits, his medical practice is less "interesting." Near the severe, but uncertain limits of his knowledge, Barry derives the pleasures of his medicine. Beyond these limits lie prominent sources not only of his patients' suffering but of his own suffering as well.

In this section I examine distinctions that Barry makes among the domains of knowledge, principally a distinction between "science" and "judgment." I then follow the course of science in Barry's composition and use of "pictures"—his metaphor for the conditions of patients. Barry conceives of pictures in strikingly different ways—in a *realism* that concretizes conditions in fixed, Platonic forms—reality—and in a *nominalism* in which pictures become whimsical illusions. When pictures fail and Barry does too, his distinction between science and judgment collapses, and all is painfully a matter of arbitrary belief.

Science and Judgment

A distinction between "science" and "judgment," or "philosophy," runs through Barry's thought and expressions. It defines what he takes to be the logical basis of his work and sets off a domain in which he works comfortably from another which he avoids, sometimes fearfully. When medical findings on a patient do not clearly indicate a course of treatment, Barry remarks, "Then we come to the philosophy of this thing—not the science. What are we doing?"

Barry uses the term *judgment* in two different senses—a generic one that includes all cognitive processes and a more specific one that includes thought processes based on value and excludes those based on science. (The term is thus like the category "animal," which, in a broad sense, includes the category "human," and in a narrower sense contrasts with "human.") The examples above illustrate the narrower, more specific usage. In the broader usage, Barry says, for example, "This is the sequence of films. They're all different techniques. It's pretty hard to judge them. They don't look strikingly different to me." These "judgments" are not distinct from his science, but are a part of it. In the analysis that follows, I focus on the narrower sense of "judgment"—that which is opposed to "science."

Barry believes that science provides the rational grounds of his medical knowledge and decision making. Medical knowledge is ultimately based on scientific facts and principles. Yet, Barry also asserts that medicine is not yet a science in fact. Current medical knowledge is vastly deficient, and it is this deficiency that makes a part of his work so excruciating: "There's a lot of unpredictability, where, you know, we're not that scientific really, in terms of what we can do with the numbers and figures that we have. . . . Oh sure, we think we're knowledgeable now, but we're very, very dumb and very ignorant; yet the knowledge that we have now is much greater than it was ten, fifteen years ago."

I am by no means fully aware of the details and links in the chains of reasoning in Barry's medicine. From his working explanations, however, I draw several inferences about the structure of his medical thinking. Many of his comments attest detailed explanatory principles as well as more systematic, theoretical knowledge. When a resident does not understand a diagnosis or a therapy, Barry may elaborate an explanation connecting a variety of findings about the patient with general principles of pathophysiology. He thus gives evidence of a larger theoretical scheme that makes sense of his observations and justifies his actions.

In contrast, much of Barry's knowledge consists of empirical patterns of correlation and sequence—in the absence of known theoretical linkage. This and that occur together such-and-such percent of the time. The events connected by these relations include not only the course of the patient's condition untreated, but the effects of intervention as well. For much of what Barry knows, he has no explanation or only a partial one. Or, he may once have had an explanation, now forgotten. "Some breast cancers may cause an elevated acid phosphatase, and I don't know why." And when a resident asks how expectorants work, he responds, "I don't know. I don't know how they work. I don't think anyone knows how they work."

Barry does not value scientific knowledge for its own sake, but because it is useful. He is a pragmatist: worth and truth are both measured by efficacy, that is, by what works in the achievement of his objectives. The objectives themselves are natural, taken for granted. Thus the details of a theory are worthy of recall when they facilitate solution of medical problems. Barry uses the term *academic* to connote knowledge that is useless and wasteful. "Academic medicine is exceedingly expensive," he will say. "No one is in a hurry to do anything." When a student asks which came first, the patient's kidney problem or his hypertension, Barry responds, "At this point, it's really very academic."

In a similar "ivory tower" idiom, Barry refers to the university committee that assured that my research would protect the "human subjects" of my study as "Knights of the Round Table," suggesting mythological unreality. Likewise, Barry thinks little of a course on the philosophy of medicine that his son is taking. His attitude toward "academics" is strong. He resents and envies the leisure of academia, its freedom from commitments to tight schedules and to the press of clinical call. I asked one morning if he thought of conducting research; he responded, "I have absolutely no desire to do so." Yet he often relies on academic consultants and on the scientific knowledge produced in academia.

To Barry's way of thinking, science most often dictates action. When one knows the relevant facts and principles, one knows how to act. "So you've got to go the route with that. . . . You've got to go to full heparinization [anti-coagulation]. You've got no choice. This could be lethal." The impulse to treat is so strong, so deeply ingrained in his thought and conduct, that it is regarded as necessity rather than choice. Choice is transformed into an immutable, natural logic. Morality becomes invisible.

Only where the facts of science indicate a close and precarious balance of risks and benefits is the mandate for action no longer clear. Science has not yet provided a unique option, "no choice." Action then becomes of matter of choice, "a judgmental thing." On the merits of kidney transplantation, he comments, "You can take either side on that. Both sides are right and both sides are wrong." Here science provides basic information. Yet, since both action and inaction have balanced risks and benefits, the choice between them is unclear. "Judgment" takes over.

Pictures

Barry refers to the conceptualization of the patient's problem as a "picture," a "story," a "thing," and less frequently with the more common medical term, "entity." He describes the processes through which characteristics of the patient come to compose a picture as "making sense." The characteristics themselves are said to "make sense," and Barry says that he "makes sense of" or "gets a handle on" them. It is the "picture" or "thing"— an explanatory hypothesis that "makes sense" of systemic physiological observations—that allows prognosis and intervention: "You know, the whole picture would fit so well with the carcinoma. I can't get out of my thought the fact that that would explain everything so logically."

In Barry's thought, pictures are fixed, in that they are more or less static generalizations about patients in whom similar sequences of events have been observed. A picture either does or does not fit the patient's condition. Pictures may be known in great detail or sketchily and better for some conditions than for others. Yet, to whatever degree known, the essence of a picture is its fixed course, a property that allows (tautologically) prediction of events occurring in patients for whom this picture is true.

To extend Barry's metaphor (my extension, not his), pictures form a gallery of many halls. Barry speaks of "sorts of things," the ways that pictures, which order facts about a patient, are themselves ordered into larger arrays. The guide to Barry's gallery would seem to be the same signs of which pictures themselves are composed. Particular signs in a patient would send Barry looking in one section of the gallery.

Barry is acutely aware of the historical changing of the pictures in his own gallery and in the gallery of the profession more widely. He is wary of currents in medical thinking. He will say, "Brompton's isn't worth a damn. Brompton's is a fad." Or "That's what a lot of people think. They think ammonia is everything, but really it means zip."

Pictures and the elementary observations (signs and symptoms) that compose them work in an interactive fashion in the diagnostic process. During early encounters with a patient, when the patient's problem may not yet be known, Barry begins by collecting increasingly detailed information from the patient and from observations of his own of the patient's physical condition. He may have vague hypothetical pictures—sketches perhaps. As his observations accumulate, a sketch may be undermined and discarded, or it may be given further credence. Barry stresses to residents the importance of maintaining several, alternative pictures. He might note, "I can't put it into any one thing yet. A lot of things come to mind."

At some point in the course of diagnosis, there is a critical perceptual event in which one picture emerges to predominate in Barry's search. The picture is tenuously pinned to the patient as hypothesis, and additional observations are then gathered in its light. Barry might now say of a patient's sign or symptom, "It makes sense with what he has." The idea that pictures are constructed artifacts is now absent from Barry's expressions.

Barry is well aware of the power of pictures in diagnosis. He commonly makes reference both to the rational guidance for which pictures are essential and to the perceptual bias to "see" what is not there and not to "see" what is there, following the picture one expects: "I can't feel it [a certain pulse in a patient]. I think I'm influenced by the fact that he shouldn't have it."

Knowing Pictures, Knowing Patients

Barry's gallery of pictures has several sources: his early medical training, "the literature," more personal information from colleagues, and his own experience. Barry is highly selective of the information he accepts to confirm and especially to revise his pictures. He is extremely skeptical about findings in the literature. He says, "The stuff you read in the literature, 90 percent is bullshit, maybe 97 percent, maybe even 98 percent. . . . You can quote me." As with laboratory results, Barry uses statistical studies to confirm what he already believes. The standing knowledge by which he works significantly shapes new knowledge he may come by.

Barry often rejects population studies inconsistent with his own beliefs. Of an epidemiological study relating low-fiber diets and intestinal cancer, he remarked, "I really don't know what the heck you can make out of studies like that." But when the conclusions of a study support his beliefs, he accepts them. He cites a large population study in support of the importance of anticoagulation in certain specific circumstances: "That's an important study, because thousands of patients were followed. Some people don't like it and say it wasn't well done. Well, if you don't like something, you can always find something wrong. But I firmly believe this is an important study." Barry suggests here that knowledge, even in science, is a matter of conviction— "firmly believing." "Not someone's chief, but statistics: two years of coumadin [an anticoagulant], 10,000 people, 10,000 MIs [myocardial infarctions—heart attacks]. They don't talk about the original study. They talk about what the chief of service says."

Barry also gives much credence to his personal experience. His experience often appears to confirm his convictions, for example, regarding anticoagulation: "Then we get a call from the wife, and she says, 'Hey, he's dead.' You know! . . . even after you've done those things. And, ah, so you become a believer." It is notable here that, while it is the patient who has died, Barry speaks of an event that has happened *to him*—Barry. The event of concern is not simply the death of the patient, but the death of a patient following Barry's best treatment.

Barry is also ambivalent about the role of personal experience. Personal experience may lead to the overreliance on one's own observations: "I wish I could be very scientific and say, 'Hey one and one is two, or two and two is three,' but ah, or 'two and two is four,' excuse me. But, ah, I think everything you do in medicine is, ah, is, is hopefully based on fact, but clouded by experience and emotion. You know, that's true of everything."

The experience Barry favors is mediated by few devices. As described earlier, he makes extensive use of direct examination of the patient's condition—by percussion, palpation, pulsing, by visual observation of the patient's body, and by assessment of the patient's "presentation": "the presentation of the patient, how they present—not only what they say, but in things they don't say or how they say it, as well as what you find. If you can listen, you can get a diagnosis most of the time. This was taught to us as students and it's true. It's very, very true."

Of the less direct, laboratory studies, Barry says they are "supportive"— the laboratory "supports and confirms what you're doing." As with population studies, when the laboratory reports contradict his prior beliefs, they are all but ignored—"thrown out." He recounts telling a medical student about the diagnosis of "a coronary": "He says, 'What were his laboratory studies yesterday?'—the first thing he said to me when we got to the floor. And I said, 'Why?' He said, 'Well, we want to know if he had a coronary.' I said, 'Is that the only way you can tell if he's had a coronary?' And he kind of looked at me startled and I said, 'You know, you have to start thinking about what you get from the patient and what you think of what the patient tells you and what you find as you look at the patient as to what he has. And if the laboratory doesn't agree with what he has, you throw the laboratory out.'"

Barry reasons carefully in his interpretation of lab reports. He is acutely aware of their technical and social sources. A measurement may, but often does not, correspond to some phenomenon of interest in the patient. Too often it corresponds more with its technical source—for example, the cuff used to measure blood pressure—or with its social source—for example, an institution that habitually produces biased results: "You might cure his high blood pressure by measuring with a big cuff." [Ironic—the patient did not have high blood pressure, but was thought to have it because of an inappropriate measurement device.] Or, "could she have had an infarct, or did the technician place the electrode differently?"

In knowing patients and looking for the proper picture, Barry insists on the importance of intuition as well as rationality. The two may be relevant at different stages: intuition as a source of hypotheses, reason in their evaluation. "The initial impression is often the right one. Very often it is," he says.

Reason also is vital and the ultimate scientific justification for action. Barry also refers to reason as "thinking," and "making sense," and to its absence as "without rhyme or reason." "Just because it's done doesn't make it the right thing to do. Think about what you're doing." The powers of reason, however, are limited. One may reason to conclusions or alternative conclusions, but the truth is validated by what works: "When you add it all up and you say this can do that, and this can do that, all you can do is measure the effect in the person."

He recommends two strategies for finding the right picture. One is the maintenance and exploration of alternative pictures. "Don't put all your eggs in one basket. I just made that up. If things aren't working the way you think they should, don't be rigid in your thinking." A second diagnostic strategy is letting a condition alone to see if the condition itself or one's conception of it then resolves. "Stand back and look at the whole thing. . . . Rely on first impression." Standing back is a posture that engages intuition. Parts may come to be seen as one picture or another.

Surprises and Shades of Doubt

Failure haunts Barry in his work—failure to discover the patient's picture, failure of the picture to predict the patient's course, and failure to know how to affect that course when known. In failure, his metaphor shifts from "pictures" and "stories" to "horror stories," "tragedies," "catastrophes," and "disasters." He recognizes that his powers are partial and tenuous: "That happens. Mr. P. did it. He wiped out his heart. Why, at this point, when they're well anticoagulated? Damned if I know. . . . You know, there is no goddamn way on the face of the earth that you can predict these things. He's on coumadin [an anticoagulant], bed rest, and what the hell can you do? It's so goddamn frustrating."

Barry is too often "surprised" by a patient's course. Even if the surprise is an unexpected improvement, it is of ambiguous worth. When a cancer patient unexpectedly feels no pain, Barry remarks that the patient's course is "just surprising as hell." Surprise is a sign of ignorance and impotence—it's "hell." Barry's assessment is dominated here by his sense of efficacy rather than by the patient's condition.

In response to perceived inefficiency, Barry's notion of knowledge shifts from the realism of pictures—fixed Platonic "entities" that are more or less apt to patients' conditions—to an increasingly groundless nominalism—in which medicine becomes a less and less useful tool, and medical practice becomes a matter of "what you believe," "what you like," that is, judgment, beyond science.

The collapse of Barry's science into subjective judgment takes place in two stages. In the first stage, Barry denies that principles true of large patient populations allow "prediction" of the course of a given individual patient. For Barry, "prediction" is not simply the assertion of expectation about a future event, but *true* assertion; assertions that turn out false are not predictions. Barry is too rarely able to predict a patient's course. He notes the absence of "crystal balls" and "clairvoyance." "The statistics don't apply to the individual. If we are told that 5 percent. . . , what do we do? . . . You're really in a squeeze. I think they all should be anticoagulated, because you can't tell. . . . And once they die, they're dead."

Barry's response to what he regards as his failures escalates to a second stage, in which the uncertainty of particular events becomes a property of the world. When a resident remarks, "Nothing's true all the time," Barry answers, "I think nothing is true any of the time anymore."

At the collapse of Barry's science of pictures, some principles of medicine, or even all of medicine, become "what you want to believe." Valid pictures and useful pictures have given way to a nihilistic vision in which nothing is secure or certain; there is no "thing" or "picture." Rather than resting on a basis of the lawful events of human physiology, medicine is anchored only in what Barry refers to as the personal "pleasures" of the practitioner. There is profound irony in such "pleasures": "I think the answer is still up in the air, and I think it depends on what you want to believe—which just proves that there are a lot of experts or authorities with different ideas about things. You do what you enjoy."

Here it seems that at heart, medicine may be founded in judgment, a realm in which no answer excludes another and all are equally good or bad. The tense opposition between science and judgment breaks down, first, when the knowledge of science indicates alternate responses that are equally promising and equally hazardous, and then, when the strategies of science fail utterly because they yield no solutions or false solutions. In the first event, judgments must be made and science can give no further help. In the second event, the solid foundation of science dissolves entirely, and all medicine slips into what is for Barry a morass of judgment.

"TREAT THE PATIENT, NOT THE LAB"

In the course of his work with residents, the predominant principle of Barry's teaching is "Treat the patient, not the lab." There are many variants of this remark, all permutations on a few themes. Alongside the explicit intent of this remark are several emotional undercurrents and hidden agenda: "Look at the numbers you're fed. Don't believe numbers." "Are we treating numbers or are we treating her? My word of wisdom today, as everyday, is 'Fuck the number.'"

Barry makes such comments in response to formulations made by his apprentices. He believes these apprentices employ a logic that approximates this (my wording):

- The patient is sick and his or her physiological function, measured on some standardized scale, is such-and-such a value.
- If we bring this value back to normal, we also will remove the pathology and restore the patient to normalcy and health.

Almost without exception, Barry rejects this logic.

Barry believes that contemporary medicine emphasizes a reliance on technology that neglects reason and the use of evidence at hand. Technology distances the physician from direct knowledge of his patients' conditions. Students are now taught to order "batteries" of tests and to respond to the results of these tests in a reflex fashion, without broader, more systematic consideration. Barry's epithetic remarks are intended as an antidote to faulty reasoning.

Though his prescriptions suggest that Barry believes numbers and laboratory values are not the sort of thing that one should treat, this inference is misleading. The essence of Barry's formulaic teachings is his insistence that patients' characteristics not be treated in isolation.

Barry does not believe that the treatment of numbers is incompatible with the treatment of patients. "We absolutely have to have the numbers," he says. Rather it is against the treatment of single numbers—numbers taken one at a time—that he inveighs. He responds to this error with another epithet: "Treat them by the company they keep." The "them" to be treated are not patients, but their signs and symptoms—that is, the characteristics of patients that include numbers and labs. And numbers and labs are treated as a group.

The logic of Barry's treatment thus runs as follows (my wording):

- Patients become diseased and systematically manifest their pathology in a variety of characteristics, including those they themselves report and others measured by various devices.
- Interpreting these characteristics and responding appropriately requires understanding the sources of knowledge and the way in which patient characteristics operate together to produce the perceptible disease.

- We don't or shouldn't treat single numbers, but rather patients.
- We treat patients by treating the system of their characteristics, their picture.
- Thus, if not identical, there is at least a close approximation of patient and syndrome. *Treating a patient is treating a syndrome.*

In exceptional instances, Barry tells a resident, "Treat the number." Two (of three) occasions on which I heard this prescription concerned high blood pressures. Very high blood pressures may be quickly fatal, and moderately high ones fatal over longer periods. But Barry's prescription in these cases was not contrary to his more common one, for he was familiar with each patient and thus knew of other features in whose "company" the blood pressure was to be treated.

The third occasion on which I heard Barry call for the treatment of a number concerned a dying patient, for whom Barry had consulted a hematologist. He tells the resident, "Just call him up and ask him for numbers to treat with." Here again, Barry will not respond simply to a single number, but to the patient's other features, which he already knows to be part of the picture.

The company kept by the patient's characteristics is an exclusive one, including many of the patient's physical or physiological features, while excluding almost all of the patient's psychological and social characteristics. The company kept is in essence physiological.

"Listen to the patient," Barry repeats emphatically and frequently to the residents. "Nine times out of ten the patient will give you the diagnosis. You don't make a diagnosis of obstruction . . . from a cardiogram. You make it from what the patient reports."

Part of what Barry listens for is current symptoms. The remainder is the patient's "history." "Your history is so damned important. . . . Take that history for what it's worth."

The history is a chronology of the patient's symptoms, activities, and environment. The history is an impersonal thing—it is "that" history and "your" (i.e., the physician's) history, and it is taken by the physician from the patient, medically translated, and medically used. The worth of this chronology, transformed from the patient's story to a medical history, is essentially diagnostic.

"Listening to the patient" and "taking the patient's history," like "treating the patient, not the lab," have the appearance of conformity to contemporary concern for the "whole person," the patient's interests, and so on. The appearance is deceptive. "Listening to the patient" and "taking the patient's history" are not efforts to sympathetically comprehend the patient's life-world, inner meanings, fears, or desires, but rather to diagnose disease conceived of by criteria independent of the patient's personal experience. Barry redirects the circumscribed information drawn from the patient to his physiological examination.

Barry by no means ignores the psychological or psychiatric characteristics of his patients. Yet his response is ambivalent. On the one hand he employs these characteristics in his medical work. On the other he anxiously avoids patients' troubles, "deferring" exploration, and "referring out" the patients themselves.

Barry uses patients' psychiatric characteristics in three distinct ways. Again, most basic is their use as diagnostic indices of physiological disturbance. The assumption justifying this usage might be described as "somatopsychic"—an assumption that physiological events have psychological consequences that may be used, like other clinical signs, to assess underlying physiological process. The manner rather than the content of the patient's presentation is indicative. The content itself is tangential, irrelevant: "What do you think of the affect? . . . Not the sensorium, but the expression on the face. It's flat. It's just flat. What meds is she on? She's normally a very astute and alert gal. This is not like her at all." Talk here is directed toward medical co-workers, and most often away from patients. It refers to the patient, sometimes naming the patient, sometimes depersonalizing the patient, as in "*the* sensorium" and "*the* expression on *the* face." Such talk may be conducted in the patient's presence, especially if the patient appears to be unaware (asleep, drowsy, or stuporous).

Patients' psychological qualities are useful also in interpreting their behavior and accounts of their conditions—that is, in "listening" and in "taking that history." Barry notes of a black woman patient, "This woman feels pain very strongly, very deeply," and of another patient, a white man, "He's a very stoic guy." Barry interprets their responses accordingly, minimizing the woman's responses and amplifying the man's.

Finally, Barry makes use of his knowledge of patients' psychological styles to predict and influence their compliance with a medical procedure he believes appropriate. In his medical listening there is no direct or primary concern for the patient's experience.

Psychiatric "Pandora's"

Barry is disturbed and anxious when he encounters the psychiatric issues of his patients. In order to illustrate Barry's encounter with psychiatry, I cite two commentaries on patients with psychiatric difficulties. The first is Barry's report on a patient's initial visit to the Hypertension Center. He dictates a note for her chart.

Chief complaint elevated blood pressure 5 years duration. . . . She was under a great deal of tension with a great deal of responsibility and initially was treated with a muscle relaxant and later with hydrochlorothiazide 50 mg. daily with apparent improvement in her hypertension. . . . She felt tired and exhausted and "supertense," not resting well, but better since her blood pressure has been controlled. The patient appears to be very, very tense, very bright, very anxious— expressed a great deal of her emotion and of her job responsibility. Expresses a great deal of anxiety regarding her mother who is very depressed.

[Stops dictation; aside to RAH] See, I get the picture of this gal not being the bright-eyed cheerful good-natured gal that she is. Underneath all that there's a great deal simmering. And I'm not so sure that this gal isn't exceedingly depressed herself and isn't exceedingly anxious about her self as she sees her mother. And I, you know, I've . . . there are a lot of things I didn't even get into with her. I'm just damned afraid of opening a Pandora's, and I wouldn't know how the hell to put the lid back on her, so I, I just circumvented a lot of areas.

[RAH asks You wouldn't want to suggest to her seeing a psychiatrist?] I'm sure . . . that this has been suggested to her, and ah, no I don't, nah, I didn't, I didn't feel now, not the initial visit. It's pretty hard sometimes to come about this. Sometimes you can antagonize an individual by the way you approach that or by what you might suggest to him, and I think you could drive them off rather than helping them get into the hands of a good therapist. And I feel very insecure about her emotionally, and I just want to play it close to the belt. I'll see her again, and we'll talk some more and see what the heck we can come up with. . . . I'm not sure how she handles other people's problems. I'm not really sure in my own mind what this all means, and, and I'm not sure that I want to get involved in that. I'm not sure that I can handle what I come up with.

[Returns to dictation] Systems review: rectal and pelvic exams are deferred at this time.

Barry "circumvents a lot of areas" and "defers" not only the intimate examination of the patient's rectum and pelvis, but exploration of psychiatric issues as well. He listens to engage the patient's trust, so that she will return. This may be a common and productive strategy, but "deferral" may also have a deeper significance for him, namely the avoidance of work that is disturbing to Barry himself. Barry's language here is highly ambiguous, referring to his patient and to himself in the same troubled phrases.

Though I believe Barry intends to refer to the patient, his word *emotionally* refers grammatically to his own mode of feeling: *he* feels emotionally insecure. In addition, *he* is insecure about how she handles other people's problems and how *he* can handle hers. His expression places his patient and himself in the same predicament. Finally, more than simply wishing to postpone exploration of her psychiatric problems, he doubts that he wants "to get involved in that" at all.

A second commentary concerns a diabetic adolescent girl he has treated for several years. Barry describes her psychiatric problems as "depression" and "suicidal tendencies," and suggests factitious illness as well—that is, illness that she has deliberately induced in herself. The rounds team has just visited her and talks in the hall.

> She's been hard to manage partly because of emotional problems. She's been depressed and has suicidal tendencies. One of her problems is her mother. . . . I finally threw up my hands and asked her to go somewhere else. . . . That's a mess. And, in addition to that, they really like medications.
>
> She's been seen by every psychiatrist in town, too. The medications can't do anything for her. We're stuck with all her problems, and we can't do anything. The only thing that's going to help this girl is letting her complete her suicide.
>
> [To the medical student:] . . . send her home. I don't know why the hell she's here. As far as I'm concerned, this gal is totally hopeless.
>
> She's been talked to by everyone. And I tell her, "I can't help you." And she says, "Don't ever leave me, 'cause you're the only one who ever talks to me."
>
> I'm impressed with these agents [psychiatric medications], that they don't help over the long haul, except in psychotics. I want to send her home, 'cause I don't want to see her anymore in the hospital.
>
> Her mother called me and said that she felt that Mary should die so she wouldn't suffer. Her mother is a large part of the problem. . . . Her father is extremely passive. . . . Her mother is quite aggressive. But I don't know how I would act with a daughter like that.

This is a litany of impotence. Barry has had difficulty treating the patient's medical problems, noting that management of the diabetes is complicated by her emotional problems. Barry also regards her depression as aggravated though not initiated by her diabetes. In addition, he suspects she may induce her own physical problems, for example, by taking milk of magnesia. He believes that no psychiatrist or psychiatric medication has done her any good. He insists that he also can and has done nothing for her. "Doing nothing" is a medical notion according to which talk with patients does not count.

As many physicians might, Barry attempts flight from the psychiatric problems of his patients. In this case, he is unsuccessful. He has thrown up his hands and asked her to go elsewhere. He says he wants to send her home, first because he doesn't know "why the hell she's" there, and then, "'cause I don't want to see her anymore in the hospital."

His strong desire to rid himself of this patient follows his adoption of her problem—"*We're* stuck with all her problems." While she herself is not yet hopeless, he now is: "As far as I'm concerned, this gal is totally hopeless." He has taken on himself the burden of her emotional problems.

Barry has no pretensions about being a psychiatrist. In contrast to his medicine, psychiatric and social issues are thought to be matters of common sense. Barry is troubled by the uncertainty of psychiatric diagnosis and theory, and the limited psychiatry he practices is highly formulaic. The lack of "black" or "white" certainty that haunts his medical practice is absent. His psychiatric categories are rigid, and patients fit or do not fit them. While Barry may have difficulty placing patients into these categories—as he admits he does not know them well—nevertheless he speaks of the categories as if they were solid and fixed. In psychiatry, Barry is at his realist extreme.

Medical versus Nonmedical

A strong dichotomy between the medical and the nonmedical pervades Barry's thought, defining the limits of his field of work and his competence. This dichotomy demarcates two domains of the universe assumed to be separable and mutually exclusive. In one domain, Barry works comfortably; in the other he is troubled.

Each side of the dichotomy has several associations. The medical domain is associated with the physical and organic, with science and objectivity. The nonmedical domain is associated with the nonphysical, or "functional," and with judgment and subjectivity. Barry refers to emotional and social problems as "some of these nonmedical, nonphysical things, situations." He reports to his partners that a patient has "more subjective complaints than objective findings"; he remarks to a resident that a patient has "really got nothing objective in his joints."

At the same time, Barry regards patients' problems as affected by both medical and nonmedical components, in a way sometimes difficult to disentangle. Problems vary in the percentage of each component present.

> *Barry:* They overlap; a good many times they overlap. But very often you can pick out the individual components of the major problem.
> *RAH:* You think there are, there are clear-cut medical problems that aren't social?
> *Barry:* Yes, there are clear-cut problems that are 99 percent medical and 1 percent social, yeah. And there are clear problems that are 99 percent social and 1 percent medical. The person who's got a marital problem and needs counseling, she may have a headache as a result of all the, you know, the problems she's got at home, but I consider that 1 percent medical and 99 percent social.
> *RAH:* What would the other end be?
> *Barry:* Well, someone who's got a metastatic cancer, for example, and that has no insurance to take care of their financial needs for their medical care. You know, they may have, I mean, their, their immediate problem is 99 percent medical. Sure they got a problem about their will and . . . going to look after the family when I'm gone and

that kind of thing, and dispose of the cat, and whatever else. But, you know, I think their problem is 99 percent medical and 1 percent social. Well, maybe not that much. Maybe it's a 90 percent and 10 percent or 80 percent and 20 percent. I think there's clear divisions where a majority fall in one sector or the other. I wish to hell I had answers. I wish to hell someone had answers.

Though Barry does not do so explicitly, we may divide causal relations into *somato-somatic* (physical outcome determined by physical cause), *somato-psychic* (psychological outcome determined by physical cause), *psycho-somatic* (physical outcome determined by psychological cause), and *psycho-psychic* (psychological outcome determined by psychological cause). Somato-somatics is Barry's proper medicine: 100 percent physical, 0 percent psychological. Somato-psychics he employs for diagnostic purposes; a psychological event may be an index of physiology. But patients may also react psychologically to their disease in ways that do not directly indicate a physiological process; such reactions are peripheral to Barry's medicine. Psycho-psychics is the realm of the "functional" and falls within the domain of psychiatry.

Barry appears to think of psycho-somatic effects as short-lived; he tells me, for example, that psychic stress affects blood pressure only transiently. It may be that psycho-somatic conditions are rare among his diagnoses because they make less sense to him. He believes that psychological explanations mask ignorance, and that when we know what really occurs, our understanding will be couched in terms of organic process. For example, he talks of changes in the understanding of "ulcerative colitis":

> They used to teach that ulcerative colitis, one of the diseases of the bowel, was an emotional disease and was treated by psychiatrists. Well, you know, if you're shittin' thirty times a day, ah, what kind of emotional problem, what kind of emotional response would you have to this illness? It, you know, it can't be complacent. If you lost a hundred pounds shittin' thirty times a day, how would you feel? You see, and I don't know. I think now we are coming around to thinking that it's, it's organic. We don't understand it fully, but it's an organic illness to which people have an emotional response. And that makes more sense to me. Merely because we don't know what causes it, we used to classify it as an emotional illness. And there was a period of time, merely because we don't know what causes it, we classify it as an allergic disease. Now we're getting another fad: If we don't know what causes it, we say it may be autoimmune, which is another thing.

I ask whether "the answers that are ultimately convincing are those that are biological in nature, microscopic?" He does not commit himself: "Well, this is more scientific, certainly. Ah, you know, how you explain what you see sometimes can be a variable thing, too. So I don't think that always applies. But I think it's more likely that's the case."

Relations with Patients

Barry describes and responds to his patients in strikingly different ways, characterizing them along three basic dimensions: their pleasantness, their medical "interest," and their personality and strength of character.

"Nice" patients are more or less agreeable; they are also called "neat," "pleasant," "lovely," and "good." They may suffer, but they do so appropriately, without exaggeration. Barry may refer to them as "poor" so-and-so, deserving of sympathy. Most often they also respond compliantly. Occasionally they are noncompliant, but still nice. When a patient is noncompliant, Barry may "tangle" or "tangle ass holes," or he may "kick him in the ass" to induce compliance. He comments on "good" patients:

- "She knows the whole bit. She's lost both her legs. But she's a lovely person." [A diabetic who has recently also lost her vision.]
- "He's a nice guy. I'm glad he's doing well."
- "She's a nice person. I have to kick her in the ass every now and then, but she's a nice person."

Barry is pleased when nice patients do well, troubled when they suffer. He works for them with urgency.

Patients may also be described as "interesting" or "fascinating." Patients are interesting because they present problems that are sufficiently complex to be intriguing and demanding: "Just a horrendous mess. . . . Every metabolic problem he can have. . . . He's fascinating. He's got every metabolic failure known."

Interesting problems (or patients) contrast with those that are simple and quickly solvable (for example, "nice juicy" pneumonias or strep throats). They allow Barry and his followers to test their medical abilities, with frequent success. Interesting problems contrast also with problems that are incurable by current means, such as sickle cell anemia and some forms of cancer.

Other patients are valued because they have strong and striking, but not offensive personalities. These patients are "characters," or "real characters": "This guy's a real character. He's got emotional problems, he and his wife. He's hard to manage sometimes."

At the negative extreme on all dimensions is the patient described as "a turd," "a nut," "a bitch," "a son of a bitch," or, rarely, "a crock." These patients are not personable, and they are regarded as of neither medical nor characterological interest. They are repugnant to Barry, as they are to many of his colleagues. Barry saw one such patient following a sleepless night on call. The patient complained of being tired. Barry later told me: "This guy I

tangled ass holes with. He's a real turd. . . . Last time he was here with his
father, and they just rubbed me wrong. . . . That was just too much."

One day while on rounds, Barry was called from the emergency room (ER)
regarding a patient of his who had just arrived there. "That gal in the emergency room, she really gets impatient. She's a nut." He mentioned to the
rounds team this patient's "semiannual bath," and he complained that for
three months she had had the same "belly pain" that now brought her into the
ER. As the patient is impatient, Barry is impatient with her. As she has delayed coming in for her "belly pain," he delays in going to see her in the ER.

Barry objects to patients he finds morally or socially offensive. He resents
patients who do not take good care of themselves and who may abuse others at
the same time; these patients seem to be the agents of their own condition.
Barry's anger toward this patient with alcoholic liver complications is thinly
veiled, and his medicine highly ambivalent—not "compulsive." He discusses forms of treatment with the residents.

> I wouldn't object to trying them [some medications] on him. After all,
> we've nothing in the world to lose, and if we bring this guy back, I
> don't know if that's good or bad. It's probably not particularly good.
> But I don't know that it's bad necessarily either. That's a philosophical
> thing you can debate all you want. But my feeling about a guy like this
> is that I think he deserves the same kind of care as someone coming the
> first crack. If he dies, well he dies, and you've tried. And I'm not just
> trying to obviate guilt. I don't have any guilt about alcoholics. Oh,
> within reason I do have guilt, of course. But I don't feel that compul-
> sive about alcoholics.

In another example of his moral repugnance, Barry saw a welfare patient
with several illegitimate children. He was offended by her promiscuity and
by his powerlessness to do anything but offer her contraceptive pills and
monitor her blood pressure. He wants her to take the pills to prevent conception; he wants her not to take them to avoid problems of hypertension. He
complains about liberal reformers:

> Unfortunately, in people who are full of ideas as to what to do with
> them, with situations in regard to them. You know the person is well-
> intentioned, and said, "Well, it's her life. She can do what she wants
> to." Well, fine, sure she can go out and screw all she wants. That's her
> business. But do we have to support her mistakes, or do we have to
> support her in the process of doing that? And do we have to pay her way,
> really, as a noncompensated prostitute, or whatever? Really! Which is
> what we're doing. . . . All you can do is beat your head against the wall.

Barry is also angry with the relatives of patients who adversely affect the
conditions of his patients themselves. He remarks about the daughter of the
patient, the "lovely person" who lost her legs as a complication of diabetes.

The patient's daughter has taken money from one man to abort the child of another. Barry says, "Bitch, I'd like to wring her tits off, honest to God." Again, vengeance is expressed in bodily metaphors.

Barry's frequent sexual metaphors indicate ambivalence toward women. A resident showed him a series of small, graded holes drilled in a plastic sheet and used as a template for measurement. Barry joked, "Is that for cervical dilation?" On another occasion, he was talking about problems of instructing patients and illustrated the difficulties with this example: "You got to instruct people in really simple things. If you give a woman a vaginal suppository, you've got to tell her to take the foil off." He makes sexual comments about nurses: "You treat the patient, and screw the machines, and, if you can catch them, the nurses." Misogyny is thinly masked by humor.

At the same time, Barry remarks often that his favorite patients are "little old ladies": "Patients get older as I do. My favorite patients are little old ladies. I love them. They're just great . . . until they start spitting at you." He enjoys their wisdom and the stories they tell. There may be other qualities as well that personally attract him to these older women. Their sexuality is greatly diminished; yet they may remain maternal and they require his close attention.

Medicine as Mirror: Patient and Self in Suffering and Healing

Barry maintains a distance from patients by listening to them in a narrowly medical way, by treating them as syndromes, and by avoiding their personal and psychiatric issues. Yet, despite his efforts, he is closely engaged in his patients' lives. He often suffers when they do. He employs his own experience, sympathetically and intuitively, to assess and respond to their conditions.

Barry is visibly anxious with patients' psychiatric conditions, but he is affected as well by their medical conditions and their social circumstances. He explicitly imagines himself in his patient's situation: "He's a nice guy," he says of a patient on dialysis. "God, he's a nice person. I often wonder how you yourself would respond to an illness like that." On another occasion, he observes, "You know, when a patient loses a couple of kids, for whatever reason, I don't think you ever recover from it. And she's like an old Jewish mother. She'd come in, 'Ach . . .' And, you know, you understand it. Shit, you know, you got any kids at all, and you think of what would happen to them, and how you'd react to that." His expression suggests ambiguously that he himself may not recover from the patient's losses.

Perhaps only rhetorically, Barry suggests that students and residents experience medical procedures, so that they will sympathize with patients they subject to these procedures and so that they will reduce their use of these procedures to a necessary minimum: "I think that everyone who wants to order a Levin tube down should have one down first." (The Levin tube is inserted through the patient's nose to his stomach for more direct feeding.)

Barry not only shares in his patient's suffering. He also uses his own experience to diagnose their conditions. He examines his own sensations, or "feelings," to achieve an intuitive assessment of the patient's condition: "There's no question in my mind what he's got, but I can't prove it to you." He speaks of fears and anxieties when things do not feel right and of feeling comfortable when they do. "Everybody's got this damned residual anxiety about this guy." Or "I don't feel comfortable. . . . It's nice to feel comfortable, and you often don't feel comfortable with a situation."

Barry also suggests that his own well-being is enhanced as his patients are healed. He may ask patients to comply with his requests and prescriptions for his benefit if not for theirs. Moreover, relief of the patient's suffering brings relief to Barry also. He is healed when they are. He is thus a subject and a patient in his own medicine.

"That's neat. That's neat," he'll say. "God, I'm pleased with her—that she can go home. She's so much better. . . . Almost came back from the other world. It's really a great feeling that you've done something like that—that you're able to do something like that. You can breathe easier."

8

DIVISIONS OF LABOR: OBSTETRICIAN, WOMAN, AND SOCIETY IN *WILLIAMS OBSTETRICS*, 1903–1989

From a biological point of view pregnancy and labour represent the highest functions of the female productive system, and a priori should be considered as normal processes. But when we recall the manifold changes which occur in the maternal organism, it is apparent that the border-line between health and disease is less distinctly marked during gestation than at other times, and derangements, so slight as to be of but little consequence under ordinary circumstances, may readily give rise to pathological conditions which seriously threaten the life of the mother or the child, or both.

It accordingly becomes necessary to keep pregnant patients under strict supervision, and to be constantly on the alert for the appearance of untoward symptoms.

—*J. W. Williams,* Williams Obstetrics (*1903*)

During the twentieth century, the developed world has witnessed a revolution in the conduct of birth.* The place of birth has moved from domestic to medical settings, while obstetrical professionals have increasingly assumed control of its events. Powerful artifacts and procedures have proliferated and appear to exert a command of their own. The monitoring and control of fertility, conception, gestation, and birth have evolved in ways unlikely to have been imagined at the beginning of the century. The revolution in childbearing has occurred in a cultural environment of deeply charged and rapidly changing values regarding sexuality and reproduction, health and health care, and the status of women.

From the first edition of *Obstetrics* in 1903 to the recent eighteenth edition of *Williams Obstetrics* in 1989, this work has been "the leading textbook

---

* At the beginning of the century fewer than 5 percent of U.S. births took place in hospitals, but by 1939 more than half occurred there, and in the 1980s more than 95 percent took place in hospitals (Wertz and Wertz 1977; U.S. Department of Health and Human Services 1984b). Also by 1939, more than 90 percent of births were attended by physicians, 39 percent outside of hospitals (Hunt and Goldstein 1964); over the past twenty years, of more than 3.5 million births per year in the United States, more than 98 percent were attended by physicians in hospitals. Coincidentally, maternal mortality has fallen by a dramatic 98 percent from 52 per 10,000 live births in 1900 to fewer than 1 per 10,000 live births in 1990. Infant

in the field" (Longo 1981:221). "No other American textbook of obstetrics, and very few texts of any other branch of medicine, have attained the popularity of *Williams Obstetrics*" (Speert 1980:81). In his preface to the eighth edition of *Williams,* H. J. Stander, the author who succeeded Williams, claimed that this text was used by "the great majority of American and Canadian medical schools, and, in its Spanish and other translations, by many foreign universities." It is estimated that more than 100,000 copies were sold during Williams's lifetime (Longo 1981:221). The only medical text of comparable genealogy is *Cecil's Textbook of Medicine,* first published in 1927 and currently also in its eighteenth edition. *Williams* has both reflected and shaped the development of belief and practice in obstetrics in the twentieth century.

Thus, examination of the development of *Williams Obstetrics* provides a window onto the profession of obstetrics and its work during this century. In this chapter, I describe the changing worldview of obstetrics visible through editions of this text, focusing on ideas and attitudes about obstetricians and women—the practitioners of this discipline, their patients, and the broader environment. Following brief notes on J. W. Williams and his successors, I review the evolution of *Williams* by considering five related topics: (1) the nature of childbearing and obstetrics, (2) the foundations and distribution of obstetrical knowledge among participants in birth, (3) notions of pain and its relief, (4) the control of reproduction, and (5) the psychological and social context of childbirth and obstetrics.

My analysis of obstetrical knowledge and attitudes is based on a review of the evolving editions of *Williams Obstetrics* themselves. I make no pretense of formulating a history of the text, its production, or its ideas; such a formulation would require broader knowledge of the cultural, social, political, and economic context than I possess. (For historical context, see Arney 1983; Leavitt 1986, and 1987; Sandelowski 1984; Speert 1980; Wertz and Wertz

---

mortality has also fallen from 159 per 1,000 live births in 1900 to 10 per 1,000 in 1990, a reduction of 94 percent (Centers for Disease Control 1993b; U.S. Bureau of the Census 1975; Woodbury 1926).

Although it is unlikely that obstetricians have been the principal source of these changes in birth outcome, they nevertheless have been in the forefront of the revolution in the conduct of birth. In 1930, obstetrics and gynecology became the third medical specialty to create a board to control training, licensure, and practice. In 1990 there were 33,697 obstetrician-gynecologists in the United States (5.5 percent of all physicians), of whom 78 percent were male (Roback 1992). Between 1977 and 1978 obstetrician-gynecologists each attended a mean of 128 births per year, 81 percent of all births in the United States, a proportion 13 percent higher than in the decade before (American College of Obstetrics and Gynecology 1979). In the United States at least 33 percent of surgical operations undergone by females are obstetrical and gynecological. In 1991, of the 100.7 surgical operations undergone per 1,000 females of all ages, 17.7 (17.4 percent) were "procedures to assist delivery," 6.5 (6.5 percent) were for cesarean sections, 5.5 (5.5 percent) for "repair of obstetrical lacerations," and 10.7 (10.6 percent) for other gynecological procedures, for a total of 5.8 million operations annually (Centers for Disease Control 1993b).

1977.) Nor do I describe in any comprehensive or detailed fashion the physiological or medical ideas or technical practice in *Williams;* such analysis should be undertaken by historians of medicine (such as Speert 1980). My cultural chronology analyzes the changing and persistent ideas for which an obstetrical history should account. I attempt to ascertain the framework of concepts, premises, logic, and values that underlie this obstetrical pedagogy.

This study has been emotionally trying. It has been my intent to portray the worldview underlying an obstetrical text. In the course of doing so, however, I have been repeatedly confronted by attitudes and practices with which I have no sympathy—essentially the reduction of the personal experience and the interpersonal relations of childbearing to an operation on the body in which the childbearing woman is deprecated or ignored.* It is likely that these attitudes were not unique to Williams and his successors, but were common in the medical and broader environments in which they practiced. I have attempted to understand the work at the same time as I reacted to it, balancing analysis and critique.

Two major phases are evident in the development of *Williams Obstetrics.* From the first edition (1903) through the ninth (1945), a view of childbearing as quasi-pathological was thought to justify pervasive obstetrical control of birth events; control was widely extended, while childbearing women and others were increasingly excluded from participation. Beginning with the tenth edition (1950), this vision of pathology and medical control has contended with another in which the centrality of social and psychological considerations in obstetrics is increasingly acknowledged. While the breadth of obstetrics is further extended, some control is also restored to childbearing women. Yet, the repetition of social and psychological ideas during the past thirty-five years has still not yielded an integration of social and psychological aspects of childbearing into biologically oriented obstetrical theory and practice.

J. W. WILLIAMS AND HIS SUCCESSORS

John Whitridge Williams (1866–1931) powerfully shaped the course of obstetrics not only through his popular text but also through his teaching, administration, and obstetrical politics. In 1914 he served as president of both the American Association for the Study and Prevention of Infant Mortality and the American Gynecological Society. At Johns Hop-

---

* The index of the fifteenth edition includes the entry, "Chauvinism, male, variable amounts, 1–923"; page 923 was the last page of text. In the sixteenth edition the entry increased to "voluminous amounts, 1–1102." In the preface to the fifteenth edition, authors Pritchard and MacDonald thank Ms. Signe Pritchard "for her myriad contributions beginning with manuscript and ending [?] with index." In the seventeenth edition, the index entry no longer appears.

kins, where he was chairman of the Department of Obstetrics from 1899 to 1931, he is said to have been a popular teacher and to have held a "virtual monopoly" over the appointment of chairmen in university departments of obstetrics and gynecology throughout the nation for three decades (Speert 1980). Because of his large physical stature, Williams was known among his students as "The Bull" (Longo 1981:223).

Williams was responsible for radical reform in obstetrics. He took as his mission the institutionalization of science in obstetrics and the maintenance of standards for obstetrical education and practice. In 1912 he issued a report (Williams 1912) paralleling the Flexner Report of 1910. At the request of the Committee on Midwifery of the Association for the Study and Prevention of Infant Mortality, Williams surveyed professors of obstetrics at 120 medical schools (of which 43 responded). He found that many academic staff who trained medical students about childbirth were themselves inadequately prepared and incompetent in obstetrical emergencies. One professor admitted that "he had never seen a woman delivered" before assuming his teaching position. Many schools had inadequate equipment and facilities and little patient "material." Williams asked (1912:6), "Why bother about the relatively innocuous midwife, when the ignorant doctor caused quite as many absolutely unnecessary deaths?" He recommended:

1. Better and properly equipped medical schools.
2. Higher requirements for the admission of students.
3. Scientifically trained professors of obstetrics with high ideals.
4. General elevation of the standards of obstetrics.
5. Education of medical practitioners.
6. Insistence by state examining boards on better training before admitting applicants to practice.
7. Education of the general public.
8. Development of lying-in charities.
9. Cheaper nurses.
10. Possibly the training of midwives.   (Williams 1912:7)

Williams was also an advocate of both prenatal care (Williams 1915) and "woman's clinics" (Williams 1914). In his 1914 presidential address to the Association for the Study and Prevention of Infant Mortality, he reported a study of 705 fetal deaths among 10,000 consecutive admissions to the Obstetrical Department of the Johns Hopkins Hospital. Syphilis caused 26.4 percent of deaths, 18 percent of deaths were from unknown causes, and 17.6 percent were attributed to "dystocia"—difficulties of labor. Williams believed that fetal mortality could have been reduced by 40 percent if patients had had prenatal care, and, he added cautiously, "with the further proviso that they had received practically ideal obstetrical care in the hospital" (1914:45). Even in the first edition of *Obstetrics,* Williams described a study showing that women who "lived comfortably in a hospital for several months

Table 8.1   A Genealogy of Editions of *Williams Obstetrics*

Year	Edition	Author(s)
1903, 1908, 1913, 1920, 1925, 1930	1–6	J. W. Williams
1936, 1941, 1945	7–9	H. J. Stander
1950, 1956	10–11	N. J. Eastman
1961	12	N. J. Eastman and L. M. Hellman
1966	13	N. J. Eastman, L. M. Hellman, and J. A. Pritchard
1971	14	L. M. Hellman and J. A. Pritchard
1976, 1980	15–16	J. A. Pritchard and P. C. MacDonald
1985	17	J. A. Pritchard, P. C. MacDonald, and N. F. Gant
1989	18	F. G. Cunningham, P. C. MacDonald, and N. F. Gant

prior to delivery" had longer pregnancies than women "poorly nourished" who were unable to "spare" themselves (1903:171). In subsequent editions, his advocacy of prenatal care grew. Williams insisted on the importance of nonmedical participants, including nurses and social workers, for comprehensive prenatal (and postnatal) care. He claimed in the fifth edition (1925:227), "One of the few creditable achievements of American obstetrics consists in the development of so-called Prenatal Care." Williams may have qualified the term *prenatal care* because of the breadth of care he advocated. "Prenatal care," he wrote, "may be defined as such supervision and care of the pregnant, parturient and puerperal woman as will enable her to pass through the dangers of pregnancy and labor with the least possible risk, to give birth to a living child, and to be discharged in such condition that she may be able to suckle it and thus afford it the greatest prospect of attaining maturity, as well as to fulfill her duties as mother and housewife with a minimal amount of invalidism" (1925:227–228).

While the authors of *Williams Obstetrics* do not say how their successors were chosen, there is evidence of patterns of succession within the editions themselves (see table 8.1). In the preface of each edition, the current author acknowledges the contributions of colleagues, and it is from among named contributors that successors have been chosen. For example, in the preface to the last edition that he authored (the sixth), Williams thanked his associates, among them Henricus J. Stander, who became editor/author of the next three editions, following Williams's death in 1931.

It was Stander who first named the text after his predecessor, but in the ninth edition (1945), "partly on the advice of my colleagues and teachers of obstetrics, many of them trained by Williams," he noted (in the passive voice) that "a change has been made in the title page." Stander deleted Williams's name from the title, renaming it *Textbook of Obstetrics; Designed for the Use of Students and Practitioners,* justifying his deletion with the assertion that recent editions embodied "the teaching and practice of the present author," who should thus "assume full responsibility."

Among those Stander thanked for assistance in the eighth edition was Nicholson J. Eastman. Following the pattern, Eastman became sole editor/author of the next two editions (the tenth and eleventh) after Stander's death, and first author of the two editions thereafter (the twelfth and thirteenth). Eastman ignored Stander's rebellion and retitled the text after the patrilineal ancestor; still the book became known to contemporary readers as *Eastman.* Succession among collaborators continued, as Louis M. Hellman, Eastman's coauthor in the twelfth and thirteenth editions, became principal author of the fourteenth edition. Jack A. Pritchard, coauthor in both the thirteenth and fourteenth editions, was first author of the fifteenth through the seventeenth editions, now succeeded by his colleague Gary Cunningham.

DEFINING CHILDBIRTH

A central theme of *Obstetrics* (1903) is forcefully portrayed by the text's first frontispiece, described as a "Vertical Mesial Section Through Body of Woman Dying in Labour, with Unruptured Membranes Protruding from Vulva" (figure 8.1). In his brief preface on the following page Williams notes, "No pains have been spared in illustrating this work"; he indicates that the text's illustrations have been drawn from photographs "taken from life" (1903:v). This icon appeared in the six editions that Williams himself authored and thus introduced many physicians to the practice of obstetrics for the first three decades of this century.*

---

* It should be recalled that the period in which Williams prepared the first few editions was indeed a dangerous one in which to bear a child and to be born. Five women out of 1,000 parturients died from "affections connected with pregnancy," and 160 out of 1,000 infants died before the age of 1 year (Woodbury 1925). It was not breech presentation, however, but the failure of hygienic practice (for which Williams was an adamant advocate) and the absence of vaccination and treatment for infection that accounted for most of these deaths. Williams himself wrote that more than 95 percent of births had a healthier, vertex presentation, and only 3.1 percent were breech. Maternal deaths from "puerperal septicemia" (blood infection from obstetric procedure or delivery) occurred at slightly increasing rates during the first two decades of the twentieth century, accounting overall for 40 percent of all maternal deaths (30,763 in states with death registration). This condition was recognized to be almost entirely preventable by aseptic procedure (Woodbury 1926) and was thus largely the result of non-aseptic obstetrical practice. Williams knew this well. He wrote, "The most usual mode of infection is by the hands of the obstetrician or the mid-wife, and no one who has observed the way in which not a few medical men conduct labours can wonder that puerperal fever occasionally occurs. The employment of dirty instruments, as well as of dirty hands, also plays an important part" (1903:770).

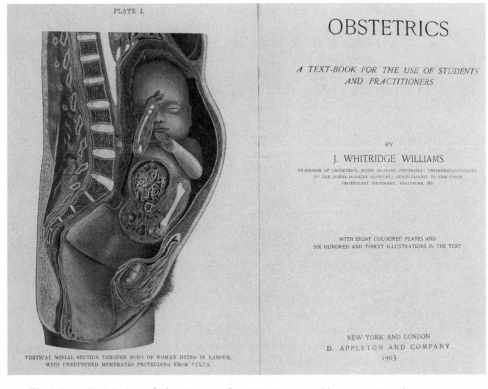

PLATE I.

VERTICAL MESIAL SECTION THROUGH BODY OF WOMAN DYING IN LABOUR,
WITH UNRUPTURED MEMBRANES PROTRUDING FROM VULVA.

OBSTETRICS

*A TEXT-BOOK FOR THE USE OF STUDENTS
AND PRACTITIONERS*

BY

J. WHITRIDGE WILLIAMS

PROFESSOR OF OBSTETRICS, JOHNS HOPKINS UNIVERSITY; OBSTETRICIAN-IN-CHIEF
TO THE JOHNS HOPKINS HOSPITAL; GYNÆCOLOGIST TO THE UNION
PROTESTANT INFIRMARY, BALTIMORE, MD.

WITH EIGHT COLOURED PLATES AND
SIX HUNDRED AND THIRTY ILLUSTRATIONS IN THE TEXT

NEW YORK AND LONDON
D. APPLETON AND COMPANY
1903

Figure 8.1   Frontispiece of *Obstetrics*, 1st ed., 1903. (Reprinted by permission of
Appleton-Century-Crofts.)

It may be that such dramatic illustrations and the techniques required to achieve them were common for medical audiences. Subsequent modifications of this frontispiece, however, suggest that later authors of the text found it inappropriate or offensive, or believed that their readers would find it so. Stander portrayed the fetus whole in the seventh edition (1936), and Williams's frontispiece disappeared thereafter. Though the figure continues to be used within the text to illustrate the complications of breech birth, it is currently reproduced as a sketch rather than a photographlike drawing. Whether or not such illustrations were conventional, this frontispiece lent to the entire text, to the work of obstetrics and the labor of childbirth, a distinctly pathological aura.

Four fundamental principles characterize Williams's conceptualization of women and childbearing. First, the childbearing woman is conceived as "the generative tract"—the organ system is abstracted from the person, so that the woman is no longer seen. Williams often writes that physicians are likely to "meet" not women with such and such a condition, nor even patients with this or that, but "cases of . . . ," or "conditions of . . . ," for example "cases of spurious pregnancy" or "pseudocyesis" (1903:168, 170).

Second, the course of childbirth is viewed as so danger-ridden as to be inherently pathological and in need of pervasive medical attention and control. Third, the parturient is ascribed an essentially passive role, while the physician assumes the central agency in delivery. In later editions of *Obstetrics,* Williams clearly indicates his belief that physicians rather than parturients deliver. The physician is not simply the attendant or counselor of a childbearing woman, but rather, the conductor of physiology and reproduction. The woman is a faintly discernible participant—the bearer of this physiological event. And fourth, where childbearing women and their consociates are ascribed any agency, it is essentially as adversaries obstructing their own childbirths.

Review of the contents of Williams's own editions of the text suggests that the events of birth, their antecedents, the delivery, and the subsequent puerperium (the period of recovery following childbirth) are in essence physiological. The chapters and contents within each section of the original edition of *Obstetrics* are overwhelmingly physical and technical in conception and focus. The first of eight sections of the book deals with anatomy, the next three with physiology, one with surgery, and the last three with the pathology of pregnancy, labor, and the puerperium. The parturient is frequently referred to as the "maternal organism," and labor is characterized as "extrusion from the maternal organism" (1903:193). A chapter segment, "Care of Patient during Puerperium," scrutinizes the woman's anatomy and its functions, but takes little or no note of the person who has just delivered. Care of the patient is care of a body: *"Care of the Patient during the Puerperium— Attention immediately after labor.* After carefully examining the placenta after its expulsion, to make sure that it is intact, the physician should devote his attention to watching the condition of the uterus" (1903:308).

Williams and his successors use the term *physiological* in two distinct, though related, senses. In the first sense, *physiological* refers to the science of bodily function—the physical, chemical, and biological workings of the body. That Williams considers childbearing a sequence of physiological events implies, by his understanding, that it is subject to no major influences other than physical, chemical, and biological ones. The mind is occasionally indicated to be minimally influential; society is not considered to affect obstetrical events significantly.

Physiological in Williams's second sense denotes at once nonpathological events of the body and events occurring without medical intervention. Thus, Williams ascribes what he believes to be excessive obstetrical intervention to a "pathological" view—contrary to the "physiological" one. In his preface to the fifth edition (1925), Williams expresses dismay that rates of maternal mortality have reportedly increased between 1916 and 1921. He notes a study indicating that, following puerperal infection, the second most common cause of maternal mortality was cesarean section. He is sobered by what he takes to be evidence that obstetrical intervention has worsened, rather than improved, obstetrical outcomes:

> As the reverse would naturally be expected, I am inclined to explain the apparent paradox by supposing that many practitioners in urban communities have been led astray by the teachings of those who regard labor as a pathological rather than a physiological process, with the result that interference upon insufficient indications is frequently undertaken by those who do not fully appreciate the risk involved.
>
> For these reasons, while the technique of the various operative procedures is described in all necessary detail, I have taken pains in stating the indications for their employment to insist upon the greatest possible conservatism consistent with the welfare of the patient and her child.   (1925:vii)

The "physiological" view, which Williams claims to hold, professes surgical conservatism and restraint—a bodily laissez-faire.

Not only are events of childbearing regarded as physiological in essence, but because of the ever-present threat of danger, these physical events come to be thought of as inherently diseaselike. Chapter 7, "The Management of Normal Pregnancy" (quoted more fully in the epigraph of this chapter), begins by referring to pregnancy and labor as the "highest functions of the female productive system," noting that these functions "a priori should be considered as normal processes." Williams then argues (1903:175) that the changes in the "maternal organism" that occur during pregnancy and labor, while ordinarily inconsequential, may become life-threatening for mother and/or child. He concludes that "strict supervision" of pregnant patients is essential.

The theme of pathology is typified by the "Printed Directions for Private Patients during Pregnancy" that Williams includes in the second edition. The last instruction informs patients, "I shall want to see you five or six weeks before you expect to be *sick* in order to ascertain your condition and to give you any desired advice" (1908:202; emphasis added). The pathological label for birth disappears in the instructions printed in Stander's 1936 edition.

Like birth itself, the events of the puerperium are also first characterized as physiological and normal; but they, too, are then recast in a pathological framework: "The puerperium or puerperal state comprises the five or six weeks following labour which are required for the return of the generative tract to its normal condition. Although the changes occurring during this period are considered as physiological, they border very closely upon the pathological, inasmuch as under no other circumstances does such marked and rapid tissue metabolism occur without a departure from a condition of health" (1903:301).

Again, it is not the mother who recovers during the puerperium, but the generative tract, and not one attached to a person, "hers," but "the" generative tract. That the puerperium is "considered as physiological" suggests that it, too, is a normal (frequently occurring) physiological event. But here, too, Williams reasons that since the only other conditions with similar metabolic characteristics are pathological, therefore the puerperium also must approximate pathology.

The understanding of childbirth as a sequence of physiological events has persisted little changed through the editions of *Williams*. Indeed, the paragraph characterizing childbirth, quoted in the epigraph, remained unchanged over fourteen editions and changed minimally thereafter:

> A priori pregnancy should be considered a normal physiologic state. Unfortunately, the complexity of the functional and anatomic changes that accompany gestation tends in the minds of some to stigmatize normal pregnancy as a disease process. . . . At times, pregnancy imposes other changes that when modest in degree are normal, but when more intense are decidedly abnormal. An example, edema of the feet and ankles after ambulation, is the normal consequence of regional forces imposed by the large pregnant uterus and by gravity. Generalized edema obvious in the face, hands, and abdomen, however, is definitely abnormal. *It is essential for the physician who assumes responsibility for prenatal care to be very familiar with the changes in normalities as well as abnormalities imposed by pregnancy.* (Pritchard, MacDonald, and Gant 1985:245; emphasis in original)

While physicians are still advised to remind patients "that labor and delivery are normal physiologic processes" (Pritchard, MacDonald, and Gant 1985:331), the "natural childbirth" or "physiologic childbirth" school of thought, which might be regarded as based on this principle, is acknowledged in neutral terms and neither criticized nor supported.

In the editions of Pritchard and MacDonald (1976, 1980), Pritchard, MacDonald, and Gant (1985), and Cunningham, MacDonald, and Gant (1989), much like their predecessors, chapters on "Maternal Adaptation to Pregnancy" consider only physiological matters and do not mention the experience or emotions of childbearing women—mothers: maternal adaptation is physiological adaptation. As in Williams's own editions, the puerperium is also still defined as the period during which the reproductive tract returns to normal. In the most recent editions (1985, 1989), postpartum depression is discussed briefly for the first time; the mother's experiential adjustment is not otherwise considered.

ISSUES OF CONTROL IN CHILDBIRTH

The possibility of malfunction shapes the enterprise of pregnancy and birth in Williams's text. Two chapter titles, "The Management of Normal Pregnancy" and "The Conduct of Normal Labor," capture the essence of the distribution of control in childbirth. While pregnancy and labor are events that women undergo, presumably also in the absence of obstetricians, Williams assumes that they require "management" and "conduct," even when normal. Such control, moreover, is thought to rest essentially, if not entirely, in the hands of the physician. The woman is cast in a passive role—the obstetrician in the active, leading role. When Williams asserts (1903:193) that in labor, either "the birth occurs spontaneously or requires external aid," no place is left for the woman as agent. Women patients are delivered; physicians—men, in Williams's day—deliver them.

Williams also exerts obstetrical control by the regime of care he recommends; control is again justified by medical principle. For example, Williams believes adamantly in the diagnostic and prognostic necessity of examining the parturient's pelvis and reproductive tract; he insists he will not treat a woman who refuses examination. Williams's remarks suggest that pelvic examinations were by no means routine at the turn of the century.

But unless the physician fully appreciates the importance of this examination, and has learned to look upon the making of it as a bounden duty, he may sometimes be deterred by feeling that it is repugnant to the patient, and that she may object to it or even refuse it. My experience, however, has always been that a few words of kindly explanation soon smooth away all such difficulties; and when, as happens fortunately in the vast majority of cases, after the examination we can reassure the woman as to the prospects of a simple and safe delivery, she will feel amply repaid for any inconvenience to which she may have been subjected. . . . If, however, it should happen that, despite the exercise of the greatest tact on the part of the physician, and his insistence that such an examination is a necessity for her own sake, the patient persists in her refusal, the former has no alternative but to decline absolutely to attend the case. (1903:178)

In Williams's view, parturients require strict supervision and direction (1903:283, 285). They are not only instructed on simple matters in simple ways; they are "allowed" to continue usual customs (1903:175) and "forbidden" sexual activity during the month before delivery. The physician is not a counselor, but a supervisor and director.

Where agency is ascribed to childbearing women, it is one of obstruction of the course of pregnancy, birth, and recovery. For example, physicians are strongly advised to disinfect and glove their hands before most pelvic examinations to avoid introducing or spreading infection, and women, "especially among the lower classes," are commonly thought to infect themselves by "fingering their genitalia or even making internal examinations" (1903:770); women may thus be a source of their own disease. Williams encourages the engagement of childbearing women in obstetrical institutions and their concomitant protection from themselves and their consociates (1903:175).

The capacities of childbearing women as informants on their own conditions are also mistrusted, perhaps because women are regarded as emotionally labile and susceptible ("nervous," 1903:166, or "hysterical," 1913:448), not fully intellectually capable (1925:228), and occasionally duplicitous. For similar reasons, their ability and motivation ("indolence," 1925:228) to comply with obstetrical regimens are also doubted.

Probably influenced by the women's movement and by the growth of the medical-legal industry, in recent editions of *Williams* attitudes toward control have shifted in tone and substance (Pritchard and MacDonald 1976, 1980; Pritchard, MacDonald, and Gant 1985; Cunningham, MacDonald and Gant 1989). As described below, women are increasingly ascribed decision-making roles in the control of reproductive events.

Recently, especially since the fifteenth edition (1976), the locus of reproductive control has been shifted in another direction by the emergence of maternal-fetal medicine. In the seventeenth edition, the fetus is said to merit "the same meticulous care by the physician that we have long given the pregnant woman" (Pritchard, MacDonald, and Gant 1985:139). The fetus is ascribed legal rights and "the status of the second patient, a patient who usually faces much greater risks of serious morbidity and mortality than does the mother" (1985:267). Though no edition of *Williams* has mentioned childbearing women in its dedication, the seventeenth highlights their babies. It is dedicated to "All Departmental Chairmen, who face the difficult task of providing for the expansion and exploitation of knowledge of human reproduction and for the application of that knowledge to the needs of society, especially the unborn and newborn, irrespective of socioeconomic status" (Pritchard, MacDonald, and Gant 1985).

In the eighteenth edition, the fetus emerges as the most powerful force in childbirth. The authors describe "the fetal-maternal communication system," in which information is exchanged through biomolecular nutrients and hormones. "The physiological and metabolic accommodations in the maternal organism that contribute to successful pregnancy are orchestrated by fetal-directed biomolecular initiatives" (Cunningham, MacDonald, and Gant 1989). Five "fetal initiatives" are described: implantation, maternal recognition in pregnancy, maintenance of pregnancy, endocrine function, and parturition. The fetus is characterized as "a benevolent, albeit self-serving, parasite . . . this rapidly growing, semiallogeneic, tumorlike graft" (1989). The authors conclude "unambiguously that the fetus, or else extraembryonic fetal tissues, direct the orchestration of the physiological events of pregnancy. The maternal organism passively responds—even to the point of her own detriment." "The high purpose of obstetrics is to ensure that every newborn is physically invested, *mens sana in corpore sano;* sound in mind and body, for the lifelong pursuit of the quintessence of earthly existence" (1989).

FOUNDATIONS AND DISTRIBUTION OF KNOWLEDGE IN OBSTETRICS

Williams describes obstetrics as an "art," based upon "scientific" foundations, with a "practical" application (1903:v). What he means by "art" is not discussed, but the term suggests an intuitive basis; it connotes the absence of fixed or rationally determined procedures. That obstetrics is an art also suggests that its principal events cannot be known or predicted with certainty.

The nature of the "scientific" foundations of obstetrics is not clarified either, though Williams makes reference to laboratory investigations of both normal and pathological anatomy. *Obstetrics* is replete with references to studies of obstetrical physiology, techniques, and their outcomes, cited to provide rationale for intervention. Art explains uncertainty, judgment, and occasional failure in obstetrics; science justifies its logic and its action.

Williams found the roots of the obstetrics he sought to establish in the United States in the science of Europe; he went to Berlin and Vienna to study bacteriology and pathology (Longo 1981). In the tenth edition (1950), the author, Eastman, deletes the numerous citations of German scientific literature in earlier editions of *Williams,* noting that they are now "only of historical interest." Eastman apparently regarded American obstetrics as having achieved autonomy.

As portrayed in *Williams,* knowledge of the events of childbirth is unequally distributed between childbearing women and physicians; moreover, the quality of knowledge possessed by each differs markedly. In general, the popular obstetrical knowledge—or rather ignorance—of women is noted to be a hindrance to effective obstetrical practice, so that physicians are advised to persuade childbearing women to avoid their "women friends" and to give full allegiance to their physicians (1903:175).

In the diagnosis of pregnancy, while the woman is thought to be often aware of her condition before she visits a physician, valid confirming knowledge resides solely with the physician. The diagnosis of pregnancy is said to be based upon particular "symptoms" and "signs." "The former are chiefly subjective and are appreciated by the patient; while the latter are made out by the physician after a careful examination, in which the senses of sight, hearing, and touch are employed" (1903:157). By definition, a childbearing

woman is said to have at best subjective knowledge of limited events in her
pregnancy, while attending physicians have the best available and definitive
knowledge.

Williams divides the signs and symptoms of pregnancy into three groups
according to their certainty and the stage of pregnancy at which they emerge.

> The *positive signs* cannot usually be detected until after the fourth
> month, and are three in number: (1) hearing and counting the fetal
> heart-beat; (2) perception of the active and passive movements of the
> fetus; and (3) the ability to map out its outlines. The *probable signs* can
> be appreciated at a much earlier period, and are: (1) changes in the
> shape and consistency of the body of the uterus; (2) changes in the cer-
> vix; (3) the detection of intermittent uterine contractions; and (4) in-
> crease in the size of the abdomen and uterus. The *presumptive evidences*,
> with a few exceptions, are subjective, and may be experienced at vary-
> ing periods. They are: (1) cessation of the menses; (2) changes in the
> breasts; (3) morning sickness; (4) quickening; (5) Chadwick's sign [the
> presence of blue or purplish coloration of the vaginal wall and open-
> ing]; (6) disturbances in urination; (7) abnormalities in pigmentation;
> (8) abnormal cravings; and (9) mental disturbances.   (1903:157–58;
> emphasis in original)

It is implied that the physician, but not the parturient, has direct access to
the "positive signs": she cannot hear and count the fetal heartbeat or perceive
the active and passive movements and location of the fetus, even after the
fourth month. While what the mother perceives as fetal movement is called
"quickening" and characterized as a weak sign ("presumptive evidence" of
pregnancy), the physician's perception of the fetal movement is classified as
"absolute," a positive sign. "This sign [maternal perception of fetal move-
ments] offers only corroborative evidence of pregnancy, and is of no value
unless confirmed by the hand of the physician, as in many nervous women
similar sensations are experienced in its absence" (1903:165).

Williams distinguishes the quality of knowledge held by physician and
patient, despite his acknowledgment that even physicians are fallible in
recognition of quickening, in cases of "false pregnancy" (1903:169). Access
to the probable signs is distributed between parturient and physician in the
same way as are positive signs. The parturient herself has direct access only to
presumptive evidence.

Through the various editions of *Williams,* the most remarkable changes in
the bases of knowledge of pregnancy are new diagnostic procedures. In 1925
Williams himself first added "laboratory studies" to his list of diagnostic
sources. Since then, the variety of tests—biochemical, radiological, and
sonographic—has multiplied, the last two now counted among the definitive "positive signs" of pregnancy.

As in earlier editions, Pritchard, MacDonald, and Gant (1985) ascribe the capacity to ascertain positive and probable signs to the "examiner" (presumably now including other types of clinicians in addition to physicians); "presumptive evidence" is still relegated to the woman whose condition is being diagnosed. Now "signs" and "symptoms" are both explicitly included among presumptive evidence, thus granting to women some objective knowledge, though still presumptive (1985:217). Again the woman's "perception" of fetal movement within her body is counted as a symptom and as presumptive evidence, whereas its "detection by the examiner" counts as a positive sign. For unstated reasons, the authors for the first time not only list as a sign the woman's self-perception of being pregnant but also emphasize its importance. Unfortunately, unlike the other presumptive evidences, they do not discuss this one further.

The eighteenth edition of *Williams* (1989) conceptualizes biochemical interactions of pregnancy as an informational exchange—a part of "fetal-maternal communication." One phase of this exchange is described as "fetal-induced maternal recognition of pregnancy." "Maternal recognition" is the biochemical, physiological response of the mother that affects the regulation of endocrine secretion. "Maternal recognition" is not a matter of the knowledge of the pregnant woman, but the reaction of her body.

In early editions of *Williams,* while information supplied to the patient by the physician is ascribed full authority, reciprocal information provided by parturient to the physician is considered suspect at best. Williams recommends that physicians "have all necessary directions written down in black and white, or preferably to use printed cards containing definite and concise instructions for the patient and nurse" (1903:275). Essential information is minimal, uniform, and thought to flow principally in one direction.

Although obstetricians are advised to provide rudimentary knowledge to parturients in routine fashion, other information is thought to require more discretion. Williams warns physicians not to make precise predictions about the duration of labor, for example, since they may be held to their predictions, even though they may be false. In addition, when the physician finds "some abnormality, even though he may not always deem it advisable to communicate his conclusions to the patient herself, he will generally do well to inform the husband or some other responsible member of her family of the existing condition" (1903:178).

Williams does not explicitly discuss the knowledge or information obstetricians should elicit from parturients, or the way in which this should be done. He nevertheless refers to information about patients useful in obstetrical decision making. During preliminary examination (recommended at least four to six weeks before the expected date of birth), physicians are advised to note "the general condition . . . particular attention being also paid to the measurements of the pelvis as well as to the presentation and position of the child" (1903:177). "The general condition" is a physical one, not involving the woman as person. Again in his chapter on the "Conduct of

Normal Labour," Williams repeats the importance of the preliminary examination in which the physician should "acquaint" himself "with any abnormality which may exist in the generative tract, but also with the general
physical condition."

PAIN AND ITS RELIEF

Williams does not mention pleasurable and satisfying experiences
in childbearing, but he is concerned with the "excruciating" pain that parturients may suffer during the course of delivery. Except for women who have
"religious objections," or for whom labor seems "almost painless," Williams
advocates a uniform approach to anesthesia.

> The patient having been instructed to give notice as soon as she feels
> a pain beginning, several drops of chloroform are poured upon an
> Esmarch Inhaler, and she is told to inspire deeply. This is repeated with
> each pain, the inhaler being removed immediately after its cessation. In
> this manner, after a short time the sensation of pain becomes markedly
> diminished, while the patient retains consciousness and is generally
> able to talk rationally. But when the head begins to emerge from the
> vulva, the chloroform should be pushed to complete anaesthesia, dur-
> ing which the head is born. This degree, however, should last only for a
> few moments.   (1903:286)

Throughout his editions of this text, Williams asserts that laboring
women experience their greatest pain when the infant's head emerges from
the vulva. In contrast, though the experience of pain is difficult to assess,
mothers commonly report the height of pain to accompany the dilation of the
cervix, before the infant's descent (Boston Women's Health Book Collective
1979; Wertz and Wertz 1977). Perhaps Williams takes for the height of pain
the visibly intense stretching of the vulva and perineum. In any case, it does
not seem that he assessed the sensations of the birth experience by inquiry of
its participants.

In the administration of anesthesia, Williams sought to balance the reduction of pain with protection of the perineum from being torn (caused by
tension and restless turning), maintenance of the woman's uterine contrac-
tions, and "a deleterious influence upon the child." He was concerned also
about the parturient's dependence on anesthesia.

In the second edition, Williams reports the recent introduction of a
compound, scopolamine hydrobromate and morphine, which promotes not
only analgesia (the dulling or alleviation of pain) but also amnesia (the
forgetting of pain and surrounding events). Pointing out that women have
"no recollection" of their labor after its use, he reports that Steinbuckel, its
discoverer, "is naturally enthusiastic concerning his results" (1908:324).

Williams, however, is cautious about use of this form of anesthesia because of inconsistent results and side effects. For these reasons, he never endorses its use. He believes "its use will eventually be restricted to a small group of neurotic patients, upon whom it is desirable to exert a psychic effect" (1930:392). He does, however, applaud the intended effects—amnesia as well as anesthesia. Childbirth is thus an experience whose pain not only merits reduction or elimination; it is an experience best forgotten.

While making the same recommendations concerning analgesia and anesthesia, Williams's successor, Stander, professes different goals. In the text's first separate chapter on "Amnesia, Analgesia, and Anesthesia in Labor," Stander indicates a belief that amnesia is not an end in itself and would be better avoided if pain could be controlled without it (1941:459). Thus, for Stander, childbirth is no longer best forgotten. Stander goes on to recommend that a patient with early pain be given analgesics "if she is a cooperative individual" (1941:476). He notes that women who respond to analgesics with increased excitation tend to be less intelligent. He adds, "In carefully selected patients excitement is reduced to a minimum." It is implied that women thought to be uncooperative or less intelligent should not be given the same analgesia as those more cooperative and intelligent.

Eastman and his colleagues do not follow the modifications of Stander, but advocate the widely used combination of amnesic and anesthetic drugs. They note that scopolamine, the amnesic, does not raise the pain threshold (thus lowering the pain experienced), but sometimes increases restlessness and expressions of pain. Again, the principal and desired effect is to make the laboring woman forget her experience. Thus, the measure of efficacy is not the woman's complaint during labor, but her dulled mental capacity and subsequent amnesia: "It is this impairment of cerebration which must be taken as an index of the action of the drug, rather than the complaints of the patient; many of them complain bitterly with every pain yet afterwards have no recollection whatsoever of what occurred" (Eastman 1950:424). Thus, it seems, it is again thought reasonable to allow the patient to experience suffering within the birth itself, if only the experience is later forgotten.

In recent editions, while the goals of pain control and amnesia are still pursued, the indications have shifted markedly. In contrast to Williams's uniform procedures for the administration of anesthesia, Pritchard, Cunningham, and colleagues recommend analgesia "initiated on the basis of the woman's discomfort." Moreover, the seventeenth edition is the first to note that though labor may be one of life's most painful experiences, it "often proves to be the most rewarding" (Pritchard, MacDonald, and Gant 1985:353). In this and the preceding edition, amnesia is not addressed as such; perhaps more subtly, it is noted that with successful analgesia and sedation, the laboring woman "does not recall labor as a horrifying experience" (1985:354).

REPRODUCTION, ABORTION,
AND THE SCOPE OF OBSTETRICS

In Williams's time, contraception was not legally available; the Comstock Law of 1873 made illegal the advertisement and sale of contraceptives.* (The Comstock Law was not reversed until 1964 by the Supreme Court case *Griswold v. Connecticut.*) On the other hand, sterilization seems to have been legal, at least in medical settings. Williams remarks that some authorities advocated sterilization of all women who deliver by cesarean section. He questions this policy and bases his own decision about sterilization on the "intelligence" or "ignorance" of each patient. If the patient is "intelligent," the decision should be left to her or her family, whereas with the "ignorant," the physician should do what he thinks is best. "Personally, I should be unwilling to sterilize the patient at the first operation, unless she comes from a district where proper operative help might not be available in a future pregnancy. On the other hand, if she is weak-minded or diseased and is liable to require repeated Caesarean sections the operation is perfectly justifiable" (1903:408).

It is Stander, in the eighth edition (1941), who first refers to "contraception" and "birth control." His concern, however, is not the general control of reproduction, but the prevention of pregnancy for women with certain specific diseases—tuberculosis, severe heart conditions, and renal failure. Stander advocates temporary or permanent sterilization of parturient women with these conditions. Like Williams, he, too, proposes that for "the unintelligent"—women thought incapable of effective contraception—"sterilization may be justified" (1941:612).

The following editions of Eastman (tenth through thirteenth) differ markedly from those of his predecessor on matters of reproductive control. For example, while Stander advocates contraception for therapeutic purposes, no discussion of sterilization whatever appears in the first two editions of Eastman (1950, 1956). Then, for the first time in 1961, authors Eastman and Hellman include information on contraception not only for the prevention of pregnancy for women with certain diseases but for the general control of reproduction. The authors cautiously assert that indications for contraception "will vary with the attitude of the attending physician" (1961:1, 124). Eastman and Hellman recommend the distribution of contraceptive knowledge and technique, quoting without comment a World Health Organization pronouncement:

---

* But for most of the first half of the twentieth century, control of fertility was a domestic, "home-made" affair, not at all within the province of physicians. "For most of this period, coitus interruptus, the rhythm method, and over-the-counter condoms were probably the primary source of contraception. With the social climate defined until the 1930s by the Comstock Law, fertility control was a private, not a public practice" (Luker 1984:51–52).

In areas in which some degree of family limitation is considered desirable because of population policies, or because the well-being of the mother and the child is being affected by excessive child-bearing, or because of social or economic reasons, the giving of appropriate advice should be included in maternity care programmes. The best time for offering such advice and instruction is during the postnatal period, due consideration being given to the family's religious and cultural background and the mother's wishes. (1961:1124–25)

In the fourteenth edition (1971), in a revised chapter on the control of reproduction ("Therapeutic Abortion, Induction of Labor, Sterilization and Contraception"), Hellman and Pritchard take a stronger position than that of previous editions, recommending that physicians, whatever their own beliefs, provide contraceptive knowledge and techniques to women and their families according to their circumstances and concerns. "Contraception is vital to the health of these women and their children. It is a requisite of good obstetric care" (1971:1100).

During Williams's lifetime, abortion was legal only when birth threatened the health or life of the mother. On Williams's recommendation, decisions concerning this procedure were to be based on a physician's evidence that the woman's life was endangered, corroborated by a second "responsible" physician. "Her [the pregnant woman's] statements are entitled to but little weight, and the decision to interfere should be based entirely upon objective symptoms [sic] and conditions" (1903:337).

The first indication for abortion that Williams describes is uncontrolled vomiting in pregnancy. Discoveries made by the time of his second edition allow, he believes, clear distinction between toxemic, neurotic, and reflex forms of vomiting. In Williams's view, only the first of these conditions is grounds for abortion. He explains, "Excellent results are sometimes obtained by treating the condition as a pure neurosis, with rest in bed, avoidance of excitement, moral suasion, and particularly the administration of small quantities of easily digestible food at frequent intervals and, when nothing is retained by the stomach, the employment of nutritive rectal enemata" (1903:462).

By the fourteenth edition (1971), while women's role in the decision is not noted, grounds for abortion had expanded to include the patient's "total environment, actual or reasonably foreseeable" (Hellman and Pritchard 1971:1088–89). Equating "social" with "nonmedical," Hellman and Pritchard remark that "the proportion of sterilizations performed primarily for social reasons is increasing quite rapidly" (1971:1095).

Attitudes toward the regulation of childbearing reflected in recent editions of *Williams* are ambivalent. On the one hand, the authors recognize problems of overpopulation and teen pregnancy; they advocate a role for obstetrics in the control of reproduction. On the other, they assert (tautologically), "the reproductive function in women is focused in a highly directed manner on the achievement of pregnancy and delivery of the mature fetus" (Cunningham, MacDonald, and Gant 1989:8). "Accordingly, menstruation must be viewed, in a physiological sense, as the end-result of fertility failure, whether chosen or naturally occurring" (1989:8). Obstruction of reproductive function may also be regarded as failure. (The implications of menopause in such a view are not considered.)

In the area of the control of reproduction by contraception, sterilization, or abortion, recent editions of *Williams* (1976, 1980, 1985, 1989) have most broadly ascribed to women substantial control. Here obstetricians are seen as serving their patients through the distribution of information and the performance of technical procedures. Editions since 1976 have included as a "transcendent objective of obstetrics" that "every pregnancy be wanted," and the preface to the 1985 edition recommends a focus on "optimal human reproduction."

THE CONTEXT OF CHILDBIRTH: MIND, BODY, AND SOCIETY

Several remarks in Williams's text indicate a strong, though mostly unspoken, sense of social order and morality. That Williams prescribes modification of the parturient's mode of living only if she has an "ill-ordered existence" suggests notions of deviance and associated problems. Williams may have believed women, or childbearing women, highly susceptible to deviance. Throughout his text are indications of the lesser capabilities ascribed to parturients, if not to women in general; as I have noted, he suggests low intellectual ability, emotionality and suggestibility, and occasional duplicity.

Williams makes several statements recommending that physicians replace the community traditionally surrounding parturients, principally family and women friends. He explicitly recommends exclusion of family from the delivery and allows their restricted entry only later. Instead, Williams believes it important both for the parturient's physical well-being and her peace of mind that she accept the commanding and exclusive confidence in her physician: "It is the duty of the physician to gain the confidence of his patient and encourage her to come to him whenever anything occurs to worry her, instead of taking advice from her women friends. A woman in her first pregnancy generally stands in need of a certain amount of reassurance with regard to the dangers of parturition, and the knowledge that she is in the hands of a competent and careful physician will contribute largely to her peace of mind as well as to her physical well-being" (1903:175).

Like Williams, Stander also insists on the importance of the parturient's confidence in her physician, a confidence he refers to as "psychic preparation"

(1941:476). Psychic preparation is to be established not by the physician himself but in maternal classes (presumably taught by nurses or other specialists). Like Williams also, Stander recommends the exclusion of family from the delivery room, because they may unduly influence the physician in his administration of anesthesia. Stander is also the first author of *Williams* to recommend that women whose pernicious vomiting does not respond to other therapies be referred to psychiatrists.

The editions of Eastman (1950 through 1966) effect a radical change from prior editions in the conceptualization of obstetrics. Beginning with the tenth edition (1950), Eastman introduces the text not with its traditional chapter on the anatomy of the female reproductive tract but with a new one on "Obstetrics in Broad Perspective." He defines "obstetrics" as "that branch of medicine which deals with parturition, its antecedents and its sequels. It is concerned principally, therefore, with the phenomena and management of pregnancy, labor, and the puerperium, both under normal and abnormal circumstances. . . . The transcendent objective of obstetrics is that every pregnancy culminate in a healthy mother and healthy baby" (1950:1–2).

Eastman attends systematically to the broad social and epidemiological environment of childbirth events. He examines maternal mortality, stillbirth, and neonatal mortality. He notes variations in maternal mortality by time, place, and person. He blames differences in medical care for the large discrepancy between the maternal mortality of whites and blacks. He also discerns relations between obstetrics and a number of other disciplines: the medical specialties of gynecology, pediatrics, and psychiatry; the "preclinical sciences" of embryology, endocrinology, immunology, pathology, bacteriology, and pharmacology; and nonmedical fields, such as nutrition, genetics, social work, and the law. Eastman believes that attention to these issues will "have an important bearing not only on many physical phenomena in pregnancy and labor but also on future mother-child relationships and on the family pattern in general" (1956:vii).

Eastman also expands consideration of psychological factors in birth, noting, "There can be little doubt that the attitude of a woman toward her confinement has a considerable influence on the ease of her labor" (1950:383). Despite this greatly broadened vision, recommended practices are not greatly changed. For example, as in medicine more generally, what Eastman calls "the personal history of the patient" is not her version of the pregnancy, but a medicalized account of her bodily condition (1950:311–12). Should this history indicate no abnormality, Eastman recommends that the woman be told that "she may anticipate an uneventful pregnancy followed by an uncomplicated delivery" (1950:313). Pregnancy and birth are characterized as "eventful" only with the occurrence of pathology.

In the 1956 edition, Eastman invited a psychiatrist, Leo Kanner, to contribute a chapter, "Psychiatric Aspects of Pregnancy and Childbirth." But, though psychiatric considerations became a part of the text during this period, they remained a separate part—not assimilated into central obstetrical theory or practice.

In his chapter, Kanner is concerned about understanding the world of parturients and their families. Perhaps optimistically or rhetorically, he asserts,

> The respect for individual needs and peculiarities, emphasized since the days of Hippocrates, has kept pace with the growth of the profession and has, in our generation, become a guiding principle in the management of sick and healthy people with regard to clinical, therapeutic, and prophylactic considerations. It is now acknowledged universally that the acquisition of skills in understanding the patient's interpersonal relationships is not less important than the mastery of technical procedures. The practice of obstetrics presents ideal opportunities for such understanding.   (1956:346)

Unlike his obstetrical colleagues and hosts, Kanner is interested in using parturients' psychological revelations not only for medical ends but also to address the concerns of parturients themselves.

> The obstetrician is indeed in a strategic position to function as the ideal mental hygienist of pregnancy and childbirth. Without being a psychiatrist he can contribute a lion's share to the emotional well-being of the mother and to the baby's comfortable start in life. For this purpose, he needs three major attributes: The ability to understand, the ability to listen, and the ability to guide. . . . The aim is voluntary compliance through insight, not blind obedience through intimidation.   (1956:360–61)

Sprague Gardiner, whose chapter replaced Kanner's in the thirteenth edition (Eastman, Hellman, and Pritchard 1966), is less sanguine than Kanner about the role of psychological considerations in medical education: "The teaching in medical school and residency programs is almost exclusively focused on the 'organic' aspects of obstetrics" (1966:335). Gardiner (who later served as president of the American College of Obstetricians and Gynecologists) is himself a strong advocate of "psychosomatic obstetrics," which "emphasizes that it is essential also for the obstetrician to learn the meaning and significance of the symptoms to the obstetric patient herself. What do these physiologic and pathologic changes and associated symptoms mean to the particular patient?" (1966:350).

Gardiner argues that when the strong emotions associated with events such as birth do not achieve satisfactory expression, their "energy" is transformed into physiologic process both through the action of smooth muscle and through endocrine function, resulting in somatic symptoms (1966:33–36). Although he titles his chapter "Psychosomatic Aspects of Obstetrics," Gardiner sketches a comprehensive theory that considers also the part played by socialization in the development of personality and by the social environment in the elicitation of social responses. He believes that women play an essentially supportive role in marital relations and that their principal sexual role is the satisfaction of their husbands (1966:341).

Gardiner also analyzes the psychodynamics of obstetrician-parturient relations. He argues that basic characteristics of this relationship are shaped by the roles of significant males in the woman's life, and that the relationship's power is determined by the meaning of birth in her life. Gardiner suggests that the obstetrician's awareness of these issues would facilitate "a greater degree of reassurance and emotional support."

In the preface to the edition following Eastman's, authors Hellman and Pritchard express their intention to integrate social and psychological considerations within their obstetrical text, rather than consigning them to a separate chapter (1971:vii). They assert that "in a broader sense obstetrics is concerned with reproduction of a society. Maternity care aims to promote health and well-being, both physical and mental, among young people and to help them develop healthy attitudes toward sex, family life, and the place of the family in society. Obstetrics is concerned with all of the social factors that greatly influence both the quantity and the quality of human reproduction. The problems of population growth are obstetrics' natural heritage" (1971:1). The authors claim that obstetrics should strive "to analyze the social factors which impinge on reproductive efficiency," noting, like Eastman, the social and economic factors that affect differences in maternal and neonatal mortality among U.S. populations. They conclude, "This concept of obstetrics as a social as well as a biologic science impels us to accept a responsibility unprecedented in American medicine" (1971:17).

Given such a broad view of obstetrics as a social as well as a biological science and a proposed resolution of the most pressing obstetrical problems through the union of two disciplines, the remainder of the fourteenth edition is remarkably unchanged. There is little evidence of an obstetrics uniting biological and social sciences. The importance of psychological factors is raised in relation to vomiting in pregnancy, spontaneous abortion, and pain in labor. Emotions are believed to exacerbate underlying physiological causes of nausea. Psychological or physical trauma are said rarely, if ever, to induce abortions. Again, total confidence of the parturient in her obstetrician is said to promote analgesia, and the woman's own society—particularly her women friends—is ascribed negative influence (1971:400). However, the relevance of an understanding of the meaning of events of pregnancy and birth in the lives of their bearers, as advocated by Gardiner, is no longer considered. And, while childbirth is explicitly said not to be a disease, but only to be "stigmatized" as one, difficulty in the "demarcation" of normal and abnormal events leaves childbearing a medical matter.

In recent editions of *Williams,* the introductory chapter, "Obstetrics in Broad Perspective," continues to claim that "obstetrics is concerned with reproduction of a society." It still professes obstetrics to be a social as well as a biological science. Still, there is no systematic consideration of the role of social organization, interaction, class, or culture (in the anthropological sense) in events of reproduction and childbearing. Nor is there more than brief mention of the psychodynamics or sociodynamics of childbearing, previously considered in the later editions of Eastman.

The eighteenth edition attempts to understand the basic nature of human reproduction by proposing a "theoretical norm," "uncluttered by social, religious, or pharmacological intervention" (Cunningham, MacDonald, and Gant 1989:893–94). The authors suggest that anthropology attempts such an uncluttering by the exploitation of "primitive societies." They cite the Kung! of the Kalahari Desert to suggest a more original state of reproduction.

VERSIONS OF *WILLIAMS OBSTETRICS*

J. W. Williams may well be regarded as the father of contemporary obstetrics. A large proportion of the 300 million U.S. births of the twentieth century (Centers for Disease Control 1992c) have probably been attended by followers of *Williams Obstetrics* in its multiple editions. Williams consolidated vast amounts of knowledge and attempted to weigh and organize this knowledge on the basis of scientific principles. He sought conceptual roots in European science of the day and incorporated his rationalized findings into a systematic, institutionalized obstetrical practice. Fundamental to his scientific system was the belief that sickness and health were essentially, if not exclusively, determined by the chemistry and physiology of the body.

Along with his reforming, scientific zeal, Williams promoted what were probably conventional notions about morality and propriety, and, more particularly, the nature of women. The synthesis of these notions with an understanding of medicine as a discipline based exclusively in the sciences of physiology, pathophysiology, and technique yielded Williams's vision of childbearing and obstetrics.

The goal of Williams's effort was the legitimized control of childbearing by Biomedical obstetrics. As this goal was achieved and physicians succeeded in expanding their purview and gaining control, women and traditional midwives lost it. Women came to be seen as having no role in defining health or in understanding, controlling, or actively participating in it. Domination and exclusion appear to have been achieved by consensus rather than by force. In sum, during the first half of this century, it became accepted both that obstetrical care should be part of a broad program of maternal, even women's health care, and that control of the ends, means, and measures of such programs should rest in the hands of physicians.

By the second half of the century, the authors of *Williams* have made broad claims about the central role of society, mind, and the behavioral sciences in obstetrical theory and practice. Psychologists and psychiatrists have contributed to this reconceptualization. Yet there remains a deep gulf dividing the claims of obstetrics as a social cum biological science and the implementation of this vision in either theory or practice. It is unlikely that social scientists would take *Williams Obstetrics* as a product of their discipline. Beyond the briefest mention, the text does not seriously consider the social or psychological context of reproduction, childbirth, or health care. *Williams's* authors have referred to the social sciences as a key to the solution of the most pressing obstetrical problems, but their promise to provide this key remains as yet unfulfilled.

Recent editions of *Williams* continue to define the events of childbearing—pregnancy, labor and delivery, and the puerperium—in essentially physical and pathological terms. Along with this focus on the body, however, another presence has emerged (or reemerged): the mother. Although recent authors continue to write of the "Maternal Adaptation of Pregnancy" in strictly physiological terms, they elsewhere refer to the mother as a sentient being—one experiencing childbearing events, expressing reactions, and making decisions. Women are no longer explicitly cast in a disparaging light. Family and society are also brought back into childbearing, as peripheral participants rather than as adversaries and obstacles. But, now also, the growth of medical knowledge, technical ability, and social-political concerns has fostered the development of maternal-fetal medicine, in which powers ascribed to the fetus dominate those ascribed to the mother, again threatening to deprive her of authority.

The largest measure of participation ascribed to women in recent editions of *Williams* involves control over reproduction—contraception, sterilization, and abortion. Beginning with the 1961 edition, obstetricians have been told that information and advice for patients on the control of reproduction should be a routine part of obstetrical care. Decision making in these matters has been increasingly ascribed to women and their families, based on their own, "sociologic interest" rather than on "medical" grounds alone. It is in reproductive control that women are ascribed the strongest roles as participants, to be served by physician advisers and practitioners.

Even at the perceived heart of obstetrical practice, in the delivery room, *Williams* increasingly recognizes the presence of childbearing women, and not simply "maternal organisms." The merits of "physiological" or "natural childbirth" are cautiously noted, and there is a modest effort to introduce some of its features into hospital settings. No longer insisting uniformly on supine, lithotomy position for delivery, physicians are now advised to allow their patients to find a posture that feels most comfortable and effective. Now anesthesia is recommended in response to the laboring woman's experience, rather than uniformly for all women. Still, in this crucial event women are seen as patients, essentially passive. Still, it is obstetricians, rather than laboring women, who are said to "deliver" babies. In the divisions of labor, obstetrics continues to cast itself in the dominant role.

9

BETWEEN TWO WORLDS:
PHYSICIANS AS PATIENTS

Between the last full moon and this, in the space of a single lunar month, I had come near to death, and been saved at the last moment; had had my mangled flesh sewn together and united; had "lost" my leg (for an eternity?) in a limbo of non-feeling; had recovered it, as by a miracle, when recovery had seemed impossible. I had had the foundations of my inner world shaken—nay, I had had them utterly destroyed.
— *Oliver Sacks (1984:169)*

Recovery uneventful.
— *Mr. Swan, Surgeon: Medical Chart of Oliver Sacks (Sacks 1984)*

While waiting for the development of an X ray of a one-year-old patient, Fitzhugh Mullan, a thirty-two-year-old pediatrician, asks the X-ray technician for a film of his own chest. He has been awakened over the last three months by an occasional pain, and he has been coughing for three weeks following the flu. He is pleased when the infant's film shows the "infiltrate" he expects, indicating a pneumonia effectively treated with antibiotics. He assumed he will find nothing pathological in his own chest film, but his first glance tells him "that something was very wrong." To the right of his heart is a "fluffy white density," the size of a grapefruit, like a "hazy cauliflower" in appearance. Mullan's first reaction is that of the physician: "This was an unusual finding, a fascinating X ray, I said to myself." He takes the X rays to the hospital radiologists, a consultation he commonly enjoys because he can show these colleagues what he knows and because he learns from them as well. When he tells the radiologists that the second film is his own, their usual friendly and casual manner abruptly turns guarded and awkward. Only then does Mullan first sense fear. Within minutes, he has been transformed from a highly competent physician, in the prime of life, productive, and seemingly very healthy, to a fearful patient, threatened by a possibly deadly disease with uncertain course.

234

Over the last thirty years a number of physicians have written accounts of various aspects of their own sickness. In this chapter, I analyze fourteen such accounts: three books, two articles in anthologies, and nine articles in medical journals. All but one (anonymously written, 1980) of the accounts I have found are by men. Among them are three surgeons (Mack, Nolen, and Cohn, a resident), a pediatrician (Mullan), a family practitioner (Geiger), an endocrinologist (Rabin), and a neurologist (Sacks). Freeman works in a hospital emergency room. Thomas has practiced pediatrics, internal medicine, and pathology, and has been president of the Sloan-Kettering Cancer Center. Stetten's specialty is unstated, but he, like most of the others, is engaged in research and/or administration.

Thomas reports three incidents of illness. Two of these and Sacks's affliction are traumatic. Sacks has further neurological complications as well. Rabin too suffers a severe and "progressive" neurological disease, ALS (amyotrophic lateral sclerosis). Todes suffers from Parkinsonism. Stetten is growing blind from "macular degeneration." Nolen has angina. Three of these physicians (Mullan, Mack, and Cohn) suffer malignant tumors. Zijlstra is afflicted with ulcerative colitis. It is notable that none of the conditions reported is psychiatric, though psychiatric issues arise in several of these accounts.

Most of us suffer affliction and become patients at some point in our lives. The intensive training of physicians in the knowledge and treatment of forms of affliction might lead one to expect that these professionals would be unusually adept as patients, or at least that their experience of the subject of their own treatment would be distinctive. The prevailing silence of physicians regarding their own affliction provokes speculation. It is possible that their training is so effective that it makes a commonly threatening experience unremarkable for them. On the other hand, perhaps their training, initial engagement, and continuing practice diminishes awareness and sensitivity to their own affliction, anaesthetically. It is possible also that public expression of the experience is not deemed appropriate or worthwhile.

Examination of physicians who publish their experiences of affliction provides a window, albeit a colored one, into this phenomenon. Indeed it provides a window into some essential features of the roles and experiences of both patients and healers in Western culture. Through this exploration I seek answers to several connected questions:

1. What patterns are there in ways in which these physicians encounter affliction? Some features may be common to patienthood in general, or to patienthood in Western society. Other features will be clearly characteristic of the medical patients examined here.
2. In these healer patients, how is the Biomedical worldview altered through the course of affliction? Does another perspective, a more person-oriented, "illness" ideology, or some other ideology, emerge

and assert itself? If so, how do the biomedical and the patient perspectives interact? Are they miscible? Does one predominate, and
what roles does each play?

3. What do these experiences tell us about being a patient, a physician,
about our medical system, about suffering and healing, about knowledge of self and the world, and about morality?

4. How do these experiences compare with the premises and practices of
non-Western ethnomedicines?

The physicians examined in this study are clearly not representative of
patienthood in the medical profession. (For a review, see chap. 6 and Pfifferling 1980.) That they write of personal matters—and before their colleagues—is itself unusual. Medical training does not encourage either introspection or its public disclosure. That most of these men write for medical
audiences, or medical audiences in addition to others, indicates that they
believe their experiences professionally distinctive and noteworthy. They are
moved to relay to their colleagues a vital message about patienthood, a
message from "the other side."

The issue of the health of physicians is of sufficient importance to the
community of physicians that it has engendered several epithetical prescriptions. One recommends to colleagues, "Physician, heal thyself!" The ambiguous prescription calls for treatment *of self,* but not *by self.* Grotjahn writes (in
Pinner and Miller 1952:95): "The demand, 'Physician, heal yourself' implies
to me: 'Learn how to be a better patient, and you will have learned how to be a
better physician in turn.'" This interpretation becomes clear in a second
prescription that suggests how this healing should *not* take place: "The doctor
who treats himself has a fool for a patient," sometimes amplified with, "and a
fool for a doctor." These attitudes are extended to the treatment of sickness in
the physician's family as well: "Don't treat the family."

There are also familiar expectations about what happens when physicians
become patients. It is said that "doctors make the worst patients." It is also
said that "if anything can go wrong, it will go wrong when the doctor is
taking care of a nurse, or physician, or a member of the physician's family."
Collectively, these epithets and customs indicate awareness of special needs,
problems, and solutions to affliction within the community of physicians.

The analysis that follows weaves these accounts into a whole, noting
differences among the afflicted physicians. Most of the studies I examine here
are linked by common features and themes. The study of Lewis Thomas
(1983), "Illness," stands apart. I analyze Thomas's account later, arguing that
while it is in the minority of reports discussed here, it is more representative
of the common reaction of physicians to their own disease. The other reports
are remarkable, and thus worthy of publication, precisely because they de-
part from the norm. Not only do they reflect on personal affliction, but they
examine medicine and its role in the light of affliction. Only for Thomas does

affliction not bear meaning beyond the bodily organ or part affected, altering conception of self or medical practice; only for Thomas does experience of the "other side" entirely reaffirm prior conviction.

ENCOUNTERING AFFLICTION

For both Mullan and Sacks, affliction descends rapidly from afar, unexpected. For both, acceptance of the affliction is met with resistance by several means: by assuming a physicianly role, by noting a troubling event (but ignoring the identity of its victim), by minimizing its import, and by intellectualizing—regarding the event as a vehicle for teaching or writing.

To reassure himself that nothing major is affecting him, to alleviate doubt, Mullan has his chest X-rayed. His youth, apparent good health, and his sense of strength and competence have fostered his belief that serious "illness—asthma, cystic fibrosis, diabetes mellitus, and cancer—happened elsewhere." Mullan reacts by setting his condition off at a distance and by medicalizing it. He notes his chest X ray to be "fascinating . . . the diagnosis seemed, at first, a total abstraction." Only after his radiological colleagues turn cool and hesitant does fear invade his consciousness. Again later, when he talks with the literary agent for his book-in-progress (*White Coat, Clenched Fist: The Political Education of an American Physician*), Mullan resists his affliction; he sees in his disease a serendipitous literary event, an opportunity for another book. His agent and friend is not so sanguine.

Oliver Sacks, a neurologist, is climbing a mountain in Norway when he comes upon a bull in the path ahead. He is seized by terror; he runs and falls. He lands with his left leg twisted beneath him, his knee in excruciating pain. He does not initially acknowledge the trauma to be his own; when he acknowledges it, he belittles it: "My first thought was this: that there had been an accident, and that someone I knew had been seriously injured. Later it dawned on me that the victim was myself; but with this came the feeling that it was not really serious" (Sacks 1984:21). When he tries to stand, his leg is totally limp, his knee flexes backward. Sacks examines himself as a surgeon examining a case. He reports his findings aloud, as if to medical students, intermittently screaming with pain as he demonstrates the damaged leg, "professionally, and impersonally, and not at all tenderly": "No movement at the knee, gentlemen, no movement at the hip. . . . You will observe that the entire quadriceps has been torn from the patella. . . . Yes, gentlemen, a fascinating case!" (1984:22). Only when he turns from his imagined audience, satisfied with a well-wrought presentation, is he struck with the realization that this "fascinating case" is himself. He is alone on a mountainside, unable to walk, fearful of death.

Some of these physician-patient-authors manifest the denial and delay commonly reported of nonphysician patients. In the summer of 1975, Nolen,

a general surgeon, played many games of tennis and racquetball, experiencing shortness of breath and chest pain, before one of his partners finally
persuaded him to see his internist. Nolen claims both to have contemplated
heart disease and not to have recognized angina even after several attacks. He
had good reason to suspect this condition, because of his family history and
his personal characteristics—imperfectly regulated hypertension, and so on.

> I can't say that the possibility my distress might be due to heart disease
> hadn't entered my head; it had, of course. I don't believe there's an
> adult male in the entire country who hasn't wondered, at one time or
> another, whether some pain or other symptom in his chest wasn't due to
> heart trouble. After all, not a day goes by that there aren't reports of
> sudden death due to "heart attacks" in the obituary columns of the
> newspapers or the news magazines. I knew it was a common ailment,
> and I knew, for reasons we'll get to soon, that I was a good candidate for
> the disease. But I did not think, at this time, my symptoms were
> coming from my heart.   (Nolen 1976:35)

BEARING AFFLICTION

For several of these physicians, acceptance of the role of patient is
deeply troubling. To Nolen's surprise, his denial of his condition continues as
both he and his internist fail to refer to the implications of the exercise test he
fails: "Oddly, at the time I'd failed my stress test, as Bill and I scheduled the
angiogram neither of us mentioned the possibility that I'd need to have a
heart operation, specifically a coronary by-pass operation. Yet it was the by-
pass operation that both of us were thinking about. Otherwise there wouldn't
have been any point in doing the angiogram" (1976:53).

Geiger (a family practitioner and researcher) writes of an illness during internship as one of three experiences profoundly shaping his medical thought
and practice. He is hospitalized on his own ward.

> In the space of only an hour or two, I went from apparent health and
> well-being to pain, disability, and fear, and from staff to inmate in a
> total institution. At one moment I was a physician: elite, technically
> skilled, vested with authority, wielding power over others, affectively
> neutral. The next moment I was a patient: dependent, anxious, sanc-
> tioned in illness only if I was cooperative. A protected dependency and
> the promise of effective technical help were mine—if I accepted a
> considerable degree of psychological and social servitude.   (Geiger
> 1975:13)

In describing the transformation, Geiger describes his experience as a
sequence of "mortification procedures" (Goffman 1958). Prominent among

these procedures is the exchange of the doctor's white coat—symbolizing authority, potency, and cleanliness—for the hospital "johnny"—symbolizing exposure, vulnerability, and helplessness. The same symbolic journey is noted also by Mullan and Sacks:

> The radiologist wanted to take X rays of my abdomen. The smock he gave me was absurdly short and as I padded down the corridor in my stocking feet with my knees showing I suddenly understood that I was a patient.   (Mullan 1983:5)

> . . . the systematic depersonalization which goes with becoming-a-patient. One's own clothes are replaced by an anonymous white nightgown, one's wrist is clasped by an identification bracelet with a number. One becomes subject to institutional rules and regulations. One is no longer a free agent; one no longer has rights; one is no longer in the world-at-large. It [is] strictly analogous to becoming a prisoner, and humiliatingly reminiscent of one's first day at school. One is no longer a person—one is now an inmate. One understands that this is protective, but it is quite dreadful too.   (Sacks 1984:46)

Sacks is further depersonalized as the surgical residents who are admitting him demand only the "salient facts" for "the history"—only a fragment of Sacks's own story, the one he wishes to tell. He feels like a "thing," "an admission." He is further silenced when, unable to tell the overbearing surgeon that he wants only spinal anesthesia, so that he can be aware and observant during his surgery, he is given "a general." This is the first of three times Sacks waits eagerly for the surgeon's visit and is severely disappointed. Deaf to Sacks's intended desperate pleas, the surgeon imposes with utter clarity, terse and cold: "Nothing to worry about. You've torn a tendon. We reconnect. Restore continuity. That's all there is to it" (1984:49).

Mullan, too, is overwhelmed with dread and helplessness. He is again reminded of his "complete subservience" as he is stripped, placed on a rolling stretcher and wheeled through the hospital corridors, covered only with a sheet. "It epitomized my vulnerability."

Mullan, Freedman, Rabin, Sacks, and Thomas all report participating early in some facet of their own diagnosis. For Mullan (and for Thomas, discussed below) this engagement involves not only examination of X rays, but also use of instrumentation to look directly into his own body. Mullan is at once diagnostician and patient. The experience is vertiginous: "The surgeon stopped partway through the exam, bent the flexible tube 180 degrees, and let me peer into my right main-stem bronchus, where I could see the tumor partially compressing the bronchus. For a crazy, order-defying moment I was doctor and patient all at once" (1983:13). Being on both ends of the bronchoscope defies order. There is something incommensurable about being physician and patient at once.

Several of these physicians report an urge to be "good patients." In part this means having a diagnosis respected by fellow medical practitioners. Geiger fears being labeled a "crock," and Rabin lies about his diagnosis to avoid the ostracism he expects intuitively. Being a good patient also means complying with prescriptions and other rules of "the sick role." Mullan notes (1983:40) that he did not "carry on as doctors sometimes do when they become patients." Cohn, a resident in surgery, dreads the epithet, "Doctors make the worst patients." It makes him "strive to be a model patient and not complain." He later feels that *he* has failed when a very strong, "aggressive" chemotherapy is discontinued because it produces systemic toxicity: "The news that my treatments were finished produced no elation. I felt that, much as I disliked chemotherapy, my lifeline has been taken away from me. I felt that I had 'failed the protocol.' This 'failure' seemed to take the onus off my physicians, since if a recurrence developed it would be my fault for not having undergone all ten courses of chemotherapy" (1982:1007). Cohn is relieved of his assumed responsibility when he is reassured that he has had at least as much medicine at this stage of disease as any patient reported in the literature.

For all of these physicians, becoming a patient means loss of control, helplessness, and assumption of a passive role. Although Sacks, Mullan, and others recognize this "regression" as necessary, "a biological and spiritual need of the hurt creature" (Sacks 1984:165), the transition is often difficult. It is resisted.

Cohn believes that the normal high competence of physicians makes it more difficult for them to "surrender to our doctors." Cohn's experience with the side effects in patients he has seen makes him still more reluctant to assume a passive posture. "After taking care of patients with a variety of illnesses, I was unable to dismiss the threat of a side-effect as an abstract concept. Many potential complications about which I was informed before consenting to chemotherapy triggered memories of patients who had had the worst imaginable complications of their diseases." He suggests that this reluctance may hinder the care of physician patients.

These physicians commonly react to the helplessness, vulnerability, and dependency of the patient role with unequivocal antagonistic emotions. There is shock, fear, dread, and anxiety, but also anger and rage and mistrust. Mullan writes that he feels he has been betrayed by his body; he is suspicious of it. His disease and treatment have "stripped me of my defenses." He becomes highly emotional, crying easily. These physicians write of their urgent needs, commonly unmet, to understand what was happening to them, to gain recognition and support from colleagues; they have needs also, sometimes explosive, for expression of their ordeals and for physical and emotional contact.

For Sacks, the course of trauma and recovery is an existential voyage, terrifying, deadly, and renewing. He writes that his sense of his injured, operated (but inoperative) leg was "something with no precedent in my entire existence." The word *inconceivable* is repeated frequently throughout his book. Sacks's literacy in Western traditions allows him to connect his personal suffering with fundamental premises of the broader culture. He refers to his experience in religious and spiritual terms of a "pilgrimage" and "grace," and in philosophical terms as "metaphysical," "ontological," "epistemological," and "moral."

Sacks discovers that the vagaries of his self and his universe follow the course of his traumatized leg. When he "recovers" from surgery, he finds that his left thigh shows no muscle tone, and that, despite intense effort, he is unable to move it. Will and effort fail. The capacities of self that he has taken for granted are themselves damaged. "But, what was not becoming frightfully, even luridly, clear was that whatever had happened was not just local, peripheral, superficial—the terrible silence, the forgetting, the inability to call or recall—THIS was radical, central, fundamental. What seemed, at first, to be no more than a local, peripheral breakage and breakdown now showed itself in a different, and quite terrible, light—as a breakdown of memory, of thinking, of will—*not just a lesion in my muscle, but a lesion in me*" (1984:67).

His powers of knowledge also fail, transforming, diminishing his sense of his own physical extent and surrounding space. At one point he awakens to be asked by the nurse to put his leg back into the bed. It has fallen out during his sleep. Yet he still believes it to lie in bed in front of him. Nor does he recognize when the nurse has moved it back. His leg has become an alien thing—a perception reinforced by its atrophy. It has become *nothing:*

> The day before, touching it, I had at least touched SOMETHING— unexpected, unnatural, unlifelike, perhaps—but nevertheless something; whereas today, impossibly, I touched nothing at all. The flesh beneath my fingers no longer seemed like flesh. It no longer seemed like material or matter. It no longer resembled anything. The more I gazed at it, and handled it, the less it was "there," the more it became Nothing—and Nowhere. Unalive, unreal, it was no part of me—no part of my body, or anything else. It didn't "go" anywhere. It had no place in the world." (1984:73).

With this transformation, an "ontological nightmare," Sacks also revises his history of himself, dismissing the history in which what had been "his leg" played an important part. Failed "proprioception" leads to a crisis in which he experiences "the existential aloneness of the patient, a sort of solitude which I hadn't felt on the Mountain." He feels again an overwhelming need for communication and reassurance.

For Sacks his mangled lost leg and reduced sense of self is a profoundly moral as well as an anatomical, conceptual, and ontological experience. He speculates that a similar alteration must affect all patients.

There had been, for me—and perhaps there must be for all patients, for it is a condition of patienthood (though, one hopes, one which can be well- and not ill-handled)—two miseries, two afflictions, conjoined, yet distinct. One was the physical (and "physical-existential") disability—the organically determined erosion of being and space. The other was "moral"—not quite an adequate word—associated with the reduced stationless status of a patient, and, in particular, conflict with and surrender to "them"—"them" being the surgeon, the whole system, the institution—a conflict with hateful and even paranoid tones, which added to the severe, yet neutral, physical affliction a far less tolerable, because irresoluble, moral affliction.   (1984:158)

In a most obvious, surface sense, Sacks's experience is quite unusual. Thus, while Mullan's superb account is said to record the "reality of what I experienced," Sacks explores the "derealizations of being in the affected, associated with an elemental anxiety and horror"—the irreality underlying the reality of profound affliction. Yet hints of existential trauma are present also in the work of Mullan and others. Although most of the authors discussed here do not formulate their pathology in philosophical and existential terms, there are clear suggestions in their writings of the threat that affliction brings to their sense of self and world.

Cohn writes, "surprise spits in the eye" (1982:1008). His inability to predict or control ever-emergent assaults, often unmitigated by medical caregivers, fosters helplessness and outrage. Yet he also writes of a new, paradoxical sense of competence formed in dealing with helplessness. Mack, too, indicates that disease that spreads despite his being a "good patient" threatens his view of the world. He is "devastated, bewildered, and very frightened." He finds his prognosis "completely intolerable." And Mullan writes, "No amount of medical training and exposure could prepare me for so sudden and drastic an alteration in self-perception." He is "ill prepared" for catastrophe. His sense of self, capacity, and the world, too, are affected by his bodily damage: "My cancer definitely affected my writing. When I could speak with such little certainty about my own body, how could I make claims about the world at large?" (1983:103).

Revision of self extends not only to the patient's present condition but to his or her past as well. Nolen examines his own past and practically prescribes habits by which other patients might avoid heart disease and recognize it. Mullan searches for the sources of his downfall in the midst of youth. "A persistent question that I spent many restless hours mulling was the explanation for my cancer. There must be a reason—some comprehensible cause—I kept telling myself. I didn't just get sick. It seemed too unlikely. The disease had to be the logical outcome of something—but what? I think I felt that the impact of the cancer would be lessened or made more bearable if I could find a rationale for it" (1983:42).

He raises a question of guilt—his own responsibility for his state. And, since his "primary" cancer, a seminoma, is congenital, he turns to scrutinize his parents. He fantasizes obsessionally of returning to the womb for a healthy new start.

Following his initial self-diagnosis, Mullan's physicianly posture loses hold, and his sense of affliction takes over. At the time of the definitive diagnostic procedure (a biopsy that goes awry, incurring much further damage), Mullan writes that he

> lived in a kind of limbo between doctor and patient. I discussed my options with several private consultants and a number of military physicians. At each visit I presented my case history and my X-rays simply and dispassionately. In fact, I discovered to my surprise, that I liked presenting my case. It felt appropriate and safe when I discussed my chest growth from a clinical point of view. The familiar role kept my fear at bay and allowed me some comfort in spite of the life-shattering diagnoses we invariably discussed. As long as I could play doctor to my disease, I learned, I could at least partially protect myself from the anxiety and feelings of helplessness that accompanied my new status. (1983:9)

Even following the "errant biopsy," Mullan can still claim to be "amused" when he awakes, following surgery, to find himself on "the other end of the respirator," a device of the technology he has practiced. He later remarks again on the bizarre fate of being a patient to his own discipline. "Weird. How weird!" Pain, fear, and subjection to common medical procedures makes maintenance of the comforting medical stance less and less possible, and less and less desirable. "As my treatments progressed, the subtleties of the doctor-turned-patient experience ceased to entertain me" (1983:41).

Later, when the radiological technician gives him his X rays to carry back to the oncologist, he no longer looks at them. "I knew as much as anyone about X-rays and easily could have examined my own on the way back to the clinic. I never did. The possibility that I would again discover trouble in my chest was so horrifying to me that it quenched my curiosity. I dutifully returned the unexamined films to the cancer specialist for his perusal" (1983:104).

Yet, while each X ray and each diagnostic label carries with it such new and personal force that his intellectual interest is markedly subdued, the medical perspective continues to assert itself. His knowledge fosters an acute attention to the slightest symptom that might indicate further disease or complication. "Not simply content to examine my scar from time to time, I put my medical knowledge to work against myself. I couldn't shave without finding a distended blood vessel or sleep without suffering a 'night sweat.' I attached a morbid diagnosis to every lump or rash I could discover. In addition, I mentally performed an examination to go with each new 'finding.'

I put myself through exploratory operations, liver biopsies, and brain scans. Unable to seize on the positive, I wallowed in the negative" (1983:63).

For Sacks also, following an initial diagnosis and an imagined lecture to medical students, pain and fear intrude, assisted by depersonalizing medical rituals, to force into consciousness and (in)action the patient posture. But for Sacks also, the medical attitude resurfaces during the course of affliction. After the crisis in which he suffers existential loss of his leg, Sacks recalls a patient more than fifteen years earlier who had had an experience very similar to the one Sacks is now suffering. Sacks had repressed this memory, because, despite its power, he was unable to grasp it. Following this remembrance, Sacks briefly imagines himself demonstrating this syndrome on himself— discoverer and patient; only then does he (again) recognize "the case" as his own, himself. He then proceeds with his self-diagnosis, contemplating several possible etiological investigations, and concluding that he had not had a stroke.

The response of physicians and other colleagues to their own afflictions is a focal concern of Rabin, Cohn, and Stetten; it is considered also by Geiger, Mullan, and Sacks. For several of these physicians, the reactions of their colleagues, both friends and strangers, is a troubling surprise. When they are severely afflicted, many of their colleagues turn away; the afflicted physicians sometimes refer to this phenomenon as "shunning." They also discover that their colleagues often are not nearly as helpful as they might be. They offer several explanations for the range of collegial responses, and they describe striking exceptions.

Rabin is an endocrinologist who was early fascinated by neurology, but who chose his current field because neurology seemed to offer patients little, if anything "in a definitive therapeutic way." For Rabin, the self-diagnosis of ALS (amyotrophic lateral sclerosis—a crippling, degenerative neurological disease) emerged logically despite his efforts at denial. Rabin senses intuitively that his colleagues' knowledge of his condition might destroy his professional career; so he lies to his colleagues, telling them he has "a disk," until his condition becomes too severe, a worsening limp, first requiring that he use a cane and then a walker. While the "disk" still seems plausible, Rabin's colleagues ask how he is doing. As his conditions worsens and the "disk" is no longer believable, his colleagues are less and less solicitous. They pretend not to see him; they turn away. "One day, while crossing the little courtyard outside the emergency room, I fell. A longtime colleague was walking by. He turned, and our eyes met as I lay sprawled on the ground. He quickly averted his eyes, pretended not to see me, and continued walking. He never even broke his stride. I suppose he ignored the obvious need for help out of embarrassment and discomfort, for I know him to be a compassionate and caring physician" (1982:508). Many former associates "disappear"; only a few become actively attentive to Rabin's plight. Rabin recalls that he himself once ignored the fatal affliction of a colleague whom he revered.

For definitive diagnosis, Rabin visits a renowned expert of ALS. The expert's diagnostic skill is superb, but his attention to Rabin's own experience of his condition is remarkably absent: "My disappointment stemmed from his impersonal manner. He exhibited no interest in me as a person, and did not make even a perfunctory inquiry about my work. He gave me no guidelines about what I should do, either concretely—in terms of daily activities—or, what was more important, psychologically, to muster the emotional strength to cope with a progressive degenerative disease" (1982:507).

The expert diagnostician manifests excitement only in showing Rabin the mortality curve for ALS. Rabin is surprised several months later when he reads an article by this physician stressing the importance of compassion and support for ALS patients; Rabin wonders if the response he has received derives from his status as physician.

Sacks too suspects that the reaction of his surgeon may result from or be exacerbated by his status as physician. When he recovers from surgery and discovers that his muscle is without tone and totally unresponsive, he longs for the surgeon's consolation. For the second time, he is severely disappointed by this man. In response to Sacks's stuttering plea, the surgeon answers insistently, "Nonsense, Sacks. There's nothing the matter. Nothing at all. Nothing to be worried about. Nothing at all!" (1984:105). Sacks is shocked. He puzzles over the surgeon's impersonality, his seeming misanthropy. "And this was sharpened and made worse by my being, and being seen as, his peer, so that neither of us really knew where we stood. And again, I could be certain that he was not really unfeeling—I had seen feeling, strong feeling, which he had to suppress, precisely as Miss Preston [a nurse] did when she saw the denervation" (1984:106).

Cohn also believes his status as colleague makes it difficult for physicians to respond adequately to him. He claims that they exhibit a "morbid curiosity," and that they seem "apprehensive about talking down to a patient with medical knowledge." Their response is to give inadequate explanations. Cohn is astonished and anxious when fellow residents discuss his "care" in his presence, but as if he were not there.

Mullan explicitly denies being shunned, but notes the depersonalization that is common to many patients, especially in hospital settings. He is particularly disturbed when a plastic surgeon discusses him as a great "case." "'This,' he said, referring to me lying on a stretcher, 'is simply a wonderful case. When the students are here, we never get a case like this, and now that the students are gone, here it is!' I felt belittled, cheapened" (1983:153).

While these physician patients are often stunned at the responses of many of their colleagues, they are also occasionally gratified by the responses of other, exceptional colleague physicians. Grotjahn (a psychoanalyst) tells of having to visit four urologists in order to finally find one who would listen to his complaint—a kidney stone. This physician described and predicted the course of the stone. Grotjahn believes the diagnosis itself had therapeutic effect. "I experienced great relief to learn that the passing of the stone, even if it is not particularly painful, causes what he called 'storms of the entire vegetative nervous system.' To be understood in these terms without psychology and psychoanalysis, without being made ridiculous or threatened by operation, gave me such relief that I passed the stone within twenty-four hours" (1952:94). Grotjahn later learns that this urologist himself has had two kidney stones removed.

Similarly, as Sacks awakes in a rural Norwegian hospital, a young surgeon enters, prances around the room, flexing his legs. He leaps onto the bedside table, takes Sacks's hands, and places them on his thighs. This surgeon too has been injured and is now healed and restored to full health. Moreover, with little talk, he embodies and enacts health; and he heals through his person and his performance. Of all the physicians encountered during his ordeal, Sacks remembers this one best and most affectionately. "His visit made me feel immeasurably better."

Toward the end of his recovery, Sacks is visited regularly in the convalescent home by another surgeon, a man with whom he finds he can talk easily. He is surprised and asks the surgeon about this unusual ease. "It's simple. Maybe you guessed the answer. *I've been through this myself.* I had a broken leg. . . . *I know what it's like.*"

Sacks hopes to finally resolve his anger toward the operating surgeon. He returns to the hospital for a checkup. No longer anguished, Sacks does not demand emotional or collegial succor. The surgeon is not friendly or effusive; he remains distant, but "allowed a remote smile."

Rabin is also surprised by the caring response of some colleagues. In the recasting of his collegial world, several physicians with whom he had had little previous contact now appear to help "unflinchingly." One remarks, "You have the illness, but we are in this together." Another of his colleagues, a former "fellow," moves into Rabin's home and helps in many ways, including daily chauffeuring.

Physicians' responses to afflicted colleagues, then, are by no means uniform. The contrast between the reactions of Rabin's colleagues when they believe he has a "disk" and when they believe he has something much "worse" suggests that the aversive response may be specific to a class of afflictions. Geiger dreads collegial response as long as his diagnosis remains uncertain. He is greatly relieved to be firmly diagnosed as having a viral pericarditis. "Good diagnoses," he asserts, have a common set of characteristics: "To survive with minimal dehumanization in a teaching hospital, there is nothing better than a moderately serious, reasonably benign, incontrovertibly organic illness with a good prognosis and just enough rarity to interest the physician" (1975:13).

As they become patients and are healed, many of these physician-patients note significant alterations in their social worlds. Beyond medical institutions as well as within them, relationships of different sorts take on new meanings, and the cast of individuals who fill these roles changes noticeably. Some of these shifts are felt as shocking impoverishment, others as deep enrichment. Affliction transforms the society of the patient, by constriction, recasting, concentration, and consolidation.

Mullan describes in detail the effects of his cancer and recovery on the life of his family. His disease both threatens and enhances the strength of his relations, first with his wife and daughter, then with a second daughter, conceived during his recovery, and finally with an adopted son. Reaffirmation of his sexual potency is crucial in restoring his embattled sense of self.

Mullan claims not to be aware of individuals in his social world who fled from his affliction. He notes on several occasions the vital importance of those who stayed, surrounding him. "It is impossible to measure the total force of this web of assistance, but I know with certainty it had much to do with my regaining my momentum. While there may have been individuals who were driven away from me by my illness, I had no awareness of it. What I remember and cherish are the people who commiserated with me, helped me, rooted for me, pinch-hit for me, and eventually cheered for me" (1983:163). An essential quality of these social effects sets them apart from those of medicine itself. He describes them as "incredibly important" and "impossible to measure."

While several of these physicians note the immeasurable importance of warmth in their plight, several also report negative facets in the responses of those around them. Sacks describes the response of a nurse, Miss Preston, who attempts to help him regain use of his operated leg, entirely without success. When she touches his inert muscle, "again I thought I saw a startled and disturbed look, and even a trace of unguarded disgust, as when one touches something which is unexpectedly soft and squirmy" (1984:60). Her horror penetrates her otherwise pleasant and hopeful demeanor.

Cohn also comments, cryptically and ambivalently, on the expectations of his close relations. As he recovers, several people from his social circle seem to resent his failure to participate actively in his career and in living arrangements. They resent also his discussions of chemotherapy. He is given little space for convalescence. But he also notes, "Being in a stable loving relationship and having several close friends and family members with whom I could share my experience helped immeasurably. So did my work, both because it was stimulating and because it allowed me to feel productive" (1982:1008).

Sacks notes a drastic segregation from caretakers and from the healthy, even as he recovers at a convalescent home. He recognizes now that, as a physician, he has fostered the same separation.

But if I rejoiced in the blessing of the sun, I found I was avoided by the non-patients in the gardens—the students, nurses, visitors who came there. I was set apart, we were set apart, we patients in white night-gowns, and avoided clearly, though unconsciously, like lepers. Nothing gave me such a sense of the social caste of patients, their being outcasts, set apart from society: the pity, the abhorrence, our white gowns inspired—the sense of a complete gulf between us and them, which courtesy and ceremony served only to emphasize. I realized how I myself, in health, in the past, had shuddered away from patients, quite unconsciously, never realizing it for a moment.   (1984:163)

Reciprocal sentiments, of physician patients toward the well, are also highly charged and ambivalent. Sacks remarks on walking by a school team practicing rugby, and feeling "virulent envy . . . the hateful spite of the sick." He is embarrassed and guilty at his own reaction. As Sacks himself is healed, gaining increasing competence and power in his leg, his hatred disappears. He is delighted to watch a dance, though not daring to participate. Some dancers grab him, and he is pulled into joyous motion without deliberation.

HEALING AND CONVALESCENCE: BECOMING A NONPATIENT

While assumption of the patient role is noted to deprive these patients of agency and society, healing, when it occurs, demands resumption of activity and social life. The return is laborious, painfully fruitful and rewarding.

Sacks describes this dark and enlightening travail in lucid detail. His renewal seems to spring, quite unexpected, from flashes of pain in the alienated leg. The reality of the limb, and its reality as his own, is further confirmed when the silent technician removes the cast. "A leg—and yet, not a leg: there was something all wrong. I was profoundly reassured, and at the same time disquieted, shocked, to the depths. For though it was 'there'—it was not really there" (1984:124). Sacks recalls again his patient of many years before who believed his leg to be a counterfeit, cleverly attached.

Later the nurse warns him when she's about to remove his stitches. When he asks if she is about to begin, she tells him she's done. Again, proprioception fails, "his" leg again alienated. Then, when the caster lifts Sacks's leg from the table, and Sacks sees that the knee no longer flexes backward, he feels "an infinite relief: a relief so sweet and intense, so permeating my whole being, that I was bathed in bliss." His leg has moved, anatomically, conceptually, from death toward rebirth. He falls asleep.

When he awakes he has an impulse to flex his leg and does so instantly. What was inconceivable is done. Sacks's sense of volition and competence is also reanimated. He is unable to repeat the motion at will, but his competence continues to grow.

Sacks regards the posture of the patient as so categorically subject that it can only end with doctor's orders, following which the patient rises. Prior to this, "one cannot see, one cannot conceive, beyond the limits of one's bed. One's mentality becomes wholly that of the bed, or the grave" (1984:133). He is forced to stand and then to put weight on "the leg." The experience is vertiginous. His sense of space is totally distorted; distances multiply and vanish: "I was infinitely unsteady. . . . The extent of transformation and change was immense—there could be a thousandfold switch between successive 'frames' " (1984:139).

He stands, and supporting weight, a sense of order returns. "I was bearing witness, even as I was undergoing it, to the very foundations of measure, of mensuration, of a world." He is forced to step, a step that is unthinkable, and so he goes. And so his sense of self and will and space are renewed.

Not all of these physicians recover. For some, their condition grows increasingly and inexorably worse. For those who recover, the path to health has common milestones. Several of these physicians write of strikingly similar difficulties in terminating a principal form of therapy. The event is profoundly ambivalent: while termination is seen as necessary in the course of recovery, the loss of therapy is feared because the patient has become accustomed to it and because he fears that it may not have worked. These patients dread failing to recover following the withdrawal of therapy. Moreover, relinquishing the role of patient means resumption of another, active role; it means fulfilling greater expectations on the part of oneself and others.

Cohn describes the "stress of termination of therapy," and the failure of both medical personnel and his personal social environment to support the difficult passage to health. Remission of the tumor that tentatively suggests medical cure only signals the beginning of his return voyage, and not, as his consociates assume, health itself.

While Mullan abhors the hospital and has suffered greatly, he fears terminating therapy and moving home: "but my last morning of radiation therapy, the day before I was to leave the hospital, I suffered an incredible spasm of anxiety. Crying did no good. Vomiting, spitting, and belching were in no way cathartic. There seemed to be no avenue of escape from the constant fear and nausea that I felt. . . . Deep within me I could not accept being cut adrift to fend for myself. I had become a slave of my therapies" (1983:57, 58). He hints at suicidal thoughts, though he does not quite say so. He is surprised and greatly relieved by a psychiatrist who responds to his needs. "His sense of succor was so spontaneous, generous, and accurate that it still astounds me. Surely it came from no textbook of psychiatry but from the man himself" (1983:59).

For Sacks also, departure from the hospital to a convalescent home is a deeply ambivalent event. He knows he must go, but he dreads leaving the protective environment. He attempts to climb onto the hospital roof, requiring a sequence of acts for which he is not yet ready. He is stopped by the hospital staff. "It was only at this point that it broke through to consciousness, and I realized—I had in fact tried to have an accident, because I was dead scared of leaving. I would not mention a purely private bit of neurotic 'acting-out,' had I not discovered that such acts were rather common among the patients. . . . We wanted, consciously, to be weaned, but unconsciously we feared, and tried to stop it, to prolong our special, pampered status" (1984:166–67).

Many of these physicians discover as patients a world of patienthood that they had not seen from "the other side" or that they had seen only dimly. Part of their new vision is through their own experiences; another part is through their encounter of other patients and patient communities. Discovery of the community of patients is informative; it is also a source of healing and a means of resocialization.

After his (failed) attempt to explain the anguish of his "lost leg" to his surgeon, Sacks calls a registrar (that is, resident). To his plea, the registrar replies, "Sacks, you're unique." Sacks becomes angry; he panics. He struggles with this remark through the course of recovery, for while it is often dehumanizing for any patient to be labeled "a case of such-and-such," it may be still more profoundly traumatic to be labeled "unique," that is, not a case of anything known, a case of nothing. Sacks's ontological nightmare is confirmed, his solitude reinforced.

For Sacks, his "brother" patients become vital companions in the path from the constricted, metamorphosed, and isolated world of affliction to restored full engagement in life and work. "This sharing of normally hidden and private feelings—feelings, indeed, often hidden from oneself—and the depths of concern and companionship evoked, the giving and sharing of priceless humor and courage—this seemed to be remarkable in the extreme, unlike anything I had even known and beyond anything I had imagined" (1984:172). Sacks's "quickening" occurs both as he again recalls the prior patient of his own and as he now comes to share experiences in a community with other convalescent patients. His isolation decreases as he discovers that other patients have suffered remarkably similar courses. He and they become "alive together." He notes that the detail in his (egocentric) diary decreases, and he communicates more directly with his fellow patients,

> as importantly, I was no longer alone, but one of many, a ward, a community, of patients. I was no longer the only one in the world, as perhaps every patient thinks in the ultimate solitude of illness. I was no longer confined to my own, empty world, but found myself in a world peopled by others—*real* others, at least in relation to each other and

me: not just role-players, good or bad, as my caretakers had been. Only now could I exorcise the fearful words of the surgeon to me: 'You're unique!' . . . for the first time, I learned that my own experience, my "case," was far from unique. Almost every patient who had had injury or surgery to a limb, and whose limb had then been casted, out of sight, out of action, had experienced, at least, some degree of alienation: I heard of hands and feet which felt "queer," "wrong," "strange," "unreal," "uncanny," "detached," and "cut off"—and, again, the phrase "like nothing on earth." (1984:161–62)

Not only had these patients had metaphysical trials akin to his own; they had also been similarly rebuffed by their caregivers.

Sacks is also surprised to find in his fellow patients "with no special knowledge" a profound wisdom. A limbless patient enlightens both his own and Sacks's suffering with a unifying explanation; he recommends an ingenious way to avoid his own dilemma—curtailing pain in a "phantom limb" by severing and anesthetizing nerves before amputation of the affected limb. "What I found with him I found with them all. They were all much wiser than the doctors who treated them! There is among doctors, in acute hospitals at least, a presumption of stupidity, in their patients. And NO ONE was 'stupid,' no one is stupid, except the fools who take them as stupid" (1984:171).

THE STRANGE BUT COMMON CASE OF LEWIS THOMAS

Of all the accounts of affliction among physicians that I have found, the account of Lewis Thomas stands clearly apart. Only for Thomas does affliction not assault the sense of self, the world, or the medicine he practices. To the contrary, the three illnesses that Thomas recounts reaffirm his sense of self and his faith in the medical system and its worldview.

Thomas tells of three incidents of illness sustained since age sixty-four: "I have had a close look from the bed itself at medicine and surgery and, as I shall relate, an even closer look at myself. On balance, I have very much liked what I have seen, but only in retrospect, once out of bed and home free. While there, I discovered that being a patient is hard work" (1983:222–23).

Two of the events are traumatic, "accidents"—a torn cartilege in his knee incurred while bathing in the surf and a dislocated shoulder following a fall during a lecture in a dark auditorium. The most threatening of Thomas's illnesses begins as pneumonia, turns into an obscure blood loss, and is effectively diagnosed and surgically treated. I focus on this most dramatic of Thomas's illnesses; it takes him by surprise and threatens his life.

When Thomas is struck by a debilitating pneumonia, his wife calls the doctor, a friend, "a real, house-calling doctor." The next day Thomas "finds himself" in the hospital. Blood tests indicate a large blood loss. To investigate the source of this loss, a hematologist neatly performs a bone-marrow biopsy.

> Despite his reassurances I could not avoid the strong sense that having one's bone marrow sucked into a syringe was an unnatural act, no way for a human being to be treated. It did not in fact hurt much, but the small crunching of bone by the trocar followed by the peculiar and unfamiliar pain in the marrow itself were strange sensations, not at all nice. I have performed bone marrow biopsies myself, long ago as an intern and from time to time since, and have always regarded the procedure as a minor one, almost painless, but it had never crossed my mind that it was, painless or not, so fundamentally unpleasant.   (1983:224)

Like Mullan, Thomas gets an opportunity to look inside his body. In search for the place of bleeding, his colon is thoroughly inspected by use of a "colonoscope"—a fiber optic device that, inserted through the rectum, illuminates regions of the lower gut and allows a more or less direct viewing.

> As a nice gesture of professional courtesy, the doctor stopped at frequent intervals during this procedure and passed the viewing end of the instrument over my shoulder and in front of my left eye. "Care to take a look?" he asked. I had never looked through this wonderful instrument before, although I had seen many photographs of the views to be had. It would have been interesting in any case, I suppose, but since it was the deep interior of my own intestine that I was looking at, I became totally absorbed. "What's that?" I cried, as something red moved into view. He took a look and said, "That's just you. Normal mucosa."   (1983:225–26)

Thomas describes the diagnostic event as a "fascinating, but negative excursion"—negative because it does not yield a (positive) diagnosis.

The definitive diagnosis is made by a gastroenterologist with a detectivelike name, Dr. Sherlock, who (with the assistance of Watson) checks out a remaining diagnostic possibility, "the new syndrome arteriovenous anomaly," in which bleeding occurs when arteries and veins do not properly connect.

> A catheter was inserted in the femoral artery, high up in the right leg, and pushed up into the aorta until its tip reached the level of the main arteries branching off to supply the large intestine. At this point, an opaque dye was injected, to fill all those arteries. Just before pressing the syringe, Dr. Robin Watson, the X-ray chief, warned me that I would feel a sense of heat, not to worry. It was a brand-new sensory impression, perhaps never experienced except by patients undergoing

this kind of arteriography: for about thirty seconds I felt as if the lower half of my body had suddenly caught fire, then the feeling was gone. Meanwhile, movies were being taken. . . . I was enchanted: there, in just one spot somewhere on the right side of my colon, was a spilled blur of dye, and the issue was settled. It struck me as a masterpiece of technological precision, also as a picture with a certain aesthetic quality, nice to look at.   (1983:227)

Thomas's descriptions of his affliction, diagnosis, and recovery are clean, colorful, cute, and passionless. It is as if he were recording the conditions of someone else, poetically writing a medical chart for a nonmedical audience. He writes of the examination of his own body in impersonal terms—"the femoral artery," "the right leg," "the aorta." His total absorption in looking at his colon is medical and intellectual. He labels his bone-marrow biopsy "fundamentally unpleasant"; while the "fundamental" suggests a profound experience, the "unpleasantness" circumscribes its depth. He is "enchanted" by his X ray—a technologic and aesthetic masterpiece. And he writes in skeptical quotation marks of "depersonalization" and "dehumanization" and denies experiencing these during his illness. Because of his undaunted faith in his physicians, his belief in medicine is reaffirmed. He fancies a technological device that would allow physicians in training to experience patienthood, without actually suffering its damage and its pain.

I know a lot more than I used to know about hospitals, medicine, nurses, and doctors, and I am more than ever a believer in the usefulness of technology, the higher the better. But I wish there were some easier way to come by this level of comprehension for medical students and interns, maybe a way of setting up electronic models like the simulated aircraft coming in for crash landings used for pilot training. Every young doctor should know exactly what it is like to have things go catastrophically wrong, and to be personally mortal. It makes for a better practice.   (1983:231–32)

Thomas's sense of "self" is also confirmed by his pathological encounters.

I have seen a lot of my inner self, more than most people, and you'd think I would have gained some new insight, even some sense of illumination, but I am as much in the dark as ever. I do not feel connected to myself in any new way. Indeed, if anything, the distance seems to have increased, and I am personally more a dualist than ever, made up of structure after structure over which I have no say at all. I have the feeling now that if I were to keep at it, looking everywhere with lenses and bright lights, even into the ventricles of my brain (which is a technical feasibility if I wanted to try it), I would be brought no closer to myself. I exist, I'm sure of that, but not in the midst of all that soft machinery. If I am, as I suppose is the case at bottom, an

assemblage of electromagnetic particles, I now doubt that there is any
center, any passenger department, any private green room where I am
to be found in residence. I conclude that the arrangement runs itself,
beyond my management, needing repairs by experts from time to time,
but by and large running well, and I am glad I don't have to worry
about the details.   (183:232–33)

Thomas's sense of "self" shows several remarkable features. First, when he
writes of seeing his "inner self," he is referring to his X-ray examination and
to colonoscopy, his joints, and his guts. Introspection here is firmly and
thoroughly literal, concrete. Second, inspection of this physical "self," even
under life-threatening conditions enhances Thomas's wonderment, but re-
veals nothing very new. Finally, Thomas's self-proclaimed "dualism" is validated. He suggests both that he is ultimately composed of atomic particles
and that he does not exist in any particular part of "the arrangement" and has,
he is satisfied, no part in its operation.

Whereas other physician writers write because patienthood has modified
or revolutionized their way of thinking and feeling about themselves, their
work, and their world, Thomas writes to express unwavering conviction in
this prior position. But though Thomas's response stands apart from those of
his colleagues as described above, I hypothesize that his response is likely to
be more fully representative of most of his profession. We can surmise, as I
suggested earlier, either that medical training and practice makes the experience of affliction unremarkable and/or that the public expression of these
reactions is not deemed worthwhile or appropriate.

THERAPEUTIC AFFLICTION:
BIOMEDICINE INSIDE OUT

With the exception of Lewis Thomas, many of these physicians are
significantly affected, if not transformed, by the events of personal affliction
and/or healing of which they write. When they return to practice, their
medical understandings and actions and their broader lives are substantially
altered.

Sacks elected a specialty in neurology because of its pure conceptual
pleasures, its "clean" distance from patients. In a previous work, *Awakenings,*
he struggled to penetrate the experience of patients with Parkinsonism. This
earlier analysis required great imagination and empathy, but his own affliction and recovery, of which he writes in *A Leg to Stand On,* gives him new
epistemological grounds.

Now I KNEW, for I had experienced myself. And now I could truly
begin to understand my patients, the many hundreds of patients with

profound disturbances of body-image and body-ego, whom I saw over the years. I could listen to them, I could understand them, and sometimes I could help, because I had traversed this region myself. I came to realize, as did my patients, that there is an absolute and categorical difference between a doctor who KNOWS and one who does not, and that this knowing can only be obtained by a personal experience of the organic, by descending to the very depths of disease and dissolution. (1984:202–03)

Sacks comes to conceive of a paradigmatic revision of his discipline in theory and practice. He reflects that neurology, as currently practiced, is "puppetology." Self and agent are absent. Following the experience with his leg, his discipline of "neuropsychology had crashed in ruins about [him]—it retained all of its practical uses and powers, but it had lost all its promises and anything deeper" (1984:217).

He observes that neurology is founded on metaphysical error, but worse, it is "deaf to anguish." His goal is to reconstruct his discipline radically for a "neurology of the soul." And, as music has played a vital part in his own healing, so he believes in the restorative powers of music in other neurological patients; the notion is literal as well as metaphorical—a healing by music, healing as reorchestration.

He describes his new approach only in broad outline. He has practiced a medicine of this form for years; only now, in the aftermath of his recovered leg, does his practice gain solid bases. His life surrounding his practice, too, is fully enriched. "The human science, the human medicine, I had glimpsed years before had rooted itself, deeper and deeper, within me, calling equally to the depths of heart and mind. And it was not just a new 'field' or even a new science that opened to me, but a new and wholly delightful sphere of life and mind" (1984:221).

Rabin has chosen *not* to become a neurologist for reasons similar to Sacks's reasons *for* this choice. While he is fascinated by neurology, he finds its ability to diagnose frustrating, since the power to cure neurological conditions is quite limited. Through the travail of affliction, Rabin's notion of "definitive therapy" is radically altered. From divergent paths, both he and Sacks arrive at consistent views of this field. He now recognizes that much can and should be done even when a condition is incurable. He calls for a response to personal suffering, for solicitation, empathy, and support, to fill the "deafening silence."

Mullan, too, discovers both an "unimagined" world of patienthood and a gulf between this world and the world of medical practitioners. He is twice struck by this distance in events that occur toward the end of his recovery, when he leaves the hospital and slowly returns to active life. He is interviewed by the *Washington Star* and is surprised that hospital personnel who treated him are offended by his account and now treat him coldly. By telling his experience of patienthood, not always recognized by treating professionals, he comes to recognize that these practitioners have been wounded.

> In all, I was stunned at the gap between the medical and the non-medical perceptions of my story. The hospital staff, on the one hand, saw my case as an exceptional cure due to good medicine and good care, and that is the story they expected to find in the newspaper article. When they discovered something different, they took exception. Laymen, on the other hand, saw me as surviving despite, not because of, the trials and risks of modern medical care. Since one reads much less about the latter circumstance than the former, they responded supportively to my even broaching the subject. (1983:160–61)

Mullan also speaks to medical students about his experience. He recommends humility and recognition of the common humanity of patient and physician. His audience is generally indifferent, except for some students who ask why he is "down" on medicine and why he did not pursue another career if he did not want to be a physician. Mullan's recommendations are antithetical to the students' understanding of the profession they are learning.

Mullan's sense of self and world as well as his medical practice are altered by his disease. "I know that I developed skills of patience and resilience that will stay with me in other crises. I think I have learned something about what it means to be elderly, since I have had to live with degrees of physical compromise and incapacity that were unknown to me before. Disease is a sober teacher that leaves its pupils wiser—if not always thankful—for the instruction" (1983:167–68).

Several of these physicians note the importance of succor in medical care. They find that, though many physicians are frustrated by an inability to help *medically,* there is a vital assistance they can render beyond the medical. Stetten and Rabin indicate the importance of assisting patients in "coping" with their disabilities. Mack advocates an "alternative" therapy—imaging—accompanied by a heightened sense of self and competence, to complement medical treatment. Several of these physicians emphasize the importance of attention to medical colleagues, whose pathology is significantly affected, they have learned, by their professional posture.

Geiger draws an insightful conclusion about the psychodynamics of doctor-patient relationships, one at odds with a postulated ideal of medical practice. He examines the stance of "affective neutrality" and "detached concern" (Fox 1957) and finds that he is more than concerned and less than detached. In medical work, he suggests, there is a profound engagement of self, an engagement against which the intense efforts of Biomedicine may "defend," without total success.

BIOMEDICINE AND OTHER MEDICINES

Biomedicine battles on various fronts to defend boundaries from patients and from their experience of sickness. Pursuit of a medical career itself most often requires unusual superior health and stamina to fulfill rigorous training and practice. It hardens as well, discouraging by various means attention to self, and training for a proper, protective distance from patients—"detached concern." There is not sufficient time both for care of self and for care of others. Nor, generally, is support offered within the institutions of training or practice for the troubles and losses suffered by physicians and trainees; rather, attention to self may be regarded as indulgence—unbecoming of the physicianly role and stigmatized. Personal attention to patients is likewise discouraged and, when acknowledged, given low priority. The (unspoken) rule of response to affliction in self and other is silence. Medical specialties that may explicitly consider personal and social facets of affliction—psychiatry and family medicine—are low-status specialties, and students who elect these specializations often do so in the face of adverse reactions from peers and teachers.

Commonly, the defenses of Biomedicine are effective in maintaining distance from disease and from the suffering of patients. Lewis Thomas, for example, evinces an apparently indomitable joy and faith in the powers of medicine, through which deep and personal fear and threat are almost undetectable. The boundary is uneasy, however; its maintenance exacts a heavy cost. In most accounts reviewed, these defenses "fail"; a new world is revealed.

When suffering breaks through, the process of translation—of the encounter within individuals of two cultures, two languages, two societies—is most often not a smooth but a cataclysmic sequence. Through this troubling course, worlds of physician and patient interact in several ways. Though not uniform, the course has several shared features:

1. The damage is initially seen as someone else's.
2. It is minimized.
3. It is intellectualized, transformed into a subject for writing and teaching.
4. Physician patients diagnose their own conditions.
5. They may treat themselves and they may delay in seeking treatment by others.
6. They evaluate the diagnoses, prognoses, explanations, treatments, and care given by their colleagues.
7. They mistrust some of their physicians or their physicians' diagnoses, therapeutic prescriptions, or prognoses.
8. They discover a special need for understanding, explanation, support, and sympathy from colleagues, beyond what is strictly "medical."

9. They strive to have non-"crock"-like conditions and to be "good patients."
10. They strenuously avoid passivity and lack of control.
11. They recall other patients whom they may have misunderstood or who may have had severe side effects with conditions similar to their own.
12. They continue to monitor themselves, medically hypervigilant for signs and symptoms indicating possible changes in their conditions.
13. They reexamine themselves and their histories in the search for etiology and broader explanation.
14. They reformulate their theory and practice of medicine in the light of their patienthood.

Among the ethnomedicines of the world, Biomedicine is distinguished by its insularity from the subject of its work. In contrast, anthropological review shows various ways in which patienthood, suffering, and therapy are incorporated within healing practices in other societies, rather than being kept apart.

In Biomedicine itself, the principal exception to unreflexive practice is found in the psychoanalytic movement, within, yet distinct from other specialties. Psychoanalytic training and practice most often requires preliminary completion of medical school and residency specialization in psychiatry. A prominent element of subsequent psychoanalytic training is the "training analysis," in which the candidate undergoes psychoanalytic therapy, not motivated by a particular affliction, but in order to better know him or herself and experience what he or she then does to patients.

Freud, in his earlier (1912) "Recommendations on Analytic Technique" and his later (1937) "Analysis Terminable and Interminable," sketched a rationale for analysis of the analysts, one that can continue beyond training throughout active practice. In 1937, Freud argued that "there is a certain advantage" in the treatment of tubercular patients by physicians who have experienced the same disease. He also claimed (1937:351) that, while for other medical specialties, affliction with a disease does not hinder treatment of that condition, the psychoanalyst "is really impeded by his own defects in his task of discerning his patient's situation correctly and reacting to it in a manner conducive to cure."

The psychoanalytic approach employs an essential reciprocity. The patient "transfers" or "projects" onto the therapist the persons of the patient's own life. The therapist "countertransfers" to the patient his or her own life scenery and cast. The therapist uses the patient's transference to understand, with the patient, the patient's past and unconscious. At the same time the therapist uses his or her own trained unconscious reactions to the patient in order to understand the patient's interactions. "To put it in a formula: he (the therapist) must turn his own unconscious like a receptive organ towards the transmitting unconscious of the patient" (Freud 1912:115). In using him or herself as an instrument of perception, it is essential that the analyst must know him or herself, so that no hidden agenda motivates interpretations and responses, unawares.

> It is not enough for this that he himself should be an approximately normal person. It may be insisted, rather, that he should have undergone a psycho-analytic purification and have become aware of those complexes of his own which would be apt to interfere with his grasp of what the patient tells him. There can be no reasonable doubt about the disqualifying effect of such defects in the doctor; every unresolved repression in him constitutes what has been aptly described by Stekel as a "blind spot" in his analytic perception. (Freud 1912:116)

While the rest of Biomedicine attempts to separate itself, "allopathically," impassively, by forms of cognitive, emotional, and practical immunization and antisepsis, from the diseases and patients it treats, many other ethnomedicines explicitly engage pathology in the healing process by several means. These ethnomedicines might thus be described as "empathetic" or "sympathetic."

In several non-Western ethnomedicines, healers-to-be are said to encounter, in distinctive and powerful ways, either the particular causal agents of afflictions or their healing counterforces. In many aboriginal North American societies, novices discovered and pursued their healing careers through meetings with the "supernatural" beings and forces associated with specific sicknesses (Hahn 1978). These meetings were achieved in "vision quests," dreams, or sometimes by "possession." Visitations were sometimes sought, sometimes regarded as involuntary.

In other ethnomedicines, the healers of certain afflictions are themselves required to have suffered those same afflictions; healers emerge or are recruited from among those healed of a particular affliction. Thus, Edgerton (1966) reports that, among the Hehe of Tanzania, shamans who treat certain psychiatric conditions must themselves have suffered (or continue to suffer) these conditions. Turner (1967) reports that among the Ndembu of Zambia, there are "cults of the afflicted" from which healers of these conditions are recruited. And Balzer (1983) describes the development of shamans among the Khanty of Siberia, among whom healing power is often manifested in "nervousness, dreaming, and sickness."

Non-Western ethnomedicines are also reported to involve close engagement of healer, patient, and affliction in the process of diagnosis. In the ancient system of Siddha medicine of India (Daniel 1984), diagnosis is believed to follow three stages. In the first stage, the diagnostician senses the patient's complex pulses (three pulses are distinguished on the right, three on the left) by application of his fingers to the patient's wrists. In the second stage, the diagnostician becomes aware of his own pulse as well as that of the patient. The diagnosis culminates in a third stage in which the diagnostician modulates his own pulse to match the patient's, and thereby knows the patient's condition by sensing it in himself, empathically.

Finally, several non-Western ethnomedicines are reported to recognize a close engagement of healer and afflicting agent in the course of healing. Balzer (1983) describes Khanty ethnomedical education, in which the focus is "learning how to send one's sickness soul into the world of spirits." Healing among the San ("Bushmen") also requires close and dangerous personal engagement with the forces of healing, a "terror-filled experience of death and rebirth" (Katz 1976:85).

In contrast to the reductionistic and individualistic tendencies of Biomedicine, many non-Western ethnomedicines recognize broader cosmic connections, part of what I refer to in chapter 1 as "disorder" accounts. The human body is seen not as discrete—an isolated entity capable and worthy of isolated treatment. It is seen rather as an element in a far broader scheme, inseparably connected to mind, person, society, and cosmos. The course of pathology and healing in "individuals" is commonly regarded as a series of events of cosmic imbalance and rebalance. In these events of cosmic imbalance and rebalance, healers are recognized to be essentially engaged as agents and as mediators of far greater forces. In several ways, these ethnomedicines recognize that healers are agents and/or patients immersed in the same nexus of affliction and healing as is "the patient" in question.

A "cult of the afflicted" has recently appeared at the heart of Biomedicine. In 1981, a group of practitioners formed the American Society of Handicapped Physicians (ASHP). The principal organizer was Spencer B. Lewis, a black family physician who practiced until his death in 1981 in Grambling, Louisiana, a town of mostly poor blacks. Lewis had diabetes and practiced blind for two years, with the assistance of his wife, a nurse midwife. According to the ASHP quarterly newsletter, *Synapse* (3;3 1984), membership comprises almost 225 people; "full membership" requires status as physician. Member Frank Zondlo estimates that there are 18,000 handicapped physicians in the United States, of which only 500 have responded to his inquiries for a directory. A study of 175 members finds 133 (76 percent) in active practice, 20 medical students, and 20 residents. Eighty-five (49 percent) suffer neurological, 37 (21 percent) musculoskeletal, 25 (14 percent) visual, and 17 (10 percent) hearing disabilities. Most frequent medical specializations (among the 133 in active practice) are internal medicine (28; 21 percent), family practice (22; 17 percent), rehabilitation medicine (16; 12 percent), psychiatry (14; 11 percent), and pediatrics (13; 10 percent); the distribution of specialty interests among the residents is similar.

American Medical News of the American Medical Association reports (Carrell 1983:37) that *beyond* the handicaps themselves, the principal difficulty of these practitioners is their colleagues: "The main problem handicapped physicians face is rejection by their colleagues, say MDs who have problems ranging from blindness to paralysis" (Wainapel 1984:1).

Their colleagues avoid encounters with them and refer fewer patients to them. The vice president of ASHP, Howard Shapiro, a psychiatrist and psychoanalyst with polymyositis, finds that "handicapped doctors are treated like doctors who are drug addicts—get them out of sight" (quoted in Carrell 1983).

These practitioners are reported to feel that their handicaps are profoundly burdensome. They must deal not only with colleagues but also with their own anger and denial, complicated by their medical knowledge. They must compensate for their handicaps with special equipment, the assistance of other personnel, or restricted practice. Compensation is commonly obstructed both because resources are not available and because the medical and broader social community resists compensatory efforts, thus multiplying difficulties.

Yet handicaps also provide a special insight into suffering and the world of patients. Handicaps often enhance the ability of these practitioners to deal with patients. Maureen Lonegan, a physician with multiple sclerosis, is herself treated in the center where she works. "We [handicapped physicians] form an interface because we are patients and physicians. I shuffle back and forth. Sometimes I don't know where I fit" (quoted in Carrell 1983:38). She finds herself more responsive and she likewise finds patients more receptive. Many of these physicians focus on the treatment of conditions akin to their own. Suggesting the proximity of the rest of society, medical and nonmedical, to themselves, some of this "handicapped" community refers to others as "temporarily able-bodied." Regarding the responses of other physicians to their handicapped colleagues, Frank Jirka, Jr., a physician, double amputee, and president of the AMA in 1983, concludes: "Other physicians are not insensitive intentionally. They just need education" (quoted in Carrell 1983:38).

10

FROM MEDICAL ANTHROPOLOGY
TO ANTHROPOLOGICAL MEDICINE

> I contend that all medicine is in crisis and, further, that medicine's crisis derives from . . . adherence to a model of disease no longer adequate for the scientific tasks and social responsibilities of either medicine or psychiatry.
> —*Engel 1977:129*

> As I see it, all the diseases which hurt the Navaho people may be divided into three kinds. There are those diseases that we medicine men have given up on. We know that you white doctors have better cures than we do. One of the diseases of that sort is tuberculosis. Then there is sickness which comes from getting too close to where lightning has struck. Right now there are probably some patients in this hospital who are sick from that illness and you doctors have no way of even finding out what is wrong with them—but we medicine men can, and we are able to cure such cases. A third type of illness is snake bite. You can cure that, and we Navaho also have our own medicines for that.
> —*Scott Preston, medicine man and vice chairman, Navaho Tribal Council,*
> *quoted in Adair and Deuschle (1970:33)*

In spite of its flourishing knowledge and expanding technique, Biomedicine in the United States is in critical condition. The system does not provide care for a large proportion of the population—34 million persons younger than sixty-five—and it discriminates in the care it gives to older persons, women, minority members, and the poor. In multiple jeopardy, those who are most likely to need care are least likely to have it. Moreover, what care is provided is commonly unsatisfactory for givers as well as recipients—though often for different reasons. The crisis in health care is generally thought to be financial—excessive, rapidly accelerating costs and unequal coverage—but the ills of Biomedicine reach far beyond matters of cost and distribution. Biomedicine suffers from false expectations, lost faith, and mistrust.

In the era of advanced scientific knowledge and technology, patients commonly expect that physicians should invariably recognize and efficiently treat their sicknesses and relieve their suffering. Patients assume that diagnoses and therapies are founded on the best science; they ignore the probabilistic and tentative foundations of much scientific knowledge. When physicians fail to meet these expectations, they are held at fault. In recent decades, patients have sued for "wrongful pregnancy" (when a recommended sterilization or contraceptive procedure has failed), "wrongful birth" (when a child is born in some way "impaired" and it is believed that the impairment could have been detected and averted by standard means), even "wrongful life" (when it is believed that the plaintiff would have been better off never having been born) (Botkin 1988), and death thought to be brought on by medical care. Thus, patients may hold their physicians responsible for the span of life events, from "medical paternity" to death (Annas 1979).

Patients are troubled not only by the outcomes of Biomedicine but by the manner of its delivery. Particularly when they come from cultural traditions or social classes that differ from those of the physicians, patients may believe they are not heard, understood, or responded to. In a nationally representative sample, 45 percent of patients recently discharged from a hospital complained of not having been informed about daily hospital routine, and 22 percent reported that their physicians spent less than five minutes explaining how they were supposed to care for themselves at home; there were substantially more complaints among minority patients, women, less educated patients, and the poor (Cleary et al. 1991). Perhaps because they were assumed unable to judge, these patients were not asked about their satisfaction with medical facets of their care.

The attitude of patients toward their physicians, once respectful if not reverential, has turned adversarial. Patients also resent physicians' earnings, though they substantially underestimate how much physicians earn (*New York Times [NYT]* Mar. 31, 1993). "This used to be a highly respected profession that we wanted to be part of," says Dr. Burton White. "Now we are the enemy" (*NYT* Mar. 9, 1993).

Profound dissatisfaction with medical practice is also reported among physicians; medicine today is often called "the troubled profession." "At some point in the past 15 years, a profound change occurred in the way doctors felt about their profession. There is now abundant evidence of serious dissatisfaction among practicing physicians, and this discontent has been mirrored in the attitudes of prospective recruits into the profession" (Schroeder 1992:583).

An AMA survey found that a remarkable 44 percent of physicians currently in practice reported that, had they known what they now know about medicine as a career, they would not have gone to medical school (Schroeder 1992). Physicians are said to be most troubled by growing bureaucratization, administrative requirements, and the loss of control to governmental and insurance agencies. A survey of professional satisfaction among internists found that "the degree of personal control these physicians perceived having over their practices" was the least satisfying facet of their work (Schroeder 1992). Thirty percent of internists are said to be willing to forgo part of their income for a reduction in administrative requirements; others are leaving their practices or retiring early (*NYT* Mar. 9, 1993). They are oppressed by the scrutiny insurers give to their medical decisions, thus diminishing their prized professional independence. The insurers may believe that they avoid unnecessary procedures and cost by carefully reviewing the medical work they pay for, but physicians perceive their judgment to be relentlessly questioned by personnel often unqualified to judge. One physician who closed his office in response to growing administrative demands and loss of independence is quoted as saying, "It's an affront every single day. I like to think that I practice good medicine, and to have someone second-guess you all the time wears you down" (*NYT* Mar. 9, 1993). Physicians protect themselves from lawsuits by practicing "defensive" medicine—selecting courses of action not for what they believe to be effective diagnosis and treatment of their patients but to avoid the possible perception of neglect. They have avoided or left medical practices, such as obstetrics, in which malpractice suits are common. Still, 8 percent of U.S. physicians are sued each year (Gonzalez 1992).

Physicians are concerned that patients are often "poor historians"—that is, they do not truly understand their own conditions or they fail to report their symptom histories in a way that would facilitate diagnosis (Coulehan 1984). Internist Richard Baron was shocked one day to hear himself say to a patient, "I can't hear you when I'm listening," revealing that he ignores the world of his patient—what the patient has to say—when he focuses on the bodily sounds he hears through his stethoscope (Baron 1985). In medical practice, the patient's story (and his or her subjective experience) may be regarded as a nuisance and a diversion from diagnosis and therapy (Brody 1987).

Physicians may also be cynical about patients who are concerned needlessly—when nothing is "really" wrong; patients may be pejoratively labeled "the worried well" or "hypochondriac." Their complaints may be thought to have no physical basis (because none is found or recognized); they may be called "crocks" or "health care abusers." Physicians are puzzled and troubled, too, by patients who do not listen or comply with their recommendations.

Reiser (1978) has claimed that medical technology has increased the distance between physicians and their patients. He argues (1993) that the intensive Biomedical focus on disease labels has led to the equation of patients and their conditions ("the carcinoma in the third bed on the left") and to a loss of concern among physicians about individuality, variation, and the experiences of patients.

In the arena of Biomedicine today, patients, physicians, nurses and others, insurers and employers, governmental payors and regulators, and administrators battle one another on fundamental matters of duty, authority, control, independence, integrity, value, and trust.

ANTHROPOLOGICAL REMEDIES

I propose *anthropological medicine* as a remedy to some of the underlying ills of Biomedicine. In brief, anthropological medicine is a theory and practice that gives primacy to sickness—conditions of patients as conceived and unwanted by themselves—that accepts the social and cultural roots of both professional and lay ideas and attitudes about sickness; that fully recognizes the etiology of sickness in social and cultural as well as physiological and environmental conditions; that also acknowledges sociocultural effects in therapy and healing processes and respects the social context of healing; and that addresses the well-being of healers and their patients alike. It integrates a sociocultural perspective with a biological one at the core of medical education, medical practice, research, and institutional arrangements.

In Biomedical settings, anthropologists are occasionally called to assist with patients whose cultural traditions appear to hinder standard practice— perhaps because the physician does not understand the patient's complaint or because the patient does not accept a prescribed therapy. Such a medical practice might be termed "cross-cultural" (Saunders 1954). I argue that, in a basic sense, *all medicine is cross-cultural*—that patient and healer inevitably conceive of the world, communicate, and behave in ways that cannot be reasonably or safely assumed to be similar or readily compatible. Use of a common language, concepts, and behavior between patient and physician gives the appearance of shared understandings and effective communication; but appearances may be deceptive. "Unless people are sensitive to such differences in purpose or unless these are explicitly discussed, meanings will not coincide since they are anchored in discrepant motives" (Barnlund 1976). As Lyle Saunders noted forty years ago in a study of Mexican-American health care in the Southwest,

> When the practice of medicine involves the application of elements of the institution of medicine in one culture to the people of another, or from one subculture to members of another subculture within the same cultural group, what is done or attempted by those in the healing roles may not be fully understood or correctly evaluated by those in the patient roles. Conversely, the responses of those on the patient side of the interaction may not conform to the expectations of those on the healing side. To the extent that this occurs, the relationship may be unsatisfactory to everyone concerned.   (1954:8)

The cultures of patient and healer should be presumed distinctive until proven otherwise.

The gulf that separates the worlds of patient and healer in Biomedicine should not be surprising, given the intensive training that persons in our society undergo in order to transform them into physicians and given the ongoing separation of Biomedical thought and practice from popular culture. As the previous chapter suggests, even physicians who become sick come to see the world in a significantly different way as patients from the way they perceive it as healers. The world may change radically from one end of the stethoscope to the other.

Elements of the medical practice I propose have recently been formulated in medical circles. Reiser (1993) claims that "the era of the patient" has begun to emerge, in which the experience of patients is engaged to shape the nature and development of medical institutions and medical practice. Delbanco (1992) writes of "enriching the doctor-patient relationship by inviting the patient's perspective," Smith and Hoppe (1991) of "the patient's story: integrating the patient- and physician-centered approaches to interviewing," Greenfield, Kaplan, and Ware (1985) of "expanding patient involvement in care." Lipkin, Quill, and Napodano (1984) describe an enhanced "medical interview: a core curriculum for residencies in internal medicine," Mathews and Feinstein (1988) "a review of systems for the personal aspects of patient care." Eric Cassell has written a two-volume theoretical and practical guide to the medical interview; he notes the importance of the interview not only for medical diagnosis but for understanding the personality of the patient and its relation to his or her condition, for examination of the role of the social environment in causing the condition, and for understanding the patient's concerns and expectations (Cassell 1985). Almy and colleagues (1992) describe a curriculum that integrates the social sciences and humanities into medical education.

These proposals are important contributions to medical thought and practice. Their very proposal, however, and the rationales that justify them indicate that what is proposed is novel and not part of current Biomedical practice. Nor are these proposals likely to be readily accepted, since their premises run counter to strong undercurrents of Biomedical thought and practice. If Reiser is suggesting that the era of the patient has arrived, his claim is premature.

Nor am I by any means the first to advocate the synthesis of anthropological and biological perspectives and/or the integration of anthropology into the practice of medicine. Though referred to in different ways, anthropological medicine has many noteworthy precedents. Trostle (1986a, 1986b) has reviewed the historical association of anthropology-like disciplines and the practice of public health in the nineteenth century and more recently. Caudill (1953) assessed the state of anthropological work on medical topics as of the first half of the twentieth century. I cite several of these contributions in the proposal that follows.

What I add to this distinguished chorus is a current review of anthropological themes, both in the abstract and as they are played out in contemporary Biomedicine. I argue that an anthropological perspective is a basic and essential component of good medical theory and practice rather than a peripheral, optional one. By means of sociocultural analysis, some of the contradictions of Biomedicine become apparent, as do opportunities for revision. I advocate anthropology both as an instrument for the examination and understanding of medical systems (Lock and Gordon 1988) and as a vital approach by which fundamental problems of Biomedical practice may be resolved. In the remainder of this chapter, I outline the theory, practice, principles, and hypothetical results of an anthropological medicine, which I believe will not only enhance the satisfaction of patients and their physicians but improve the efficacy of medical practice.

THE THEORY OF ANTHROPOLOGICAL MEDICINE

In the first half of this book I outlined the foundations of an anthropological medicine whose central tenets are as follows:

1. *Sickness is, in essence, a condition of persons unwanted by themselves, and conceptions, theories, and experiences of sickness are elements of socially transmitted cultural systems.* In Biomedicine, sickness and pathology are conceived of as cellular, biochemical, physical disturbances of normal function; it is assumed that the presence or absence of sickness can be empirically defined and determined by laboratory or other biological or physical tests. At best, the accounts given by patients can be used as clues to underlying physiological process.

In contrast, the anthropological perspective conceives of sickness in terms of the perceptions and experiences of patients. And the perception and experience of sickness by individuals is fundamentally shaped by their cultural setting. As individuals grow up in society, they are taught how to label their sickness experiences; they learn the cultural explanations of these conditions, the standard treatments, and the appropriate responses to others with the same conditions. It is the patient's experience and life goals that define the distinction of normal and abnormal function that may then be explained, in part, by cellular, biochemical, physical events.

In given cultural traditions, distinctions among different sicknesses and theories about the causes and treatment of sicknesses form systems known as ethnomedicines. Biomedicine is one such system, distinct though related to the system of popular conceptions in Western society, and distinct as well from the numerous perspectives of other cultural traditions. In chapter 1, I referred to ethnomedicines that focus on biological function as the arena of sickness and healing—of which Biomedicine is a prime example—as "disease" theories. In contrast, "illness" ethnomedicines focus on persons and their immediate environments as the domain of sickness and healing, whereas "disorder" ethnomedicines focus on broader cosmic forces.

2. *The organization of societies is significantly responsible for the distribution of sickness in populations and for the availability and utilization of healing resources.* The Biomedical disease theory conceives of the basic causes of sicknesses as "pathogens"—that is, microorganisms or toxins whose contact with or entry into the body leads to pathology. The causes of sickness are regarded as "natural" phenomena. The events of a pathological condition untreated by medicine are likewise referred to as the "natural course." To this list of causes may be added traumatic events, such as automobile crashes or gunshot wounds.

In the anthropological perspective, the way societies organize their members in time, place, and activity is held to be a fundamental cause of sickness. Automobile crashes or gunshot wounds are obvious products of social relations and behavior; but infectious—"communicable"—and chronic diseases are also powerfully affected by how society is organized and how people interact. Social relations may not only indirectly influence exposure to "pathogens" but more directly have pathogenic effects, as in the pervasive placebo phenomenon. Sickness is a social as well as a natural event.

3. *Diverse approaches to healing are cultural systems, and healing is a sociocultural as well as a biological process.* In the Biomedical perspective, healing is a matter of applying the best available technical methods to diagnose and treat the medical conditions of patients. The healing process is regarded as a physical one in which bodily malfunction is altered by the medical introduction of physical materials or the surgical modification of bodily arrangements. Subjectivity on the part of physicians (and of patients) is regarded as an obstacle to effective therapeutic practice. Healing in which medical intervention plays no role is referred to as "spontaneous" or "natural remission," as if the physical actions of Biomedical intervention and nature were the only possible sources of healing. And the scientific foundations of medical practice are thought to differ radically from the commonsense beliefs of patients and the presumably nonscientific medical principles found in more traditional non-Western societies.

In the anthropological perspective, the scientific beliefs of Biomedicine, like those of patients and non-Western medical traditions, form a cultural system of principles and practices, based on shared assumptions about how the world is, on standards of knowledge acquisition, and on valued goals and methods. Healing is a process in which social interaction and societal organization play a prominent role, along with medical or surgical procedures. "The first point is that the practice of medicine is a social activity" (Saunders 1954:7). The social and psychodynamic interrelations of physicians and patients are recognized as critical elements in the healing process. As in processes of sickness, societal organization and social relations may indirectly mediate healing effects through the distribution of healing resources, or they may more directly cause healing through the physiological effects of beliefs and emotions. As Saunders has written, "The social relationship is not something apart from medical practice which, like the icing on a cake, can be included or left out at the discretion of the practitioner. It is rather an integral and necessary part of medical practice, without which there is no practice" (1954:243).

If the healing process invariably requires an understanding of different perceptions of the world; if understandings of sickness are culturally given and organized; if sickness is caused in part by social organization and social relations; if healing depends on effective relationships across cultural boundaries; if, in other words, social and cultural conditions and events underlie the healing process, then healers—Biomedical and others—unwittingly make anthropological assumptions about themselves, their patients, and their interactions in the course of medical practice. Unknowingly but inevitably, physicians practice a form of anthropology in their work; as they encounter, analyze, and direct their patients, physicians implicitly conduct ethnographic inquiries (Stein 1982). A goal of anthropological medicine is to make the anthropological assumptions and ethnographic practices of medical work explicit and responsive to the best available theory, concepts, and evidence—to transform the anthropology implicit in medicine from a commonsense practice into an informed one.

THE PRACTICE OF
ANTHROPOLOGICAL MEDICINE

In advocating an anthropological medicine, I am recommending not the employment of anthropologists in medical settings but something more radical—the adoption of anthropological principles and practices into the core institution and practice of medicine. This transformation might initially require an army of anthropologists; their ultimate challenge, however, would be to make themselves dispensable.

Here I outline several settings in which an anthropological medicine might be implemented and briefly describe examples of strategies that have been used in doing so. I examine the role of anthropological medicine in clinical, public health, and international health settings, formulate general principles that apply to the practice of anthropological medicine, and suggest the possible effects of such a practice.

Clinical Medicine

In the late 1970s, responding to patient dissatisfaction, rising costs, and the sometimes questionable effectiveness of Biomedicine in reaching and healing its patients, internist George Engel (1977) proposed a "biopsychosocial model" and psychiatrist and anthropologist Arthur Kleinman and colleagues formulated a "clinical social science" (Kleinman, Eisenberg, and Good 1978). Engel noted the inadequacy of the basic tenets of contemporary Biomedicine, principally the narrow premise that sickness is in essence a pathobiological phenomenon. He asserted that effective medical practice must recognize the centrality of the patient's perspective and social environment in defining and explaining his or her condition and in designing and implementing medical response. Engel (1980) used case studies to illustrate the role of social and psychological context in the origins, course, and outcome of sickness and healing of individual patients.

Kleinman, Eisenberg, and Good recommended specific steps to enhance the communication of physician and patient and thereby increase satisfaction and improve outcomes. They described the basic elements of the "explanatory models" (EMs) that both patients and physicians bring to the clinical encounter. An EM is the way in which persons understand sickness conditions, including their ideas about (1) the causes of conditions, (2) the circumstances of their onset, (3) how sickness produces its effects, (4) the course of sickness, and (5) possible treatments. Kleinman, Eisenberg, and Good (1978) recommend that physicians first carefully elicit the EMs of patients, then articulate for patients their own Biomedical EMs, discuss with patients differences and similarities between their respective models, and finally negotiate an approach to the patient's condition (Katon and Kleinman 1981). They also suggested that physicians elicit and acknowledge their patients' fears and expectations regarding their conditions. And they advocated the teaching of clinical social science as part of basic medical education.

Building on the work of Engel and Kleinman, Eisenberg, and Good, anthropologists have developed guidelines to assist clinicians in responding to the ethnic backgrounds of their patients. Harwood (1981) has proposed general principles and described the ethnic traditions, health conditions, and cultural beliefs and practices of seven U.S. ethnic populations. Harwood (1971) has also described the health culture of Puerto Ricans and approaches that might be used by Biomedical practitioners to enhance success in the care of Puerto Rican patients. Physician-anthropologist Cecil Helman (1990) has formulated questions that clinicians may use in understanding and responding to the cultural traditions of patients. Nurse-anthropologist Marjorie Muecke (1983) has described problems likely to arise around the treatment (and nontreatment) of Southeast Asian refugee populations in Biomedical settings; she proposes practical solutions to these problems. In another study, Muecke and I (Hahn and Muecke 1987) focused on one health issue, childbearing, examined its treatment in five U.S. ethnic populations, and proposed ways in which health care personnel and patients might deal with ethnic variations in childbirth practices.

Others have described the relevance of their experience in specific cultural settings for the provision of Biomedical health care. Physician-anthropologists Alexander and Dorothea Leighton (1944) formulated ways in which standard Biomedical practices might be adapted to the Navaho setting, and Adair and Deuschle (1970) described a project that deployed anthropological methods and findings to enhance the use of Biomedicine in a Navaho community.

Public Health and International Health

While clinical medicine generally treats people one at a time, Western society also draws on the principles of Biomedicine to improve the health of populations. This practice is often termed "public health" when the populations of interest reside within (Western) national boundaries and "international health" when the populations treated live elsewhere. The division between clinical medicine and public health may be tenuous, particularly for poor patients who attend public health clinics staffed or financed by government agencies.

Broadly speaking, public health in the United States comprises programs that shape the pathogenic exposures and health resources of constituent populations. Principal components are Medicare and Medicaid, which administer health resources to the elderly, disabled, and poor; agencies like the Centers for Disease Control and Prevention, which investigates and responds to infectious disease "outbreaks," intentional and unintentional injuries, chronic diseases, and risk factors, monitors conditions of sickness, and supports prevention programs like immunization campaigns; such agencies as the Indian Health Service and the Department of Defense that arrange for the health care of their constituents; diverse agencies that regulate and monitor drugs, the food supply, and such environmental conditions as water, sewage, work places, and highways; legislation regulating health behavior, such as smoking, alcohol, and drugs, seat belt use, and abortion services; and schools and media programs that educate the public about health matters.

International health is the effort by wealthier, technologically "developed" nations to assist "underdeveloped" nations address their—the underdeveloped nations'—health problems (Rubinstein and Lane 1990). The State Department's Agency for International Development (AID) is the principal government institution of international health in the United States. It has been argued (Brown 1979) that international health grew not from altruistic concerns but from the interest of colonial nations in maintaining the health of "human capital," that is, the workers whose labor produced profits for the colonial powers. Others have argued that contemporary international health continues to promote underdevelopment and to perpetuate the unequal distribution of wealth and health within developing nations and between developing and developed nations (Navarro 1976; Taussig 1978). For example, AID serves the interests of U.S. foreign policy and requires use of American personnel and consumption of American products; thus the United States is an immediate beneficiary of its foreign assistance. Regardless of motives, international health efforts since World War II are thought to have resulted in diminished rates of disease and death in developing nations (G. Foster 1984).

It should be noted, however, that although development may bring benefits to less developed nations, it may also have severe side-effects on the health of populations. Hughes and Hunter (1970) documented a wide range of such effects in Africa even twenty years ago. The change of the landscape brought about by land clearing, irrigation, and damming for hydroelectricity facilitated the growth and spread of parasites. Altered agriculture reduced the availability and consumption of traditional foods. In addition, changing patterns of labor, migration, residence, urbanization, and crowding facilitated the spread of parasites and infections. More recently, processes of development in Africa have contributed to the rapid dissemination of AIDS.

It is also important to note that the technical means to prevent a large proportion of early deaths in the developing world are known, available, and relatively inexpensive (Foster et al. 1990). Some diseases, such as measles, neonatal tetanus, and whooping cough, are preventable by immunization; others, such as diarrhea, malaria, and acute lower respiratory tract infection, are readily treatable once they have occurred (Foster et. al. 1990). Much less is known about how to implement technical knowledge where it might be useful. The obstacles appear to be political, bureaucratic, and cultural; they lie not only within the boundaries of the developing nations but in developed nations as well and in the relations between the two.

Anthropologist George Foster (1987a) discerns three epochs in the evolution of programs of international health. In earlier years, planners and technical assistants adopted the "silver platter model," which assumed that when developing nations are offered a technique known to work in the donor's setting, potential recipients would rationally and readily accept this offering. The silver platter model has also been described as the "empty vessel" approach—based on the premise that the recipient nation has no knowledge or practices regarding the proposed intervention, so that the donor simply fills a void.

The difficulties of the silver platter approach are illustrated in anthropologist Brigitte Jordan's (1989) study of the training of traditional birth attendants in rural Mexico. In 1979, Jordan was invited by the Mexican Ministry of Health to be a consultant on this training. She decided to attempt to understand the classes from the perspective of the traditional midwives whose beliefs and practices she had closely observed for years (Jordan 1993). And so she stayed with the midwives and talked with them between and after the training sessions.

Physicians and nurses lectured, showed standard diagrams, and gave tests in these classes; there were no practical exercises and there was no contact with materials that were demonstrated, such as contraceptive devices. Lectures addressed such abstract questions as "What is a family?" and "What is a home visit?" Jordan noticed that the midwives paid little attention to the lectures and seemed to wait patiently for them to end.

The trainers failed to recognize that some midwives were not fluent in Spanish and that some could not read or write. The program ignored traditional ideas, such as the belief that the menstrual period is the time of greatest fertility, thus missing an opportunity to teach more effective contraception. It failed to note that midwives lacked the material resources recommended in the course. It ignored the benefits of traditional practices, such as external cephalic version, the participation of family members at birth, and the use of squatting and other birthing positions. And it ignored

the traditional mode of learning among the midwives—namely, apprenticeship and hands-on practice.

The midwives learned a new vocabulary for talking about elements of their
work but little if anything of practical value. Yet this vocabulary did not
correspond to Biomedical understandings; some midwives, for example,
began to refer to the uterus as "prolapso," borrowing from the Spanish phrase
for prolapsed uterus (a weakening of uterine muscles, which may hinder
birth). They also learned that some traditional practices, such as external
cephalic version of breech fetuses, were "bad."

This silver platter approach had critical flaws—assuming that the standard Biomedical approach to knowledge and teaching was the only valid
method and that the trainees' approach was irrelevant. The result was the
transfer of a different way of talking, the enhancement of the midwives' status
and authority for having attended the course, and a report by the trainers that
an additional number of rural midwives had been "upgraded" in effective
obstetric practice. Symbolic of this failed effort was an episode at the end of
the course: the midwives were asked to pose for a photograph holding midwifery kits, but the kits were empty, and had to be returned after the photograph.

By the mid-1950s, Foster asserts, a "sociocultural model" had gained cur-
rency. The sociocultural model postulated that recipients commonly failed to
accept proposed interventions because of conflicting beliefs or practices in
their cultural tradition; their traditions were thus regarded as "cultural
barriers." Foster argues that whereas the sociocultural model was a substantial advance over the silver platter model because it recognized the importance of the recipients' social and cultural organization, it, too, failed because
it did not take into account the critical role of the organization of the agencies
that propose and conduct the interventions.

Foster describes a "bureaucratic model," which examines the social and
cultural organization of bilateral and multilateral agencies like AID and the
World Health Organization that conduct international health. These agencies have achieved notable successes, but barriers of bureaucratic culture
impede effective work. In order to justify budgets, for example, international
agencies may exaggerate past accomplishments as well as current problems
and the possibility of their solution. They may look for short-term, quantifi-
able results rather than long-term, deeper changes. Bureaucracies also have
"limited corporate memories," forgetting the failures and successes of earlier
periods. They often promote doctrines without clear evidence for their efficacy, and they pursue programs in which their personnel are skilled rather
than programs that may be appropriate.

Foster also indicates that the Biomedical model of research predominates
in international health. With its focus on discrete, testable hypotheses and
countable "variables," this quantitative approach to knowledge often precludes the qualitative research needed to understand what might make pro-

grams work in different settings. Foster concludes pessimistically, "Probably it is unrealistic to expect that behavioral information will ever play much of a role in policy and planning activities" (1987a:1047).

PRINCIPLES OF ANTHROPOLOGICAL MEDICINE

Several principles underlie the integration of anthropological thought and practice in clinical medicine, public health, and international health. The practice of anthropological medicine requires that such principles be taught alongside Biomedical knowledge.

Listening

Listening to others of all traditions is the hallmark of the anthropological perspective and practice; a central goal is to understand how things look from the other's point of view. Although the importance of listening is most obvious with patients from non-Western traditions, the inevitable cultural gap between physicians and patients makes the anthropological approach pertinent in all interactions between physicians and patients. Listening serves multiple purposes in the process of healing, including the establishment of rapport with the patient, the understanding of the patient's condition, the recognition of the patient's goals in healing, and assessment of effective modes of therapy. As Leighton and Leighton wrote, "The thing to keep in mind is that the Navaho knows something as well as the doctor, and if the doctor pays him the compliment of inquiring about it in an interested way, he will not only learn a good deal about Navahos and their point of view, but he will enlist the loyalty and confidence of his patient, who will then do his utmost to follow instructions" (1944:74–75).

Listening is a social activity associated with rules and attitudes that vary greatly from society to society. For example, "A quiet, unhurried but purposeful demeanor is a part of normal professional decorum that is particularly reassuring to Southeast Asians because it symbolizes characteristics that are highly valued among them, such as wisdom, good judgment and dignity" (Muecke 1983:433). Southeast Asian patients may be reluctant to question or contradict the authority of physicians, though they may later disregard physician recommendations. The clinician's elicitation of the patient's point of view may minimize misunderstanding. In addition, initial comments in interviews with Southeast Asian patients should be addressed to an elder, since elders often make decisions for the patient. Similarly, among the Navaho, the family commonly speaks for the patient (Leighton and Leighton 1944). In the clinical setting, it may be helpful for the practitioner to modify his or her usual manner of listening to patients from different ethnic traditions.

Listening is critical not only in understanding the patient's perspective and goals but also in the pursuit of medical information and diagnoses. A study of an outpatient clinic in Britain found that 82 percent of final diagnoses were achieved from the patient's medical history alone, while physical and/or laboratory examination added essential information in the remaining 18 percent of cases (Hampton et al. 1975). Similar results have recently been reported among physicians diagnosing the medical conditions of their patients in the United States (Peterson et al. 1992).

At least in the case of Southeast Asian refugees, Muecke points out, "taking a history" may be difficult. Southeast Asian patients may expect healers to be sufficiently wise and knowing not to require the elicitation of detailed information or the administration of multiple, sometimes invasive, tests to arrive at a diagnosis. They may not have been informed of previous diagnoses or treatments. Moreover, patients may conceive of their conditions quite differently from their clinicians; for example, because many Southeast Asians do not consider the fetus human, they may underreport losses in childbearing. They may also reckon time differently. Southeast Asians commonly do not use the Gregorian calendar, and age calculations may differ by as many as two years (Muecke 1983). The elicitation of even routine medical information and the formulation of a chronology of events relevant to a Biomedical diagnosis may thus be difficult, if possible.

Elicitation of medical information may also be difficult among other patient populations, though not always for the same reasons. Because Navaho diagnosticians do not ask questions when making diagnoses, Navaho patients may suspect that clinicians who ask many questions do not really "know" their conditions. Moreover, Navaho patients have a great fear of the dead and their influence over the living; this reluctance to talk of deaths and past sicknesses may make it difficult to elicit a medical history (Leighton and Leighton 1944).

Understanding the patient's concepts of bodily (and mental and spiritual) function may also be critical to treatment. Among Southeast Asian populations, for example, particular spiritual significance is attached to the head; thus, such procedures as the use of intravenous lines in the scalp of infants—a standard Biomedical procedure for premature births—may be highly threatening to parents (Muecke 1983). Harwood (1981) indicates that ideas about blood, "hot" and "cold" substances, drafts and winds, and psychosomatic causation vary widely and may be essential to understand in diverse populations. In treating Puerto Rican patients, for example, Harwood recommends that the clinician understand whether conditions and proposed therapies are considered "hot" or "cold," so that proposed treatments will be used. The practitioner who does not respect cultural norms of interaction may be ineffective in explaining conditions or treatments to patients and may fail to achieve the patient's acceptance of recommended therapies.

Attitudes toward death and suffering are also critical. Muecke points out that Southeast Asian patients may appear unconcerned with severely sick relatives because of a "preference for quality of life over length of life because of the expectation of less suffering in one's next reincarnation" (1983:437). Southeast Asian patients may also greatly prefer that their relatives die at home rather than in the hospital. In contrast, because of their great fear of the dead and their abhorrence of disposal of the dead, Navahos are said to bring dying patients to hospitals so that the whites can take care of them (Leighton and Leighton 1944).

The effect of concepts of sickness on compliance is demonstrated by anthropologist Suzanne Heurtin-Roberts's study of the beliefs of black women attending a hypertension clinic in New Orleans (Heurtin-Roberts, Reisin, and Wilson 1990). Blacks in the United States have 1.5 times the prevalence of definite hypertension as do whites. Though not generally symptomatic, hypertension may lead to stroke and other cardiovascular events. In the New Orleans clinic, some patients (41 percent) believed in the Biomedical disease, "hypertension"; others, however, believed either in "high blood" or "high pertension." "High blood" was regarded as an inherited condition in which the blood was thick or hot; "high blood" was thought to be appropriately treated by diet. In contrast, "high pertension" was regarded as an emotional state of stress and anxiety; remedy was thought to lie in control of the emotions and the social environment. (Similar beliefs have been reported by physician-anthropologist Dan Blumhagen among white patients in a veterans hospital [Blumhagen 1980].) Whereas 27 percent of the women who believed in hypertension complied poorly with the recommendations of their physicians, 63 percent of women who believed in either high blood or high pertension complied poorly; that is, patients who did not share their physicians' beliefs about their condition were 2.3 times more likely not to comply with their physicians' recommendations. The physicians who treated these patients were either unaware of their patients' beliefs or thought that patients simply referred to the phenomenon of hypertension with another word (Heurtin-Roberts et al. 1990).

The importance of listening applies not only to patients in clinical settings but to health care in communities. Anthropologist Susan McCombie worked as an infection control epidemiologist in a county health department in Arizona. Her charge was to investigate outbreaks of infectious diseases in order to control their spread. In the course of her work, she found that physicians as well as patients had ideas about sickness that differed from epidemiological ideas, that impeded disease control, and that, in some instances, allowed the further spread of disease (McCombie 1987).

McCombie found that patients had a concept of flu (which she called "folk flu") that included various gastrointestinal conditions. Since patients believed their flu would soon pass, they may have failed to seek treatment, thereby prolonging their condition and facilitating transmission to others. Physicians diagnosed "viral syndrome" when they had not isolated an infectious agent associated with their patient's condition and when they believed the condition would quickly resolve on its own, "spontaneously." Because they had no precise diagnosis, they also may have failed to give appropriate treatment, prolonging the patient's condition and allowing the infection of others. (Paradoxically, McCombie notes, physicians sometimes gave an antibiotic that would *not* have treated a viral condition they believed their patients had but that *did* treat another condition the patient is more likely to have had.) Recognition of these beliefs and practices among patients and physicians would enhance effective public health response to outbreaks of infectious disease.

In the practice of public and international health, the assessment of community views of health needs is uncommon. There have been outstanding exceptions, however. In 1940, South African physicians Sidney and Emily Kark organized a health center for Zulus in the rural community of Polela in Natal Province (Trostle 1986b). They recruited Zulus from the community as health workers and nursing assistants in the project (Kark and Kark 1962). Health teams for groups of families consisted of a physician, a nurse, and a health educator. In what they called a "community health diagnosis," the Karks studied the perceptions of health problems within the community and integrated their findings with epidemiological studies of community disease patterns. They attempted to transform "unfelt" health needs—as they assessed them—into "felt" health needs (Cassel 1955). Their investigations indicated, for example, that standard pit latrines were unacceptable owing to attitudes regarding the privacy of defecation and people's fears that enemies might use their feces for sorcery. (Practical resolution of this dilemma was not noted.) The Karks also found that although the Zulus believed themselves to be following a traditional diet, their ancestors had enjoyed a far more varied diet; the health team used this information to introduce additional foods (Cassel 1955). Within the first ten years of the establishment of the Polela Health Center, infant mortality rates fell from the extremely high rate of 276 per 1,000 livebirths to fewer than 100 per 1,000 livebirths (Cassel 1955).

The Karks founded the Institute of Family and Community Health to develop and teach the practice of "social medicine." Although the institute failed after the apartheid government took power in the late 1940s, the Karks influenced the training of physicians and epidemiologists and the development of community and family medicine in the United States and elsewhere (Susser 1993).*

A project similar to the Polela Health Center was implemented in the United States among the Navaho in 1955, coincidental with the establish-

---

*My work in anthropology and public health is a third-generation descendant of the influence of the Karks, through their collaboration with physician John Cassel at Chapel Hill, anthropologist Arthur Rubel's training with Cassel, and my postdoctoral training with Rubel in 1978 and 1979.

ment of the Indian Health Service (McDermott et al. 1960; Adair and Deuschle 1970). From its inception, this project, at Many Farms, involved the collaboration of physicians and social scientists. It was recognized that "those members of the donor society concerned with planned change must have a comprehensive knowledge of the culture of those for whom the innovations are designed. . . . The innovations must meet a felt need of the recipient society which must share in making decisions which will affect the community" (Adair and Deuschle 1970:xiv). The objectives of the Many Farms project were threefold: "to define the proper concerns of a health program among a people such as the Navaho"; to make Biomedical practices acceptable to the Navaho; and to study the consequences of the introduction of contemporary Biomedical practice in a traditional society (McDermott et al. 1960:199).

Listening was a key to the project's adaptation of Biomedical practice to Navaho circumstances. Researchers learned in their survey of community health problems, for example, that the Navaho had a high rate of "congenital dislocation of the hip"—a rate almost three hundred times that of residents of New York City (where the prevalence of the condition happened to have been studied). This condition may result in stiffness of the hip and a limp among young persons and in painful and disabling arthritis among persons older than forty. The researchers suspected that the condition might be exacerbated among the Navaho by use of the cradleboard among infants. Biomedicine treats this condition nonsurgically in young children but surgically in older children; in teenagers, congenital dislocation of the hip is treated by fusion of the hip joint.

As researchers listened to the Navaho, they recognized that the Navaho felt this condition to be relatively benign; in the spectrum of evil events, many worse things could have happened, and the Navaho were grateful that nothing worse had happened. In addition, the limp associated with hip disease was not stigmatizing; researchers noted that persons with the limp married at approximately the same ages as those without it. Further, some of the surgical procedures recommended by Biomedicine were themselves disabling in the Navaho setting, since persons with fused hips could not sit on the ground, as is common in hogans; neither could they ride horses or walk on uneven terrain. Moreover, Navaho were troubled by the idea of treating children who manifested no symptoms in a manner that disrupted the use of cradleboards. Finally, they were relatively unconcerned about events that might occur thirty or forty years later. "In reality," concluded the team, " 'health' is a relative matter and signifies the degree to which a person can operate effectively within the particular circumstances of his heredity *and environment*" (McDermott et al. 1960:281). The project limited its interventions to infants.

On a national scale, the U.S. government began to support the development of community health centers in the mid-1960s (Geiger 1984). Based on models from elsewhere (including the Polela project), community health centers were revolutionary in U.S. health care in that they responded to community needs, were intended to provide a basis for redress of the social conditions underlying community health problems, and provided medical and other services rather than simply serving as a financing mechanism (Geiger 1984). For example, Delta Health Center, in a largely black county in Mississippi, not only provided basic medical services but fostered the growth of an agricultural cooperative, assisted in the construction of housing and sanitary facilities, operated a bus service, and provided assistance for the professional training of people from the community. This community's social perspective on health is reflected in one physician's writing prescriptions for food (as a remedy for malnutrition); patients had their prescriptions filled at groceries (Geiger 1993). By 1982, there were 872 health centers around the country serving approximately 4.2 million people; in 1993, approximately 7 million persons were served in 2,000 centers (Geiger 1993). The national program has been deemed successful by many measures (Davis, Gold, and Makuc 1981).

A common objection to the use of anthropology in public and international health is the length of time required by many anthropological studies—generally at least one year of full-time research. "Traditional" in-depth study can be useful in designing and implementing public and international health programs, but anthropologists have developed rapid assessment methods to accelerate the process (Scrimshaw and Hurtado 1987). In preparation for a campaign to control acute respiratory infections among children in Lesotho, for example, anthropologist Ruth Wilson and her colleagues (1992) applied rapid assessment techniques in several communities to learn about indigenous concepts of respiratory disease, theories of etiology, and treatment practices; with the help of local investigators, this study took just three weeks. They learned, for example, that Basotho mothers found the cost of attending medical clinics prohibitive yet would spend even more money (or barter goods, such as goats) to see traditional healers.

Using another rapid technique, a multidisciplinary team administered a brief questionnaire in several Yoruba communities in western Nigeria to assess priority development concerns, their rationales, and knowledge of different diseases (Brieger et al. 1984). To the team's surprise, it was discovered that malaria, though prevalent, was not regarded as a serious problem. Schistosomiasis was rarely mentioned. And onchocerciasis, or river blindness, a parasitic disease with multiple manifestations, was thought of as four distinct diseases, each associated with a different set of symptoms occurring at different stages of "the disease" (Adeniyi, Brieger, and Ramakrishna 1984). Listening to the concerns of the communities assisted the team in designing community projects as well as in enlisting community participation. As one researcher noted, "Successful health care programs should be designed to address both biomedical considerations, which health care professionals recognize as critical, and local concerns, which the community considers critical" (Weiss 1988:11).

Physician Fitzhugh Mullan recommended in 1984 that community-oriented primary care, with ongoing attention to community needs, should become the standard of medical practice in the United States. As precedents Mullan cited the Karks' project in South Africa and the Many Farms project among the Navaho: "Perhaps, a decade or two hence, we will look back on this epoch and wonder about our current practices. Providing primary care without evaluating the community will appear to us, in retrospect, like treating dysuria without a urinalysis or using vitamin B_{12} for an undifferentiated anemia. Logic, science, and economy argue that we can do better" (Mullan 1984:1078). A decade later, there is little evidence that this vision will soon be realized.

Understanding Context

Anthropologists attempt not only to understand the perspective of others but to recognize how this perspective fits the others' social environment. In understanding the patient's (or the community's) context, the physician is an ethnographer: "the successful clinician (as measured, say, in terms of patient compliance and satisfaction) must *prima facie* be *an astute ethnographer of his or her patients*" (Stein 1982:62).

Recognition of context may indicate the origins of a patient's condition. Waitzkin (1981), for example, cites many ways in which the maldistribution of resources in U.S. society leads to an increased burden of suffering among poor, often minority populations, among them farmworkers who for years suffered back pain and degenerative joint disease because they were supplied with short- rather than long-handled hoes and workers exposed to carcinogens in the work place. As I have described in chapter 4, a person's social environment, including family, may also affect the origin, manifestation, and persistence of sicknesses.

It may also be important in healing to understand how a sickness fits into the patient's life and how a recommended treatment may or may not fit the patient's circumstances. Patients told to take a medication with meals on the assumption that they eat three meals each day may not receive adequate doses if, in fact, they eat less often. For some patients, poverty and day-to-day survival may take precedence over the treatment and, in particular, the long-term prevention of sicknesses. A survey conducted in 1988 of tuberculosis patients in a public hospital in New York indicated that 82 percent of patients were unemployed, 53 percent were alcoholic, 40 percent had AIDS or its precursor ARC (AIDS-related complex), 45 percent were homeless, and an additional 23 percent were "unstably" housed (Brudney and Dobkin 1991).

Under any of these circumstances, tuberculosis may not be the patients' primary focus, and remembering to take medications regularly may be a relatively minor concern and a major challenge. Among the Navaho, more than 75 percent of conditions were found to be infectious and most effectively addressed by preventive measures. However, the great distances, isolation, and difficult environment hindered the development of a prevention program (McDermott et al. 1960).

Awareness of the social and cultural context of sickness facilitates the design of effective treatment. Public health physician Michael Deming and his colleagues (1989) used a survey in Togo, West Africa, to explore village practices in responding to malaria in children. Researchers asked mothers what they did when their child had a fever. Only 20 percent of mothers reported taking their child to a health center; when they did so, treatment was often delayed by a day, presumably because of the distance to the centers and/or the waiting once there. Of mothers who did not take their children to health centers, 90 percent gave the treatment—chloroquine—at home. Sixty-five percent of the women acquired this medicine from street or market vendors, the remainder from local pharmacists. Only 5 percent of mothers consulted traditional healers. One percent of home dosages were in excess of recommended levels and may have been toxic, whereas 70 percent were below recommended levels. With this knowledge, the National Malaria Service designed posters indicating proper dosages to display in pharmacies; it also planned to train pharmacists to educate their clients.

The relevant context may also include the political environment. Researchers in the Navaho project at Many Farms recognized the importance of collaboration with Navaho political leaders. The project received substantial funding from the tribal council and was "blessed" by Navaho medicine men.

Recognizing Intraethnic Variability

Variation within cultural traditions must be recognized. An individual's identification with an ethnic group by no means determines his or her beliefs, values, or behavior in line with the norms of that group. Harwood (1981) lists a wide range of social characteristics that may influence the patient's thought, values, and behavior, aside from cultural tradition: level of formal education, nativity, place of origin within country of birth, generation since immigration, age at immigration, urban or rural origin, return migration to country of origin, degree of engagement in ethnic networks, prior medical experience, income, occupation, and religion. In a review of ideas about "hot" and "cold" among Puerto Rican patients in New York, Harwood (1971) notes that Puerto Rican patients, unlike many other Hispanic cultures, add a third category, "cool," to this system of classification that powerfully affects much of their dietary and health behavior. He also notes that individuals may categorize specific foods differently from the cultural norm "if it idiosyncratically produces physical symptoms which are typically classified as hot or cold" (Harwood 1971:1154).

Recent birth statistics indicate substantial variation among ethnic groups that are sometimes lumped together, among them "Asian/Pacific Islander," "Hispanic," and "Black" (CDC 1993a). Among Asian/Pacific Islanders, for example, fertility rates range from 40.8 births per 1,000 women ages 15–44 among the Japanese to 115.1 among native Hawaiians. Births to unmarried mothers range from 5 percent of mothers of Chinese ancestry to 45 percent among native Hawaiian mothers. Among "Hispanic" women, fertility rates range from 52.6 per 1,000 women among Cubans to 118.9 among Mexican Americans. Births to unmarried mothers range from 18.2 percent of mothers of Cuban ancestry to 55.9 percent among Puerto Rican mothers.

There is also great variation among populations classified as "black." In Massachusetts in 1987–1988, 32.4 percent of childbearing Haitian women were unmarried, compared with 70.5 percent of self-classified American blacks (CDC 1991a). Among American blacks, 21.7 percent of mothers were younger than 20 years, compared with 2.8 percent of Haitian mothers. Similar variations are found among American Indian populations, for example, reported rates of infant mortality ranging from 6.0 per 1,000 livebirths in the Oklahoma Region (of the Indian Health Service) to 19.8 per 1,000 livebirths in the Aberdeen Region (Indian Health Service 1991). It has also been shown that among different "racial" groups foreign-born mothers generally have better birth outcomes than do mothers born in the United States (Kleinman et al. 991). Such statistics leave unexplored the cultural and social milieu that may explain them.

In an international context, assessment of concerns among three communities in western Nigeria revealed substantially divergent priorities—despite a common Yoruba ethnic identity (Brieger et al. 1984). Whereas electricity was of primary concern in one town, water was the primary concern in two villages; residents of one village believed that their scattered settlement pattern made it unlikely that they would be given electricity. One village was far more interested in a hospital than the other two sites, most likely because of its distance from other medical facilities. Guinea worm was mentioned as a concern by 1.6 percent of the residents of one village, 22.8 percent of the residents of the other village, and 40.9 percent of the residents of the town; the investigators suggest that these differences may be due both to variations in the prevalence of infection and to attitudes toward the inevitability of this condition.

Explaining, Translating, and Brokering

Beyond legal requirements of informed consent, the explanation of proposed treatments is a moral imperative of medical practice, at least when patients are conscious and rational. Explanation does not require that the patient receive years of medical training, but should respond to the patient's level of cultural background and education. As Scott Preston, vice chairman of the Navaho Tribal Council, stated, "There is a missing bridge between the Navajo patients and the (white) doctors. The bridge is adequate interpretation. The only way that you doctors can put across your message is through better interpretation" (Adair and Deuschle 1970:67). In particular, the strategies of preventive medicine, the use of diagnostic tests, and the treatment of asymptomatic conditions are not commonly understood and may require explanation to allow valid patient consent and to achieve compliance. For example, because many Southeast Asian patients do not know that blood cells normally die and that the body routinely regenerates blood, they may be reluctant to have their blood drawn for diagnostic tests; informing them of the need for the tests and of the body's capacity to regenerate blood may relieve their anxiety and increase their willingness to participate (Muecke 1983).

Anthropologists have recommended that bilingual and bicultural translators be used when patients do not speak English (and the clinician does not speak the patient's language). In addition to interpretation and translation, anthropologists have also advocated the use of "culture brokers" to negotiate understanding and compromise between disparate cultural perspectives and practices. "*Culture brokerage* relates to the process of establishing meaningful, strategic, or significant linkages between separate cultural or sub-cultural systems" (Weidman 1982:211). Translators and culture brokers should be familiar not only with the languages of patient and clinician but with the Biomedical environment. Patients may prefer practitioners from their own backgrounds, when available; however, traditions that appear similar to an outsider may in fact be hostile to one another (Muecke 1983). Acquaintance with the physical settings of Biomedicine can also be useful. Muecke and I (1987) recommend that patients who are about to spend time at a hospital, for example, pregnant women planning to deliver, should be introduced to the settings, personnel, and procedures they are about to face.

Respecting, Responding, and Accommodating

The patient's traditional practices should be respected and accommodated when they are not known (by the clinician) to be harmful. As Adair and Deuschle write, "A vital aspect of the art of cross-cultural medical service and research, or of any newly introduced technology, is ascertaining which of the native institutions are still vital and highly valued in their present form by the recipient society. These must be taken into consideration by the innovators in designing their program" (1970:93).

Some traditional practices are clearly harmful. In the summer of 1981, for example, cases of acute lead poisoning among Mexican-American children were reported in clinics in the Southwest (CDC 1982). After negative investigations of usual sources of lead poisoning, it was discovered that Mexican Americans used two lead compounds known as "azarcon" and "greta" to treat a digestive disorder they called "empacho." In a survey of several Hispanic communities and clinics in Texas, New Mexico, and Arizona, anthropologist Robert Trotter (1985) found that although azarcon and greta were not the most common remedies for empacho, they were used by about 10 percent of the population. Usage varied widely among communities. The drugs were available locally but were also brought by family members who traveled between Mexico and the United States. The lead content of these medicines was found to range from 70 percent to greater than 90 percent, and lead levels in children treated with azarcon were many times the acceptable limit (which has since been lowered). Public health personnel feared that these treatments might reproduce the symptoms they were supposed to relieve, thus possibly leading to greater use. Because of the debilitating and even deadly consequences of chronic lead exposure, a campaign by radio, television, and poster was mounted and efforts were made to restrict the availability of these drugs (CDC 1983a; Trotter 1985). Unfortunately, a survey conducted in 1992 of lead levels in poor children in Orange County, California, reports that all of the children with lead levels two or more times the recommended maximum are Hispanic; investigation indicates that some of these children are exposed to azarcon or greta, some to use of unglazed pottery in food preparation, and others to the ingestion of dirt, encouraged by their mothers as a source of nutrients (CDC 1993d; Gellert et al. 1993). Similar lead-based remedies (for fever and rash) have been reported among Hmong refugees (from northern Laos) living in Minnesota (CDC 1983b), among East Indians, and among Tibetans (CDC 1993d).

In many instances the traditional practices of patients, if not efficacious by various measures (Etkin 1990), are not harmful and may be used to enhance standard therapies (Harwood 1981). Harwood (1981) recommends, for example, that clinicians build on the patient's ideas about diet by complementing or choosing from among his or her dietary preferences; when prescribing increased liquid consumption, for example, recommending traditional herbal teas in addition to juices may increase the likelihood that the recommendation is followed. And where hospitals generally recommend that formula for infants be administered hot, Puerto Rican mothers associate hot milk with rashes and are far more likely to follow a recommendation of cool milk (Harwood 1971).

Recognition of attitudes toward the body may suggest the modification of standard procedures. Among Southeast Asian populations the pelvic area of the body is almost never exposed to others. Muecke (1983) recommends pelvic exams of unmarried Southeast Asian women only when medically indicated, and then by women practitioners in the presence of the patient's husband, if desired. The Leightons (1944) make similar recommendations for Navaho women.

Recognition and response to patients' use of non-Biomedical healers, particularly (though not only) patients from non-Western cultural traditions, is also critical (Harwood 1981). Patients may seek care from non-Western healers because they recognize and trust these modes of healing, because they believe that Biomedicine is inappropriate for their conditions, and because their access to Biomedical healing may be limited. According to Harwood (1981), clinicians should be aware of their patients' use of "alternative" healers so that they may better understand the responses of patients to their prescriptions. He writes that alternative healers often complement the work of Biomedical practitioners and may refer patients to Biomedicine when they believe their skills are of limited use. He proposes collaboration and the adoption of some of the practices of alternative healers, particularly their manner of interacting with patients and patients' families: "Respect for the patient's tradition and an ability to work with the therapeutic choices inherent in it allows for the development of a treatment regimen with the patient which does not contravene his deeply held ideas about illness and will therefore stand a much better chance of success" (Harwood 1971:1158). As a Navaho singer, Sam Yazzie, told physicians on the Many Farms project, "After all, the medicine man and your doctors are working towards the same goal. They are both trying to cure the patient, so why should there be any feeling of rivalry between them?" (Adair and Deuschle 1970:11).

Adaptation may be useful not only for treatment but for such apparently mundane procedures as record-keeping. In the Many Farms project, researchers became aware that standard methods of record-keeping were not effective in the Navaho setting. Standard records "are based on the 'facts of life' of Western society and are simply 'imposed' on everyone else" (McDermott et al. 1960:202). Because of Navaho naming practices, for example, the medical information for more than one person was recorded on a single record. The Many Farms project responded to Navaho concepts of identity and relationships by adding clan names, kinship information, and aliases to their records and arranging their files in terms of Navaho units of residence.

To bridge gaps in cultural communication and reach patients in remote settlements, the Many Farms project initiated a program of "health visitors." Several Navahos familiar with Navaho language and culture but not so young that they would not be respected in the community were selected; several had been tuberculosis patients and could communicate about their experiences of this common condition with the families they visited.

Health visitors were trained to assess family and health conditions in households, perform elementary diagnosis, administer basic medications, refer for further help when necessary, and record health events and their circumstances. Each health visitor was supervised by a public health nurse.

Training was carried out in a manner that respected Navaho sensibilities, for example, the shame experienced with indication of personal failure, such as failure to understand concepts being taught.

Because of their responsiveness to the Navaho, the project's effort to introduce contemporary Biomedicine was "perceived by the community as being vastly different from the medical service they had been used to receiving from many physicians and nurses in the government service of a previous era and, in fact, which still persisted in some regions of the reservation" (Adair and Deuschle 1970:166).

Also among the Navaho (though independent of the Many Farms project), psychiatrist Robert Bergman, chief of mental services for the Indian Health Service in the early 1970s, collaborated in a "School for Medicine Men" (Bergman 1973). To address the problem of declining numbers of traditional healers, the Navaho school gave scholarships to support the training of singers—the traditional Navaho healers. Bergman greatly respected the theory, practice, and efficacy of Navaho healing and was asked to teach in the school. He taught Biomedical ideas and practices while learning from Navaho healers about their traditions. Thomas Largewhiskers, a one-hundred-year-old singer, told Bergman, "I don't know what you learned from books, but the most important thing I learned from my grandfathers was that there is a part of the mind that we don't really know about and that it is that part that is most important in whether we become sick or remain well" (Bergman 1973:664). A Biomedical practice the Navaho healers found especially insightful and useful was hypnosis, which they compared to their diagnostic practice of "hand trembling."

Bergman took the students on a tour of a medical center. They were shocked by a pediatric ward in which children were left for prolonged periods without their parents. The students recommended that a hogan be built at the hospital so that Navaho ceremonies could be performed. Bergman remarks that his collaboration resulted in a more effective process of referral from the medicine men to Biomedical practitioners as well as a greater respect for Navaho practices on his part and the adoption of some of them in his medical practice.

Caring for Practitioners

The physician is a critical element in healing. "The self as medical instrument, and the clinician-client relationship," notes anthropologist Howard Stein, is "the most important 'medicine' " (1982:62). The importance of the healer's perspective is also recognized in the thesis that the "disease" models of Biomedicine play a critical role in the interaction of physicians and their patients (Kleinman, Eisenberg, and Good 1978). Although the self of the healer is explicitly used and is a basic focus of training in psychoanalysis, the healer's self is generally ignored if not avoided in most

Biomedical practice: "for the most part we instruct future clinicians as though they, as persons, were not really present. We hope that their years in professional training have effectively socialized *out* of them any and all subjectivity—the bane of scientific, objective medicine" (Stein 1982:65).

Medical education, internship, residency, and medical practice can be highly stressful. Both trainees and practitioners work long hours, often requiring constant attention to vital matters, and witness personal, private, and sometimes profound events in patients' lives. Consciously and unconsciously, trainees and practitioners may be deeply affected by the conditions and courses of their patients. Yet routine ways of caring for physicians themselves, particularly as they are affected by the demands of their work, have not been widely established. Biomedicine has commonly been blind to the needs of its practitioners and neglectful in their care. Or worse, medical training has been described as "abuse" (Rosenberg and Silver 1984) and compared to the denigrating rituals of hazing (Cousins 1981). Biomedicine's failure to attend to its practitioners may result in harm not only to the practitioners themselves but, because the well-being of physicians affects their medical practices, to patients as well. A survey of medical schools conducted in 1993 indicated that although 61 percent of schools address the "personal growth" of their students, the time devoted to such programs amounts to little more than ten hours a year of medical school (Novack et al. 1993).

Two approaches have been taken to resolve practice-related anxieties and promote well-being among physicians. Both have roots in the psychoanalytic perspective. One approach is to hold meetings in which medical students, residents, or practicing physicians review interactions with patients who have troubled them. Such groups were first instituted by psychoanalyst Michael Balint and social worker Edith Balint in the 1950s and are now called "Balint groups." Though the Balints' initial purpose was to enhance the capacity of general practitioners to explore the psychiatric issues of patients, their attention turned one step back to enhance medical practice by bringing its psychodynamic processes to the consciousness of practitioners; at the same time, the Balint meetings relieved some of the emotional difficulties of medical practice by allowing physicians to express and share their experiences. Balint groups have been used among practicing physicians in England, but in the United States they are more commonly used during residency (Scheingold 1988). A survey of 1993 indicates, however, that only 4 percent of medical schools use Balint groups with their students (Novack et al. 1993).

Making unconscious facets of medical practice conscious has also been pursued by Howard Stein in his teaching of medical students, family practice residents, and others. The key in Stein's approach is countertransference—the persistent force of the physician's psychodynamic processes in his or her healing of others. As Stein notes, "My constituency is the system, not a member or subunit of it; this likewise is my advocacy, loyalty, and the focus of ethnographic (i.e., clinical) attention" (1985a:66). Stein examines at least three arenas: the patient in his or her environment, the interaction of physician and patient, and Stein's interaction with the physician in training. In each arena, Stein asks what history, understandings, and feelings participants bring that affect their presence, participation, and response. He seeks "to help clinicians become competent ethnographers in their own right" (p. 65). Like the Balints' approach, this mode of teaching enhances self-awareness and communication and provides some relief from the anxieties and pressures of personal involvement in medical work. I refer to its underlying principle as "You are what you treat"—that is, in taking care of yourself you take care of others; in taking care of others, you take care of yourself; you are like those you treat.

Attention to the context of Biomedical practice is relevant not only in clinical medicine but in public and international health as well. The "bureaucratic model" recognizes the role of the practitioner's and institution's cultural self-awareness in the facilitation of public and international health programs (Foster 1987a).

The need for attention to "the culture of the innovator" was a deliberate element of the Navaho Many Farms project. Project designers noted, "There must be constant awareness on the part of those planning change of their own culture (or subculture), its values, structure, predilections, and biases. . . . In large measure, change is due to the interchange that takes place when any two societies are in contact. There must be knowledge of the attitudes and beliefs that have shaped the behavior of the one society towards the other. What has the one society accepted from the other? Or rejected?" (Adair and Deuschle 1970:xiv–xv). The researchers report in retrospect that they failed to achieve full self-awareness during the project, but they analyze the facets of their own diverse culture, or rather cultures, and the effects of this diversity on the project (Adair and Deuschle:chap. 9). They describe how governmental regulations about drivers (requiring government licenses) threatened the development of the health visitor program and how the clinical orientation of physician recruits initially conflicted with the public health orientation of the project. Anthropologists were not accustomed to intervention; the clinicians were. "At Many Farms, the medical team and the social scientists each had their own subculture, and just because the doctor, nurse, or anthropologist had the same national background and spoke the same language, it should not be assumed that there would be no communication problems" (p. 149). Cultural boundaries had to be bridged not only between project personnel and the Navaho but among project personnel themselves.

HEALING BIOMEDICINE

Anthropological and kindred studies of the experience of sickness, the interaction of patients and healers, and the effects of the social and cultural environment on sickness and healing reveal the fundamental roles of culture and society in sickness and healing. On the basis of such studies, I have proposed that medical anthropology can address some of the ills of contemporary Biomedicine in a revised practice that I have called "anthropological medicine."

Were anthropological medicine an established practice, what kinds of relations would exist between physicians and their patients? To consider alternate outcomes, I review Ezekiel and Linda Emanuel's (1992) four models of the physician-patient relationship, distinguished on the basis of goals of the physician-patient interaction; the physician's obligation; the role of the patient's values; and the underlying concept of patient autonomy.

Like the silver platter model, in the "paternalistic" model, on the assumption that "there are shared objective criteria for determining what is best, . . . the physician presents the patient with selected information that will encourage the patient to consent to the intervention the physician considers best" (p. 2221). The physician is guardian to the patient. Patient autonomy is limited to assent. In the "informative" model, the physician provides all relevant factual information, which the patient then uses to determine how best to fulfill his or her own values. In this model, the physician's values are not relevant, nor need the physician understand the patient's values. The patient's autonomy consists in control over medical decisions that physicians then execute. This model assumes that the patient's values are clear and fixed.

In the "interpretive" model, the physician not only provides the patient with information, as in the informative model, but assists the patient in discovering his or her values regarding choice among alternative approaches. Here it is assumed that the values of the patient are not fully developed, well formulated, or self-consistent. The physician takes on the task of clarifying values. In this model, autonomy is thought to be based on growing patient self-understanding. Last, in the "deliberative" model, "the aim of the physician-patient interaction is to help the patient determine and choose the best health-related values that can be realized in the clinical situation. . . . By engaging in moral deliberation, the physician and patient judge the worthiness and importance of the health-related values" (p. 2222). Although the physician's values play a prominent role here, the deliberative model differs from the paternalistic model in addressing the values of the patient and allowing the patient greater choice among alternatives. The physician acts as teacher or friend and, based on his or her values, encourages "moral self-development" and the reconsideration of "unexamined preferences" by the patient.

The Emanuels note the relevance of each model to specific circumstances, for example, paternalism in the case of emergency. Except in such circumstances, however, they reject paternalism on the grounds that "it is no longer tenable to assume that the physician and patient espouse similar values and views of what constitutes a benefit" (p. 2224). The Emanuels object to the informative model because it does not show the caring reflected by interest in "understanding what the patient values or should value" (p. 2224). They also assert (for reasons that are not clear to me) that the informative model does not allow for changes in patient values; perhaps they assume that, if the physician plays no role in elucidating or altering the patient's values, those values will not change. They object to the interpretive model because "technical specialization militates against physicians cultivating the [necessary] skills" (p. 2224) and because they believe that physicians *should* evaluate and judge the values of patients.

Although they consider the objection that "patients see their physicians to receive health care, not to engage in moral deliberation or to revise their values" (p. 2225), the Emanuels give overall credence to the deliberative model because they believe that physicians should be not only providers of medical knowledge and technique but educators of health values.

My objections to the deliberative model are two. First, it assumes that there is a "best" *clinically based* decision, perhaps constant for all patients and all circumstances; the focus is on the clinical condition rather than *the patient's life*. Second, it proposes that the physician should attempt to persuade the patient to adopt the physician's values. The deliberative model assumes that physicians have clarified their own values and that patients have not. Moreover, it ignores the plurality of values in our society and others, assuming health as a universal. It encourages physicians to advocate their own values rather than to understand the patient's circumstances. For these reasons I support a model closer to the informative or interpretive ones, in which the physician either provides relevant information for the patient's informed decision or provides information *and* assists the patient in clarifying the patient's values. This is the likely outcome of an anthropological medicine which focuses on the patient's world and context in the definition of sickness and the orientation of healing. I have argued that skills in understanding the patient's circumstances and perspective on a condition may be necessary to understand and treat the condition and satisfy the patient. Physicians' efforts at health education should likewise address the patient's values and context.

Informative or interpretive approaches do not directly apply in several circumstances. First, they require that patients be conscious; thus they may exclude emergency situations, such as severe injury, in which the patient's participation is not possible. Yet even in this setting, the patient's values and context may play a decisive role by means of "advance directives," "living wills," or appointed guardians. Second, as I describe in chapter 1, people suffer conditions that impair their ability to recognize or communicate their own unwanted conditions; I refer to such conditions as metapathologies because they constrain patients' capacity to establish their own sicknesses. In states of metapathology, patients cannot be the principal representatives of their own conditions; their representatives should then attempt to speak to their interests as best they can be known. Finally, patients may surrender self-representation and decision-making powers to others, such as their physicians. A sizable portion of the population wish, at least when sick, to have decisions made for them (Cassileth 1980; Strull 1984). In such cases their physicians or other representatives should attempt to speak to their interests as best they can.

The values of physicians do play a critical role in the organization and practice of medicine. Physicians choose the career of medicine and particular forms of practices, patients, settings, and so on. They may choose to perform or not to perform certain procedures (provision of contraception, abortion, termination of life support, euthanasia), and they may choose the circumstances in which they do so. Such choices may reflect the practitioners' values.

The establishment of anthropological medicine as standard practice will require substantial revisions in the way physicians are taught. It will also demand a reorientation of current practice. The first and perhaps greatest challenge will be to achieve the Biomedical community's acceptance of the validity and legitimacy of an anthropological approach to medicine. The concept of anthropological medicine contradicts the common Biomedical assumption that the essence of sickness is disturbed biological process and that social and cultural characteristics of patients are not central in the etiology and treatment of sickness. Implementation of an anthropological medicine will necessitate the translation of anthropological concepts and practice into medical language. Translation, in turn, will require substantial moderation of the jargon common to anthropology and the linkage of anthropological concepts and theory with real or realistic problems and practical action.

The current position of anthropology and other behavioral sciences in medical training is ambiguous and peripheral. A survey of U.S. medical schools conducted in 1978 found that 50 percent of departments of internal medicine and 60 percent of departments of pediatrics and family medicine had no formal teaching of medical sociology (or presumably of any behavioral science of medicine) (Feinstein and Petersdorf 1981). Only in departments of family medicine was "substantial" time devoted to medical sociology; most instruction was given in grand rounds or conferences. Among schools of medicine that did not teach medical sociology, the most common reasons given for this lack were "low priority," "lack of faculty," "lack of time in the curriculum," and "no need for subject." Departments of internal medicine reported "lack of relevance." This survey only hints at the status of the behavioral sciences in medical training; it does not indicate the attitudes of faculty and students to behavioral disciplines. A survey of the communication skills of residents in internal medicine reports that residents believe that their role is to care for medical not psychosocial problems; that they have insufficient time to discuss social and psychological problems; that such discussion is too stressful for patients; and that such talk is beyond the internist's capacity to solve and thus a waste of time (Duffy et al. 1980).

More recently researchers in a survey of the teaching of interpersonal skills in medical schools noted that "the remarkable scientific advances in medicine have not changed the fact that physicians' core clinical skills are interpersonal" (Novack et al. 1993). Novack and colleagues' survey of 1991 indicated that although 83 percent of schools taught students about the medical interview in introductory courses, the proportion of schools that had instruction about basic social and cultural issues was smaller: the doctor-patient relationship (37 percent), family issues in the medical interview (23 percent), the biopsychosocial model (24 percent), cultural differences (17 percent), and interpersonal skills (17 percent). Among perceived barriers to the teaching of interpersonal skills, 61 percent of respondents asserted insufficient time in a crowded curriculum, 39 percent cited lack of faculty interest, and 31 percent mentioned a lack of institutional commitment.

Anthropologists have employed diverse approaches in introducing anthropological concepts and methods to medical students and residents. Robert Ness has participated in a one-hundred-hour required lecture series on the behavioral sciences for first-year students; he has taught elective seminars on alternative healing strategies and on social factors in health; and he has taught an introduction to clinical medicine in which students learn by discussion and by experience how to elicit medical information and to understand the patient's perspective (Ness 1982). As described earlier, Howard Stein deploys an "ethnographic mode of teaching clinical behavioral science" to residents in family medicine (1982:61); by examination of the ongoing practice of medicine as a social and cultural process, Stein fosters the habit of contextual analysis as a way to enhance medical practice.

The following are critical elements in the training for practice of an anthropological medicine.

1. Physicians in training must recognize that the conception of sickness rests fundamentally with the patient. It is the patient's perception that ultimately determines the existence of sickness. Biomedical understanding may or may not be able to explain given conditions. This is not to deny the essential role of human physiology and the physical environment but only to note that human values determine which conditions are problematic and which are not. The integrity of the patient's life should guide decisions about care.

2. Physicians-in-the-making must learn to recognize the multiple sources of sickness in the social and cultural environment. Patients' notions of sickness may be significantly shaped by their culture; social circumstances may play a critical role in their becoming sick or avoiding sickness.

3. The social and cultural environment likewise plays a critical role in healing. The patient's beliefs and social conditions may powerfully affect health-related behavior and medical outcomes. The patient's interaction with the physician may be an important element in this environment.
4. Physicians must, finally, learn to care for themselves, both because of the multiple hazards of their work and its potential for harm to self and others.

Anthropological medicine would shift the focus of agency in health care toward patients and their communities and away from physicians. Patients and their communities would assume a central role in defining sickness, explaining their conditions and circumstances, determining courses of action, and following through. They would have better understanding and more choice and control. They would have fewer complaints about their treatment and greater satisfaction. They would better comply with the recommendations of physicians, and for this, and perhaps for other reasons, they would have better outcomes.

In anthropological medicine, the role of physicians would be the understanding of patient conditions and circumstances, the development of etiological and therapeutic knowledge and technique, the effective communication of this knowledge and expertise to patients, and the application of this knowledge for the assistance of patients and their communities in treating sickness and achieving patient and community goals. The ultimate burden of control and decision-making would rest with patients and their communities. Common sources of an adversarial environment would be eliminated. The stresses and anxieties of medical practice would be buffered by a sharing among physicians. By listening, by understanding context, by recognizing ethnic variation, by explaining Biomedicine, by respecting, responding to, and accommodating patient traditions, and by recognizing healers themselves, the practice of anthropological medicine would substantially enhance the condition of medicine in Western society.

REFERENCES

Adair, J., and K. W. Deuschle. 1970. *The People's Health: Medicine and Anthropology in a Navajo Community.* New York: Appleton-Century-Crofts.

Adeniyi, J. D., and W. R. Brieger. 1984. Involving communities in tropical disease control. *Education for Health* 1:39–47.

Alland, A., Jr., 1970. *Adaptation in Cultural Evolution: An Approach to Medical Anthropology.* New York: Columbia University Press.

Almy, T. P., K. K. Colby, M. Subkoff, D. S. Gephart, M. Moore-West, and L. L. Lundquist. 1992. Health, society, and the physician: Problem-based learning of the social sciences and humanities. *Annals of Internal Medicine* 116:569–574.

American Board of Medical Specialists (ABMS). 1992. *Annual Report and Reference Handbook.* Evanston, Ill.: ABMS.

American College of Obstetricians and Gynecologists (ACOG). 1979. *Manpower Planning in Obstetrics and Gynecology.* Section H. Washington, D.C.: ACOG.

American College of Physicians. 1984a. American College of Physicians Ethics Manual. Part 1: History of medical ethics; the physician and the patient; the physician's relationship to other physicians; the physician and society. *Annals of Internal Medicine* 101:129–137.

———. 1984b. American College of Physicians Ethics Manual. Part 2: Research; other ethical issues; recommended reading. *Annals of Internal Medicine* 101: 263–274.

———. 1989a. American College of Physicians Ethics Manual. Part 1: History; the patient; other physicians. *Annals of Internal Medicine* 111:245–252.

———. 1989b. American College of Physicians Ethics Manual. Part 2: The physi-

295

cian and society; research; life-sustaining treatment; other issues. *Annals of Internal Medicine* 111:327–335.

———. 1992. American College of Physicians Ethics Manual. 3d ed. *Annals of Internal Medicine* 117:947–960.

American Medical Association (AMA). 1991. *Women in medicine in America: In the mainstream.* Chicago.

AMA Council on Ethical and Judicial Affairs. 1990. Black-white disparities in health care. *Journal of the American Medical Association (JAMA)* 263:2344.

———. 1991a. Gender disparities in clinical decision making. *JAMA* 266:559–562.

———. 1991b. Sexual misconduct in the practice of medicine. *JAMA* 266:2741–2745.

———. 1992a. *Code of Medical Ethics: Current Opinions.* Chicago: AMA.

———. 1992b. Decisions near the end of life. *JAMA* 267:2229–2233.

———. 1992c. Conflicts of interest. *JAMA* 267:2366–2369.

———. 1993. Caring for the poor. *JAMA* 269:2533–2537.

AMA Council on Mental Health. 1973. The sick physician: Impairment by psychiatric disorders, including alcoholism and drug dependence. *JAMA* 223:684–687.

AMA Council on Scientific Affairs. 1992. Induced termination of pregnancy before and after *Roe v. Wade. JAMA* 268:3231–3239.

American Psychiatric Association. 1980. *Diagnostic and Statistical Manual of Mental Disorders,* 3d ed. Washington, D.C.: APA.

Anderson, J. R. 1985. *Muir's Textbook of Pathology.* Baltimore: Edward Arnold.

Anderson, N., and S. Marks, 1988. Apartheid and health in the 1980s. *Social Science and Medicine* 29:667–681.

Angell, M. 1985. Disease as a reflection of the psyche. *New England Journal of Medicine (NEJM)* 312:1570–1572.

———. 1987. Medicine: The endangered patient-centered ethic. *Hastings Center Report* 17:12–14.

Annas, G. J. 1979. Medical paternity and "wrongful life." *Hastings Center Report* 9:15–17.

Anonymous. 1980. I had a phaeochromocytoma. *Lancet* 8174:922–923.

Antman, E. M., J. Lau, B. Kupelnick, F. Mosteller, and T. C..Chalmers. 1992. A comparison of results of meta-analyses of randomized control trials and recommendations of clinical experts. *JAMA* 268:242–248.

Antonovsky, A. 1977. Social class and infant mortality. *Social Science and Medicine* 11:453–470.

Asken, M. J., and D. C. Raham. 1983. Resident performance and sleep deprivation: A review. *Journal of Medical Education* 58:382–388.

Association of American Medical Colleges (AAMC). 1987. *Medical School Admission Requirements, 1988–89: United States and Canada.* Washington, D.C.: AAMC.

———. 1992. *Data Book.* Statistical Information Related to Medical Education. Washington, D.C.: AAMC.

Baer, H. A. 1981. The organizational rejuvenation of osteopathy: A reflection of the decline of professional dominance in medicine. *Social Science and Medicine* 8:701–711.

Baer, H. A., M. Singer, and J. H. Johnsen. 1986. Toward a critical medical anthropology. *Social Science and Medicine* 23:95–98.

Baker, D. W., C. D. Stevens, and R. H. Brook. 1991. Patients who leave a public hospital emergency department without being seen by a physician. *JAMA* 266:1085–1090.

Balzer, M. 1983. Doctors or deceivers? The Siberian Khanty shaman and Soviet medicine. In L. Romanucci-Ross, D. E. Moerman, and L. R. Tancredi, eds., *The Anthropology of Medicine.* South Hadley, Mass.: J. F. Bergen.

Banta, H. D., and S. B. Thacker. 1979. Assessing the costs and benefits of electronic fetal monitoring. *Obstetrical and Gynecological Survey* Suppl. 34:627–642.

Barinaga, M. 1991. How the nose knows: Olfactory receptor cloned. *Science* 252: 209–210.

Barnes, B. A. 1977. Discarded operations: surgical innovation by trial and error. In J. P. Bunker, B. A. Barnes, and F. Mosteller, eds., *Costs, Risks, and Benefits of Surgery.* New York: Oxford University Press.

Barnlund, D. C. 1976. The mystification of meaning: Doctor-patient encounters. *Journal of Medical Education* 51:716–725.

Baron, R. J. 1985. An introduction to medical phenomenology: I can't hear you while I'm listening. *Annals of Internal Medicine* 103:606–611.

Barsamian, E. M. 1977. The rise and fall of internal mammary artery ligation in the treatment of angina pectoris and the lessons learned. In J. P. Bunker, B. A. Barnes, and F. Mosteller, eds., *Costs, Risks, and Benefits of Surgery.* New York: Oxford University Press.

Bazzoli, G. J., E. K. Adams, and S. L. Thran. 1983. Race and socioeconomic status in medical school choice and indebtedness. *Journal of Medical Education* 61:285–292.

Beard, G. M. 1880. Experiments with the "Jumpers" or "Jumping Frenchmen" of Maine. *Journal of Nervous and Mental Diseases* 7:487.

Becker, H., and B. Geer. 1958. Student culture in medical school. *Harvard Educational Review* 28:70–80.

Becker, H., B. Geer, E. C. Hughes, and A. Strauss. 1961. *Boys in White: Student Culture in the Medical School.* Chicago: University of Chicago Press.

Becker, M. H., and N. K. Janz. 1990. Practising health promotion: The doctor's dilemma. *Annals of Internal Medicine* 113:419–422.

Beckman, H. B., and R. Frankel. 1984. The effect of physician behavior on the collection of data. *Annals of Internal Medicine* 101:692–696.

Beecher, H. K. 1955. The powerful placebo. *JAMA* 159:1602–1606.

Belloc, N. B. 1973. Relationship of health practices and mortality. *Preventive Medicine* 2:67–81.

Belloc, N. B., and L. Breslow. 1972. Relationship of physical health status and health practices. *Preventive Medicine* 1:409–421.

Bentley, M. E. 1988. The household management of childhood diarrhea in rural North India. *Social Science and Medicine* 27:75–85.

Berg, J. K., and J. Garrard. 1980. Psychosocial support in residency training programs. *Journal of Medical Education* 55:851–857.

Berger, P. L., and T. Luckmann. 1966. *The Social Construction of Reality.* Garden City, N.Y.: Doubleday.

Bergman, R. L. 1973. A school for medicine men. *American Journal of Psychiatry* 130:663–666.

Bergner, L., and M. Susser. 1970. Low birth weight and prenatal nutrition: An interpretative review. *Pediatrics* 46:946–966.

Berkman, L. 1984. Assessing the physical health effects of social networks and social support. *Annual Review of Public Health* 5:413–442.

Berkman, L. F., and L. S. Syme. 1979. Social networks, host resistance, and mortality: A nine-year follow-up study of Alameda County residents. *American Journal of Epidemiology* 109:186–202.

Black, H. C. 1979. *Black's Law Dictionary.* St. Paul, Minn.: West.

Bloom, S. W. 1965. The sociology of medical education. *Milbank Memorial Fund Quarterly* 43:143–184.

———. 1986. Institutional trends in medical sociology. *Journal of Health and Social Behavior* 27:265–276.

Blumhagen, D. 1980. Hypertension: A folk illness with a medical name. *Culture, Medicine and Psychiatry* 4:197–227.

Bloomfield, A. L. 1959. Origin of the term "internal medicine." *JAMA* 168:1628–1629.

Bolsen, B. 1982. Strange bedfellows: Death penalty and medicine. *JAMA* 248:518–519.

Boone, M. 1989. *Capital Crime: Black Infant Mortality in America.* Beverly Hills, Calif.: Sage.

Bosk, C. L. 1979. *Forgive and Remember.* Chicago: University of Chicago Press.

———. 1980a. Occupational rituals in patient management. *NEJM* 303:71–76.

———. 1980b. The doctors. *Wilson Quarterly* 4:75–86.

Boston Women's Health Book Collective. 1979. *Our Bodies, Ourselves.* New York: Simon and Schuster.

Botkin, J. R. 1988. The legal concept of wrongful life. *JAMA* 259:1541–1545.

Braveman, P., G. Olivia, M. G. Miller, R. Reiter, and S. Egerter. 1989. Adverse outcomes and lack of health insurance among newborns in an eight-county area of California, 1982 to 1986. *NEJM* 321:508–513.

Brennan, T. A., L. L. Leape, N. M. Laird, L. Hebert, A. R. Localio, A. G. Lawthers, J. P. Newhouse, P. C. Weiler, and H. H. Hiatt. 1991. Incidence of adverse events and negligence in hospitalized patients: Results of the Harvard Medical Practice Study I. *NEJM* 324:370–376.

Brenner, H. M. 1973. Fetal, infant, and maternal mortality during periods of economic instability. *International Journal of Health Services* 3:145–159.

———. 1981. Importance of the economy to the nation's health. In L. Eisenberg and A. Kleinman, eds., *The Relevance of Social Science for Medicine.* Dordrecht: D. Reidel.

———. 1983. Mortality and economic instability: Detailed analysis for Britain and comparative analysis for selected industrialized countries. *International Journal of Health Services* 13:563–619.

———. 1987. Economic change, alcohol consumption and heart disease mortality in nine industrialized countries. *Social Science and Medicine* 25:119–132.

Brewster, J. M. 1986. Prevalence of alcohol and other drug problems among physicians. *JAMA* 248:518–519.

Brieger, W. R., J. D. Adenyi, O. Oladepo, J. Ramakrishna, and D. C. Johnson.

1984. Impact of community need differentials on health education planning. *Hygie* 3:42–48.

Brody, H. 1977. *Placebos and the Philosophy of Medicine.* Chicago: University of Chicago Press.

———. 1987. *Stories of Sickness.* New Haven: Yale University Press.

———. 1992. Assisted death—A compassionate response to a medical failure. *NEJM* 327:1384–1388.

Brody, H., and D. S. Sobel. 1979. A systems view of health and disease. In D. Sobel, ed., *Ways of health.* New York: Harcourt Brace Jovanovich.

Brody, I. A. 1955. The decision to study medicine. *NEJM* 252:130–134.

Brooks, D. D., D. R. Smith, and R. J. Anderson. 1991. Medical apartheid. *JAMA* 266:2746–2749.

Brown, E. R. 1979. *Rockefeller Medicine Men: Medicine and Capitalism in America.* Berkeley: University of California Press.

Brown, G. W., and T. Harris. 1978. *Social Origins of Depression.* London: Tavistock.

Brown, S. S. 1988. *Prenatal Care: Reaching Mothers, Reaching Infants.* Washington, D.C.: National Academy of Sciences.

Brudney, K., and J. Dobkin. 1991. Resurgent tuberculosis in New York City. *American Review of Respiratory Disease* 144:745–749.

Bucher, R., and J. G. Stelling. 1977. *Becoming Professional.* Beverly Hills, Calif.: Sage.

Buehler, J. W., D. F. Stroup, D. N. Klaucke, and R. L. Berkelman. 1989. The reporting of race and ethnicity in the National Notifiable Diseases Surveillance System. *Public Health Reports* 104:457–465.

Cannon, W. B. 1942. Voodoo death. *American Anthropologist* 44:169–181.

Carlson, E. D. 1984. Social determinants of low birth weight in a high-risk population. *Demography* 21:207–215.

Carr, J. E. 1978. Ethno-behaviorism and the culture-bound syndromes: The case of amok. *Culture, Medicine and Psychiatry* 2:269–293.

Carr, J. E., and P. Vitaliano. 1982. The theoretical implications of converging research on depression and the culture-bound syndromes. In A. Kleinman and B. Good, eds., *Culture and Depression.* Berkeley: University of California Press.

Carrell, S. 1983. Rejection by peers issue for handicapped MDs. *American Medical News* 26:1, 37–38.

Carrick, P. 1985. *Medical Ethics in Antiquity.* Boston: D. Reidel.

Cassel, J. 1955. A comprehensive health program among South African Zulus. In B. D. Paul, ed., *Health, Culture and Community.* New York: Russell Sage Foundation.

———. 1964. Social science theory as a source of hypothesis in epidemiological research. *American Journal of Public Health* 54:1482–1488.

Cassell, E. 1985. Talking with patients. Vol. 1: *Theory of Doctor-Patient Communication.* Vol. 2: *Clinical Technique.* Cambridge: MIT Press.

Cassidy, C. M. 1982a. Protein energy malnutrition as a culture-bound syndrome. *Culture, Medicine and Psychiatry* 6:325.

———. 1982b. Subcultural prenatal diets of Americans. In Committee on Nutrition of the Mother and Preschool Child, *Alternative Dietary Practices and Nutritional Abuses in Pregnancy.* Washington, D.C.: National Academy Press.

Cassileth, B. R., R. V. Supkis, K. Sutton-Smith, and V. March. 1980. Information and participation preferences among cancer patients. *Annals of Internal Medicine* 92:832–836.

Caudill, W. 1953. Applied anthropology in medicine. In A. L. Kroeber, ed., *Anthropology Today: An Encyclopedic Inventory*. Chicago: University of Chicago Press.

Centers for Disease Control (CDC). 1981. Use of lead tetroxide as a folk remedy for gastrointestinal illness. *Morbidity and Mortality Weekly Report* 30:546–547.

———. 1982. Lead poisoning from lead tetroxide used as a folk remedy—Colorado. *Morbidity and Mortality Weekly Report* 30:647–648.

———. 1983a. Lead poisoning from Mexican folk remedies—California. *Morbidity and Mortality Weekly Report* 32:554–555.

———. 1983b. Folk remedy–associated lead poisoning in Hmong children—Minnesota. *Morbidity and Mortality Weekly Report* 32:555–556.

———. 1989a. Deaths from chronic obstructive lung disease—United States, 1986. *Morbidity and Mortality Weekly Report* 38:549–552.

———. 1989b. State-specific smoking-attributable chronic obstructive pulmonary disease mortality. *Morbidity and Mortality Weekly Report* 38:552–554, 559–561.

———. 1989c. Deaths from stroke—United States, 1986. *Morbidity and Mortality Weekly Report* 38:191–193.

———. 1989d. Advance report of final mortality statistics. *Monthly Vital Statistics Report* 38, no. 5:1–48.

———. 1990a. *Health United States, 1989*. Hyattsville, Md.: U.S. Public Health Service.

———. 1990b. *Vital Statistics of the United States, 1988;* Vol. 1: *Natality*. Washington, D.C.: National Center for Health Statistics.

———. 1991a. Ethnic variation and maternal risk characteristics among Blacks—Massachusetts, 1987 and 1988. *Morbidity and Mortality Weekly Report* 40:403, 409–411.

———. 1991b. Infant mortality by marital status of mother—United States, 1983. *Morbidity and Mortality Weekly Report* 39:521.

———. 1991c. Current estimates from the National Health Survey, 1990. *Vital and Health Statistics*, Ser. 10.181:1–212.

———. 1992a. *Health United States 1991 and Prevention Profile*. Hyattsville, Md.: U.S. Public Health Service.

———. 1992b. Ethnic variation and maternal risk characteristic among Blacks—Massachusetts, 1987 and 1988. *Morbidity and Mortality Weekly Report* 40:403, 409–411.

———. 1992c. *Vital Statistics in the United States, 1989:* Vol. 1: *Natality*. Hyattsville, Md.: National Center for Health Statistics.

———. 1993a. Childbearing patterns among selected racial/ethnic minority groups—United States, 1990. *Morbidity and Mortality Weekly Report* 42:398–403.

———. 1993b. *Health United States 1992 and Healthy People 2000 Review*. Hyattsville, Md.: U.S. Public Health Service.

———. 1993c. *Monthly Vital Statistics Report* 42, no.2(S).

———. 1993d. Lead poisoning associated with use of traditional ethnic remedies—California, 1991–1992. *Morbidity and Mortality Weekly Report* 42:521–524.

Chalmers, I., M. Enkin, and M. J. N. C. Keirse, eds., 1989. *Effective Care in Pregnancy and Childbirth*. New York: Oxford University Press.

Chalmers, T. C. 1974. The impact of controlled trials on the practice of medicine. *Mount Sinai Journal of Medicine* 41:753–759.

Chalmers, T. C., J. B. Block, and S. Lee. 1972. Controlled studies in clinical cancer research. *NEJM* 287:75–78.

Chappel, J. N. 1981. Physician attitudes toward distressed colleagues. *Western Journal of Medicine* 134:175–180.

Chase, R. A. 1976. Proliferation of certification in medical specialties: Productive or counterproductive? *NEJM* 294:497–499.

Chrisman, N. 1977. The health seeking process: An approach to the natural history of illness. *Culture, Medicine and Psychiatry* 1:351–377.

Cleary, P. D., S. Edgman-Levitan, M. Roberts, T. W. Moloney, W. McMullen, J. D. Walker, and T. L. Delbanco. 1991. Patients evaluate their hospital care: A national survey. *Health Affairs* 10:254–267.

Clouser, K. D., C. M. Culver, and B. Gert. 1981. Malady: A new treatment of disease. *Hastings Center Report* 11(3):29–37.

Cohn, K. H. 1982. Chemotherapy from an insider's perspective. *Lancet* 8279:1006–1009.

Colombotos, J. 1969. Social origins and ideology of physicians: A study of the effects of early socialization. *Journal of Health and Social Behavior* 10:16–29.

Couch, N. P., N. L. Tilney, A. A. Rayner, and F. D. Moore. 1981. The high cost of low-frequency events. *NEJM* 304:634–637.

Coulehan, J. L. 1984. Who is the poor historian? *JAMA* 252:221.

Cousins, N. 1981. Internship: Preparation or hazing? *JAMA* 245:377.

Crane, D. 1975. *The Sanctity of Social Life: Physicians' Treatment of Critically Ill Patients*. New York: Russell Sage Foundation.

Crapanzano, V. 1990. Traversing boundaries: European and North American perspectives on medical and psychiatric anthropology—Introduction. *Culture, Medicine and Psychiatry* 14:145–152.

Cunningham, F. G., P. C. MacDonald, and N. F. Gant. 1989. *Williams Obstetrics*. 18th ed. New York: Appleton-Century-Crofts.

Daniel, E. V. 1984. The pulse as an icon in Siddha medicine. *Contributions to Asian Studies* 18:115–126.

Dansak, D. 1973. On the tertiary gain of illness. *Comprehensive Psychiatry* 14:523–534.

Davis, K., M. Gold, and D. Makuc. 1981. Access to health care for the poor: Does the gap remain? *Annual Review of Public Health* 2:159–182.

Davis-Floyd, R. 1992. *Birth as an American Rite of Passage*. Berkeley: University of California Press.

Delbanco, T. L. 1992. Enriching the doctor-patient relationship by inviting the patient's perspective. *Annals of Internal Medicine* 116:414–418.

Deming, M. S., A. Gayibor, K. Murphy, T. S. Jones, and T. Karsa. 1989. Home treatment of febrile children with antimalarial drugs in Togo. *Bulletin of the World Health Organization* 67:695–700.

Dercum, F. X. 1916. Untitled transcript. *Transactions of American Congress of Internal Medicine: First Scientific Session*, Dec. 28–29.

Dismuke, S. E., and S. T. Miller. 1983. Why not share the secrets of good health? The physician's role in health promotion. *JAMA* 249:3181–3183.

Dreyfus, H. L., and S. E. Dreyfus. 1986. *Mind over Machine.* New York: Harper and Row.

Dubler, N. N. 1993. Commentary: Balancing life and death—proceed with caution. *American Journal of Public Health* 83:23–25.

Dubos, R., and J. Dubos. 1952. *The White Plague.* Boston: Little, Brown.

Duffy, D. L., D. Hamerman, and M. A. Cohen. 1980. Communication skills of house officers. *Annals of Internal Medicine* 93:354–357.

Dumont, L. 1965. The modern conception of the individual: Notes on its genesis. *Contributions to Indian Sociology* 8:13–61.

Dunn, F. 1979. Behavioural aspects of the control of parasitic diseases. *Bulletin of the World Health Organization* 57:499–512.

Durkheim, E. 1966/1895. *The Rules of Sociological Method.* New York: Free Press.

Eastman, N. J. 1950. *Williams Obstetrics.* 10th ed. New York: Appleton-Century-Crofts.

———. 1956. *Williams Obstetrics.* 11th ed. New York: Appleton-Century-Crofts.

Eastman, N. J., and L. M. Hellman. 1961. *Williams Obstetrics.* 12th ed. New York: Appleton-Century-Crofts.

Eastman, N. J., L. M. Hellman, and J. A. Pritchard. 1966. *Williams Obstetrics.* 13th ed. New York: Appleton-Century-Crofts.

Edgerton, R. B. 1966. Conceptions of psychosis in four East African societies. *American Anthropologist* 68:408–425.

Edwards, J. W. 1985. Indigenous Koro: A genital retraction syndrome of insular Southeast Asia; A critical review. In R. C. Simons and C. C. Hughes, eds., *The Culture-Bound Syndromes.* Boston: D. Reidel.

Eiler, M. A. 1984. *Physician Characteristics and Distribution in the United States.* Chicago: Survey and Data Resources, AMA.

Eisenberg, D. M., R. C. Kessler, C. Foster, F. E. Norlock, D. R. Calkins, and T. C. Delbanco. 1993. Unconventional medicine in the United States: Prevalence, costs, and patterns of use. *NEJM* 328:246–252.

Elling, R. H. 1981. The capitalist world-system and international health. *International Journal of Health Services* 11:21–51.

Emanuel, E., and L. Emanuel. 1992. Four models of the physician-patient relationship. *JAMA* 267:2221–2226.

Emanuel, I. 1986. Maternal health during childhood and later reproductive performance. *Annals of the New York Academy of Sciences* 477:27–29.

Emerson, J. P. 1970. Behavior in private places: Sustaining definitions of reality in gynecological examinations. In H. P. Dreitzel, ed., *Recent Sociology* No. 2. New York: Macmillan.

Engel, G. L. 1960. A unified concept of health and disease. *Perspectives in Biology and Medicine* 3:459–485.

———. 1968. A life setting conducive to illness: The giving-up-given-up complex. *Annals of Internal Medicine* 69:292–300.

———. 1971. Sudden and rapid death during psychological stress: Folklore or folkwisdom? *Annals of Internal Medicine* 74:771–782.

———. 1977. The need for a new medical model: A challenge for biomedicine. *Science* 196:129–136.

————. 1980. The clinical application of the biopsychosocial model. *American Journal of Psychiatry* 137:535–544.

Etkin, N. L. 1990. Ethnopharmacology: Biological and behavioral perspectives in the study of indigenous medicines. In T. M. Johnson and C. F. Sargent, eds., *Medical Anthropology: Contemporary Theory and Method.* New York: Praeger.

Evans-Pritchard, E. E. 1937. *Witchcraft, Magic, and Oracles among the Azande.* London: Oxford University Press.

Eyer, J. 1977. Prosperity as a cause of death. *International Journal of Health Services* 7:125–150.

Federation of State Medical Boards of the United States. 1992. Official 1991 Federation Summary of Reported Medical Board Actions Released. News release. Boston.

Feinstein, A. R. 1964. Scientific methodology in clinical medicine, II: Classification of human disease by clinical behavior. *Annals of Internal Medicine* 61:757–781.

————. 1967. *Clinical Judgment.* Huntington, N.Y.: Robert E. Krieger.

Fielding, J. E. 1978. Successes of prevention. *Milbank Memorial Fund Quarterly/ Health and Society* 56:274–302.

Fineberg, H. V., and H. H. Hiatt. 1979. Evaluation of medical practices. *NEJM* 301:1086–1091.

Ford, E., R. Cooper, A. Castaner, B. Simmons, and M. Mar. 1989. Coronary arteriography and coronary bypass survey [sic] among Whites and other racial groups relative to hospital-based incidence rates for coronary artery disease: Findings from NHDS. *American Journal of Public Health* 79:437–440.

Foster, G. M. 1984. Anthropological research perspectives on health problems in developing countries. *Social Science and Medicine* 18:847–854.

————. 1987a. Bureaucratic aspects of international health agencies. *Social Science and Medicine* 25:1039–1048.

————. 1987b. World Health Organization behavioral science research: Problems and prospects. *Social Science and Medicine* 24:709–717.

Foster, G. M., and Anderson, B. G. 1978. *Medical Anthropology.* New York: John Wiley and Sons.

Foster, S. O., J. Shepperd, J. H. Davis, and A. N. Agle. 1990. Working with African nations to improve the health of their children. *JAMA* 263:3303–3305.

Fox, R. C. 1959. *Experiment Perilous.* Philadelphia: University of Pennsylvania Press.

————. 1979. *Essays in Medical Sociology.* New York: John Wiley and Sons.

————. 1989. *The Sociology of Medicine.* Englewood Cliffs, N.J.: Prentice Hall.

Frake, C. O. 1961. The diagnosis of disease among the Subanun of Mindanao. *American Anthropologist* 63:113–132.

Fraser, W., R. H. Usher, F. H. McLean, et al. 1987. Temporal variation in rates of cesarean section for dystocia: Does "convenience" play a role? *American Journal of Obstetrics and Gynecology* 156:300–304.

Freedman, S. 1984. Treat yourself, right? *JAMA* 252:1541.

Freidson, E. 1970. *The Profession of Medicine.* New York: Dodd, Mead.

Freud, S. 1958/1912. Recommendations to physicians practising psycho-analysis. In James Strachey, ed., *Standard Edition of the Complete Psychological Works of Sigmund Freud,* Vol. 23. London: Hogarth.

————. 1958/1937. Analysis terminable and interminable. In James Strachey, ed.,

Standard Edition of the Complete Psychological Works of Sigmund Freud, Vol. 12. London: Hogarth.

Funkenstein, D. H. 1979. Factors affecting career choices of medical students, 1958–1976. In E. C. Shapiro and L. M. Lowenstein, eds., *Becoming a Physician*. Cambridge, Mass.: Ballinger.

Gartrell, N., J. Herman, S. Olarte, M. Feldstein, and R. Localio. 1987. Reporting practices of psychiatrists who knew of sexual misconduct by colleagues. *Am. J. Orthopsychiatry* 57:287–295.

Gartrell, N., N. Milliken, W. H. Goodson III, S. Thiemann, and B. Lo. 1992. Physician-patient sexual contact. *Western Journal of Medicine* 157:139–143.

Geertz, C. 1973. *The Interpretation of Cultures*. New York: Free Press.

Geertz, H. 1968. Latah in Java: A theoretical paradox. *Indonesia* 3:93.

Geiger, H. J. 1975. The causes of dehumanization in health care and prospects for humanization. In J. Howard and A. Strauss, eds., *Humanizing Health Care*. New York: Wiley.

———. 1984. Community health centers: Health care as an instrument of social change. In V. W. Sidel and R. Sidel, eds., *Reforming Medicine: Lessons of the Last Quarter Century*. New York: Pantheon.

———. 1993. Community-oriented primary care: The legacy of Sidney Kark. *American Journal of Public Health* 83:946–947.

Gellert, G. A., G. A. Wagner, R. M. Maxwell, D. Moore, and L. Foster. 1993. Lead poisoning among low-income children in Orange County, California. *JAMA* 270:69–71.

Gerber, L. A. 1983. *Married to Their Careers: Career and Family Dilemmas in Doctors' Lives*. New York: Tavistock.

Ginsburg, F. 1989. *Contested Lives: The Abortion Debate in an American Community*. Berkeley: University of California Press.

Glymour, C., and D. Stalker. 1983. Engineers, cranks, physicians, magicians. *NEJM* 308:960–964.

Gomez, E. A. 1982. Voodoo and sudden death: The effects of expectations on health. *Transcultural Psychiatric Research Review* 19:75–92.

Gonzalez, M., ed. 1992. *Socioeconomic Characteristics of Medical Practice*. Chicago: AMA Center for Policy Research.

Good, B., and M. Del Vecchio Good. 1982. Patient requests in primary care clinics. In N. J. Chrisman and T. W. Maretzki, eds., *Clinically Applied Anthropology*. Boston: D. Reidel.

Goodwin, J. S., J. M. Goodwin, and A. V. Vogel. 1979. Knowledge and use of placebo by house officers and nurses. *Annals of Internal Medicine* 91:106–110.

Gordon, D. R. 1988. Tenacious assumptions in Western medicine. In M. Lock and D. R. Gordon, eds., *Biomedicine Examined*. Boston: D. Reidel.

Gortmaker, S. L. 1979. The effects of prenatal care upon the health of the newborn. *American Journal of Public Health* 69:653–660.

Green, E. C. 1985. Traditional healers, mothers and childhood diarrheal disease in Swaziland: The interface of anthropology and health education. *Social Science and Medicine* 20:277–285.

Greenfield, S., S. Kaplan, and J. E. Ware. 1985. Expanding patient involvement in care: Effects on patient outcomes. *Annals of Internal Medicine* 102:520–528.

Grotjahn, M. 1952. A psychoanalyst passes a small stone with big troubles. In M.

Pinner and B. Miller, eds., *When Doctors Are Patients*. New York: W. W. Norton.

Gurwith, M., and C. Langston. 1980. Factitious Munchausen Syndrome. *NEJM* 302:1483–1484.

Haas, J., and W. Shaffir. 1987. *Becoming Doctors: The Adoption of the Cloak of Competence*. Greenwich, Conn.: JAI Press.

Hackman, E., I. Emanuel, G. van Belle, and J. Daling. 1983. Maternal birth weight and subsequent pregnancy outcome. *JAMA* 250:2016–2019.

Hahn, R. A. 1973. Understanding beliefs: An essay on the methodology of the statement and analysis of belief systems. *Current Anthropology* 14:207–229.

———. 1978. Aboriginal American psychiatric theories. *Transcultural Psychiatric Research* 15:29–58.

———. 1984. Rethinking "disease" and "illness." In E. V. Daniel and J. Pugh, eds., *Contributions to Asian Studies: Special Volume on Southasian Systems of Healing* 18:1–23.

———. 1985. A sociocultural model of illness and healing. In L. White, B. Tursky, and G. E. Schwartz, eds., *Placebo: Clinical Phenomena and New Insights*. New York: Guilford Press.

Hahn, R. A., ed. 1987. Obstetrics in the United States: Woman, physician, and society. *Medical Anthropology Quarterly* 1:227–334.

Hahn, R. A., and A. D. Gaines, eds., 1985. *Physicians of Western Medicine: Anthropological Approaches to Theory and Practice*. Dordrecht: D. Reidel.

Hahn, R. A., and A. M. Kleinman. 1983a. Biomedical practice and anthropological theory. In B. J. Siegal, A. A. Beals, and S. A. Tyler, eds., *Annual Review of Anthropology*, Vol. 12. Palo Alto, Calif.: Annual Reviews.

———. 1983b. Belief as pathogen, belief as medicine: "Voodoo death" and the placebo phenomenon in anthropological perspective. *Medical Anthropology Quarterly* 14:3, 16–19.

Hahn, R. A., and M. A. Muecke. 1987. The anthropology of birth in five U.S. ethnic populations: Implications for obstetrical practice. *Current Problems in Obstetrics, Gynecology, and Fertility* 4:133–171.

Hahn, R. A., J. Mulinare, and S. M. Teutsch. 1992. Inconsistencies in coding of race and ethnicity between birth and death in U.S. infants. *JAMA* 267:259–263.

Hahn, R. A., L. S. Magder, S. O. Aral, R. Johnson, and S. Larsen. 1989. Race and the prevalence of syphilis reactivity in the U.S. population: A national seroepidemiologic study. *American Journal of Public Health* 79:467–470.

Hahn, R. A., S. M. Teutsch, R. B. Rothenberg, and J. S. Marks. 1990. Excess deaths from nine chronic diseases in the United States, 1986. *JAMA* 264:2654–2659.

Hall, J. A., D. L. Roter, N. R. Katz. 1988. Meta-analysis of correlates of provider behavior in medical encounters. *Medical Care* 26:657–675.

Hall, J. A., D. L. Roter, and C. S. Rand. 1981. Communication of affect between patient and physician. *Journal of Health and Social Behavior* 22:18–30.

Hampton, J. R., M. J. G. Harrison, J. R. A. Mitchell, J. S. Pritchard, and C. Seymour. 1975. Relative contributions of history-taking, physical examination, and laboratory investigation to diagnosis and management of medical outpatients. *British Medical Journal* 2(5969):486–489.

Hardy, J. B., and E. D. Mellits. 1972. Relationship of low birth weight to maternal characteristics of age, parity, education, and body size. In D. M. Reed and F. J. Stanley, eds., *The Epidemiology of Prematurity*. Baltimore: Urban and Schwarzenberg.

Harris, H. W., and J. H. McClement. 1983. Pulmonary tuberculosis. In P. D. Hoeprich, ed., *Infectious Diseases*. New York: Harper and Row.

Harris, L. 1982. Views of informed consent and decisionmaking: Parallel surveys of physicians and the public. In *President's Commission for the Study of Ethical Problems in Medicine and Biomedical and Behavioral Research: Making Health Care Decisions*. Vol. 2: Appendices (Empirical Studies of Informed Consent). Washington, D.C.: U.S. Government Printing Office.

Harris, M. 1968. *The Rise of Anthropological Theory*. New York: Thomas Y. Crowell.

———. 1974. *Cows, Pigs, Wars, and Witches*. New York: Vintage.

———. 1977. *Cannibals and Kings: The Origins of Cultures*. New York: Random House.

———. 1979. *Cultural Materialism: The Struggle for a Science of Culture*. New York: Vintage.

Harwood, A. 1971. The hot-cold theory of disease: Implications for treatment of Puerto Rican patients. *JAMA* 216:1153–1158.

Harwood, A., ed. 1981. *Ethnicity and Medical Care*. Cambridge: Harvard University Press.

Hauck, G. H., and D. W. Louisell. 1978. Medical malpractice. In W. T. Reich, ed., *Encyclopedia of Bioethics*. New York: Free Press.

Haug, M. R., and B. Lavin. 1981. Practitioner or patient—Who is in charge? *Journal of Health and Social Behavior* 22:212–229.

Hearst, N., T. B. Newman, and S. B. Hulley. 1986. Delayed effects of the military draft on mortality. *NEJM* 314:620–624.

Hellman, L. M., and J. A. Pritchard. 1971. *Williams Obstetrics*. 14th ed. New York: Appleton-Century-Crofts.

Helman, C. G. 1990. *Culture, Health and Illness*. Boston: Wright.

Helsing, K. J., M. Szklo, and G. W. Comstock. 1981a. Mortality after bereavement. *American Journal of Epidemiology* 114:41–52.

———. 1981b. Factors associated with mortality after widowhood. *American Journal of Public Health* 71:802–809.

Hemminki, E., and B. Starfield. 1978. Prevention of low birth weight and pre-term birth: Literature review and suggestions for research policy. *Milbank Memorial Fund Quarterly/Health and Society* 56:339–361.

Henslin, J., and M. Biggs. 1971. Dramaturgical desexualization: The sociology of the vaginal exam. In J. Henslin, ed., *Studies in the Sociology of Sex*. New York: Appleton-Century-Crofts.

Herbst, A. L., P. Cole, T. Colton, S. J. Robboy, and R. E. Scully. 1977. Age-incidence and risk of diethylstilbestrol-related clear cell adenocarcinoma of the vagina and cervix. *American Journal of Obstetrics and Gynecology* 128:43–50.

Herbst, A. L., H. Ulfelder, and D. C. Poskanzer. 1971. Adenocarcinoma of the vagina: Association of maternal stilbestrol therapy with tumor appearance in young women. *NEJM* 284:878–881.

Heurtin-Roberts, S., E. Reisin, and R. Wilson. 1990. Health beliefs and com-

pliance with prescribed medication for hypertension among Black women—
New Orleans, 1985–86. *Morbidity and Mortality Weekly Report* 39: 701–704.

Ho, M., et al. 1988. Diarrheal deaths in American children. *JAMA* 260:3281–3285.

Honzak, R., E. Horackova, and A. Culik. 1972. Our experience with the effect of placebo in some functional and psychosomatic disorders. *Activitas Nervosa Superior (Prague)* 14:184–185.

Hough, D. E., and G. J. Bazzoli. 1985. The economic environment of resident physicians. *JAMA* 253:1758–1762.

House, J. S., K. R. Landis, and D. Umberson. 1988. Social relationships and health. *Science* 241:540–545.

Hughes, C. C., 1968. Ethnomedicine. In *International Encyclopedia of the Social Sciences*. New York: Free Press.

———. 1985. Culture-bound or construct-bound? The syndromes and DSM III. In R. C. Simons and C. C. Hughes, eds., *The Culture-Bound Syndromes*. Boston: D. Reidel.

Hughes, C. C., and J. M. Hunter. 1970. Disease and "development" in Africa. *Social Science and Medicine* 3:443–493.

Hunt, E. P., and S. M. Goldstein. 1964. *Trends in Infant and Childhood Mortality.* Children's Bureau, Statistical Series 76. Washington, D.C.: U.S. Department of Health, Education, and Welfare.

Indian Health Service. 1991. *Regional Differences in Indian Health, 1991.* Rockville, Md.: Indian Health Service.

Ingelfinger, F. J. 1980. Arrogance. *NEJM* 303:1507–1511.

Institute of Medicine. 1973. *Preventing Low Birthweight.* Washington, D.C.: National Academy Press.

Irish, D. P., and D. W. McMurry. 1965. Professional oaths and American medical colleges. *Journal of Chronic Diseases* 18:275–289.

Iyasu, S., D. L. Rowley, J. E. Becerra, and C. J. R. Hogue. 1992. Impact of very low birthweight on the black-white infant mortality gap. *American Journal of Preventive Medicine* 8:271–277.

Janes, C. R., R. Stall, and S. M. Gifford, eds. 1986. *Anthropology and Epidemiology.* Dordrecht: D. Reidel.

Jinabhai, C. C., H. M. Coovadia, and S. S. Abdool-Karim. 1986. Socio-medical indicators of health in South Africa. *International Journal of Health Services* 16:163–176.

Jordan, B. 1977. The self-diagnosis of early pregnancy: An investigation of lay competence. *Medical Anthropology* 1(2):1–38.

———. 1989. Cosmopolitical obstetrics: Some insights from the training of traditional midwives. *Social Science and Medicine* 28:925–937.

———. 1992. Technology and social interaction: Notes on the achievement of authoritative knowledge in complex settings. Palo Alto, Calif.: Institute for Research on Learning.

———. 1993. *Birth in Four Cultures.* Prospect Heights, Ill.: Waveland.

Justiniani, F. R. 1984. Iatrogenic disease: An overview. *Mount Sinai Journal of Medicine* 51:210–214.

Kaplan, G. A., M. N. Haan, S. L. Syme, M. Minkler, and M. Winkleby. 1987.

Socioeconomic status and health. In R. W. Amler and H. B. Dull, eds., *Closing the Gap*. New York: Oxford University Press.

Kark, S. L., and E. Kark. 1962. A practice of social medicine. In S. L. Kark and G. W. Steuart, eds., *A Practice of Social Medicine*. London: E. and S. Livingstone.

Karp, I. 1985. Deconstructing culture-bound syndromes. *Social Science and Medicine* 21:221–228.

Kasiske, B. L., J. F. Neylan III, R. R. Riggio, G. M. Danovitch, L. Kahana, S. R. Alexander, and M. G. White. 1991. The effect of race on access and outcome in transplantation. *NEJM* 324:302–307.

Katon, W., and A. Kleinman. 1981. Doctor-patient negotiation and other social science strategies in patient care. In L. Eisenberg and A. Kleinman, eds., *The Relevance of Social Science for Medicine*. Boston: D. Reidel.

Katz, J. 1984. Why doctors don't disclose uncertainty. *Hastings Center Report* 14:35–44.

Katz, R. 1976. The painful ecstasy of healing. *Psychology Today* 10:81–86.

Kellerman, A. L. 1991. Too sick to wait. *JAMA* 266:1123–1125.

Kendall, C., D. Foote, and R. Martorell. 1984. Ethnomedicine and oral rehydration therapy: A case study of ethnomedical investigation and program planning. *Social Science and Medicine* 19:253–260.

Kenny, M. G. 1978. The symbolism of a putative mental disorder. *Culture, Medicine and Psychiatry* 2:209.

———. 1983. Paradox lost: The latah problem re-visited. *Journal of Nervous and Mental Diseases* 171:159.

Kissel, P., and D. Barrucand. 1964. *Placebos et effet placebo en medecine*. Paris: Masson.

Kitagawa, E. M., and P. M. Hauser. 1973. *Differential Mortality in the United States*. Cambridge: Harvard University Press.

Kleinbach, G. 1974. Social structure and the education of health personnel. *International Journal of Health Services* 4:297–317.

Kleinman, A. M. 1980. *Patients and Healers in the Context of Culture*. Berkeley: University of California Press.

———. 1988. *The Illness Narratives: Suffering, Healing and the Human Condition*. New York: Basic.

Kleinman, A. M., and B. Good, eds. 1985. *Culture and Depression: Studies in the Anthropology and Cross-Cultural Psychiatry of Affect and Disorder*. Berkeley: University of California Press.

Kleinman, A. M., L. Eisenberg, and B. Good. 1978. Culture, illness, and care. *Annals of Internal Medicine* 88:251–258.

Kleinman, J. C. 1990. Infant mortality among racial/ethnic minority groups, 1983–1984. *Morbidity and Mortality Weekly Report* 39(SS-3):31–39.

Kleinman, J. C., and J. H. Madans. 1985. The effects of maternal smoking, physical stature, and educational attainment on the incidence of low birth weight. *American Journal of Epidemiology* 121:843–855.

Kleinman, J. C., L. A. Fingerhut, and K. Prager. 1991. Differences in infant mortality by race, nativity status, and other maternal characteristics. *American Journal of Diseases of Childhood* 145:191–199.

Knafl, K., and G. Burkett. 1975. Professional socialization in a surgical specialty: Acquiring medical judgment. *Social Science and Medicine* 9:397–404.

Korsch, B. M., and V. Negrete. 1972. Doctor-patient communication. *Scientific American* 227:66–74.

Koskenvuo, M., J. Kaprio, A. Kesaniemi, and S. Sarna. 1980. Differences in mortality from ischemic heart disease by marital status and social class. *Journal of Chronic Diseases* 33:95–106.

Lakshmanan, M. C., C. O. Hershey, and D. Breslau. 1986. Hospital admissions caused by iatrogenic disease. *Archives of Internal Medicine* 146:1931–1934.

Landy, D. 1983. Medical anthropology: A critical appraisal. In J. Ruffini, ed., *Advances in Medical Social Science*. New York: Gordon and Breach.

———. 1985. Pibloktoq (hysteria) and Inuit nutrition: Possible implications of hypervitaminosis A. *Social Science and Medicine* 21:173–185.

Langness, L. L. 1965. Hysterical psychosis in the New Guinea highlands: A Bena Bena example. *Psychiatry* 28:58.

———. 1967. Rejoinder to R. Salisbury. *Transcultural Psychiatric Research* 4:125.

Lanphear, J. H. 1986. Rural medicine/Urban responsibilities. *JAMA* 256:2567–2568.

Latour, B., and S. Woolgar. 1986. *Laboratory Life: The Construction of Scientific Facts*. Princeton: Princeton University Press.

Laudan, L. 1977. *Progress and Its Problems*. Berkeley: University of California Press.

———. 1990. *Science and Relativism*. Chicago: University of Chicago Press.

Leach, E. R. 1984. Glimpses of the unmentionable in the history of British social anthropology. *Annual Review of Anthropology* 13:1–23.

Leape, L. L., T. A. Brennan, N. M. Laird, A. G. Lawthers, A. R. Localio, B. A. Barnes, L. Hebert, J. P. Newhouse, P. C. Weiler, and H. H. Hiatt. 1991. The nature of adverse events in hospitalized patients: Results of the Harvard Medical Practice Study II. *NEJM* 324:377–384.

Leavitt, J. W. 1986. *Brought to Bed: Childbearing in America, 1750–1950*. New York: Oxford University Press.

———. 1987. The growth of medical authority: Technology and morals in turn-of-the-century obstetrics. In R. A. Hahn, ed., *Obstetrics in the United States: Woman, Physician, and Society, Medical Anthropology Quarterly* 1:230–255.

Lebowitz, M. D., and B. Burrows. 1975. Tucson epidemiologic study of obstructive lung diseases. Part 2, Effects of in-migration factors on the prevalence of obstructive lung diseases. *American Journal of Epidemiology* 102:153–163.

Lee, R. L. M. 1981. Structure and anti-structure in the culture-bound syndromes: The Malay case. *Culture, Medicine and Psychiatry* 5:233.

Lehrman, D. 1970. Semantic and conceptual issues in the nature-nurture problem. In L. R. Aaronson et al., *Problems in the Development and Evolution of Behavior*. San Francisco: Freeman.

Leighton, A. H., and D. C. Leighton. 1944. *The Navaho Door: An Introduction to Navaho Life*. Cambridge: Harvard University Press.

Leighton, A. H., and J. M. Murphy. 1965. Cross-cultural psychiatry. In J. Murphy and A. H. Leighton, *Approaches to Cross-Cultural Psychiatry*. Ithaca, N.Y.: Cornell University Press.

Levine, J. D., N. C. Gordon, and H. L. Fields. 1978. The mechanism of placebo analgesia. *Lancet* 2(8091):654–657.

Levinson, D. 1967. Medical education and the theory of adult socialization. *Journal of Health and Social Behavior* 8:253–264.

Lévi-Strauss, C. 1963. The sorcerer and his magic. In C. Lévi-Strauss, *Structural Anthropology.* New York: Basic.

Levit, K. R., H. C. Lazenby, C. A. Cowan, and S. W. Letsch. 1991. National health expenditures, 1990. *Health Care Financing Review* 13:29–54.

Lewis, C. E. 1969. Variations in the incidence of surgery. *NEJM* 281:880–884.

Lewontin, R. C. 1982. *Human Diversity.* New York: W. H. Freeman.

————. 1983. The corpse in the elevator. *New York Review of Books* 29:34–37.

Lewontin, R. C., S. Rose, and L. J. Kamin. 1984. *Not in Our Genes: Biology, Ideology, and Human Nature.* New York: Pantheon.

Lidz, C., and A. Meisel. 1983. Informed consent and the structure of medical care. In *President's Commission for the Study of Ethical Problems in Medicine and Biomedical and Behavioral Research: Making Health Care Decisions.* Vol. 2: *Appendices (Empirical Studies of Informed Consent).* Washington, D.C.: U.S. Government Printing Office.

Lieberman, E., K. J. Ryan, R. R. Monson, and S. C. Schoenbaum. 1987. Risk factors accounting for racial differences in the rate of premature birth. *NEJM* 317:743–748.

Light, D. 1979. Uncertainty and control in professional training. *Journal of Health and Social Behavior* 20:310–322.

————. 1980. *Becoming Psychiatrists.* New York: W. W. Norton.

Linton, R. 1956. *Culture and Mental Disorder.* Springfield, Ill.: Charles C. Thomas.

Lipkin, M., Jr., T. E. Quill, and R. J. Napodano. 1984. The medical interview: A core curriculum for residencies in internal medicine. *Annals of Internal Medicine* 100:277–284.

Livingstone, F. B. 1958. Anthropological implications of sickle cell gene distribution in West Africa. *American Anthropologist* 60:533–562.

Localio, A. R., A. G. Lawthers, T. A. Brennan, N. M. Laird, L. Hebert, J. P. Newhouse, L. M. Peterson, P. C. Weiler, and H. H. Hiatt. 1991. Relation between malpractice claims and adverse events due to negligence: Results of the Harvard Medical Practice Study II. *NEJM* 324:377–384.

Lock, M., and D. Gordon, eds. 1988. *Biomedicine Examined.* Boston: D. Reidel.

LoGerfo, J. P. 1977. Variation in surgical rates: Fact vs. fantasy. *NEJM* 297:387–389.

Longo, L. D. 1981. John Whitridge Williams and academic obstetrics in America. *Transactions and Studies of the College of Physicians of Philadelphia* 5(3):22, 1–254.

Low, S. M. 1985. Culturally interpreted symptoms or culture-bound syndromes: A cross-cultural review of nerves. *Social Science and Medicine* 21:187–196.

Luce, J. M., and R. L. Byyny. 1979. The evolution of medical specialism. *Perspectives in Biology and Medicine* 22:377–389.

Luker, K. 1984. *Abortion and the Politics of Motherhood.* Berkeley: University of California Press.

Lutz, C. 1985a. Depression and the translation of emotional words. In A. M. Kleinman and B. Good, eds. *Culture and Depression: Studies in the Anthropology and Cross-Cultural Psychiatry of Affect and Disorder.* Berkeley: University of California Press.

————. 1985b. Ethnopsychology compared to what? Explaining behavior and consciousness among the Ifaluk. In G. M. White and J. Kirkpatrick, eds., *Person, Self, and Experience.* Berkeley: University of California Press.

Lyden, F. J., H. J. Geiger, and D. L. Peterson. 1968. *The Training of Good Physicians.* Cambridge: Harvard University Press.

Mack, R. M. 1984. Lessons from living with cancer. *NEJM* 311:1640–1644.

MacMahon, B., M. G. Kovar, and J. J. Feldman. 1972. *Infant Mortality Rates: Socioeconomic Factors.* Rockville, Md.: National Vital Statistics System, ser. 22, no. 14.

Manning, P., and H. Fagbrega. 1973. The experience of self and body: Health and illness in the Chiapas highlands. In G. Psathas, ed., *Phenomenological Sociology.* New York: John Wiley and Sons.

Marieskind, H. I. 1980. *Women in the Health System: Patients, Providers, and Programs.* St. Louis: C. V. Mosby.

Martin, W. 1957. Preferences for types of patients. In R. K. Merton, G. G. Reader, and P. L. Kendall, eds., *The Student Physician.* Cambridge: Harvard University Press.

Massey, J. 1980. Using interviewer-observed race and respondent-reported race in the Health Interview Survey. *Proceedings of the American Statistical Association Meetings: Social Statistics Section.* Alexandria, Va.: American Statistical Association, 425–428.

Mathews, D. A., and A. R. Feinstein. 1988. A review of systems for the personal aspects of patient care. *American Journal of the Medical Sciences* 295:159–171.

Mawardi, B. H. 1979. Satisfactions, dissatisfactions, and causes of stress in medical practice. *JAMA* 241:1483–1486.

Mayer, J. D. 1984. Medical geography. *JAMA* 251:2680–2683.

McCombie, S. 1987. Folk flu and viral syndrome: An epidemiological perspective. *Social Science and Medicine* 25:987–993.

McCue, J. D. 1982. The effects of stress on physicians and their medical practice. *NEJM* 306:458–463.

———. 1985. The distress of internship. *NEJM* 312:449–452.

McDermott, W., K. Deuschle, J. Adair, H. Fulmer, and B. Loughlin. 1960. Introducing modern medicine in a Navajo community. *Science* 131:197–205, 280–287.

McFarlane, J., B. Parker, K. Soeken, and L. Bullock. 1992. Assessing for abuse during pregnancy. *JAMA* 267:3176–3178.

McKinlay, J. 1981. From "promising report" to "standard procedure": Seven stages in the career of a medical innovation. *Milbank Memorial Fund Quarterly/Health and Society* 59:374–411.

McQuillan, G. M., T. R. Townsend, H. A. Fields, M. Carroll, M. Leahy, and B. F. Polk. 1989. Seroepidemiology of hepatitis B virus infection in the United States, 1976–80. *American Journal of Medicine* 4;87(3A):55–105.

McWhinney, I. R. 1972. Beyond diagnosis: An approach to the integration of behavioral science and clinical medicine. *NEJM* 287:384–387.

Meade, M. S. 1986. Geographic analysis of disease and care. *Annual Review of Public Health* 7:313–335.

Mechanic, D. 1972. Social psychological factors affecting the presentation of bodily complaints. *NEJM* 286:1132–1139.

Melzack, R., and P. D. Wall. 1982. *The Challenge of Pain.* New York: Basic.

Merton, R. K., S. Bloom, and N. Rogoff. 1956. Studies in the sociology of medical education. *Journal of Medical Education* 31:552–565.

Merton, R. K., G. G. Reader, and P. L. Kendall, eds. 1957. *The Student Physician.* Cambridge: Harvard University Press.

Miller, C. A. 1988. Prenatal care outreach: An international perspective. In S. S. Brown, ed., *Prenatal Care: Reaching Mothers, Reaching Infants.* Washington, D.C.: National Academy Press.

Miller, S. J. 1970. *Prescription for Leadership: Training for the Medical Elite.* Chicago: Aldine.

Mintz, M. 1979. If there are no side effects, this must be Honduras. *Mother Jones* 4:32–33.

Moerman, D. E. 1983. General medical effectiveness and human biology: Placebo effects in the treatment of ulcer disease. *Medical Anthropological Quarterly* 14:3, 13–16.

Mold, J. W., and H. F. Stein. 1986. The cascade effect in the clinical care of patients. *NEJM* 314:512–514.

Morsy, S. 1990. Political economy in medical anthropology. In T. M. Johnson and C. F. Sargent, eds., *Medical Anthropology.* New York: Greenwood Press.

Muecke, M. A. 1983. Caring for Southeast Asian refugee patients in the U.S.A. *American Journal of Public Health* 73:431–438.

Mullan, F. 1982. Community-oriented primary care. An agenda for the '80s. *NEJM* 307:1076–1078.

———. 1983. *Vital Signs.* New York: Dell.

Muller, J. H., and B. A. Koenig. 1988. On the boundary of life and death: The definition of dying by medical residents. In M. Lock and D. Gordon, eds., *Biomedicine Examined.* Boston: Kluwer.

Mumford, E. 1970. *Interns: From Students to Physicians.* Cambridge: Harvard University Press.

Myer, M. B. 1977. Effects of maternal smoking and altitude on birth weight and gestation. In D. M. Reed and F. J. Stanley, eds., *The Epidemiology of Prematurity.* Baltimore: Urban and Schwarzenberg.

Myer, M. B., and G. W. Comstock. 1972. Maternal cigarette smoking and perinatal mortality. *American Journal of Epidemiology* 96:1–10.

Myer, M. B., B. S. Jonas, and J. A. Tonascia. 1976. Perinatal events associated with smoking during pregnancy. *American Journal of Epidemiology* 103:464–476.

Myers, J. D. 1981. Preventing iatrogenic complications. *NEJM* 304:664–665.

National Academy of Sciences. 1990. *Nutrition during Pregnancy.* Washington, D.C.: National Academy Press.

Nations, M. 1986. Epidemiological research on infectious disease: Quantitative rigor or rigormortis? Insights from ethnomedicine. In C. R. Janes, R. Stall, and S. M. Gifford, eds., *Anthropology and Epidemiology.* Dordrecht: D. Reidel.

Navarro, V. 1976. *Medicine under Capitalism.* New York: Prodist.

———. 1990. Race or class versus race and class: Mortality differentials in the United States. *Lancet* 336:1238–1240.

Ness, R. C. 1982. Medical anthropology in a preclinical curriculum. In N. J. Chrisman and T. W. Maretzki, eds., *Clinically Applied Anthropology.* Boston: D. Reidel.

New York Times. Sept. 3, 1985. Medical discipline laws: Confusion reigns.

———. Feb. 9, 1993. Dutch move to enact law making euthanasia easier.

———. Mar. 9, 1993. Sensing a loss of control, more doctors call it quits.

————. Mar. 31, 1993. Doctors' pay resented, and it's underestimated.

Nichter, M. 1982. Idioms of distress. *Culture, Medicine, and Psychiatry* 5:379–408.

Nightingale, E. O., K. Hannibal, H. J. Geiger, L. Hartmann, R. Lawrence, and J. Spurlock. 1990a. *Apartheid Medicine: Health and Human Rights in South Africa.* Washington, D.C.: American Association for the Advancement of Science.

————. 1990b. Apartheid medicine: Health and human rights in South Africa. *JAMA* 264:2097–2102.

Nolen, W. 1976. *Surgeon under the Knife.* New York: Dell.

Novack, D. H., G. Volk, D. A. Drossman, and M. Lipkin, Jr. 1993. Medical interviewing and interpersonal skills teaching in U.S. medical schools. *JAMA* 269:2102–2105.

Obeyesekere, G. 1985. Depression, Buddhism, and the work of culture in Sri Lanka. In A. M. Kleinman and B. Good, eds., *Culture and Depression: Studies in the Anthropology and Cross-Cultural Psychiatry of Affect and Disorder.* Berkeley: University of California Press.

Onoge, O. F. 1975. Capitalism and public health: A neglected theme in the medical anthropology of Africa. In S. R. Ingman and A. E. Thomas, eds., *Topias and Utopias in Health.* The Hague: Mouton.

Otten, M. W., S. M. Teutsch, D. F. Williamson, and J. S. Marks. 1990. The effect of known risk factors on the excess mortality of black adults in the United States. *JAMA* 263:854–860.

Overpeck, M. D. 1991. Children's exposure to environmental cigarette smoke before and after birth. *Advance Data* 202:1–12.

Park, L. C., and L. Covi. 1965. Nonblind placebo trial: An exploration of neurotic outpatients' responses to placebo when its inert content is disclosed. *Archives of General Psychiatry* 12:336–345.

Parsons, T. 1951. *The Social System.* Glencoe, Ill.: Free Press.

Parsons, T. 1967. *Sociological Theory and Modern Society.* New York: Free Press.

Paul, B. D., ed. 1955. *Health, Culture, and Community.* New York: Russell Sage Foundation.

Petersdorf, R. G., and A. R. Feinstein. 1981. An informal appraisal of the current status of "medical sociology." In L. Eisenberg and A. Kleinman, eds., *The Relevance of Social Science for Medicine.* Boston: D. Reidel.

Peterson, M. C., J. H. Holbrook, D. Von Hales, N. L. Smith, and L. V. Staker. 1992. Contributions of the history, physical examination, and laboratory investigation in making medical diagnoses. *Western Journal of Medicine* 156:163–165.

Pfifferling, J. H. 1980. *The impaired physician: An overview.* Chapel Hill, N.C.: Health Sciences Consortium.

Phillips, D. P. 1972. Deathday and birthday: An unexpected connection. In J. M. Tanur, F. Mosteller, W. H. Kruskal, R. F. Link, R. S. Pieters, and G. R. Rising, eds., *Statistics: A Guide to the Unknown.* Cambridge, Mass.: Holden-Day.

————. 1974. The influence of suggestion on suicide: Substantive and theoretical implications of the Werther effect. *American Sociological Review* 39:340–354.

————. 1977. Motor vehicle fatalities increase just after publicized suicide stories. *Science* 196:1464–1465.

Phillips, D. P., and D. G. Smith. 1990. Postponement of death until symbolically meaningful occasions. *JAMA* 263:1947–1961.

Phillips, D. P., and E. W. King. 1988. Death takes a holiday: Mortality surrounding major social occasions. *Lancet* 2:728–732.

Phillips, D. P., and L. L. Carstensen. 1986. Clustering of teenage suicides after television news stories about suicide. *NEJM* 315:685–689.

Physician Advocate. 1981. My brother's keeper. *Journal of Iowa Medical Society* 71(10):414–419.

Pinner, M., and B. F. Miller. 1952. *When Doctors Are Patients.* New York: W. W. Norton.

Piper, J. M., W. A. Ray, and M. R. Griffin. 1990. Effects of Medicaid eligibility expansion on prenatal care and pregnancy outcome in Tennessee. *JAMA* 264:2219–2223.

Porkert, M. 1974. *The Theoretical Foundations of Chinese Medicine.* Cambridge: MIT Press.

Pratt, W. F., and M. C. Horn. 1985. Wanted and unwanted childbearing: United States, 1973–82. *Advance Data* 108:1–8.

Pritchard, J. A., and P. C. MacDonald. 1976. *Williams Obstetrics.* 15th ed. New York: Appleton-Century-Crofts.

———. 1980. *Williams Obstetrics.* 16th ed. New York: Appleton-Century-Crofts.

Pritchard, J. A., P. C. MacDonald, and N. F. Gant. 1985. *Williams Obstetrics.* 17th ed. New York: Appleton-Century-Crofts.

Quick, J. D., M. R. Greenlick, and K. J. Roghmann. 1981. Prenatal care and pregnancy outcome in an HMO and general population: A multivariate cohort analysis. *American Journal of Public Health* 71:381–390.

Quine, W. V. O. 1960. *Word and Object.* Cambridge: MIT Press.

Rabin, D. 1982. Compounding the ordeal of ALS: Isolation from my fellow physicians. *NEJM* 308:506–509.

Rappaport, R. 1967. *Pigs for the Ancestors: Ritual in the Ecology of a New Guinea People.* New Haven: Yale University Press.

Reichel-Dolmatoff, G. 1971. *Amazonian Cosmos: The Sexual and Religious Symbolism of the Tukano Indians.* Chicago: University of Chicago Press.

Reiser, S. J. 1978. *Medicine and the Reign of Technology.* New York: Cambridge University Press.

———. 1993. The era of the patient: Using the experience of illness in shaping the missions of health care. *JAMA* 269:1012–1017.

Reuben, D. B. 1990. Psychologic effects of residency. *Southern Medical Journal* 76:380–383.

Richards, S. 1987. *Philosophy and Sociology of Science.* Oxford: Basil Blackwell.

Ritenbaugh, C. 1982. Obesity as a culture-bound syndrome. *Culture, Medicine and Psychiatry* 6:347–364.

Roback, G., L. Randolph, and B. Seidman. 1992. *Physician Characteristics and Distribution in the U.S.* Chicago: Division of Survey Resources, AMA.

Robbins, S. L., M. Angell, and V. Kumar. 1981. *Basic Pathology.* Philadelphia: W. B. Saunders.

Robinson, J. C. 1989. Exposure to occupational hazards among Hispanics, blacks, and non-Hispanic whites in California. *American Journal of Public Health* 79:629–630.

Rogoff, N. 1957. The decision to study medicine. In R. K. Merton, G. G. Reader, and P. L. Kendall, eds., *The Student Physician*. Cambridge: Harvard University Press.

Roos, N. P., L. L. Roos, and P. D. Henteleff. 1977. Elective surgery rates—Do high rates mean lower standards? *NEJM* 297:360–365.

Rorty, R. 1979. *Philosophy and the Mirror of Nature*. Princeton: Princeton University Press.

Rosenberg, D. A., and H. K. Silver. 1984. Medical student abuse. *JAMA* 251: 739–742.

Roter, D., and R. Frankel. 1992. Quantitative and qualitative approaches to the evaluation of the medical dialogue. *Social Science and Medicine* 34:1097–1103.

Roter, D. L., and J. A. Hall. 1989. Studies of doctor-patient interaction. *Annual Review of Public Health* 10:163–180.

Roter, D. L., J. A. Hall, and N. R. Katz. 1988. Patient-physician communication: A descriptive summary of the literature. *Patient Education and Counseling* 12:99–119.

Rubel, A. J. 1964. Epidemiology of a folk illness: Susto in Hispanic America. *Ethnology* 3:268–283.

Rubel, A. J., C. W. O'Nell, and R. Collado-Ardon. 1984. *Susto, a Folk Illness*. Berkeley: University of California Press.

Rubinstein, R. A. 1984. Epidemiology and anthropology: Notes on science and scientism. *Communication and Cognition* 17:163–185.

Rubinstein, R. A., and S. D. Lane. 1990. International health and development. In T. M. Johnson and C. F. Sargent, eds., *Medical Anthropology: Contemporary Theory and Method*. New York: Praeger.

Sacks, O. 1984. *A Leg to Stand On*. New York: Summit.

———. 1985. *The Man Who Mistook His Wife for a Hat*. New York: Harper and Row.

Sahlins, M. 1976. *The Use and Abuse of Biology*. Ann Arbor: University of Michigan Press.

———. 1978. Culture as protein and profit. *New York Review of Books* 25:45–53.

Salisbury, R. F. 1966. Possession in the New Guinea highlands: Review of literature. *Transcultural Psychiatric Research* 3:103–116.

———. 1967. Salisbury replies. *Transcultural Psychiatric Research* 4:130–134.

Sandelowski, M. 1984. *Pain, Pleasure, and American Childbirth: From the Twilight Sleep to the Read Method, 1914–1960*. Westport, Conn.: Greenwood Press.

Saunders, L. 1954. *Cultural Difference and Medical Care: The Care of Spanish Speaking People of the Southwest*. New York: Russell Sage.

Savitt, T. L. 1978. *Medicine and Slavery*. Chicago: University of Illinois Press.

Scheiber, S. C. 1983. Emotional problems of physicians: Nature and extent of problems. In S. C. Scheiber and B. B. Doyle, eds., *The Impaired Physician*. New York: Plenum Medical.

Scheiber, S. C., and B. B. Doyle. 1983. *The Impaired Physician*. New York: Plenum Medical.

Scheingold, L. 1988. Balint work in England: Lessons for American family medicine. *Journal of Family Practice* 26:315–320.

Schmidt, K., L. Hill, and G. Guthrie. Running amok. *International Journal of Social Psychiatry* 23:264–274.

Schoendorf, K. C., C. J. R. Hogue, J. C. Kleinman, and D. Rowley. 1992. Mortality among infants of black as compared with white college-educated parents. *NEJM* 326:1522–1526.

Schroeder, S. A. 1992. The troubled profession: Is medicine's glass half full or half empty? *Annals of Internal Medicine* 116:583–592.

Schwartz, E., V. Y. Kofie, M. Rivo, and R. V. Tuckson. 1990. Black/white comparisons of deaths preventable by medical intervention: United States and the District of Columbia, 1980–1986. *International Journal of Epidemiology* 19:591–598.

Scrimshaw, S., and E. Hurtado. 1987. Rapid assessment procedures for nutrition and primary health care: Anthropological approaches of improving programme effectiveness. Los Angeles: UCLA Latin American Center.

Selik, R. M., K. G. Castro, and M. Pappaioanou. 1988. Racial/ethnic differences in the risk of AIDS in the United States. *American Journal of Public Health* 78:1539–1545.

Seravalli, E. P. 1988. The dying patient, the physician, and the fear of death. *NEJM* 319:1728–1730.

Shapiro, A. K. 1960. A contribution to the history of the placebo effect. *Behavioral Science* 5:109–135.

Sharpe, J. C., and J. P. Brown, Jr. 1962. Physician heal thyself. *JAMA* 182:234–237.

Sheehan, T. J. 1991. A structural equation model of factors affecting neonatal outcomes. Paper presented at the International Workshop on Statistical Modeling and Latent Variables, Fifth New England Statistics Symposium, Storrs, Conn., Apr. 27, 1991.

Shortell, S. M. 1974. Occupational prestige differences within the medical and allied health professions. *Social Science and Medicine* 8:1–9.

Simons, R. C. 1980. The resolution of the latah paradox. *Journal of Nervous and Mental Diseases* 168:195–206.

———. 1983. Latah II—Problems with a purely symbolic interpretation: A reply to Michael Kenny. *Journal of Nervous and Mental Diseases* 171:168–175.

———. 1985. Sorting the culture-bound syndromes. In R. C. Simons and C. C. Hughes, eds., *The Culture-bound Syndromes*. Boston: D. Reidel.

Simons, R. C., and C. C. Hughes, eds. 1985. *The Culture-bound Syndromes*. Boston: D. Reidel.

Singer, M. 1989. The coming of age of critical medical anthropology. *Social Science and Medicine* 28:1193–1203.

Siu, A. L., W. G. Manning, and B. Benjamin. 1990. Patient, provider and hospital characteristics associated with inappropriate hospitalization. *American Journal of Public Health* 80:1253–1256.

Smith, R. C., and R. B. Hoppe. 1991. The patient's story: Integrating the patient- and physician-centered approaches to interviewing. *Annals of Internal Medicine* 115:470–477.

Snow, L. F. 1983. Traditional health beliefs and practices among lower-class black Americans. *Western Journal of Medicine* 139:820–828.

Snow, L. F., and S. M. Johnson. 1978. Folklore, food, female reproductive cycle. *Ecology of Food and Nutrition* 7:41–49.

Sonnenberg, A., K. Keine, and K. B. Weber. 1979. Prevention of duodenal ulcer recurrence with cimetidine. *Deutsche Medizinische Wochenschrift* 105:152.

Speert, H. 1980. *Obstetrics and Gynecology in America: A History.* Chicago: ACOG.

Spodick, D. H. 1973. The surgical mystique and the double standard. *American Heart Journal* 85:579–583.

Stack, C. B. 1974a. *All Our Kin.* New York: Harper and Row.

―――. 1974b. Sex roles and survival strategies in an urban black community. In M. Z. Rosaldo and L. Lamphere, eds., *Woman, Culture, and Society.* Stanford, Calif.: Stanford University Press.

Stander, H. J. 1936. *Williams Obstetrics: A Textbook for the Use of Students and Practitioners.* 7th ed. New York: Appleton-Century-Crofts.

―――. 1941. *Williams Obstetrics: A Textbook for the Use of Students and Practitioners.* 8th ed. New York: Appleton-Century-Crofts.

―――. 1945. *Textbook of Obstetrics: Designed for the Use of Students and Practitioners.* 9th ed. New York: Appleton-Century-Crofts.

Starr, P. 1982. *The Social Transformation of American Medicine.* New York: Basic.

Stedman's Medical Dictionary. 1976. Baltimore: Williams and Wilkins.

Steel, K., P. M. Gertman, C. Crescenzi, and J. Anderson. 1981. Iatrogenic illness on a general medical service at a university hospital. *NEJM* 304:638–642.

Stein, H. F. 1982. The ethnographic mode of teaching clinical behavioral science. In N. J. Chrisman and T. W. Maretzki, eds., *Clinically Applied Anthropology.* Boston: D. Reidel.

―――. 1985a. Principles of style: A medical anthropologist as clinical teacher. *Medical Anthropology Quarterly* 16:64–67.

―――. 1985b. *The Psychodynamics of Medical Practice: Unconscious Factors in Patient Care.* Berkeley: University of California Press.

―――. 1990. *American Medicine as Culture.* San Francisco: Westview.

Steinbock, B. 1986. The logical case for "wrongful life." *Hastings Center Report* 16:15–20.

Stelling, J. G., and R. Bucher. 1979. Professional cloning: The patterning of physicians. In E. C. Shapiro and L. M. Lowenstein, eds., *Becoming a Physician.* Cambridge, Mass.: Ballinger.

Stern, H., and E. E. Cornwall, eds. 1918. *Transactions of the American Congress on Internal Medicine; First Scientific Session; New York City, December 28–29, 1916.* New York: Burr Printing House.

Stetten, D., Jr. 1981. Coping with blindness. *NEJM* 305:458–460.

Stevens, R. 1971. *American Medicine and the Public Interest.* New Haven: Yale University Press.

Stroudmire, A., and J. M. Rhoads. 1983. When the doctor needs a doctor: Special considerations for the physician-patient. *Annals of Internal Medicine* 98:654–659.

Strull, W. M., B. Lo, and G. Charles. 1984. Do patients want to participate in medical decision making? *JAMA* 252:2990–2994.

Sullivan, L. W. 1983. The status of blacks in medicine. *NEJM* 309:807–808.

Surgeon General. 1989. *Reducing the Health Consequences of Smoking: Twenty-five Years of Progress.* Rockville, Md.: U.S. Department of Health and Human Services.

Susser, M. 1993. A South African odyssey in community health: A memoir of the impact of the teachings of Sidney Kark. *American Journal of Public Health* 83:1039–1042.

Susser, M., and Z. Stein. 1977. Prenatal nutrition and subsequent development. In D. M. Reed and F. J. Stanley, eds., *The Epidemiology of Prematurity.* Baltimore: Urban and Schwarzenberg.

Syme, S. L., and L. F. Berkman. 1976. Social class, susceptibility and sickness. *American Journal of Epidemiology* 104:1–8.

Taffel, S. 1978. *Prenatal Care, United States, 1969–1975; Data from National Vital Statistics System,* ser. 21, no. 33. Hyattsville, Md.: U.S. Department of Health and Human Services.

———. 1980. *Factors Associated with Low Birth Weight; Data from National Vital Statistics System,* ser. 21, no. 37. Hyattsville, Md.: U.S. Department of Health and Human Services.

———. 1986. *Maternal Weight Gain and the Outcome of Pregnancy, United States, 1980; Data from National Vital Statistics System,* ser. 21, no. 44. Hyattsville, Md.: U.S. Department of Health and Human Services.

Taffel, S. M., and K. G. Keppel. 1993. Medical advice on maternal weight gain and actual weight gain: Results from the 1988 National Maternal and Infant Health Survey. Annals of the New York Academy of Sciences 678:293–305.

Taussig, M. T. 1978. Nutrition, development, and foreign aid: A case study of U.S. directed health care in a Colombian plantation zone. *International Journal of Health Services* 8:101–121.

Thacker, S. B., and H. D. Banta. 1983. Benefits and risks of episiotomy: An interpretative review of the English language literature, 1860–1980. *Obstetrical and Gynecological Survey* 36:322–338.

Thielens, W. 1957. Some comparisons of entrants to medical and law school. In R. K. Merton, G. G. Reader, and P. L. Kendall, eds., *The Student Physician.* Cambridge: Harvard University Press.

Thomas, L. 1978. Notes of a biology-watcher: On magic in medicine. *NEJM* 299:461–463.

———. 1983. *The Youngest Science.* New York: Viking.

DeTocqueville, A. 1966. *Democracy in America.* Garden City, N.Y.: Doubleday.

Todes, C. 1983. Inside Parkinsonism . . . a psychiatrist's personal experience. *Lancet* 8331:977–978.

Trostle, J. 1986a. Early work in anthropology and epidemiology: From social medicine to the germ theory, 1840 to 1920. In C. R. Janes, R. Stall, and S. M. Gifford, eds., *Anthropology and Epidemiology.* Boston: D. Reidel.

———. 1986b. Anthropology and epidemiology in the twentieth century: A selective history of collaborative projects and theoretical affinities, 1920 to 1970. In C. R. Janes, R. Stall, and S. M. Gifford, eds., *Anthropology and Epidemiology.* Boston: D. Reidel.

Trotter, R. 1985. Greta and Azarcon: A survey of episodic lead poisoning from a folk remedy. *Human Organization* 44:64–72.

True, W. R. 1990. Epidemiology and medical anthropology. In T. M. Johnson and C. F. Sargent, eds., *Medical Anthropology: Contemporary Theory and Method.* New York: Praeger.

Trupin, S. 1986. When the obstetrician gets pregnant. In R. H. Coombs, D. S.

May, and G. W. Small, eds., *Inside doctoring: Stages and outcomes in the professional development of physicians.* New York: Praeger.

Turner, V. W. 1967. *The Forest of Symbols.* Ithaca, N.Y.: Cornell University Press.

U.S. Bureau of the Census. 1975. *Historical Statistics of the United States; Colonial Times to 1970.* Washington, D.C.: Bureau of the Census.

———. 1989. Money income and poverty status in the United States: 1988. *Current Population Reports: Consumer Income.* Washington, D.C.: Bureau of the Census.

U.S. Department of Commerce. 1990. *Statistical Abstract of the United States, 1990.* Washington, D.C.: Bureau of the Census.

Unschuld, P. 1985. *Medicine in China.* Berkeley: University of California Press.

Vaillant, G. E., N. C. Sobowale, and C. McArthur. 1972. Some psychologic vulnerabilities of physicians. *NEJM* 287:372–375.

Valentine, C., and B. L. Valentine. 1974. Missing men: A comparative methodological study of underenumeration and related problems. Unpublished manuscript. Author's collection.

Vallee, F. G. 1966. Eskimo theories of mental illness in the Hudson Bay region. *Anthropologica* 8:53.

Veatch, R. 1980. Professional ethics: New principles for physicians. *Hastings Center Report* 10:16–19.

Wainapel, S. F. 1984. President's corner. *Synapse* 3:1, 6.

Waitzkin, H. 1979. Medicine, superstructure and micropolitics. *Social Science and Medicine* 13A:601–609.

———. 1981. A Marxist analysis of the health care systems of advanced capitalist societies. In L. Eisenberg and A. Kleinman, eds., *The Relevance of Social Science for Medicine.* Boston: D. Reidel.

———. 1985. Information-giving in medical care. *Journal of Health and Social Behavior* 26:81–101.

———. 1989. A critical theory of medical discourse: Ideology, social control, and the processing of social context in medical encounters. *Journal of Health and Social Behavior* 30:220–239.

Watson, B., trans. 1964. *Chuang Tzu.* New York: Columbia University Press.

Weber, E. 1984. Review of P. Veyne, *Writing History,* and P. Ricoeur, *Time and Narrative. New York Times Book Review,* July 22.

Wechsler, H., S. Levine, R. K. Idelson, M. Pohman, and J. O. Taylor. 1983. The physician's role in health promotion: A survey of primary care practitioners. *NEJM* 308:97–100.

Weidman, H. H. 1982. Research strategies, structural alterations, and clinically relevant anthropology. In N. J. Chrisman and T. W. Maretzki, eds., *Clinically Applied Anthropology.* Boston: D. Reidel.

Weiss, M. G. 1988. Cultural models of diarrheal illness: Conceptual framework and review. *Social Science and Medicine* 27:5–16.

Weiss, N. S. 1973. Marital status and risk factors for coronary heart disease: The United States Health Examination Survey of Adults. *British Journal of Preventive and Social Medicine* 27:41–43.

Wennberg, J., and A. Gittelson. 1982. Variations in medical care along small areas. *Scientific American* 246:120–134.

Wertz, R. W., and D. C. Wertz. 1977. *Lying-In: A History of Childbirth in America.* New York: Schocken.

West, C., ed. 1984. *Routine Complications: Troubles with Talk Between Doctors and Patients.* Bloomington: Indiana University Press.

White, G. M., and J. Kirkpatrick. 1985. *Person, Self, and Experience.* Berkeley: University of California Press.

White, K. L., T. F. Williams, and B. G. Greenberg. 1961. The ecology of medical care. *NEJM* 265:885–892.

Wilcox, R. W. 1918. The field of internal medicine. In H. Stern and E. E. Cornwall, eds., *Transactions of the American Congress on Internal Medicine; First Scientific Session; New York City, December 28–29, 1916.* New York: Burr Printing House.

Williams, J. W. 1903. *Obstetrics: A Textbook for the Use of Students and Practitioners.* 1st ed. New York: D. Appleton.

———. 1908. *Obstetrics: A Textbook for the Use of Students and Practitioners.* 2d ed. New York: D. Appleton.

———. 1912. Medical education and the midwife problem in the United States. *JAMA* 58:1–7.

———. 1913. *Obstetrics: A Textbook for the Use of Students and Practitioners.* 3d ed. New York: D. Appleton.

———. 1914. The place of the maternity hospital in the ideal plan. *Transactions of the Fourth Annual Meeting of the American Association for the Study and Prevention of Infant Mortality* 4:35–59.

———. 1915. The limitations and possibilities of prenatal care. *Transactions of the Annual Meetings of the American Association for the Study and Prevention of Infant Mortality* 5:32–48.

———. 1920. *Obstetrics: A Textbook for the Use of Students and Practitioners.* 4th ed. New York: D. Appleton.

———. 1925. *Obstetrics: A Textbook for the Use of Students and Practitioners.* 5th ed. New York: D. Appleton.

———. 1930. *Obstetrics: A Textbook for the Use of Students and Practitioners.* 6th ed. New York: D. Appleton.

Wilson, E. O. 1975a. *Sociobiology: The New Synthesis.* Cambridge: Harvard University Press.

———. 1975b. The origins of human social behavior. *Harvard Magazine* 77:21–26.

———. 1977. Biology and the social sciences. *Daedalus* 106:127–140.

———. 1979. *On Human Nature.* New York: Bantam.

Wilson, R. P., M. M. Shale, and K. A. Parker. 1992. Rapid anthropological procedures in the early planning for control of paediatric acute respiratory infections: Lesotho, 1989. In N. S. Scrimshaw and G. R. Gleason, eds., *Rapid Assessment Procedures.* Boston: International Nutrition Foundation for Developing Countries.

Winch, P. 1958. *The Idea of a Social Science.* New York: Humanities Press.

Winn, J. R., D. G. Breaden, and K. A. Shelton. 1991. Official 1989 federation summary of reported board actions. *Federation Bulletin* 78:44–50.

Winzeler, R. 1984. The study of Malayan latah. *Indonesia* 37:77–104.

Wittgenstein, L. 1958. *Philosophical Investigations.* Translated by G. E. M. Anscombe. New York: Macmillan.

Woodbury, R. M. 1925. *Causal Factors in Infant Mortality.* Children's Bureau, publication 142. Washington, D.C.: Department of Labor.

―――. 1926. *Maternal Mortality.* Children's Bureau, publication 158. Washington, D.C.: Department of Labor.

World Health Organization (WHO). 1973. *Report of the International Pilot Study of Schizophrenia.* Geneva: WHO.

―――. 1978. *The International Classification of Diseases, 9th Revision.* Ann Arbor, Mich.: Commission on Professional and Hospital Activities.

―――. 1979. *Schizophrenia: An International Follow-up Study.* New York: John Wiley and Sons.

―――. 1983. *Apartheid and Health.* Geneva: WHO.

―――. 1985. *The Management of Diarrhoea and Use of Oral Rehydration Therapy.* Geneva: WHO.

―――. 1987. Unintended pregnancy and infant mortality/morbidity. In R. W. Amler and H. B. Dull, eds., *Closing the Gap: The Burden of Unnecessary Illness.* New York: Oxford University Press.

Wyshak G., G. A. Lamb, R. S. Lawrence, and W. J. Curran. 1980. A profile of the health-promoting behaviors of physicians and lawyers. *NEJM* 303:104–107.

Yap, P. M. 1962. Words and things in comparative psychiatry, with special reference to the exotic psychoses. *Acta Psychiatrica Scandinavica* 38:163.

―――. 1969. The culture-bound reactive syndrome. In W. Caudill and T. Lin, eds., *Mental Health Research in Asia and the Pacific.* Honolulu: East-West Center.

Young, A. 1980. The discourse on stress and the reproduction of conventional knowledge. *Social Science and Medicine* 14B:133–146.

Zijlstra, F. J. 1982. Ulcerative Colitis. *Lancet* 8265:215–216.

Zimny, G. H., and T. R. Thale. 1970. Specialty choice and attitudes toward medical specialists. *Social Science and Medicine* 4:257–264.

INDEX